The Inquisition

The Inquisition

A History

Michael C. Thomsett

McFarland & Company, Inc., Publishers
Jefferson, North Carolina, and London

Library of Congress Cataloguing-in-Publication Data

Thomsett, Michael C.
    The Inquisition : a history / Michael C. Thomsett.
      p.   cm.
    Includes bibliographical references and index.

    ISBN 978 0 7864 4409 0
    softcover : 50# alkaline paper ∞

    1. Inquisition — History.   I. Title.
  BX1713.T46   2010
  272'.2 — dc22

                           2010013312

British Library cataloguing data are available

Front cover images ©2010 Photos.com and Shutterstock

Manufactured in the United States of America

McFarland & Company, Inc., Publishers
 Box 611, Jefferson, North Carolina 28640
  www.mcfarlandpub.com

Acknowledgments

Thanks to the many people who have provided advice and suggestions in the development of this book. These include the invaluable resources provided by the Jean and Alexander Heard Divinity School Library at Vanderbilt University in Nashville, Tennessee, and especially librarian Chris Benda; and Helmut Smith, Professor of European Studies at Vanderbilt University, with gratitude for his support of this project.

Also my thanks go to Professor Mark Schwartz of Grand Valley State University, Allendale, Michigan; and to Christine Caldwell Ames, Professor at the University of South Carolina, Columbia.

Before submitting the book, I relied on the indispensible first-read edits of two family members. My wife, Linda Rose Thomsett, and my son, Eric J. Thomsett, have both helped me to shape and expand my treatment of this complex topic, and I appreciate their support and belief in the project.

Table of Contents

Acknowledgments   v

Introduction: A Four-Stage, 400-Year History   1

Stage One of the Inquisition

1. Pope Gregory IX, 1227 to 1241: Stage One Begins 11
2. Cathar Beginnings: Challenges in Heresy 36
3. The Dominican Order 53
4. The Cathars' End and Expanded Inquisitions 69
5. The Age of Wyclif and Hus 84
6. The Great Witch Hunt 97

Stage Two: The Spanish Inquisition

7. The Jews and Conversos of Spain 117
8. Conversos in the Fifteenth Century 131
9. The Age of Torquemada, the Grand Inquisitor 147
10. The Spanish Inquisition after Torquemada 163

Stage Three: The Reformation and the Roman Inquisition

11. Martin Luther 177
12. Anglicanism and Calvinism 191
13. The Roman Inquisition 206
14. Galileo and the Center of the Universe 216

Stage Four: The Modern Inquisition

15. The End of Inquisitions 233

16. The Modern Office of the Inquisition 247

Epilogue   263

Chapter Notes   267

Bibliography   273

Index   277

Introduction:
A Four-Stage, 400-Year History

But, say you, the State cannot punish in the name of God. Yet was it not in the name of God that Moses and Phineas consigned to death the worshippers of the Golden calf and those who despised the true religion?
— St. Optatus of Mileve, *De Schismate Donntistarum*, III, cc. 6–7, 4th C.

Any attempt at writing a history involves a series of judgment calls and decisions. The greatest judgment call is to determine the proper tone and emphasis. How can a history be compiled without any bias? It cannot, especially when dealing with a topic as controversial as the Inquisition. There is absolutely no doubt that the Church and its representatives went to extremes in treatment of suspects under the Inquisition, at times with great relish and sadism. But this does not condemn the entire institution of the Church.

In spite of the centuries of abuse of suspected nonbelievers, heretics, witches, and eventually Jews and Muslims, not to mention scientists and artists, there remains the institution of the Roman Catholic Church, which has had a colorful and varied history. Mixed in with many evil popes and inquisitors have been inspired missionaries and saints whose lives were devoted to the cause of Christianity and of saving souls. This work continues to this day and, with an ever-present paradox, so does the institution of the Inquisition itself, now given a gentler name and with greatly scaled-back authority, but still in existence nonetheless.

The challenge in writing a history of this complex institution, with its good works and bad works mixed together, with a series of inspired popes and some very evil and corrupt ones, is to attempt to report the facts as they unfold. Everyone has a bias, and no historian can expect that his or hers will not come through. In trying to honestly report factual information about events and thoughts in the context of their times, it may be possible to avoid only the extremes of bias. In the case of the Inquisition, there are two such extremes one especially strives to avoid.

The first bias is that of the unquestioning faithful who become apologists for the Church and even for the acts of inquisitors in ancient torture chambers around Europe. The apologist tends to argue that the abuses were not as widespread as many believe, or that torture rarely resulted in death for the accused, or that other types of punishment in the same era were at least as extreme as those of the Inquisition. The apologist bases such claims on a belief that the Church has always existed to do God's work and that casting the Inquisition in a negative light is contrary to that purpose. For such a believer it may be very difficult to accept that the institution of the Church has at times, during its 2,000-year history, been ruled by some bad players.

At the opposite end is the individual who is completely anti–Church and specifically anti–Catholic. The tendency for this individual is to find the worst examples of the extremes and to highlight the evil players in the Inquisition's history, casting the entire Church in the same light of evil and abuse.

The effect of both biases is to cloud history and increase the difficulty of documentation. For this reason, the telling of history involves a balancing act, an attempt to remain somewhere in between the extremes in bias as one searches out the facts that not only tell the story fairly, but also provide explanations in background matters that further cast light not only on what has occurred, but also on why.

A reader with an appreciation for politics will understand the motives of many of the popes and Church leaders, as well as the opponents of the Church, in how this history unfolded. However, it is equally important to recognize the unique point of view among popes concerning the role of the papacy and of the Church, even in temporal and political matters. The Church has always seen itself as the sole representative of Christ on earth, with the task of promoting Christ's message. Any questioning of this role or of Church authority to pursue it is the height of offense. This is augmented further by the Church's claim to supreme authority in *all* matters, even over monarchs. The pope himself believes in his own infallibility, which means that his decisions are made under God's inspiration and cannot be mistaken or questioned.

This attitude of perfection in the pursuit of God's work has made the Church single-minded in its pursuit of heretics throughout its history. The popes invariably cited infallibility and supreme authority as justification for the entire Inquisition and for individual decisions. From a political point of view one might reasonably argue that when faced with a well-organized and popular heretical movement, the smart thing to do would be to negotiate a compromise, or to align with one heretical movement against another. While such strategies would make sense from a military or political perspective, the Church has never considered such a policy. In its own view, all heresy is simply evil and has to be eradicated; and if a heretic cannot be convinced even under torture, he has to be executed to save his soul. This single-minded approach to a chronic problem of schisms and individual heretics became a blind spot for the Church. As the incidence of heretical movements spread in the Middle Ages, the Church never considered anything other than an escalation of its battle to destroy those breakaway movements. The Church did not employ strategic methods to fight heresy; it only increased its efforts to destroy it and even expanded the definition of heresy to include more than those whose beliefs were at odds with those of the Church. Over time, the Inquisition's victims included people accused of witchcraft, alchemy, questionable scientific claims, non-acceptable art, and even non–Christian belief. By the early 16th century, the Inquisition had grown into a highly organized institution with authority throughout Europe to exercise judicial powers, arbitrarily and with tragic results.

How did the Church evolve from the representative of peaceful philosophy of Christ into such an authoritarian worldly power? In the matter of its response to heresy, the Church's progression from nonviolence all the way to burning people at the stake has to be traced through the time when the Church aligned itself with the power of the Roman Empire to become the *Roman* Catholic Church. The point of view that heresy and other crimes against God or the Church deserved a death sentence emerged around the end of the 4th century. Before that, excommunication was considered an appropriate punishment for non-temporal crime. St. Optatus of Mileve was the first to cite Old Testament examples to justify a sentence of death.

From the early Church and its initial temporal tolerance of heresy, changes in opinion led, over the course of some 1,000 years, to the founding of the Inquisition (from the Latin *inquiro*, to inquire) as a permanent Church-based judicial institution. Originally based on the search for heretics, alchemists, and witches, the Inquisition system soon became useful as a means for punishing political enemies or seizing land and wealth. Punishments varied over time based on the approach of individual inquisitors and guidelines from various popes.

The evolution of the Inquisition can be traced through three schools in Church thinking. As expressed by notables of the 4th and 5th centuries including St. Augustine, St. Ambrose, and Pope Leo I (440–461), the earliest prevailing view was that it was contrary to Christian belief to punish heretics physically, with excommunication the preferred response. The second stage, which applied through the worst periods of the Inquisition, was based on the writings of Optatus of Mileve, who first cited Old Testament scripture as justification for the death penalty as punishment for heresy. The outlook was applied in the punishment of Priscillian, 4th century Bishop of Avila, generally thought to be the first Christian executed for heresy. This execution, in 385, marked a significant change in direction from the earlier belief shunning temporal punishment. In the third stage, the death penalty was viewed once more as contrary to Christian belief.

Augustine's early explanation of the Church view on this matter, as he wrote in the 5th century, was, "We wish them corrected, not put to death; we desire the triumph of discipline, not the death penalties that they deserve" (*Corrigi eos volumus, non necari, nec disciplinam circa eos negligi volumus, nec suppliciis quibus digni sunt exerceri*). In the Eastern Church, St. John Chrysostom (also known as John of Antioch), Archbishop of Constantinople, confirmed the same viewpoint in the late 4th century. He wrote in *Homilies* (a collection of his sermons), "To consign a heretic to death is to commit an offence beyond atonement." Although it took 15 centuries for Church policy to return to these original concepts in opposition to physical punishment, without these great early thinkers of the Church the sway of the Inquisition might have endured even longer than it did.

The origins of Inquisition have to be studied with evolving attitudes over many centuries. No Inquisition is likely to spring up suddenly or without being rationalized in doctrine and belief. In the case of the Church, the sense throughout the first 10 centuries was that any dissent from a singular interpretation of theology presented a very real threat. The ideal of a single Christian Church was envisioned from the time of Constantine, who in 312 converted to Christianity and ended the state persecution of Christians. In 380, Emperor Theodosius went a step farther, outlawing pagan practices and declaring the Roman Empire to be fully Christian.

This decision granted great power to Christianity, which from that point forward was known as the *Roman* Church, protected by the wealth and military might of empire. It also transformed the spiritual church into a temporal power.

The empowerment of the Church under Rome's protection made the Church leaders bolder than they could have ever hoped to be as a young religion with no temporal power at all. From that early 4th century onward, doctrine concerning the treatment of heretics was given not only executable power, but sanction under Roman law, where capital punishment was an accepted solution. The "just war" of the Christian, based partly in Judaic teachings, now merged with the might of Rome, and a new idea of a "Holy Rome"—blessed by Christianity—merged Church beliefs with the state's policies on capital punishment. Nonbelievers and heretics were viewed with the same disdain as those who committed treason against the state; the Church and the state became one and the same, institutionalized and permanent. In spite of Augustine's later rationale against physical punishment, the Church evolved a new principle based on Rome's state policies, declaring the mission of a holy war (*bellum sacrum*) and a just war (*bellum justum*). From that point onward, war itself became an accepted form of Christian faith.

Thus, the Inquisition was the offspring of the union of Church and State in the single entity of the Holy Roman Empire. Given the power inherent in this union, it is easy to understand how the Inquisition grew and expanded.

The entire history can be broken down into four distinct stages.

Stage One

By the 13th century, the Church was struggling with numerous internal problems and external threats. Europe was in social chaos at the time, and Church political control was disrupted by several groups' attempts at breaking away from the strict doctrine of Rome. The perceived threat from these groups was what led to development of policies meant to prevent and punish any breakaway movements.

The first stage of the Inquisition began with the efforts of Pope Gregory IX to do away with heretical movements. For hundreds of years of the Church had contended with one heretical movement after another. Growing splinter groups in Europe posed a serious threat to the primacy of the Church. Gregory empowered the Dominican Order to operate an Inquisition aimed at identifying and destroying the heretical movements of the day.

Most prominent among these movements was the Cathars. The Cathar rebellion against the Church and its Inquisition was centered in Southern France, in an area called Languedoc. During the 12th and 13th centuries, the movement was widespread and posed a direct challenge to Church doctrine. Cathars believed in a temporal evil in the form of a fallen angel or a deity dominating temporal matters and representing an eternal power with a benevolent God. Cathars thought of the central Church as a false religion more interested in political power than in promoting the interests of God. By crushing the Cathar movement, the Church perfected its Inquisition and the techniques for destroying heretics. The newly developed system remained in effect for three centuries.

The Inquisition began as a means for quelling breakaway groups. The Church sought out nonbelievers with a view to changing their mind or eliminating them through tribunal and execution or imprisonment. As time went on, a growing enthusiasm for neighbor-to-neighbor accusations created a state of terror among all communities falling within the Church's realm. The Inquisition expanded its mission from quelling heresy to eliminating any non–Christian influence, including Jews, Muslims, and pagans (witches, for example).

Stage Two

The second stage, and perhaps the best known, was the 15th century Spanish Inquisition. Spain had long been geographically shared by Spanish Christians, Jews and Muslims. A recurring theme in Christian circles was the desire to convert all of Spain to Christianity, conquer the Moors, and either convert Jews to Christianity or expel them. This movement began in the 10th century and continued until the height of the Spanish Inquisition.

During the reign of Ferdinand and Isabella (15th century), disputes arose between the ruling monarchs and the Church. King and queen insisted it was their right to appoint Church bishops. A compromise conceded to the monarchs' desire that Spain be cleansed of all Jews. By this time, Muslim influence in Spain had declined, and the Church agreed with Ferdinand and Isabella that Spain needed to become fully Christian. In 1478, the monarchs established the Inquisition of Castile to end heresy and to expel Jews and force them into the Church.

Pope Sixtus IV authorized a new Inquisition in 1478 to help in the Spanish invasion of the Muslim kingdom of Grenada. As part of this authorization a good friend of Isabella's, the infamous Tomás de Torquemada, was appointed Grand Inquisitor. Torquemada's reign has come to represent the entire Inquisition for many people even to this day. Torquemada developed the most extreme methods for forcing confessions from his victims. Most infamous among these methods was the *auto-da-fé*, or "act of faith." This was a ritual including prayer and mass, followed by the reading of findings. After the ritual, those found guilty were given their punishments, including burning at the stake. Under such extreme torture many confessed to heresy. Although Torquemada succeeded at driving the Jews out of large areas of Spain, he eventually turned his attention to dissenting Spanish clergymen, and this turn led to his downfall. He was replaced with a tribunal of four clergymen. But the precedents Torquemada set lasted long after his death in 1498.

Stage Three

In 1542, Pope Paul III established a new movement, the Roman Inquisition. Its initial purpose was to ensure that the Protestant movement did not spread to Italy, but this purpose soon evolved into serving as a permanent judicial system, part of the Vatican government. The Inquisition set rules and laws for clergy. It became a 20th century subdivision of the Holy Office, and in 1965 it was merged into the Congregation for the Doctrine of the Faith. Although this office originated with the Inquisition 400 years earlier, it functioned as an administrative office mainly concerned with interpretation of matters of faith, more a legal office than an enforcement movement.

As the Inquisition ran its course in seeking out heretics and Jews as threats to the Church, emphasis changed. Scientists were beginning to recognize concepts such as heliocentrism, an idea that directly contradicted the long-held Christian belief that Earth was the center of the universe. As late as the 17th century, scientists, artists and writers could be found guilty of heresy and forced to agree to censorship or face the possibility of death. But the extremes of the Spanish Inquisition were rarely matched by this late date, and the movement faded away.

Stage Four

The historical extremes of past Inquisitions were gradually replaced with a more legalistic and administrative version of Inquisition, including attempts to regulate science, the arts, and the clergy through various forms of pressure and censorship. The modern Church continues to hold on to the remains of this system; however, it has returned largely to the original ideas about punishment and today relies on the threat of excommunication as the most appropriate but extreme response to disobedience. Additional threats, such as loss of retirement security for aging clergy or isolation from their congregation, keep most in line with Church doctrine. However, the investigative and legal arms of the Congregation for the Doctrine of the Faith exert great influence today.

The purpose of this book is to document the origins of the Inquisition, and to provide explanations of how the movement expanded and changed over many centuries. The book is divided into the four stages described above. Stage One examines the first phase of the Inquisition from the mid–13th century to the middle of the 15th century. Stage Two covers the second phase of this movement, the Spanish Inquisition. Stage Three looks at the third segment, the Roman Inquisition, and Stage Four is involved with the Inquisition in modern times.

In attempting to document such a complex and lengthy history, it is obviously not possible to tell the complete history of each important element. Entire books have been written on the many discrete subtopics within the history, such as the Cathars or Galileo. Larger topics such as overall Church history, the papacy, and European political history have inspired even more and larger works. Bringing all of these sources together in a single history involved an examination of Church policies and beliefs about matters that are basic to Church dogma. Many disagreements on these basic ideas persist, and many misconceptions about Church history remain in place. The history of the Church is not a history of one single, true, and universally accepted series of beliefs. It involves multiple interpretations, which over centuries have inspired breakaways as small as the tiniest cults and as large as the splits between Rome and Constantinople, or between Catholic and Protestant.

The controversies involved in these disagreements lie at the core of the Inquisition. Many thousands have died or been otherwise threatened or punished for what the Church has defined as heresy. Given other names (pagans, infidels, nonbelievers, or witches) or persecuted on the basis of religious differences, disputed scientific observations or artistic expression, the many forms of Inquisition evolved over time as the Church tried to eliminate any and all dissent. Today the Catholic Church co-exists with other Christians and with other religions out of necessity, but strict Church thinking still holds that there is no salvation apart from the Catholic Church. Whatever co-existence is tolerated today, many centuries passed in which the Church tried to enforce its point of view with threats, excommunication, banishment, imprisonment, seizure of lands, torture and death.

This history of the Inquisition may be interesting to readers not only for a study of the events as they occurred, but also for an evolving Church philosophy. The Church has developed with the involvement of dozens of intellectual and philosophical giants of theology, and much of the credit for the evolution of doctrine belongs to so-called heretics. Augustine, for example, developed opinions in his writings that were responses to heretical challenges; and these points of view were then folded into the basic doctrines and codified at Church councils and synods. These doctrines were further influenced by the partnership between the papacy and the Roman Empire, which shaped the early legal formation of the Church in every respect, including responses to heretical movements. It was this partnership that converted the early Church into a political power, and with this power the Church became convinced that its task was to rid the world of nonbelievers. With all such instances of absolute power in the hands of the few, the concept of infallibility invariably leads to a tragic, far-reaching and devastating application of force.

Stage One
of the Inquisition

CHAPTER 1

Pope Gregory IX, 1227 to 1241: Stage One Begins

The pope did not establish the Inquisition as a distinct and separate tribunal; what he did was to appoint special but permanent judges, who executed their doctrinal functions in the name of the pope. Where they sat, there was the Inquisition.

— The Faith Database, "Inquisition"

The condition of life in Europe in the 13th century was a paradox. Technology and farming methods were improving rapidly even while medicine was rudimentary and brutal. The Church continued to exercise near absolute control over the Christian world while people were beginning to gain education outside of Church control (often at universities established by the Church throughout Europe). These new centers of learning in England, Spain, Portugal, France and Germany added to an expanding desire for knowledge. At the same time, the Church was trying to maintain its control over thought and belief. Meanwhile, scholars moved throughout Europe and, using the common language of Latin, were able to spread ideas on many topics, including medicine, mathematics, science, and even religion.

Travel during the 13th century was a perilous undertaking. There were few roads, no organized transportation, and little in the way of amenities. Population was spread among farms and villages but densely concentrated in cities. The lack of sewers, running water, or even paved streets made living conditions filthy and accelerated the spread of disease. Medicine was virtually ineffective. The most popular "cure" for any disease was bleeding or treatment of wounds with boiled oil. Disease was blamed on witchcraft or punishment from God. Polluted water and tainted meat were common and frequent outbreaks of smallpox, typhus and cholera defined life. A majority of newborns did not survive their first year of life and adult life expectancy averaged only 35.

At the same time, advancements in clock making were making time-keeping a rapidly improving science. Eyeglasses were developed and used. Navigation was improving as sailors learned how to read the stars. In spite of primitive travel conditions and short lives, European trade was improving quickly. The Church was the most important institution of the century, and was not only providing a central source for spiritual belief and education, but also enjoyed virtually unlimited power in the continent.[1]

It was under these contradictory conditions—primitive social culture and expansion of science and education—that the Church initiated its first formal Inquisition, with the intention of putting an end to growing heretical movements. Ironically, questioning Church authority and doctrine was only one feature of expanded learning and social and scientific development. In a sense, the Church wanted to encourage social improvements while also maintaining complete control. It was an impossible task, built on fundamentally conflicting goals; but the Church would persist in it for hundreds of years, during which thousands of people would be convicted of heresy, lose their property and their lives, face long prison terms, or be killed in Crusades or at the stake, all in God's name. During these centuries, too, the intent to maintain control of belief evolved into a more sinister form in which zealous inquisitors held and abused uncontrolled power.

It all began with concern over a localized movement of a Christian sect that, ironically, took Christianity more to heart and practiced a higher level of devotion than most Catholic priests of the day. The problem, however, was not with levels of piety but with the challenge this movement presented to the Church's authority.

The threat the Church perceived from this movement—Catharism—was serious enough for the pope to take strong and decisive action with the intention of destroying the challenge completely and ensuring that the Church, and only the Church, had the right to set doctrine.

The First Inquisition

Like so many important events, the first formal Inquisition (known today as the Medieval Inquisition*) came into existence quietly, with little notice. Certainly no one knew that it would lead to hundreds of years of abuse, tragic loss of life for many innocent people, and a permanent association of persecution with the Church.

Pope Gregory IX (1227–41) launched the Inquisition when he authorized investigations of the Cathars in Southern France. A crusade to destroy the move-

---

*It was also known as the Dominican Inquisition because the primary inquisitors were drawn from the Dominican Order.

ment (called the Albigensian Crusade) did not succeed (see Chapter 2), so Gregory was determined to rid Europe of the Cathars by direct investigation, tribunals, and executions. This effort did not occur in a vacuum; it was the result of decades of struggle between the Church and the Cathars, and of centuries of disputes with heretics, both real and imagined. From the time the Church was created, it was constantly besieged by sects and breakaway movements. Gregory's Medieval Inquisition was originally intended to serve as the solution to this problem.

A half-century before the Medieval Inquisition officially was initiated by Pope Gregory IX, a lesser-known Inquisition was put into place. Known as the Episcopal Inquisition, it was instituted by the pope and operated by local bishops. However, while it was not effective at rooting out heresy, the Episcopal Inquisition laid the groundwork for what would come later.

Pope Lucius III (1181–5) declared the Episcopal Inquisition on November 4, 1184, through his papal bull* *Ad abolendum* (On Abolition). Also referred to as the Charter of the Inquisition, the bull stated the pope's intention:

> To abolish the malignity of diverse heresies which are lately sprung up in most parts of the world, it is but fitting that the power committed to the church should be awakened, that by the concurring assistance of the Imperial strength, both the insolence and mal-pertness of the heretics in their false designs may be crushed, and the truth of Catholic simplicity shining forth in the holy church, may demonstrate her pure and free from the execrableness of their false doctrines.... [W]e likewise declare all entertainers and defenders of the said heretics, and those that have showed any favor or given countenance to them, thereby strengthening them in their heresy, whether they be called comforted, believers, or perfect, or with whatsoever superstitious name they disguise themselves, to be liable to the same sentence.... And as for a layman who shall be found guilty either publicly or privately of any of the aforesaid crimes, unless by abjuring his heresy and making satisfaction he immediately return to the orthodox faith, we decree him to be left to the sentence of the secular judge, to receive condign [deserved] punishment according to the quality of the offense.... [B]ut those who after having abjured their errors, or cleared themselves upon examination to their bishop, if they be found to have relapsed into their abjured heresy — We decree that without any further hearing they be forthwith delivered up to the secular power, and their goods confiscated to the use of the church.[2]

This bull specifically instructed bishops to turn unrepentant heretics over to civil authorities for punishment. Many years later, the future Pope Gregory IX would conclude that this was not effective. More aggressive measures would be required.

Lucius was an exceptionally honest individual of advanced age when he became pope, and has been described as "well-meaning, but weak."[3] Born

---

*A papal bull is a formal letter, decree or ruling issued by the pope. It is named for the metal seal, the *bulla*, that is used only on this document. In modern times, a bull is the only document the pope signs by referring to himself as bishop, servant of the servants of God (*episcopus servus servorum Dei*).

approximately 1110 at Lucca, he entered the Cistercian Order under Bernard of Clairvaux and attained the post of cardinal deacon in 1141, then cardinal bishop in 1159. From 1159 to 1181 he was dean of the Sacred College of Cardinals (*Decanus Sacri Collegii*) with the rank of cardinal bishop, a very influential post. The dean has a primary responsibility for calling a new conclave upon the death of the pope, and to preside over the conclave while in session. The college convenes only when a pope has died, and has no powers except during a papal vacancy (*sede vacante*). The pope may also call upon the College of Cardinals, at his discretion, to advise him on Church matters.

As pope, Lucius was involved in a dispute regarding the disposition of territories of the Countess Matilda of Tuscany. The inheritance had been left originally to the Roman Curia,* but after the death of the countess, Emperor Frederick I (Barbarossa) proposed that the Curia renounce its claim in exchange for 20 percent of the estate's income. This was the first of several disputes between Frederick and the pope, including a refusal by the pope to grant the emperor regulatory powers over Episcopal elections in Germany. Just as Lucius and Emperor Frederick I were at odds, many years later Pope Gregory IX would spend a good part of his career in disagreements with Emperor Frederick II.

An Early Target: The Waldensians

Among the targets of the initial Episcopal Inquisition enacted by Lucius III were the Waldensians. This was a movement that began in about 1177 in Italy, based on the beliefs of Peter Waldo.

Waldo (alt. Pierre Vaudès or de Vaux) was born ca. 1140 and died ca. 1218. Although his life preceded the Episcopal Inquisition, the Church was intent on curtailing the beliefs of his followers, all of whom were deemed to be heretics. In about 1170, Waldo gave away all of his possessions and began preaching simplicity and poverty. He memorized the Gospels, which had been translated by a priest into Waldo's native language, Provençal. Soon Waldo had a large following who also gave away their worldly possessions and lived lives of poverty. They called themselves the Poor Men of Lyons. This movement soon came to the attention of priests in Lyons, who tried to prevent the preaching from continuing. Waldo appealed directly to Pope Alexander III (1159–81),* who was the first prominent lawyer pope and a theological scholar.

Even though Waldo's beliefs were very similar to those of Saints Francis

---

*The *Curia* is the governing body of the Roman Catholic Church, which shares with the pope the governing functions of Church government and operations.

*Alexander presided over the Third Lateran Council and many of his decisions were later incorporated in canon law. He was the first to suggest a two-thirds vote by Cardinals to elect a new pope, a rule remaining in effect today.

and Dominic, Waldo had not been trained within the Church, and for this reason the Church classified his preaching as "without divine inspiration." Hence even though Alexander praised Waldo and his followers for their vows of poverty and sympathized with their simple Christian ideals, he concluded that the Waldensians could continue to preach only if they gained permission from the archbishop of Lyons. Waldo and his followers rejected the pope's limitation on their activities, and as a result Pope Lucius III later excommunicated* all members of the sect at the Council of Verona in 1184 on the charge of "contempt for ecclesiastical power." At this council, Lucius declared that the Poor Men of Lyons were to be included on a formal list of known heretics on the charge of preaching without permission or ordination from the Church.

The Waldensians were once again condemned by the Fourth Lateran Council (also known as the General Council of Lateran), held in 1215. This council was called by Pope Innocent III (1198–1216). Innocent, like Alexander many years before, appreciated the humble lifestyle and evangelical poverty practiced by many heretical groups but also condemned them. In 1199, Innocent called heresy "high treason against God," and at the 1215 Council, he issued numerous decrees condemning heresy (including a call to secular authorities to aid the Church in suppressing and punishing heretics).[4]

Among the important theological differences between the Waldensians and the Church was the former's refusal to accept the concept of purgatory (*purgare*, meaning to make clean), since it is not mentioned in the Bible. They also refused to venerate the saints. Perhaps most offensive to the Church, the Waldensians believed that anyone, not only priests, had the right to consecrate sacramental bread and wine. In short, the Waldensians thought of the Church as unbiblical in much of its dogma.

Waldensians also refused to swear oaths, so that in a tribunal aimed at presenting evidence of heresy, a member of this sect was treated as a suspect refusing to tell the truth. Both Church and secular authorities were troubled as well by the Waldensians' refusal to go to war.

Waldo himself faded into history after he was excommunicated, but the Church continued to pursue his followers through the Episcopal Inquisition as well as later tribunals. Waldensians escaped to the mountainous regions of Northern Italy to avoid Church inquisitors, and the movement survived over many centuries, its followers finally becoming prominent in the Protestant Reformation movement. The Waldensians were later accused of practicing witchcraft and were among those persecuted in Europe's Great Witch Hunt (1450–1750), a variant of the Inquisition focused on witches as heretics.

Today, some sub-groups of Mennonites, Anabaptists and Baptists claim that their history can be traced back to the original apostles through the Waldensian movement. However, these sects are minor:

---

*A person when excommunicated is deprived of access to the sacraments of the Church.

The theory of Waldensian origin of the Anabaptists was popular among Dutch and German Mennonites in the 17th-19th centuries, though never proposed by the 16th-century Anabaptists themselves.... The tempting and romantic theory of apostolic succession from the apostles down to the Anabaptists through successive Old Evangelical groups, which has been very popular with those among Mennonites and Baptists who feel the need of such an apostolic succession, always includes the Waldenses as the last link before the Anabaptists.[5]

A spin-off of the Waldensian sect began in 1207 when Durand of Huesca, an early follower of Waldo, converted to Catholicism. He wrote a text, "The Anti-Heresy Book" (*Liber Antihæresis*), and gained permission from Pope Innocent III in 1208 to establish a new mendicant order, the Poor Catholics (*Pauperes Catholici*). Members of the Poor Catholics preached throughout Southern France and Northern Italy. However, after five years the order began to fall apart. The pope discontinued his support in 1212, shifting his support to the Dominican (Preaching Friars) and Franciscan (Friars Minor) mendicant orders. In 1237, Pope Gregory IX directed the Dominicans to compel the Poor Catholics to adopt the approved rules of one of the other mendicant orders. Nearly 20 years later, the order was dissolved when the Poor Catholics were united with and merged into the Order of St. Augustine (*Ordo Sancti Augustini*). Although the origins of the OSA went back to Augustine of Hippo, the order was not formally organized into a single entity until the 13th century. This order is based largely on the "Rule of St. Augustine" and on his writings and codices (specifically in his *De opere monachorum*). This rule includes many sections, most significant among them being the requirement to live within a monastic community and take a vow of poverty. So the best-known attempt of Waldensians to reconcile with the Church led to formation of an order that was later dissolved.

Popes and Emperors at Conflict

The growth of heretical movements sparked a desire by the Church to enact strict anti-heretical measures. However, equally responsible for what would eventually become a full-scale Inquisition was a power struggle between Pope Gregory IX and Emperor Frederick II.

Power struggles between popes and emperors were nothing new in the 13th century. From the moment Emperor Constantine embraced Christianity eight centuries earlier, the issue of which side was supreme was raised and remained a source for conflict without ever being resolved. Constantine converted to Christianity in the year 312 after winning the battle of the Milvian Bridge. According to ancient historians, Constantine saw a vision of the cross in the sky, which he took as a sign from God that Constantine's army would win the battle. As a result of this sign and his victory, Constantine converted and ended

Rome's persecution of Christians, a new rule formally mandated by the 313 Edict of Milan (*Edictum Mediolanensium*). In 380, Emperor Theodosius outlawed pagan practices in the Roman Empire and declared Christianity its sole and official religion. This put the whole might of Rome behind the Church.

For several years after his conversion, Constantine continued to have coins issued carrying images of Roman gods. Constantine saw the embracing of the Church as politically advantageous to him as emperor, and the Church continued to promote its own supremacy while viewing Constantine and his temporal power as a means toward its own ends.

Constantine dreamed of uniting all of Christianity under a sole leader, but he soon faced many obstacles. Not only were there divisions between Rome and Constantine's newly established base of Constantinople; the Church was also struggling with North African sects of the Church and seemingly endless heretical breakaway movements.

In Rome, the ruling class of bishops saw Constantine's partnership as a means to increase their own social standing. Bishops competed for wealth and power with Roman senators, serving in political as well as in Church roles. Ironically, Rome remained primarily pagan, so another source of conflict between Church and the ruling class was pagan versus Christian belief. The struggle for influence had begun, each side wanting to hold onto its position and expand it at the expense of the other. A turning point occurred during the reign of Pope Leo I (440–61), who declared the papacy the supreme and universal authority within the Church, and the Church the supreme and universal authority over all matters, both spiritual and temporal.

In August 449, the Council of Ephesus passed several new canons, one of which recognized the ruler of Constantinople as holding the same ruling status as Rome's (canon 28). Leo disagreed strongly and did not endorse the council's findings until 453, declaring canon 28 to be invalid and a violation of the earlier conclusions of the canons of the First Council of Nicaea. Leo interpreted the Nicaean rulings as granting absolute power to the pope to the exclusion of all others. This was the beginning of the concept of the infallibility of the Church, defined as

> [i]n general, exemption or immunity from liability to error or failure; in particular in theological usage, the supernatural prerogative by which the Church of Christ is, by a special Divine assistance, preserved from liability to error in her definitive dogmatic teaching regarding matters of faith and morals.[6]

Because Leo strongly claimed papal jurisdiction over all of Christendom and Rome exerted political and military might over the same regions, conflict between the two was inevitable. By the 5th century, Italy was largely ruled by Theoderic, a Goth who decided to become Roman as he claimed the title of emperor. Theoderic ruled over the bishops in his realm who belonged to the breakaway Arian sect and did not respond to the pope's mandates. Arians held that Christ was subordinate to, rather than of the same essence as, the Father

Believed to be a portrait of Pope Leo I, one of only two popes called "The Great" (the other was Gregory I). Leo declared that the Church was the supreme and universal authority in all matters. (Detail from the manneristic frescos by Carlo Urbino on the ceiling of the altar chapel in the Cappella di sant'Aquilino in the Basilica di San Lorenzo Maggiore in Milan, Italy. Photograph by Giovanni Dall'Orto, May 18, 2007.)

God — that there was a time when the Son did not exist. In 484, the Eastern Orthodox patriarch Acacius defied Rome and the pope by adopting a pro-monophysite belief (denial of the dual nature of God as Father and Son). Pope Felix III (483–92) excommunicated Acacius and warned Emperor Zeno to stay out of Church affairs. Zeno's successor, Emperor Euphemius, asked Pope Felix to restore communion between the two churches, but Felix refused until Acacius' name was take from the diptychs (relief carvings or panels of paintings of patriarchs). The matter was not resolved until the reign of Gregory the Great many years later.

In spite of Rome's protection of the Church, its leaders and its properties, the papacy regarded the temporal Roman leaders as supporters of heretical movements. As a result, popes tried to draw a clear distinction between secular and Church powers and jurisdiction. This became especially marked when emperors attempted to claim political authority, a recurring theme in Church history. This distinction was expressed most clearly by Pope Gelasius (492–6), who wrote to newly elected Byzantine Emperor Anastasius:

> There are, most august Emperor, two powers by which this world is chiefly ruled: the sacred authority of bishops and the royal power. Of these the priestly power is much more important because it has to render account for the kings of men themselves at the judgment seat of God. For you know, most gracious son, that although you hold the chief place of dignity over the human race, yet you must submit yourself in faith to those who have charge of divine things, and look to them for the means of your salvation. You know that it behooves you, in matters concerning the reception and reverent administration of the sacraments, to be obedient to ecclesiastical authority, instead of seeking to bend it to your will.[7]

The early struggles to define the limitations between Church and State were set by this strong message for many decades to follow. Emperors generally refused to be dictated to by the Church, while the Church generally insisted on its superiority over emperors. But the Church needed the protection of the Empire. By the year 500, after being repeatedly attacked and plundered, Rome's population had fallen from 800,000 down to 30,000 and the city's great aqueducts were no longer working, having been destroyed by invading Goths. Pope Gregory I (Gregory the Great, 590–604) inherited a Christian empire in ruins. Italy was under the rule of the Lombards, pagan tribes who had invaded from what today is Austria. Gregory was able to negotiate a truce with the Lombards while asking Byzantine Emperor Maurice for support that never came. Even while balancing the temporary and Church power, Gregory continued to insist on papal supremacy over all churches, East and West, and over the entire empire.

Gregory was forced to administer Rome in the most basic of ways, including providing food to its starving citizens and taking control of the local military. He negotiated treaties, paid soldiers, and became virtual governor, diplomat and military leader of the area. As head of the Church, he set new rules for elections of bishops, celibacy of priests, and negotiations with the Church in the East. With exceptional talent and broad interests, Gregory was an outstanding leader; even so, he never resolved the struggle for power that lasted not only into the 7th century, but for the next 600 years as well.

The Church-State conflict rested on the desire for power and control by both sides. The Church position had consistently remained one of seeking protection and military support while insisting that emperors bow to its greater authority. The position of emperors remained one of exploiting the Church as a useful institution for political influence and prestige, but outside of its political realm of control and power.

The conflict grew into a theory of politics, the *divine right of kings*. This is a combined political and theological doctrine claiming that monarchs derive their power directly from God and do not answer to any temporal authority, not even the Church. From the monarch's point of view, any attempts to restrict these powers are contrary to God's will and are acts of heresy. The Church, on the other hand, continually asserted the doctrines of universal supremacy and papal infallibility, claiming that it had total authority over monarchs and all other humans. The differences in these two opposing points of view came to a head with the conflict between Pope Gregory and Emperor Frederick II.

The Medieval Inquisition's Origins

Gregory IX was faced with a dilemma. He realized that the Church's authority was falling due to two forces. First, the Episcopal Inquisition had lacked a central authority and failed to gain control over heretics as Lucius had hoped. Second, Gregory found himself unable to bend monarchs to his will simply on the basis of authority. The threat of excommunication seemed to have little power to control the behavior of others, and Gregory found that lack of power frustrating. As a result, he set into motion an idea that evolved over several centuries. The formal Medieval Inquisition can be traced to many causes: a recurring battle between the Church and various movements deemed heretical by the Church (such as the Waldensians), the desire to rid the Holy Land of nonbelievers (which also served as justification for the many crusades to the Middle East), and growing frustration among Church leaders at not being able to control others through excommunication. Gregory IX spent much of his papacy trying to bring Roman Emperor Frederick II into line, without success.

Excommunication had originally been used to punish heretics, those who defied the tenets of Christianity or challenged the authority of the Church to determine beliefs. By the 13th century, the punishment was extended beyond heretics to anyone who defied the pope. So as time passed, the power to excommunicate moved beyond a reaction to the crime of heresy, and was used in an attempt to keep citizens and even rulers in line with what the Church wanted.

Ultimately, the power of the Church, exerted through the Inquisition, would be further extended to include all nonbelievers of many types, and those who did not bend to the will of the pope.

The concept of excommunication was intended as the ultimate threat available to pontiffs. For Church members the sacraments, especially communion, are all-important; they keep Christians in touch with God. To be excluded from communion is thought to be the most severe of punishments, and in fact, throughout the history of the Church, the earliest belief was that the most severe punishment for heresy was excommunication. This belief has gone out of favor many times; during the first 1,000 years of Church history, a debate continued between those favoring excommunication and those preferring capital punishment. When the Church merged with the Roman Empire and became the Roman Catholic Church, the appropriate punishments for heresy were also merged, and Roman law prevailed.

By the 13th century, heresy had begun to emerge once more after a relatively quiet period. The newly emerged movements took many forms. However, the greatest problem for the papacy grew from the fact that excommunication, or the threat of it, seemed to no longer hold the power it had once held, even over monarchs. Roman Emperor Frederick II (reigned as emperor 1220–50) created a problem for the Church and specifically for Pope Gregory IX. Gregory was politically skilled but not able to control Frederick. Gregory excom-

Emperor Frederick II, known both as "the Pioneer of the Renaissance," and "the Wonder of the World" (*Stupor Mundi*), defied Pope Gregory IX and was excommunicated by the pope three times.

municated the emperor three times but was still unable to force him to obey the Church's commands. On the contrary, Frederick defied the pope directly and even tried to have Gregory removed from office. Frederick was a highly intelligent man who spoke six languages and was a patron of the arts and sciences. He was known during his life by the title "wonder of the world" (*Stupor Mundi*), making him a formidable opponent of the Church of the 13th century. The clash between Gregory and Frederick was one of two great intellects with equally great political aspirations.

The first of three excommunications occurred in 1228, when Fredrick had become ill and abandoned the Sixth Crusade. Citing abandonment as a cause, Gregory in fact was fearful of Frederick's political ambitions. The condemnation was reversed in 1230 after Frederick vowed to not make any attempts at ruling in the papal territories of Italy.

Gregory excommunicated Frederick a second time in 1231 after the emperor reorganized the laws of Sicily, including curtailing Church mandates against heretics. A truce was entered soon afterwards and once again, Frederick was granted absolution. However, in 1239 Gregory entered a ruling of excommunication for a third time after discovering that Frederick had political ambitions to take over rule of all of Italy, including Rome. This instance was the most contentious to date. Frederick called for a general council hoping to overrule the pope, comparing the pontiff to the "red horse" of Revelation who would destroy peace on earth:

> And another horse came forth, a red horse: and to him that sat thereon it was given to take peace from the earth, and that they should slay one another: and there was given unto him a great sword.[8]

Gregory retorted by calling Frederick the wild beast (*belua*, term for the antichrist). The war of words finally resulted in Frederick's invading Rome, and in 1241 his forces surrounded the city; but while Rome was under siege, Gregory passed away.

The problems caused by Frederick's lack of response to excommunication or threat, as much as other causes, led to the establishment of a formal policy for punishment of heresy: the Inquisition. Once Frederick went to the extreme of attempting to overtake Rome by force of arms, the Church realized that it needed more than the threat of excommunication to maintain its hold on power.

To understand how the preference for physical threats came to replace the long-preferred separation of believers from the sacraments requires a brief explanation of excommunication.

The Concept of Excommunication

The word *excommunication* is derived from the Latin words *ex* (away from or out of) and *communio* (communion). A basic premise in Christianity, based on Christ's message at the Last Supper, is the idea of shared blessings with God in the form of Holy Communion (symbolically receiving the Eucharist, representing body and blood of Christ):

> During supper, Jesus took bread and having said the blessing he broke it and gave it to the disciples with the words, "Take you and eat, this is my Body." Then he took a cup, and having offered thanks to God he gave it to them with the words, "Drink from it, all of you. For this is my blood, the blood of the covenant, shed for many for the forgiveness of sins."[9]

In its original form, excommunication was meant as a corrective measure, aimed at bringing a wrongdoer back into compliance. In comparison, physical punishment, especially the death penalty, was aimed at controlling people by example, and at finally and permanently punishing behavior. So the transition from the relatively gentle and well-intended excommunication to the death penalty was a significant and extreme change in how heresy and other wrongs were treated by the Church.

Historically, excommunication has been applied both to clerics who did not follow the strict doctrines of the Church, and to Church members who were deemed to be acting outside of the prescribed manner. This could mean everything from pagan worship to outright rebellion, and at times even punishment for un–Christian thought.

The institution of excommunication is one of several degrees. Two separate forms of excommunication have evolved, one each for clerical and lay offenses. The *forum externum* was an ecclesiastical court or tribunal aimed at enforcing Church rules in the public. The *forum sacramentale* was designed to impose penance primarily among the clergy.

Another distinction is when excommunication takes effect. If it is *latæ*, then the guilty person is excommunicated immediately and by reason of the act committed, without the requirement that a person actually be declared excommunicated. A second classification, excommunication *ferendæ sententiæ*, is a penalty in ecclesiastical law and is imposed by sentence of a judge (pope or bishop). The popes have used this second type traditionally as a threat, to induce the accused to obey the pope's commands. A public excommunication is further subject to degrees of punishment. Some excommunicated persons are shunned (*vitandi*) whereas others are simply tolerated (*tolerati*).

An excommunication can also be either reserved or non-reserved. Any confessor can grant absolution to someone in a non-reserved excommunication. But if someone's excommunication is reserved, then absolution can come only from a specific person. Some acts of excommunication are reserved only for the pope; others require an act of the pope or a bishop.

The ability to excommunicate is also subject to a series of restrictions and rules. In general, any cleric with jurisdiction can excommunicate someone, but this right is limited only to persons within the jurisdiction. This right extends to papal legates, vicars and other authorities in addition to bishops and popes.

However, a local priest is not allowed to impose excommunication officially, nor can a priest declare that someone has been excommunicated. The act must go through the formal process in ecclesiastical law.

The consequences of excommunication depend on the person subjected to it. For clerics, excommunication deprives them of the right to administer the sacraments. For laymen, it deprives guilty people from receiving any of the sacraments, meaning achieving a state of grace is made impossible. The range of consequences resulting from excommunication is summarized as *Res sacræ, ritus, communion, crypta, potestas, prædia sacra, forum, civilia jura vetantur* (loss of the sacraments, Church rites including Mass, communion, and prayers of the Church; ecclesiastical burial, jurisdiction, canonical rights and social intercourse with other Christians).

The institution has been abused and misused many times through Christian history. Thus, a rule concerning improperly excommunicated persons states that such acts are immediately void and invalid. This includes excommunication by a person who lacks jurisdiction or imposes the penalty incorrectly; it also includes instances where the act is defective in form.

Excommunication has been imposed at times for a specific period only, after which absolution (forgiveness) was automatic; but these instances have been rare. Although the word "absolution" is also used for forgiveness of sins as one of the sacraments, it has a different meaning for those excommunicated. Absolution in this case requires a judicial action and has nothing to do with the sacraments. By absolution, a previously excommunicated person is reinstated in good standing with the Church and the rights previously lost are returned. First and most important among these is the right to receive the sacraments. While under excommunication, a person cannot be absolved of sins, by definition. Thus, for a faithful believer, upon being absolved of excommunication, the next step would be to visit a confessor and obtain the other type of absolution, from all sins. (This subsequently requires performance of penance, and then the person is able to receive communion.)

Some variations of absolution from excommunication have historically varied in terms of conditions imposed as part of the act. In order to complete absolution, a person might be required to spend time on a pilgrimage, pay a fine, or even embark on a holy crusade. If these acts of penance are not performed in advance, then absolution will have been granted conditionally and within a specified timeframe. The individual who originally imposed the sentence can grant absolution. However, this right can be delegated to a secondary judge, such as a bishop who succeeds a previous bishop or pope. The pope can overrule excommunications imposed by those under him, and even by previous popes.

Pope Gregory IX created a distinction between what was termed *minor* and *major* excommunication. A minor excommunication as defined by Gregory was a prohibition against receiving the sacraments. In theory, any priest could impose a minor excommunication; for example, a member of the Church could be refused communion on the basis that he or she was not penitent for sins. To remove this restriction, the offender had to receive absolution from the priest.

As applied to priests, minor excommunication remained a serious restriction. For example, a priest under minor excommunication could not legally perform a mass or administer sacraments to others. Minor excommunication was abolished by the Church through the *Apostolicæ Sedis* (Acts of the Apostolic See), a bull issued by Pope Pius IX (1856–78) in 1869. This bull became the basis of modern-day penal law of the Church; the Church formally adopted the elimination of minor excommunication in 1884.

Major excommunication, the only remaining form of the institution, was originally reserved for the most serious offenses. Today, distinctions of excommunication are no longer recognized. Exclusion from the sacraments exists without degrees. An individual can be excommunicated under the law — *a jure* — or by an ecclesiastical prelate — *ab homine* — usually as part of a criminal proceeding or following conviction. For example, if a priest is convicted of a criminal offense in a public court, he may be excommunicated *ab homine* even if a specific Church law has not been violated.

In Church history, excommunication has at times been used in the extreme, and this is largely the reason for so many cautious restrictions and qualifiers in modern ecclesiastical law. Many of the original uses of excommunication served as the original basis for inquisitorial practices, and so the institution has been reformed and carefully restricted in modern use.

Among the extremes of the past was one of the most unusual acts in Church history. Pope Stephen VI (896–7) considered the late Pope Formosus (891–4) an enemy. Nine months after the death of Formosus, Stephen ordered his remains dug up to be placed on trial. The body was dressed in papal vestments and placed on the throne, and Stephen presided at the trial. Formosus was found guilty of a range of offenses. The three fingers of the corpse's right hand used to grant blessings were cut off and the body flung into the Tiber River. The removal of the important blessing fingers was the ultimate ban on issuing of the sacraments. Finally, the corpse was also assigned to the river, with Pope Stephen satisfied that he had made his point.

Excommunication was applied even against dumb animals. During the course of the Inquisition, cows, horses, and other animals were accused and subsequently tried, convicted, tortured and executed for a range of offenses. St. Bernard (12th century) was said to be interrupted during a service by an invasion of flies. He excommunicated them en masse and the flies immediately fell dead, so the story goes. Many other anecdotes tell of excommunication against grasshoppers and locusts as punishment for ruining crops. Even as late as the 18th century, an edict was issued in the Municipal Register of Thonon, France, excommunicating crop-damaging insects.

The Church has more clearly defined excommunication and narrowed its application in modern times. It can be applied only to people who are living and who have been baptized. Many people have confused excommunication with exorcism, but these rituals are not the same. Exorcism applies to nonentities such as demons, which cannot be excommunicated because they are not Christians. The act also cannot be applied against living non–Christians, broadly classified as infidels. The act of excommunication against the dead is not allowed; however, this restriction can be avoided by a post mortem declaration that the individual is retroactively deemed to have been excommunicated while living. By the same argument, a previously excommunicated person can be declared absolved after his or her death. The rite of absolution of a previously excommunicated person is called *ritus absolvendi excommunicatum jam mortuum.*

The act of excommunication is specifically limited in these ways. However, the act has been applied against entire communities. For example, in the past a dissenting sect charged with heresy or identified as a schism against the doctrine of the Church has been excommunicated en masse, including individuals born into the communities at issue. By definition, a breakaway schism that remains Christian but is no longer Catholic is subject to excommunication under the Church definition.

A Catholic can be excommunicated only upon being charged with a specific act or fault. An internal failing, such as doubt or error, is not enough to lead to excommunication under modern Church law. The fault must be external, meaning the commission of an intentional act of heresy or other offenses. Three groups are excluded from the possibility of excommunication. In the first group are people who do not possess knowledge that the act or belief is wrong; people who are unable to reason, including young children until they have reached the age of reason; and the mentally ill. In the second group are those acting from extreme fear; they are excluded on the basis that fear affects free will. In the third group are those acting out of ignorance; someone who is not aware of the law cannot suffer a penalty.

These distinctions become very complicated and even the Church acknowledges that "ignorance" comes in many forms. Although modern-day excommunication is absolute and does not contain degrees of guilt, culpability itself is not as clear. The consequences of excommunication are significant insofar as it restricts behavior rather than preventing future acts, and this is the crux of the problem the Church faced in the 13th century.

The Life of Pope Gregory IX

Gregory IX was a skillful politician and legal scholar, energetic in the pursuit of Church interests, and very religious. He was a friend to two of the individuals who began the major mendicant movements, Dominic and Francis.

Gregory was born Ugolino de Conti in Anagli, to the southeast of Rome.

His birth year is not known, but it is usually cited as 1145 or 1147. He was educated at the universities of Paris and Bologna. A nephew of Pope Innocent III, Ugolino was appointed papal chaplain when his uncle became pope (some sources claim Innocent was not an uncle but a cousin). In 1206, Ugolino was also appointed cardinal-bishop of Ostia and Velletri. The following year, he was sent to negotiate a truce between Philip of Swabia and Otto of Brunswick, who both claimed the German throne. The negotiations were not successful; but in 1209 Ugolino returned to Germany and succeeded in convincing the German prices to accept Otto as rightful king.

When Innocent III died in 1216, Ugolino played a key role in the election of a successor, Honorius III. The next year, the new pope appointed Ugolino plenipotentiary legate for Lombardy and Tuscia. Among his duties was promoting a new crusade. He was appointed dean of the College of Cardinals in 1219. In 1220, a new Roman Emperor, Frederick II, was crowned. Frederick immediately pledged to go on a crusade to the Holy Land. This pledge was the basis for later conflicts between Frederick and Ugolino.

In 1227, Honorius passed away and a new conclave began. The cardinals first elected Conrad of Urach, but Conrad refused to accept the position. This led to election of Ugolino, who took the title Gregory IX. He adopted this name because he was elected at the monastery of Saint Gregory ad Septem Solia.

Even though he was in his eighties, the new pope was energetic and pursued his duties vigorously. His background in many diplomatic posts made Gregory an exceptionally skilled politician and statesman. One of his first acts was to order Frederick II to fulfill his vow to embark on a crusade to the Holy Land. Although Frederick did set sail as instructed, he returned after only a few days, citing serious illness as the cause. This was the beginning of decades of conflict between pope and emperor that largely defined Gregory's reign.

Gregory was instrumental in many decisions creating and furthering the Inquisition. Among these was a continuation of the belief in papal supremacy, an idea promoted by previous popes, notably by Gregory VIII (1073–85) and Innocent III (1198–1216). This concept — that the pope and his decisions were beyond reproach — was based on a statement made by Christ to Saint Peter:

> And I say to you: you are Peter, the rock, and on this rock I will build my church, and the powers of death shall never conquer it. I will give you the keys of the kingdom of Heaven; what you forbid on earth shall be forbidden in heaven; and what you allow on earth shall be allowed in heaven.[10]

This citation was used by many popes to claim papal supremacy and to justify decisions that could not be questioned or challenged by opponents.

Papal supremacy strengthened the influence and role of the papacy from the 11th through the 13th century. Even though the Crusades were not permanently successful, when Pope Urban II (1088–99) launched the era of the Crusades in 1095, it brought European powers together under a unified cause, led by the pope. The growing influence of popes preceding Gregory brought papal authority to a zenith with Gregory's reign. This empowered him to create the Inquisition, not only as a means for punishing heretics, but also to control temporal rulers and to force them to obey the pope. The papacy thus expanded its long-standing authority over spiritual affairs, and now included domain over temporal politics as well. One of Gregory's major accomplishments was publication of his bull *Parens scientiarum* (The Mother of Sciences) in 1231. This settled a dispute among university scholars in Paris. As part of the settlement, the pope took direct control over the university, including the right to suspend lectures on the premise of some provocation (for example, "monstrous injury or offense").

In the same year, Gregory established the formal Papal Inquisition. Unsatisfied with the progress made toward stamping out heresy, Gregory took away from Church bishops the authority to manage punishment, and claimed it to be within the pope's authority to set rules. Thus, the Medieval Inquisition replaced the earlier, less formal Episcopal Inquisition that had been established by Lucius III. The failure of the Episcopal Inquisition influenced Gregory's decision to create a more encompassing Inquisition under the control of the papacy itself. He determined to staff investigations with professionals, primarily from the Dominican Order. Gregory's Inquisition had an organized, systematic character and was far more effective in gaining the desired result, the punishment of heretics.

It was Gregory's support of the Dominican and Franciscan orders that is cited as his most notable achievement as pope. However, creation of the first effective and long-standing Inquisition, while not as positive an accomplishment, has to be considered an equally important one. In fact, in large measure, Gregory's support for the well-educated mendicant orders was largely responsible for the high degree of organization in the Inquisition and its legal processes.

Gregory canonized St. Francis of Assisi in 1228, and St. Dominic in 1234. Among those canonized by Gregory, these two are the most significant, not only in terms of history but also for the role the mendicants played in future inquisitorial tribunals and investigations.

In the first truly organized Inquisition, Gregory took fast action. In 1233, he extended his mandate through the Monastic Inquisition, in which he formally named the Dominican Order as the Church's official inquisitors.

Origins of the Inquisition Movement

Gregory's battles with Frederick dominated his papal reign and were partially responsible for Gregory's desire to strengthen the legal standing and rules of the Church. Before his death, Gregory took several steps that made the Inquisition a permanent institution within the Church. His decretals became part of the Church's statutes. A decretal is a papal letter including a decision, frequently a legal one (*epistola decretalis*), or a written opinion by the pope on an issue of discipline. Such writings were derived from a request for the pope to make a decision on an issue of law, specifically Church law. The decretal is not the same as a Church law, but historically popes have directed local authorities to conform to their decretals and the conclusions reached. In the year 1230 Gregory ordered his confessor, St. Raymond of Peñaforte, to organize his decretals into a new set of canonical writings.[11]

The compilation of Gregory's decretals into a body of Church law (*corpus juris canonici*) was an important step in creating the legal framework for the tribunals that became standard in the ensuing Inquisition movement. The compilation of church documents had been under way for over 100 years, begun by the legalist Gratian, who had been commissioned by the papacy. Gratian's "Concord of Discordant Canons" (*Concordia discordantium canonum*) was an attempt to resolve contradictory canons previously published. Gratian had cited the Bible, church fathers such as St. Augustine, and decisions made during the Second Lateran Council. Gregory's desire for a legalistic basis for his interpretation of Church law helped create the legal justifications for later decisions within the Inquisition movement, including rules of trial, inadmissibility of statements by defense witnesses or the accused, and the use of torture to exact confessions.

Gregory's desire to strengthen Church law was inspired not only by Frederick's defiance, but also by the growth and spread of heresy in many forms. Indeed, heresy had become as much a problem by Gregory's day as it had been many hundreds of years earlier, when movements like Gnosticism, Dynamism, and Donatism had severely threatened the power of the Church. The 13th century movement called Catharism was perhaps the most serious heretical movement the Church had ever faced. The Church social trend toward extreme measures (beyond excommunication) began to grow, even beyond Pope Gregory's influence. The Council of Toulouse in 1229 issued a decree approving death at the stake as punishment for heresy. Similarly, in Germany the "Mirror of Saxon Laws" (*Sachsenspiegel*) was compiled in 1235 and approved execution of heretics and nonbelievers by burning at the stake (*sal man uf der hurt burnen*). Prior to approximately 1224, it seems there were no formalized Church or civil laws allowing the death sentence for heresy. In that year, the first known imperial law allowing death by burning at the stake for heretics was found in the rescript* of Lombardy. This was published by Gregory IX's predecessor, Honorius III (1216–27). The introduction of legalized burning at the stake opened the avenue to the Inquisition, which was then formalized by Gregory IX.

Gregory also institutionalized a belief in the Church in the inferiority of Jews, a belief that certainly added to the anti–Jewish fervor in later Inquisitions, notably the Spanish Inquisition, and even to anti–Jewish sentiment in relatively

---

*A rescript is a response by a pope, made in writing, to questions or petitions raised by individuals; these usually involve granting favors, issuing legal opinions, or interpretation of Church law.

modern times. In Gregory's 1234 decretals, he cited the doctrine "perpetual servitude of the Jews" (*perpetua servitus iudæorum*) and incorporated this concept into canon law. Under this doctrine, Jews were assigned to political servitude and deserved humiliation until the final judgment. This led to an elaboration of the concept, expressed as servitude under authority of the emperor (*servitus cameræ imperialis*), a concept first promoted by Frederick II.

This was one area of belief where Gregory and Frederick agreed. However, the ongoing conflict over other matters of temporal authority between Gregory and Frederick was, indeed, the turning point in Church history leading to the Inquisition. This was an era in which temporal authority of the Church itself was widely challenged and questioned. However, Gregory did not simply set up a new tribunal specifically to deal with dissent. Instead, he appointed "special judges" whose mandate was to represent Church law in the name of the pope. They operated within the existing law and courts, but had the power to bring charges and hold hearings. Departing from the long-established concept that a charge required an accuser separate from those sitting in judgment, these special judges were allowed to question witnesses in secret and issue indictments against an accused person, even in instances where the accusation came from the judges themselves.

In their original form, Inquisition hearings were allowed to impose punishments including imprisonment, confiscation of property, and burning at the stake. But who was to serve as the investigators and judges in Inquisition hearings? Because such hearings were considered part of the existing legal system and not as a separate court, judgment was to be made by well-educated and properly trained theologians. For this argument, Dominicans and Franciscans were assigned the primary role of inquisitors. The priests within these movements were trained in both theology and law and, unlike most people of the times, they knew how to read, which increased their ability to acquire additional knowledge. Another reason for appointing these mendicant priests to the role of inquisitors was their widespread popularity. By the 1230s, many priests set out on inquisitorial missions. The Dominican Alberic traveled through Lombardy in 1232 as an inquisitor, investigating instances of heresy. Later the same year, Dominicans at Strasbourg, Würzburg, Bremen and Ratisbon held inquisitorial hearings. The following year, a rescript from Gregory IX was sent out to bishops in Southern France and to the Dominican Order. The tribunals spread and by 1235, all areas of Central and Western Europe were affected.

The most important aspect of this growing movement was that Gregory removed the role of suppressing heresy from civil courts and granted it almost solely to the special judges who were mostly members of the Franciscan and Dominican orders. This absolute power did not continue unabated; in 1254, Pope Innocent IV (1243–54) banned perpetual imprisonment or burning at the stake of accused heretics without the consent of the Episcopal authorities. Popes Urban IV in 1262, Clement IV in 1265, and Gregory X in 1273 placed several similar restrictions on inquisitional tribunals. Clement V declared that all judgments issued in trials concerned with charges of heresy were void unless approved by the local bishop.

The Procedure of Inquisition

The usual procedure for examining a district was a summoning of local residents to appear before the judge. The purpose was not necessarily to respond to a specific charge, but to determine (in the judge's opinion) whether heretics were active within the community. If anyone appearing before the tribunal admitted to heresy, a penance was imposed. This consisted of a pilgrimage or other act of atonement, but did not usually lead to imprisonment or loss of property. However, to avoid being accused themselves, residents often accused their neighbors, so that what might have begun as a relatively small investigation expanded quickly.

When an accused person denied the charge of heresy, a trial was held. Four methods were used in these early tribunals for extracting information. First was threat of death, usually including the choice of a confession or being burned at the stake. Second was confinement combined with little or no food. Third was visitation from others who had been tried, with the idea that they would encourage the accused to confess. And fourth was the most extreme: one or more methods of torture, which usually resulted in the accused confessing. (In spite of the common belief that torture was used as a punishment for heresy, it was not; torture was used to gain a confession.)

Witnesses were easy to find. Personal rivalries and resentments brought people forward without hesitation. According to the Church law set forth in the early days of the Inquisition, at least two witnesses were required for identification of a heretic. But this rule could be overlooked when a foregone conclusion of guilt was in play. Any testimony offered by an accused heretic was considered worthless on the premise that a heretic would, naturally, lie to avoid punishment. Ironically, this meant that a falsely accused person had no chance to offer defense through testimony.

The identification of the witness was frequently withheld from the accused person. This practice was first legalized in 1205 when Pope Innocent III (1198–1216) published a papal bull, *Si adversus vos*, writing that any and all legal assistance for heretics was forbidden:

> We strictly prohibit you, lawyers and notaries, from assisting in any way, by council or support, all heretics and such as believe in them, adhere to them, render them any assistance or defend them in any way.[12]

The practice was confirmed and continued by Gregory IX and approved by subsequent popes, notably Innocent IV (1243–54) and Alexander IV (1254–61).

However, Pope Boniface VIII (1294–1303) reversed this practice in a papal bull, *Ut commissi vobis officii*. Boniface ruled that from that moment onward, all trials (including inquisitorial trials) required the naming of witnesses, opportunity for cross examination, and inclusion of witnesses for the defense (which had not been allowed previously).

Before the reversal of this rule banning testimony by defendants or introduction of witnesses, Church law allowed the accused to name his or her enemies. If the inquisitor determined that the accusation had been made falsely, the accuser could be punished severely. The crime of perjury was viewed as a serious offense, especially in a Church-sponsored court. The major safeguard in behalf of defendants in these early trials was a requirement — approved by Innocent IV, Alexander IV, and Urban IV — that the inquisitor work directly with the local bishop in consulting with local men of esteem (*boni veri*) in order to determine that the decision was fair and justified. Essential qualifications for the *boni veri* included education in theology and canon law. Trial documents were usually delivered personally for review by the *boni veri*, and one of the most important functions of these men was to determine whether witness testimony was reliable and credible.

Attempted safeguards for the accused were extensive during this early stage of the Inquisition. Often, more than 50 *boni veri* were called upon, including both priests and laymen. After a review of trial documents and witnesses, they were finally asked to determine guilt or innocence and suggest an appropriate sentence. While the opinions expressed were only advisory and not final, the tribunal vote usually conformed to what the *boni veri* recommended.

Even though the Church attempted to include safeguards through what amounted to an independent review of witnesses, evidence, and documents, the fact that the accused was not allowed to present testimony (more to the point, the accusation itself negated the value of testimony by an accused heretic) made these tribunals far from fair. The early history is a study of irony. For example, many sects suspected of heresy rejected the taking of oaths as a matter of dogma. However, the inquisitorial courts tended to view an accused who was unwilling to swear an oath as more likely to be guilty of heresy.

Punishments Imposed on Heretics

The range of punishments for those found guilty by tribunals was broad. No single standard was applied in any region, and a finding of guilt might easily result in an entirely different level of punishment in one place and another. Punishments did not include torture, which was used as a method for forcing confessions but rarely as a punishment for the crime itself. Of course, the favorite form of capital punishment was burning at the stake, which is an especially painful and slow death; and in many instances, slow burning included removing the condemned from the fire when near death, reviving them, and then returning them. Clearly, the fact that torture was not codified as an appropriate sentence did not always prevent its use.

Innocent IV first authorized the use of torture in the investigative phase of a trial in 1252, published in his bull *Ad extirpanda* (alt. *Ad exstirpanda*). Pope Alexander IV confirmed this later in 1259 and Pope Clement IV in 1265. The pontiffs were cautious, however; they wanted to limit the use of this interrogation so that accused heretics did not suffer permanent injury or death. This legal restriction was called *citra membri diminutionem et mortis periculum*. In addition, torture was to be used only once and as a last resort, meaning that the accused did not confess voluntarily. However, this provision was conveniently ignored or interpreted to mean that although a particular method could be used only once, subsequent and even more extreme methods were allowed.

Although torture was applied widely, many doubted its value, recognizing that most people will confess to anything under extreme pain. A well-known Dominican inquisitor, Nicolas Eymeric, wrote on theological and philosophical topics during his lifetime. His opinion concerning the use of torture is similar to the opinion held by many people in modern times. He wrote that torture is deceptive and ineffectual (*Quæstiones sent fallaces et inefficacies*).[13]

At first, clerics were forbidden to even be present during interrogations including torture, because the practice was considered to be so horrible. In 1260, in an ironic mixture of jurisprudence and Church law, Pope Alexander IV authorized inquisitors to absolve one another of any sin attached to the practice of torture. (Pope Urban IV confirmed this later.) The absolution provision led to many abuses and much extreme treatment of accused heretics.

A problem arose when the accused, having confessed while under torture, later contradicted the confession. Some, like Eymeric, argued that in this case the accused should be released. Others argued that when an accused withdrew previous statements, the torture should be continued because the previous confession had been incriminating. Ultimately, the practice was abused to the point where even witnesses could be tortured to get additional information or to confirm what they had previously claimed in front of the tribunal. Furthermore, even after confessing, a heretic could be tortured further to induce accusations against his friends or family members. Torture could be used as long as the inquisitors believed additional information could be gained, at their sole discretion.

Invariably the tribunals concluded that the confession was given true and free of coercion (*confessionem esse veram, non dactam vi tormentorum*). This wording was included in the judgment even when torture had been used. Because the actual torture was used away from the formal courtroom, the judges set up the system to protect themselves from knowing whether or not a confession had truly been gained voluntarily. The paradox of the tribunals was that only voluntary confessions were considered valid, but the use of torture was rarely mentioned in actual trial transcripts.

After conviction, punishments handed down by the inquisitorial courts included imprisonment for a number of months or years, or for life (perpetual imprisonment was termed *in perpetuum carcerem retrudi* or *perpetuo commorari*). In some cases, the severity of the heresy was deemed exceptional and the sentence included isolation from others, a form of solitary confinement; this may have included the exceptional cruelty that the condemned heretic would serve out the sentence wearing irons or being chained to a cell wall. The place of confinement was popularly referred to as "a place where one grows wise" (*sophronisterion*). Other convictions were as mild as payment of a fine or being required to go on a pilgrimage or a crusade. Some of the milder punishments could be rescinded when family members pleaded with inquisitors, especially when the accused was of advanced age or physically ill.

The popes of this age were cautious to not be included in the sentencing of heretics. Officially, the Church restricted itself to penal remedies, the most extreme being excommunication. Criminal penalties were the venue of the inquisitorial tribunals. So while the Church insisted that it had the legal right to define heresy, it was not at all willing to sentence those found guilty; rather, the Church preferred handing over the guilty to secular authorities for punishment (*sæculari judicio relinquere*), thus enabling the Church to wash its hands of imposing the death penalty. Punishment, especially the death sentence, was to be determined by the courts and not by the Church. In the papal bull *Ad extirpanda* published in 1252, Pope Innocent IV explained:

> When those adjudged guilty of heresy have been given up to the civil power by the bishop or his representative, or the Inquisition, the podestà or chief magistrate of the city shall take them at once, and shall, within five days at the most, execute the laws made against them.[14]

Innocent instructed that this directive be sent to every jurisdiction, and declared that any judge failing to carry through on this requirement would be excommunicated. Even though Innocent knew fully that "the laws made against [heretics]" included burning at the stake, the wording was designed carefully to exclude the Church from involvement in capital punishment. Alexander IV, Clement IV, Nicholas IV and Boniface VIII confirmed the requirement placed by Innocent IV over the next 50 years, and a consequence of the decree was that local officials, themselves fearing excommunication, became increasingly likely to impose death sentences on condemned heretics. In this manner, freeing the papacy from direct association with or involvement in application of the death penalty resulted in a higher incidence of the most extreme sentences.

The passing of final judgment was quite a solemn affair, and judgment was given the name *auto-da-fé* (act of faith). Within this ritual, three sections were involved. First was the *sermo*, a brief reading of the charges and conclusion of guilt. This was followed by the "decrees of mercy," including consideration of commutation, reduction of sentence, and forgiveness by removal of previously imposed penalties. Finally, the punishment was announced, ranging from public penance, payment of a fine, or a required pilgrimage, through to periods of imprisonment, life in solitary confinement, or death by burning at the stake.

The death penalty was controversial within the Church even when popes ensured free rein to its inquisitorial tribunals and to individual inquisitors. Pope Gregory IX's confessor, St. Raymond of Peñaforte, preferred the penalties of confiscation, imprisonment, or exile rather than application of the death penalty. And Saint Thomas Aquinas advocated the use of capital punishment as a remedy for heresy, but in such a way that the punishment was a secular matter beyond the jurisdiction of the Church and its merciful intentions. Aquinas wrote that

> on the side of the Church there is mercy, with a view to the conversion of them that are in error; and therefore the Church does not straightway condemn, but after a first and second admonition, as the Apostle teaches.[*] After that, if he be found still stubborn, the Church gives up hope of his conversion and takes thought for the safety of others, by separating him from the Church by sentence of excommunication; and, further, leaves him to the secular court, to be exterminated from the world by death.[15]

Punishments for heresy extending to the extreme were justified by the basic belief in the Church that Christ's kingdom was perfect and divine and that heresy was not only a violation of law, but also a direct invasion on the basic belief itself. So in the early stages of the Inquisition, there was little sentiment for showing mercy or for under-playing the severity of the crime or of the justification for penalties to be imposed. The intertwined Church and State of the day extended to the melding of ecclesiastical and civil society. Heresy was viewed as the worst crime a person could commit, and while the papacy kept itself at arm's length from carrying out penalties, it also required civil authorities to do so, under threat of excommunication.

The Church view that heresy was the worst possible crime was tested in the 13th century by the emergence of a widespread movement. The Cathars of Southern France defied the Church in dogma and actively sought to convert Catholics to their beliefs. The differences in theology were so extreme that the Church embarked on a 21-year crusade to wipe out the movement. This crusade did not succeed, but it did set a tone for the Medieval Inquisition that followed.

---

*Reference to the Apostle is to Titus 3:10–11, which states, "If someone is contentious, he should be allowed a second warning; after that, have nothing more to do with him, recognizing that anyone like that has a distorted mind and stands self-condemned in his sin" (*Revised English Bible*).

CHAPTER 2

Cathar Beginnings: Challenges in Heresy

> We live a hard and wandering life. We flee from city to city like sheep in the midst of wolves. We suffer persecution like the Apostles and the martyrs because our life is holy and austere. It is passed amidst prayers, abstinence, and labors, but everything is easy for us because we are not of this world.
>
> — Cathar Everwin of Steinfeld, quoted in Charles Schmidt, *Histoire et doctrine de la secte des cathares ou albigeois*, 1849

The most serious threat the Church faced by the 13th century was a movement in the Languedoc region of France. The Cathars became so popular and well organized that the Church believed it had to respond with more than the threat of excommunication. To destroy the threat the Church perceived in this popular movement would require a crusade.

The Cathar movement began in the 11th century and grew over time. The word "Cathar" comes from the Greek *katharos*, which means "pure." The term first appeared in print at the Third Lateran Council in 1179, when heretical movements described in Southern France were termed Cathari, Patrini and Publicani. The Council tried to outlaw the Cathar movement with the following statement:

> We decree that [the Cathars] and their supporters and abettors lie under an anathema, and we prohibit, under pain of anathema, anyone to dare to keep them in his house or on his land, or to support them or to have dealings with them.[1]

Many terms have been used to describe this movement, but "Cathars" is the most commonly used. Cathars referred to themselves as "good men and women" or as "good Christians."

Cathars were slandered by their enemies with fabricated versions of the origin of their name. Accusations made against them were lurid and crude in

36

nature. One outspoken critic was Alain de l'Isle (alt. Alan of Lille), a monk and preacher who in 1179 attended the Third Lateran Council. He imaginatively wrote, "The Cathars are so called from the cat, whose posterior parts they are said to kiss and in whose form, as they say, Lucifer appears to them."[2]

The definition of Cathar as "pure" is commonly misunderstood as well. The Cathars did not consider themselves pure, but rather strived for the ideal of living lives devoted to God. They tried to live in accordance with the advice Jesus gave to a young man who asked him, "What good must I do to gain eternal life?" Jesus replied, "If you wish to be perfect, go, sell your possessions; and give to the poor, and you will have treasure in heaven; then come and follow me."[3] The highest designation among members of the Cathar faith was *Perfecti*, a spiritual elite devoted to a life of vegetarian diet and celibacy. The perfecti were believed to be walking angels. The perfecti were a small group; the larger body of followers was called the *Credentes* (believers).

However, use of the term "pure" is derived from the Church itself, which described members of the movement as *pure* in the heretical sense. This is distinguished from lesser degrees of heresy, meaning that the Church viewed Cathars as *perfect heretics*; the Cathars themselves know their beliefs were heretical, making them the worst kind of dissenters in the Church view.

The Church also referred to members of the Cathar movement as Albigenses (alt. Albigensians). The Church came up with this name at the Council of Tours in 1163, called by Pope Alexander III. At this council, the groundwork was laid for the later Albigensian Crusade, called to wipe out the Cathar movement. Because the Church believed the Cathars had begun their movement in and around the French town of Albi, this title stuck.

The Cathar Theology

Suggestions that the Cathar movement was tied to previous heretical belief systems are in some ways supportable. There was no shortage of heretics in the centuries preceding the rise of the Cathars. Many people were burned at the stake for refusing to compromise their beliefs in matters like rejection of infant baptism, the nature of God as Father and Son versus Christ as a human but not the Son of God, and similar theological tenets.

During the 12th century, the Church was always willing to burn heretics at the stake to enforce acceptance of the central beliefs, with varying punishments at times proposed as alternatives. A few examples of Cathars being punished are found in this time period without a formal program to extinguish the movement. For example, in 1161, thirty German men and women were accused of being against marriage, baptism, and the Church. A council of bishops sentenced them to branding on the forehead and flogging. Some monarchs forbade burning at the stake, preferring the guilty be blinded and castrated. Nevertheless, the Cathar movement persisted, apparently on the strength of popular support.

A Dominican named Rainerius, a former heretic who converted and joined the Dominican Order, was an inquisitor of the age. He estimated the number of Cathars at four million, and followers were believed active in over 1,000 cities. The movement actively preached and sought recruits with great success. They had even established their own schools for children in many regions.

The popularity of the Cathar movement was based in both its beliefs and its high level of organization. The beliefs of the Cathars proclaimed that the devil created the temporal world and controlled it. They further believed that the Church sacraments were false and deceptive. They taught that the Church itself was evil and did not represent God's message as it had been intended or expressed in the Bible. The Cathars also denied the resurrection of Christ's body, which is a central theme in the Church.

Many Cathar beliefs were stricter than those of their Catholic foes. For example, Cathars thought that eating meat, eggs or cheese was a mortal sin, and that swearing oaths was forbidden in any circumstances. Among these controversial differences with the Church, Cathars argued that secular authorities committed a mortal sin when they attempted to punish heretics. Like many sects, Cathars also believed that the only way to achieve salvation was through their particular faith. The Cathar religion had only four sacraments (as opposed to the Church's seven): the imposition of the hand, the blessing of bread, penance, and consecration.

The imposition of the hand (*Consolamentum*) was spiritual baptism, also called baptism by the Holy Spirit. Only Cathars could provide the salvation granted through this form of baptism, and no sins could be forgiven without the imposition of the hand. Varieties of this sacrament existed in both Latin and Occitan, a Romance language spoken in the Lanuedoc region. (Occitan is the official co-language of Catalonia, Spain.) The ceremony involved two steps. First, a blessing was spoken in Latin: "Bless us; have mercy upon us. Amen. Let it be done unto us according to Thy word. May the Father, the Son, and the Holy Spirit forgive all your sins." This blessing was recited three times; the Lord's Prayer followed, and then a reading of John 1:1–17 ("In the beginning was the word..."). After this came another reading (found in the Occitan version but not in the Latin ceremony), consisting of a series of invocations to God.[4]

The second part of the ritual was a repeat of the Lord's Prayer presided over by a perfecti or elder, with detailed explanations of each of its parts. The Book of John was placed on a table and covered with a cloth while a ritual greeting was made. Replacing the better known phrase "daily bread" was "super-substantial bread," a change to the prayer that the Church cited as evidence of heresy. This was followed by the laying on of the hands on the individual being initiated. The new member was told to abstain from adultery, killing, lying, stealing or swearing of oaths. As each senior member also laid hands on the book or the person being initiated, the ceremony concluded with requests for forgiveness of sins (the Pardon) and embracing one another with kisses to the check (the Act of Peace). This was the primary Cathar ritual for about 200 years from the mid–12th through mid–14th centuries.[5]

The blessing of bread (*Fraction du Pain*) was performed twice every day, at morning and evening meals, and was a simplified version of the Catholic mass. The blessing consisted of remaining standing upon arrival at the table and reciting the Lord's Prayer before bread was shared among those in attendance.

The sacrament of penance, also called confession and absolution (*Appareil-amentum*), was required as atonement for sins and was similar to the better-known Catholic penance, consisting of prayer in most circumstances. The last of the four sacraments, consecration, was the act of declaring a member a bishop of the Cathar faith.

The entire Cathar routine was highly ritualized. This enabled even the uneducated masses to participate in practice of the faith even without grasping all of the theological implications and distinctions involved. Although different Cathar sects disputed many of the beliefs, all agreed that the Church establishment was evil and corrupt and did not represent God's intentions or message. The Cathar philosophy was that there were two distinct Churches. The Catholics, whom they called Romanists, were evil, and only the Cathars were righteous and in God's grace.

The Church believed that much of the Cathar doctrine was a compilation of beliefs among earlier heretical movements, notably those of the Paulicians and Bogomils. Paulicians were originally found in the fifth century in Asia Minor, and the Bogomils were more contemporary, a 12th-century movement primarily located in the region of Constantinople. Paulicians rejected the Old Testament completely and believed in strict dualism (a belief in good and evil as separate realities governed over by God and the devil). The Bogomils rejected baptism by water and were the originators of the alternative imposition of hands. They also rejected the use of images, including the cross and icons of Jesus or the saints.

Those Cathars dedicated completely to the faith (the *perfecti*) vowed lives of simplicity, frugality and poverty. The believers (the *credentes*) were not expected to take the same vows. The distinction is the same as that between clergy and lay members of the Catholic Church, in which believers are expected to adhere to the doctrine but are not expected to take vows. So the ideal life, which included a purely vegetarian diet, was practiced by Cathar clerics but not always by the faith's believers and supporters.

The differences of opinion in both ritual and sacraments formed the core of Catholic opposition to the Cathars, in addition to the threat posed by the Cathar disdain for the Church. One of the most troubling practices to the

Catholic view was the consolamentum, baptism without benefit of water. Catholic opinion was that this ritual was not a true sacrament and was an "initiation into heresy" (*hæreticatio*). The Church also objected very strongly to the Cathar provision allowing women to perform this rite. Only men were allowed to serve in the role of priests under Catholic rules.

It was not only that Cathars had different sacraments than the Catholic faith; they specifically condemned the seven Catholic sacraments. They called baptism by water a form of corruption and the work of an evil god. John the Baptist's invention of baptism was called the work of the devil in the Cathar Church. Cathars thought of Catholic communion as ungodly because it involved the use of the Eucharist, which is not an accepted form of consecrated host because it passes through the human belly, considered vile and dirty. The Cathar equivalent of this sacrament, breaking the bread, was a ritual of prayer and not of consumption, even though it took place prior to meals.

The sacrament of matrimony was also rejected by Cathars, on the argument that the concept was against God's word. Because Cathars believed that the human body was created by the devil to corrupt mankind with carnal desires, the purists among the Cathars preferred a life of celibacy and self-denial. The Cathars took literally the warning from the Bible that "if a man looks at a woman with a lustful eye, he has already committed adultery with her in his heart."[6] So to live by the Cathars' ideal, the love between married partners should be much like the love that Jesus had for his Church, and this should not include sex. The Cathar belief was that if a man and a woman had a sexual relationship, they could not be saved.

Abstaining from eating meat, eggs and cheese also was based on a Biblical citation, "I have never eaten anything profane or unclean" (Acts 10:14). Cathars did eat fish, however, based on the example set by Jesus in feeding the multitude and, after resurrection, feeding fish to the Apostles.

Cathars were also opposed to Catholic rituals and symbols. They shunned the wearing of vestments by their priests, worship using altars, and the cross, all called symbols of idolatry. In fact, the cross was termed the mark of the beast because, as the instrument of Christ's murder and shame, it should not be used in worship under any circumstances. Cathars also rejected the Catholic belief in purgatory and forbade the use of indulgences. The use of indulgences in the Catholic Church was criticized as a form of corruption, notably because Catholic priests and bishops sold indulgences to their faithful as a way to raise money. As a form of remission of sins, indulgences could be "saved up" and used to reduce the time a person had to spend in purgatory. This was described by Cathars as evidence of corruption in the Catholic Church, the primary point raised centuries later by Martin Luther that led to the Protestant Reformation.

The obvious disputes between Catholic and Cathar were deep and profound. But it was the popularity of the Cathar movement that alarmed the

Church even more than the heretical beliefs they promoted, and this led to an organized effort by the Church to destroy the Cathar movement completely.

The Concept of Dualism

The enduring popularity of Catharism can be traced, at least partially, to the mass appeal of dualism as a belief system. Dualists were defined by an anonymous author of the late 12th century as those who

> believe and preach that there are two gods or lords without beginning and without end, one good, the other wholly evil. And they say that each created angels: the good God good angels and the evil one evil ones, and that the good God is almighty in the heavenly home, and the evil one rules in all this worldly structure.[7]

Dualism, which predated the Cathars by many centuries, further taught that Lucifer was the son of the evil god, and Lucifer corrupted many of the heavenly God's angels as part of a huge battle for dominance. The battle ended when God expelled Lucifer from Heaven and placed his followers into physical bodies to live on earth. Dualists believe that Christ came to earth to save only the souls of these fallen angels.

The Cathar faith, like many other dualist sects, included beliefs that many Christians held to be true, even if not specifically expressed. The debate over the nature of God has been an unending one, and dualist ideas are found today among many Christian sects, including Catholicism. Duality even characterized basic tenets of Christianity. Early Church thinkers debated the issue of God's own duality and disagreed as to whether or not He was a single being (the Father) or possessed of two parts (Father and Son). This debate had grown to serious proportions by the 11th century to the extent that in 1054, the Western and Eastern Churches split (the Great Schism). The debate over the singularity of God (the Eastern view) or His duality (the Western view) was only one of many issues at dispute between the two great Church centers. An equally serious cause of the split was difference in language, with Western Churches employing Latin as a primary language and Eastern Churches relying on Greek. The schism is defined largely on the basis of geography and language, with the two major Christian Churches known as the Roman Catholic Church and the Eastern Orthodox Church. This dispute came to the forefront when Pope Leo IX (1049–54) and Patriarch Michael Cerularius (1043–58) each banned the language of the other Church in their regions.*

Another cause of the Great Schism was a long-standing conflict between

---

*Leo's emissary, Humbert, traveled to Constantinople in an attempt to resolve these differences. On July 16, 1054, Humbert placed a bull of excommunication on the altar of the Hagia Sophia. Leo's bull included Cerularius and all of his supporters. Although Leo had died before this date, it is used as the start of the Great Schism between Roman Catholic and Eastern Orthodox Churches.

pope and patriarch based on which one ruled the other. Sharing power proved an unacceptable middle ground when the Western Church began promoting the idea of papal primacy, a promotion that would culminate many years later in the expanded theory of Church and papal infallibility.

Even with the many problems based on language barriers, geographic distance, and power struggles, the central issue leading to the Great Schism was based on the *Filioque*, a clause inserted into the Latin version of the Nicene Creed. The word *Filioque* is derived from the Latin "and from the son." The Eastern Orthodox belief rests on the singularity of God, whereas the Roman Catholic version identifies Jesus as the Son of God, co-existing with an equal divinity with the Father (and from these two, the Holy Spirit is derived). So the basic Christian faith itself was split into East and West based on a theological dispute over the question of God as a singular being or a dualistic one. The Catholic Filioque statement that caused the controversy was "And in the Holy Spirit, the Lord, and giver of life, who proceeds from the Father and the Son." (*Et in Spiritum Sanctum, Dominum, et vivificantem: qui ex Patre Filioque procedit.*)

The dispute makes dualism more readily comprehensible to Christians. In modern Church theology, the belief in the forces of good and evil, good God and evil god or devil, rulers of Heaven and Earth, remain widespread. Modern-day Christian practice has incorporated many of the older dualist beliefs practiced by the Cathars and others before them, whether official Church doctrine agrees or not.

The distinctions of good and evil gods or forces of benevolence and malignance are encompassed in the term *moral dualism*. Separating the personalities of spiritual beings from the debate, moral dualism recognizes that in all things there is a natural conflict between good and evil (or, right and wrong). In Christianity today, moral dualism has become ingrained in most sects in the theory of temptation. A sinner is constantly tempted to respond to evil and to do the wrong thing, but the ideal Christian practice involves resisting temptation and then, when that fails, gaining absolution through penance and forgiveness. An individual is only able to resist the temptation of evil by accepting Christianity, the doctrine tells Christians. So dualism is at the core of the Christian faith, even though Church tenets argue against dualists like the Cathars.

The distinction might not seem important in modern-day spiritual belief, but over the history of the Church these differences have been treated as matters of survival, and the Inquisition was formed to stamp out the Cathars and the ideas they preached. However, dualism preceded Christianity itself. In ancient religions, binary distinctions were very appealing and were expressed as creative versus destructive deities, a belief called theodicy. In some ancient faiths, different gods were described as male and female or as summer and winter (or drought and rain). One early Christian sect the Church called heretical, Marcionism, argued that the Old and New testaments were written by two opposing gods. Most Christian-based forms of dualism are absolute (or, radical) dualism, meaning that the two opposing gods exist without beginning or end.

Cathars in Historical Context

The Church viewed the Cathars as a serious threat to its authority, because the movement gained popularity and was growing rapidly. However, Catharism was only the latest version of a long history of dualistic beliefs. In ancient Persia, Zoroastrianism was one of the earliest recognized dualist beliefs. Tenets include distinctions between one universal creator who practices truth and order (*asha*) and a lesser god who focuses on lies and disorder (*druj*). The conflict between these two forces is universal. Zoroastrians continue to practice today, and are found mostly in Iran and India.

The enduring appeal of dualism springs from its simplified rationale that many Christians find comforting, notably in response to the question, "How can a benevolent God allow such suffering in the world?" The Church has not been able to provide an answer based on its insistence of a supreme God (even with several aspects in Father, Son and Holy Spirit). But a dualist can convincingly argue that worldly suffering is not allowed by the good God, but caused by the evil god. Because the temporal existence is within the evil god's realm, human suffering is more readily comprehended. In fact, reliance on a spiritual God and afterlife is made more imperative through dualistic belief, because existing in the temporal world is hopeless without the promise of better things to believers, who accept on faith the premise that God as a universal and all-powerful force is enough to hold the Church together. This is accepted by many, but many others find more comfort in explaining away the evils of the world by recognition of good and evil as opposing forces, maintained by conflicting but equally powerful gods. This idea, originating with Zoroastrianism, is quite different from the belief in many Christian sects in what is terms *mitigated dualism*. Under this version of the concept, the spiritual, good God is more powerful than the temporal, evil God. Within this mitigated dualistic belief, some sects go a step further, identifying some exceptionally enlightened or inspired members as co-existing in both physical and spiritual worlds. This is seen in the Cathar distinction between the *perfecti* who, as a spiritual elite within the faith, were walking angels; and the typical followers, the *credentes*. Even though the Catholic Church does not accept the premise of dualism, descriptions of its most inspired saints also fit this description. Able to accept the pain of martyrdom and perform amazing miracles, the saints are without any doubt a special category of inspired Christians even in the Church view. Evidence of miracles as a prerequisite for sainthood creates a very specific form of dualism, especially in the sense that the typical Catholic is not able to perform miracles even with a great deal of faith and piety.

It may be a great irony of the Cathar movement that the true believers had much in common with the Church itself, beginning with the Cathar philosophy that Lucifer was cast out of Heaven, which conforms closely to the Christian explanation of the Fall. It was not so much a difference in dogma that caused the Church to actively seek to destroy the Cathars, but what Cathars were saying to the people to convert them. The primary threat was derived from the Cathar description of the Church as false. Once Cathar preachers began telling the multitudes that they could achieve salvation only through them and not through the Church and its baptism of water, it was inevitable that the conflict would lead to persecution.

Gnosticism and Dualism

Dualism is not easily detached from Christian belief and assigned only to heretics. Aspects of dualism exist in ancient and modern Christianity in many forms. These include the disputed but widely practiced belief in the duality of God between Father and Son; the existence of the devil that tempts mankind endlessly and in opposition to God; and the duality among classes of believers as either saints or sinners.

A variation of the Christian-based dualistic belief is described as Gnosticism. This movement is traceable back to belief in a *demiurge*, a purely evil being coexisting with God. The term "Gnosticism" is derived from the Greek word *gnōsis*, meaning knowledge. This form of knowledge is esoteric and relates to spiritual wisdom passed from God to humans, a form of attaining a higher consciousness. Gnostic movements cite this perception of a higher reality as a necessary attribute for salvation. Many Gnostic sects have been identified well before the birth of Christ, so Gnosticism is not uniquely Christian. Sects have also been attached to Judaism and to older Eastern faiths.

Gnostic beliefs incorporate several basic tenets, many of which can be seen as the origins for the dualistic beliefs of the Cathars. These tenets include recognition of a supreme, divine being as well as one or more secondary sub-deities, distinguished in terms of degrees of evil (versus the pure good in the primary God). Second, the Fall of Man recognized as the basis for Judaic and Christian theology is seen among Gnostics as being a divine incident that was played out in human form (as opposed to the more Christian belief in the incident as original sin of mankind). In Gnostic belief systems, the temporal world is inferior to a separate, higher-level spiritual world, and the human body is evil and serves as a prison for the spiritual being inside. (This particular belief conforms very closely to the Christian view of body versus soul.) The most significant duality occurs when a divine attribute or awareness is manifested in the physical consciousness of an enlightened human. Through this deep awakening, the inspired human begins the path toward salvation. The ability to achieve this enlightened state requires the help of a redeemer (such as Christ) or, in the Greek Church, the embodiment of wisdom through Sophia.

A modern Judaic version of Gnostic belief is found in Kabbalah. There are many similarities between Christian Gnostic beliefs such as the Cathars and the Judaic Gnostics like the Kabbalah; in fact, both beliefs originated in the Provence region of France at approximately the same time. It may be that the two sects influenced one another. For example, Kabbalah includes a belief in multiple levels of Heaven, mystical beings and deities, and creation of the Hebrew Bible by an inferior and evil deity — teachings contrary to the monotheism expressed in the Pentateuch.[8]

The Society of the Cathars

The Languedoc region of France was the center of Cathar belief as described by a chronicler of the 13th century, Peter, a Cistercian monk who was an eyewitness to the conflict between the Church and the Cathars. He described the region as "the source and origin of every form of heresy." A cleric from Toulouse named William of Puylaurens told Peter that the region was the location "in which, through the heretics, the Devil had prepared a seat for himself."[9]

Cathar society was highly organized. Meetings were held in a series of households. Homes were even set up for Cathar women. The movement was not initially underground and, in fact, public debates were frequent events. During the early 13th century, meetings between Waldensians and Cathars were common occurrences. The Cathar movement was far from isolated and as it grew, it amassed powerful friends and supporters. In that region of France, the countryside was spotted with a series of fortified villages and controlled by feudal nobles, often with small armies of their own. Because the Cathar preachers were able to gain many of these nobles as allies, they were able to preach over wide areas with the protection of a central, fortified town. Believers bolstered the preachers with provision of shelter, food, clothing and funds.

It became difficult for the Church to counter the influence of the Cathars in this complex feudal society. Many of the nobles formed alliances with one another, so that the combined vassals available for armed conflict and protection of Cathar preachers constituted a formidable opposing power to be dealt with. The Church, which initially relied on local bishops and its own traveling preachers, was not as well organized as the Cathars. Many Church bishops were unprotected by armed might, and congregations were poorly informed, disorganized, and completely dependent on the Church for moral leadership. So the highly organized, well-educated Cathar preachers, especially under protection of nearby nobles, were better equipped to gain support among the population. Usually better informed than the Church bishops on matters of scripture, the Cathars easily won many debates with relatively unprepared clerics.

The region was not urban for the most part. The majority of people lived in very small towns or on farms. Consequently, urbanized areas where the Church was more likely to establish its own strongholds did not play an important role in the spread of Catharism. On the contrary, the disbursed, rural population favored the Cathars largely because of the well-organized personal missions that preachers undertook. The Cathars were poor and a stark contrast to the wealthy bishops dressed in their fine silks, perhaps the most important observation Dominic made when he traveled through the region. The Cathar movement was strong enough and widespread enough that even though it was deemed heretical, it flourished in the open in the 13th century. The movement was more rural than urban in nature and was focused on providing peasants with information. In comparison, Catholic bishops were intent on keeping the poor uninformed and dependent on their leadership.

Yet an appeal focused on peasants and other lower-strata occupations only partially defines the kind of movement that the Cathars represented. Of greater threat to the Roman Church was its popularity among all levels of society and its rate of integration within the society itself. The traditional Roman Catholic believer, especially among the peasant classes, had no theological education and the Church had no interest in improving the knowledge base of its flock. Cathars, in comparison, were more likely to approach the preaching mission by imparting wisdom and knowledge, and encouraging people to study for themselves. The frequent meetings, discussions, debates, and challenges to established belief were a big part of what made Catharism a populist movement. At a time when there were more illiterate than literate citizens, even among the nobility, the enlightened message of the Cathars was welcomed.

The resistance by the Church to the development of an educated and informed public only helped the Cathars to gain more and more influence. Nearly 200 years after the Cathar movement began, Johannes Gutenberg printed his first book, the Bible. The response among the clergy to the existence of many *identical* copies of the Bible in circulation and for sale betrayed their own ignorance and resistance to change. One story tells of a visitor who met with an archbishop in his palace. Upon seeing the visitor's Bible and noticing that the print was identical to the one he had recently purchased, the archbishop said, "This is the work of the devil." The cleric did not comprehend the advance in printing and could

> arrive at no other conclusion. The Bible is a dangerous book. None but the priests should be permitted to read it. But here is the Evil One selling it everywhere; or, if not himself in person, some man has sold himself to Satan for that purpose. [Upon finding the man's identity, the archbishop told him] "You have sold yourself to the Evil One, and must be burned to death."[10]

The printing press and its implications were highly threatening to the educated of the day, especially to the clergy. For centuries they had relied on their

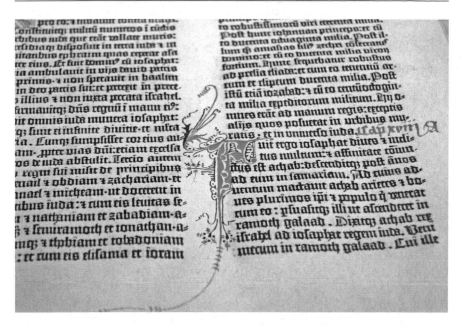

Detail of Gutenberg Bible at Yale University. Once it became widely available, the Bible was called a "dangerous book" by the Church. (Photograph by Kelly McCarthy, March 16, 2008.)

complete control of book publication by hand-lettering every edition in monasteries while, at the same time, keeping the population illiterate. The initial response to the printed Bible is instructive: If it did not come from the Church, it must be the work of the devil. Meanwhile, the movement towards widespread literacy may be partially credited to the Cathars who, in spite of the Church's claim over all Christianity, accepted the title *heretic* and advanced the message of enlightened and informed Christianity throughout the region.

Cathar Literature

One problem with describing the theology of the Cathar movement is that it varied over time and from place to place. Just as the Christian religion contains many variations, the Cathar faith also varied by social class and evolved geographically. Furthermore, modern scholarship on the Cathars must take into account not only Cathar writings and histories of the time, but also the records of inquisitors. Information gained under the extremes of inquisitorial methods must be carefully weighed and tested, since it often represents only what inquisitors desired to portray.

The unreliability of admissions given under interrogation extended beyond the immediate confession, and included the tendency for accused persons to later recant, or to offer admissions fearing that others might later accuse them. As one inquisitor explained:

> When they are converted, they tell everything, reveal the truth, and betray their confederates, whence results a great harvest. Also, as long as such perfected heretics are held, their believers and accomplices more readily confess and expose themselves and others, fearing to be betrayed by the heretics if the latter are converted.[11]

The "conversion" (which often meant no more than confession under torture) of Cathars and others accused of heresy has led to the development of a Cathar theology as understood by the Church, but that might be the result of inquisitorial demands rather than fact. However, when recurring themes evolve even under interrogation, there is probably a basis in fact. A lot of Cathar theology is derived from or influenced by the Bogomils. This Gnostic sect came from modern-day Bulgaria in the 10th century, and many Bogomil beliefs are close to Cathar teaching. The word "Bogomil" means "Dear to God" in Bulgarian.[12]

The historical record of Cathar beliefs relies heavily on Bogomil literature of the 12th century, but after this era Cathars began developing their own writings as well. Early Bogomil texts included *The Secret Supper* (or, *The Book of St. John*) and *The Vision of Isaiah*. These both appeared around 1170, originally in Greek and later translated into Latin. In *The Secret Supper*, the Bogomil theology is laid out including an explanation of Satan's dispute with God and creation of the earth by Satan and not by God; in this dualistic theology, Satan is creator of earth and all living beings. The theology rests on the duality of God and Satan, Heaven and Hell, good and evil, ideas that led to development of the Cathar view of Christianity as well. In the Cathar and Bogomil views, Christ came to earth to make God's name known and to repent for mankind's sins. The belief in two deities— one good and the other evil — is common to Bogomils and Cathars, and both are at odds with the Catholic view of *one* God who is creator of all things including the earth and life. To argue otherwise is, in the Church view, a very specific form of heresy.

Cathar literature includes *The Book of Two Principles*, written in the mid–13th century. This text documents biblical authority for Cathar beliefs. For example, the description of the universe consisting of two separate kingdoms relies on John 18:36 ("My kingdom does not belong in this world") and Isaiah 66:22 ("new heavens and the new earth"). The Church's greatest point of disagreement with the dualist beliefs of both Bogomil and Cathar rests on this very issue. The dualists argue that the Catholic belief that God created everything is simply incorrect. The recurring rejection of the Old Testament by dualist theology returns to the argument presented in *The Book of Two Principles*. The argument is made that a single, all-powerful God was impossible because

> for one who knows fully all things that shall come to pass is powerless, in so far as he is self-consistent, to do anything except that which he himself has known

from eternity that he shall do. [With knowledge of evil, a single God would have] knowingly and in full awareness created and made His angels of such imperfection from the beginning that they could in no way escape evil. [Thus, God has to be] the whole cause and origin of evil, which is obviously to be denied.[13]

In other words, the Cathar logic argued, if God is the all-powerful and *only* power in the universe, then God is responsible not only for all good, but also for all evil. The Cathars and other dualists maintained that instead there are two realms, one ruled by God (the good, heavenly one) and the other by the Devil (the evil, earthly one). This theology supports the traditional story of the great conflict between God and the Devil. That belief is that the Devil and his army invaded God's Heaven and had a great battle with the Archangel Michael. In *The Book of Two Principles*, this coexistence of God and the Devil is explained by citing a parable from the Gospels:

> The kingdom of heaven is like this. A man sowed his field with good seed; but while everyone was asleep his enemy came, sowed darnel among the wheat, and made off. When the corn sprouted and began to fill out, the darnel could be seen among it. The farmer's men went to their master and said, "Sir, was it not good seed that you sowed in your field? So where has the darnel come from?" "No," he answered. "This is an enemy's doing."[14]

The Cathars make a strong argument for dualism by citing this passage. Christ in his own words described Heaven through parable as having its own conflicts and enemies. According to one authority on the Cathars, Cathars further believed that the two worlds of heaven and earth coexist as separate realities; and that in heaven as on earth, "marriages, fornications and adulteries take place there, from which children are born."[15]

The Church Reaction: The Albigensian Crusade

The Church not only disputed the Cathar belief system but tried to vilify those who subscribed to it. A Church writer of the day described the Cathars:

> The "perfected" heretics wore a black robe, claimed (falsely) to practice chastity, and renounced meat, eggs, and cheese. They wished it to appear that they were not liars although they lied, especially about God, almost unceasingly! ... Those called "believers" were dedicated to usury, robbery, murder and illicit love — and to all kinds of perjury and perversity....[16]

Church writers tried to describe Cathars as illiterates, fools or dupes, who had been seduced by cunning serpents. The problem for the Church was that Cathars were well educated, at times better educated than Church priests or bishops. The two theologies also had considerable overlap in beliefs, so condemning Cathars in their entirety was not possible. In many aspects, the self-imposed rules of fasting and prayer among Cathars were more stringent than the Catholic self-sacrifice even among the most dedicated mendicant orders. Attempts to portray Cathars as self-indulgent sinners did not stick.

The Cathar movement was appealing and popular because Cathar preachers truly led by example. In comparison, many of the Church bishops of the day thought of themselves as the elite and were not ashamed to exhibit their wealth. Cathar preachers liked to point to the contradiction between the clergy's rich lifestyles and Christ's own humility. The dualist explanations of the origins of heaven and earth also were appealing even for many Catholics, to whom the idea of two universes made a lot of sense. Separating God, heaven and good from the Devil, earth and evil made sense, especially when selected scripture verses bolstered the case.

As the Cathar movement spread, the Church escalated its response. A papal legate, Peter of Castelnau, had been murdered in January 1208 in Toulouse. In response, two months later Pope Innocent III (1198–1216) called the Albigensian Crusade with the command, "Attack the followers of heresy," and put out the call, "Forward then, soldiers of Christ! Forward, brave recruits to the Christian army! Let the universal cry of grief of the Holy Church arouse you, let pious zeal inspire you to avenge this monstrous crime against your God!"[17]

This crusade predated Gregory's formal founding of the Inquisition by 25 years, but the events that followed led directly to it. The crusade, a "just war" originally based on the writings of Augustine as regrettable but necessary, was further incited by lurid descriptions, including so-called eyewitness accounts, of the Cathars' sexual immorality. One account by Paul of St. Père de Chartres claimed that

> heretics [who] were discovered in Orléans in 1022 [a half century before this account was written] ... held orgies at night in which indiscriminate sexual intercourse took place and that the ashes derived from the cremation of children born of such unions were used as viaticum for the terminally ill.[18]

The crusade was lengthy. It extended from 1209 until signing of the Treaty of Paris in 1229; and the final outcome was far from successful for the Church, with no discernible reduction in heresy in the target area of Languedoc. It began with the assembly of two armies, described by Peter of Les Vaux-de-Cerney:

> With so many thousands of the faithful in France already taking up the cross to avenge the wrong done to our God, and others yet to join the Crusade, nothing remained but for the Lord God of Hosts to dispatch his armies to destroy the cruel murderers.... [T]he heretics and their supporters ... persisted in their perversity and were obstinate in their wickedness....[19]

The Albigensian Crusade was just as bloody as those fought to take Jerusalem. In many battles, civilians as well as soldiers were slain when captured. In the infamous Battle of Baziège (alt. name Béziers) in 1209, crusaders overtook the city and slaughtered Cathars as well as Catholics; between 10,000 and 20,000 people were killed. When the commander of the crusaders, Cistercian

Abbot and papal legate Arnaud Amaury (alt. Amalric), was asked by his men, "What shall we do? We cannot tell the good from the wicked," he replied, "Kill them all. God will recognize his own."[20]

The Pope had given all crusaders full indulgence, plus the right to seize and occupy any lands seized from heretics.* Pope Innocent described heresy as the equivalent of treason defined under Roman law in his decretal *Vergentis*, and the punishment was loss of all property and disinheritance of all descendants.

The crusade continued concurrently with the Episcopal Inquisition which began in 1184 but which had been ineffective in curtailing the Cathar movement or other forms of heresy. In contrast with the legalistic approach to heresy through the Episcopal Inquisition, the Albigensian Crusade was outright warfare on Cathar strongholds. But this approach to heresy was different from previous Church efforts. The Church was moving away from peaceful dealings with heresy and toward more aggressive methods, a movement that would lead, eventually, to the enactment of the Inquisition as a means for combating anti–Church dissent.

The motivations for this particular crusade were primarily among the "true believers" in the Church. The commitment was not as strong among the soldiers themselves, even with the granting of indulgences. Many soldiers signed up merely to acquire forgiveness with the idea that once it was received, they could simply return home with the promise of salvation in hand:

> The 1208 offer of indulgences invited a rather casual approach, if not blatant abuse. Recruits showed little commitment or staying power, judging a brief appearance in the field adequate to gain spiritual reward, and perhaps hoping for a share of the clerical taxes being raised for the project.[21]

Thus, Pope Innocent's desire for a fast campaign aimed at establishment of a strict and orthodox Catholic regime and complete elimination of heresy was not fulfilled. In 1213, Innocent temporarily rescinded the promise of indulgences since it was not working as a recruitment tool. Victories by the crusading army were frequently reversed, and clear identification of friends and foes became muddled as the crusade stretched into years without decisive outcome. Infighting among the lay supporters of the crusade (who were primarily responsible for raising armies) and problems raising funds to finance the effort led the crusade into disunity. The long-lasting war created great resentment toward the Church on the part of the population, augmented by bad behavior among the crusaders in regions they occupied. Innocent wrote that the "protectors and defenders ... are more dangerous than the heretics themselves."[22]

The campaign deteriorated into guerilla war with mercenary groups taking part and widespread executions of captured soldiers and civilians on both

---

*This "forgiveness in advance" forgave any and all sins crusaders committed during the struggle. This had been used in previous crusades to the Holy Land and, like those previous cases of full indulgence, it led to many atrocities committed in the name of the Church.

sides. Massacres were common. Captured heretics were in some cases burned at the stake without benefit of a hearing; and Cathar perfecti were quickly executed as soon as they were captured by crusading armies. The defenders were equally violent. Captured soldiers were likely to be blinded or otherwise mutilated en masse, including amputations of hands and feet. Captured soldiers were tortured, starved and held for ransom by local ex-nobles whose lands had been seized by crusaders. The long crusade was chronically short of money and manpower and defined by escalating atrocities on both sides.

Pope Innocent III died in 1216 and was replaced by Honorius III (1216–27). The new pope intensified the Albigensian Crusade with the support of France's King Louis VII. Honorius also published new ordinances increasing and clarifying punishments for heresy and taking steps leading to the formal Inquisition by his successor, Gregory IX. Honorius formally sanctioned the Dominican Order on December 22, 1216. In spite of his desire for peace, his efforts accelerated the violence of actions in France. It would not be until Gregory's reign that the crusade was finally wound down and the Cathars put to rest—for the moment.

In fact, Gregory IX used the Dominican Order as the primary weapon to continue finding Cathar heresy and wiping it out and expanding the investigations to many other groups and individuals. Gregory instituted the Medieval Inquisition after the failure of two decades of war and untold death and suffering, believing that with diligent investigation and punishment of heretics, heresy would never again pose a serious threat to Church authority. He could not have been more wrong.

CHAPTER 3

The Dominican Order

Seeing you wrapped in the whirlwind of cares, and scarce able to breathe
under the pressure of overwhelming anxieties, we think it well to divide
your burdens, that they may be more easily borne. We have therefore determined to send preaching friars against the heretics of France and the adjoin-
ing provinces.

— Pope Gregory IX, letter to bishops announcing
his decision to appoint the Dominican Order to
assume responsibility for the Inquisition, 1233[1]

The Dominican Order, officially called the Order of Preachers (*Ordo Prædicatorum*), became the primary source of inquisitors and managers of the
Medieval Inquisition. The Dominicans were chosen for expertise in theology,
philosophy and the law, combined with a religious zeal and dedication unknown
to most other clerics.

The intention in granting this authority to the Dominican Order was to
make sure that the Cathars would never again pose a threat to the Church, and
that no other heretical movements could rise as effectively in the future.

Pope Gregory IX reasoned that because they had taken a vow of poverty,
the Dominicans would be above temptation to accept bribes. However, along
with the many worthy causes the Dominican Order has pursued in its history,
it is also known as the source for the extreme interrogation of accused heretics,
and for punishments that included, as a particular favorite, the penalty of burning at the stake.

The Life of St. Dominic

Dominic de Guzmán (also known by the names Dominic of Osma and
Domingo de Guzmán Garcés) was born in 1170 in Caleruega (alt. Calaroga) in
Old Castile, Spain. He was named for Saint Dominic of Silos, who lived from
1000 to 1073. A Benedictine monk, Dominic of Silos was prior of the monastery

of San Millán de Cogolla. He eventually specialized in book design, scholarship and charity and his order raised money to pay ransom for Christians imprisoned by the Moors.

Dominic de Guzmán was aptly named. His name serves as a play on words in the Latin, *Dominicanus*, or *Domini canis* (God's hound). In managing and operating the Inquisition for the papacy, he and his followers lived up to the name in the pursuit of heretics; he earned the nickname "the hammer of the heretics."

As a young man, Dominic was schooled in the arts and theology. In 1191, during a famine in Spain, he finished his studies and gave away all of his money and possessions, including his clothing and valuable manuscripts. When his contemporaries asked him why he had given away his books, Dominic replied, "Would you have me study off these dead skins, when men are dying of hunger?" This statement has become one of the most famous of Dominic's sayings. In 1194, Dominic joined the Canons Regular, a sect that follows the Augustinian Rule, calling for a monastic life and vows of poverty.

Legend holds that Saint Dominic gave away his book collection and, when asked why, explained, "Would you have me study off these dead skins, when men are dying of hunger?" (Stained-glass window in Santuario Madonna della Guardia di Tortona. Photograph by Vincenzo de Tortona, August 30, 2008.)

On a journey to Denmark in 1203 or 1204 to find a bride for Alfonso VIII, King of Castile, Dominic encountered members of the Cathars for the first time. Dominic immediately saw them as heretics who showed no respect for the Church or for the pope. This encounter created in Dominic a desire to fight heresy in behalf of the Church. He noted that much of the heretical preaching he heard was made not by ignorant men, but by those who were well-educated and cultured. On a second journey to Denmark two years later, Dominic stayed for several years in Southern France and worked among the Cathar communities there. He established a new monastery in Prouille (alt. Prouilhe), a small hamlet in Languedoc. Because this small monastery led eventually to the founding of an influential order within the Church, Prouille became known in later years as the "cradle of the Dominicans." A primary function of Dominic's monastery was to provide shelter to women who were previously living in Cathar homes.

In 1208, Dominic greeted papal legates returning to Rome, who had tried unsuccessfully to do away with the Cathars. Noting their display of wealth and pomp, Dominic chastised the legates, saying,

> It is not the display of power and pomp, cavalcades of retainers, and richly-houseled palfreys,* or by gorgeous apparel, that the heretics win proselytes; it is by zealous preaching, by apostolic humility, by austerity, by seeming, it is true, but by seeming holiness. Zeal must be met by zeal, humility by humility, false sanctity by real sanctity, preaching falsehood by preaching truth.[2]

After seeing how disconnected the papal legates were from the common people, Dominic gathered a few fellow monks and began formulating a major tenet of the future Dominican Order: to resolve to find truth wherever it is to be found. Setting himself up in Toulouse, he devoted himself to a life dominated by monastic rule, prayer and penance. He also obtained permission from the local bishop to preach in the Toulouse region. Dominic for the first time envisioned a movement of preaching friars. He attended the Fourth Lateran Council, called by Pope Innocent III, in 1215. This council is important in the history of the Inquisition. Out of it came a series of ecclesiastical canons defining beliefs and practices acceptable under Christianity, canons that could be used to punish heretics and other dissenters. This council was an attempt to exert total papal control over the Christian world, even to include the Eastern Orthodox Church, which was warned in the writings of the council to "conform themselves like obedient sons to the holy Roman church, their mother, so that there may be one flock and one shepherd [or] be struck with the sword of excommunication."[3]

Dominic's request to create an order was denied by the council because it had been decided that no new orders would be established. However, he appealed

---

*"Houseled palfreys" refers to those who administer the Eucharist (houseled) while traveling around on expensive and highly-bred riding horses (palfreys).

to the pontiff once more, and on December 22, 1216, Dominic received authorization from Pope Honorius III (1216–27) through the papal bull *Religiosam vitam* (The Religious Life). Honorius named the newly formed group the Order of Preachers. The order adopted the motto, "to praise, to bless, to preach" (*Laudare, benedicere, prædicare*). In England, Dominicans are called Blackfriars, a reference to the black cloak (*cappa*) worn over their white habits. This distinction distinguishes Dominicans from members of the Carmelites (Whitefriars) and Franciscans (Greyfriars). The French refer to Dominicans as Jacobins, as the first Dominican convent in Paris was Saint Jacques (in Latin, *Jacobus*). Members of the order include the initials O.P. after their names, signifying Order of Preachers (*Ordo Prædicatorum*).

In 1217, Dominic was named master of the sacred palace (the pope's theologian). From that time until the modern day, the office has always been held by a member of the Dominican Order.

Throughout his life, Dominic practiced a regimen of self-denial. He never ate meat; he fasted and imposed periods of silence on himself. He always chose the least comfortable and poorest accommodations wherever he stayed, and never allowed himself to sleep in a bed, preferring a bare floor. He removed his shoes in order to endure stones and thorns along the road. When encountering cold weather and other hardships, he never complained but only expressed thanks to God. Although his Dominican Order is associated with many of the worst abuses of the accused heretics of the Medieval Inquisition, Dominic was a deeply pious man who believed in his cause. His reputation for humility and piety was borne out by his own actions. From 1212 to 1215, at least three attempts were made to promote Dominic to the role of bishop, based on his high level of intellect and inspiration. He refused them all, however, due to his dedication to poverty, simple preaching, and the common man.

Remaining with the members of his order rather than advancing within the Church, Dominic relocated the headquarters of his new order to Rome, but continued to travel extensively in preaching his mission. While visiting Bologna in 1218, he established a convent at the Church of San Nicolò of the Vineyards. He died there in 1221 at the age of 51. This church was later renamed the Basicila of Saint Dominic and, in 1251, was consecrated by Pope Innocent IV. Pope Gregory IX signed his bull canonizing Dominic on July 13, 1234.

Dominicans and Franciscans Contrasted with Other Orders

Two major mendicant orders both began in the 13th century, the Dominicans and the Franciscans. Although both orders were supported and promoted by the papacy and especially by Gregory IX, the two orders were quite different. Both orders considered vows of poverty to be at the core of their mission.

This was not a new idea in Christianity. Saint Francis incorporated an absolute rule forbidding any monk in his order to hold any personal property and also to give away any ownership of business property. This followed the example of many previous sects, including the Humiliati, the Poor Men of Lombardy, and the Poor Men of Lyons. Absolute poverty was believed essential in order for a Franciscan to find God. Francis was referred to as Christ's poor man (*pauper Christi*). Dominic instilled the same ideas in the Dominican Order, although Francis preceded him in requiring absolute poverty of his members.

While previous monks had created orders to take vows of solitude and avoided society, even to the extent of living their lives out as hermits, both Franciscans and Dominicans were very involved in all aspects of their societies and considered education and preaching essential parts of their mission. Both orders also formed secondary orders, or tertiaries such as the Franciscan Penitential Brothers (*fratres de poenitentia*). Both orders also relied on many lay members who, in addition to continuing to pursue their daily occupations, volunteered to take part in preaching, sharing monastic life, and otherwise supporting the work of the friars.

One of the most enduring attributes of both mendicant orders was their focus on education. Friars taught at the major universities from the schools' earliest days and continued to do so through to modern times. This is odd for the Franciscans given the fact that St. Francis himself was opposed to "too much" education. He once predicted, "The time of tribulation will come when books will be useless and be thrown away."[4]

Even though Francis had doubts concerning the value of education, his successors received grants and privileges from the papacy for establishing schools and for teaching in them. In comparison, the Dominicans were dedicated from their very beginning to the value of teaching and were prominent in the two major universities of the 13th century, in Paris and Bologna. Expanding to universities at Oxford and Cologne, the Dominicans produced the great scholars Albertus Magnus and Thomas Aquinas, among others. The Franciscans also produced notable scholars, including John of St. Giles, Alexander Hales, Adam Marsh, Bonaventura, Duns Scotus, Ockham, and Roger Bacon.

Perhaps the most important attributes of both orders, from the point of view of the papacy, was that they both were willingly subjugated to the will of the pope. In fact, both orders vowed allegiance to the pope directly as the result of a papal bull of 1260 issued by Pope Alexander IV (1254–61). This bull ordered that both Franciscans and Dominicans were to swear an oath of allegiance directly to the pope, and both orders came to be known affectionately as "our cherished and faithful children in Christ."[5]

This unqualified allegiance helped the papacy to strengthen its authority over all bishops, who previously had been known to question the absolute authority of the papacy in all matters. The Church's loyalty to both orders was the result of their effective pursuit of heretics, especially among Dominicans serving as inquisitors. In the future, mendicants would become infamous not for their scholarly works or pious nature, but for their abuses of accused heretics. For example, Tomás de Torquemada, the much-feared Inquisitor General of Spain in the era of the Spanish Inquisition, was a Dominican, and so was the sadistic Conrad of Marburg.

Gregory IX had assigned the Dominicans most of the inquisitorial posts, but by 1232, the Franciscans demanded a share as well. A bitter dispute developed between the two orders, both desiring papal approval and power. In 1254, the rivalry became so severe that Pope Innocent IV (1243–54) issued what is known as his "terrible bull," restricting privileges for members of both orders. The pope died the same year, however, and the next pope, Alexander IV (1254–61), retracted all of the restrictions. The rivalry between Dominicans and Franciscans continued for at least two centuries, until each established itself as a permanent institution within the Church. In modern times, the two orders distinguish themselves with continued missionary work, teaching, and work for the poor.

The Dominican Order and Its Mission

Because Pope Gregory did not declare his Inquisition until 10 years after Dominic's death, Dominic certainly was not involved in the extreme interrogations and tribunals that followed. In the 15th century, Dominic was inaccurately depicted in art presiding over a burning at the stake, an image used to characterize Dominic as directly involved in passing judgment and presiding over the execution of heretics. Another fanciful legend involves Dominic at a book burning, in which heretical books (of the Cathars) burned up while Dominic's books survived the flames.

In 1231, Pope Gregory IX officially appointed the Dominican Order, specifically the convent at Regensburg, as official managers of the Papal Inquisition (replacing the previous but ineffective Episcopal Inquisition). His order included the instruction to "seek out diligently those who are heretics or who are inflamed of heresy" and also authorized the convent's prior to appoint other Dominicans or "other discreet people known to you" to assist in the investigation and eradication of the Cathars and other heretics. When found and convicted, Gregory instructed, heretics were to be punished according to both ecclesiastical and civil law.[6]

Gregory's directive to the Dominicans was quite specific: "When you arrive in a town, you will summon the prelates, clergy and people, and you will preach a solemn sermon." After this, the inquisitors were to "begin your enquiry into the beliefs of heretics and suspects with diligent care." Those "recognized as guilty or suspected of heresy must promise to obey the orders of the Church absolutely [but if they do not] you should proceed against them, following the statutes that we have promulgated against the heretics."[7]

Dominicans and the Origins of the Inquisition

Certainly, one factor in the development of the Inquisition was a desire to rid the Christian world of heresy. However, this became a catch-all excuse for the persecution of political enemies and for attacks on breakaway movements. Inquisitional movements soon moved far beyond the limited realm of heresy to attack witches and, in later years, scientists, artists and members of non–Christian faiths. The inspiration became anything the pope and his inquisitors desired, and anyone who challenged Church authority was at risk.

In this evolving movement, the Dominicans were the primary enforcement agency for the pope. The relatively benign early practices of coercion to force confessions eventually gave way to extreme methods of torture, including drawing and quartering, flaying, ripping out of the tongue, and burning in caldrons of boiling oil. In fact, the lines between inducing confession and outright sadism became indistinguishable over time, and the Dominican Order served either as interrogators or supervised the activities of those they hired to perform this work.

The distinction between passing sentence (by Church tribunal) and executing the guilty (by secular authorities) became important in the Inquisition. An old maxim states, "The Church abhors blood" (*ecclesia non sitit sanguinem*). Church leaders even allowed Dominican interrogators to employ torture and then to absolve one another of the guilt for inflicting pain upon suspects. This unparalleled power assumed by the Church not only to mistreat victims, but to also allow the guilty to absolve one another, perhaps epitomizes the abuses of the Inquisition.

Even among the highly intellectual members of the Dominican Order, the death penalty was strongly supported. Popes, their councils, and even Thomas Aquinas argued in favor of the death penalty for heretics, citing heresy as the worst crime against God. Innocent III had started the defense of execution of heretics (*ad hæreticorum exterminium*), and even outside of the Inquisition, absolution could be granted. For example, soldiers of the Crusades were granted absolution, sometimes in advance, for killing heretics and infidels. During the height of the Inquisition, bishops were instructed to travel through their dioceses and look for cases of heresy, or risk being deposed.

During the first 100 years since the origins of the Inquisition, the various popes issued endless bulls and decretals concerning detection and punishment of heretics. Pope Alexander IV alone wrote over 100 bulls on the subject. An important aspect of the way the Inquisition was set up by Gregory IX was the distinction between official inquisitors and local priests. While it was assumed that priests would care for the souls of their local flocks, inquisitors held special powers and even had the right to overrule local priests and bishops. In cases where priests were under suspicion (or simply resisted the holding of interrogations and tribunals), the Dominican inquisitors had the power to suspend priests from the performance of their sacramental duties. The only avenue of appeal for deposed priests was the papal court, and of course, once the priest had been removed in this manner, he risked being accused of heresy himself.

The populace did not always go along quietly. The origins of the Inquisition involved a long-standing and growing dissent by the Cathars in Southern France, and it took a great effort to finally wipe out that movement. Smaller rebellions against inquisitors also occurred. In 1235, citizens of Narbonne drove inquisitors out of their city. In 1242, several inquisitors were murdered in Avignon. In 1279, citizens in Parma broke into a Dominican convent and killed two friars in retaliation for the burning at the stake of a noble lady and her servant. The prominent inquisitor Peter of Verona (also known as Peter Martyr) was murdered in Como in 1252.

The Dominican Contradiction

The Dominican Order is, in a sense, a study in contradiction. On the one hand were vast efforts put forth in missionary work; on the other were the operations of the Inquisition, an activity which is at odds with the intellectual pursuits normally associated with Dominicans, and with the highest level of philosophy and theology associated with the order's founders and prominent thinkers. The formal Inquisition — and the Dominican contradiction — are based largely on the goal of the pope as expressed in the Fourth Lateran Council's canons, to rid the world of "heretical filth." The document essentially declares war on heresy: "We condemn all heretics, whatever name they may go under. They have different faces indeed but their tails are tied together inasmuch as they are alike in their pride.... [W]henever anyone is promoted to spiritual or temporal authority, he shall be obliged to confirm this article with an oath."[8]

The canon not only allowed, but required inquisitors to act against heretics. And so, even the worst of the inquisitors, while attempting to coerce confessions from accused heretics, must have believed that their effort was truly God's work. Two years later, in 1233, Gregory published a bull, *Excommunicamus*, which was used as a constitution for inquisitional procedure. In this document, Gregory recommended a penalty of life in prison for even repentant heretics and capital punishment for "obstinate heretics," who were to be turned over to secular authorities for carrying out of the punishment. The papal bull was significant in development of the Inquisition because it formalized the rules of conduct as a law, calling for punishment of enemies of the faith.

Gregory's papal bull further outlawed the right of appeal for convicted heretics. This decision resulted from complaints made to the pope concerning the frequent appeals made to the pope and others, resulting in reduction of sentences. The formal rules for conducting tribunals were augmented by other writings, including guidebooks and written opinions. The *Processis inquisitionis* (1248–9) was a short guide for procedures at tribunal. A more extensive manual, the *Pracuca officii inquisitionis heretice pravitatis*, was written by Bernard Gui, a Dominican inquisitor in Toulouse between 1307 and 1324.

Events in the early Inquisition were formalized by these writings. Expanding even beyond accusations against individuals, at times they encompassed entire communities. These "general inquests" were frightening occurrences because they invariably led to individual interrogations and resulted in convictions and executions, at times on a large scale. The arriving inquisitor would gather an entire village or town together and explain his mission. An indulgence or period of grace was announced, usually 40 days. All males over the age of 14 and females over the age of 12 were required to appear on a specified day before the inquisitor. Those who appeared as instructed and who provided what were believed to be true depositions were usually excused from more severe penalties if and when found guilty. But this approach presented a dilemma. The incentive was to confess to minor heresy in order to avoid harsh punishments, whether guilty or not.

Anyone suspected of heresy who had not confessed during this state of grace could be summoned and interrogated. A failure to appeal resulted in a "provisional" excommunication. After one year, the person would be officially considered a heretic. So traveling inquisitors would subject an entire community to a process of investigation in the search for heretics. Even though no specific accusations were made in many cases, the inquisitors had complete power to make any determinations they wanted, including finding someone guilty simply because they did not confess when offered the chance. Why would a true believer not want to repent? This was the logic applied by inquisitors.

A Rationale for Harsh Measures

If the intention of the Inquisition was to save souls by convincing heretics to confess and repent, then the motivation, if not the method, is more readily understood. However, this is a way of applying intellectual rationale to what became a study of excess. Torture was used to gain confession, with the idea that after confession comes repentance and a return to the "ideal" grace of the Church. Only in those cases where the crime was extreme or when confession was refused or recanted was the death sentence supposed to be applied. Even then, the concept of burning at the stake as an *auto-da-fé* (act of faith) was meant to purify the soul and to either save the accused through suffering or demonstrate to others the consequences of heresy itself. The acts of penance and repentance on the part of the accused through the *auto-da-fé* included reading a confession in public, pilgrimages, imprisonment, and execution, usually by burning at the stake. This occurrence drew large and enthusiastic crowds, so that the *auto-da-fé* itself is associated with burning at the stake, even though burning was only one of many possible sentences.

Whether the purpose of the original Inquisition was to purify souls and redeem the guilty, or to quell breakaway movements like the Cathars or Waldensians, the apparent contradiction between intellectual study and physical punishment is a glaring one. Complicated by a veil of theology, the physical aspects of the Inquisition can be understood on one level (specifically, that the *intention* was to save the accused from his own bad decisions); but on another level, it remains a paradox that the best educated, most enlightened, and most pious members of the Church were capable of the extremes of torture and execution. The fact is that the Church and its leaders were specifically concerned with widespread dissent and used the Dominican Order as an enforcement arm and also as a means for discouraging people from exposing themselves to accusations of heresy.

It would seem that an order of dedicated and pious Dominicans would not perform well as inquisitors; but in fact, they excelled at this task. It may have been the religious zeal that led men to the order that augmented their focus on gaining confessions from accused heretics by any means available. This zeal and absolute faith combined with education made the Dominicans effective as interrogators. Most of their victims were poorly educated and illiterate and, additionally, held the clergy in very high esteem. So with superior knowledge of Christian dogma and the respect people naturally had for priests, Dominican inquisitors had tremendous advantages over the accused who faced them. For these reasons, inquisitors were likely to be chosen from among "wise and mature men capable of asserting their authority."[9]

The training of Dominican Order inquisitors went beyond theological matters, and was also aimed at identifying and punishing heretics. Primary among the interests of Dominican inquisitors was getting a confession from the accused. From a legal point of view, it would be difficult to condemn a heretic on the word of a personal enemy alone or on suspicions among local clergy. Beyond this legal requirement, however, the Dominican inquisitors believed that a confession was necessary in order for the accused to gain absolution for the sin of heresy itself. The extreme measures that were used to gain confessions were not punishment of a convicted person, but a means for gaining either a conviction or absolution.

Burning at the stake was the usual method of execution under Roman law; crucifixion, the older method, had been banned since the fourth century. The Church and its inquisitors were not allowed under the law to execute a heretic; that sentence could be imposed and carried out only by the secular court. So upon a finding of guilt for the crime of heresy, the accused person was turned over to the courts for execution. If the accused confessed before the fires were lit, the sentence could be altered to strangulation. In some parts of Europe, such as Venice, guilty heretics were drowned rather than burned at the stake. The point is, the way that the secular law and the Church-run Inquisition worked together enabled the Dominicans to maintain a distance from carrying out any actual executions. Their task was to identify the unrepentant guilty; what the secular law determined to be an appropriate sentence was out of their hands. Although the Dominican inquisitors knew without any doubt what the outcome would be, this system allowed them to keep their hands clean — if not in the judgment of history, at least in their own minds.

Inquisitors, in investigating charges of heresy, were not involved directly in carrying out executions. But among the worst offenses of the Inquisition, in addition to passing sentences that led to execution, were the methods employed to get confessions. Pope Gregory IX approved of the use of torture by allowing "free faculty of the sword against enemies of the faith." An accusation of heresy usually led to the immediate arrest of the accused and confiscation of his or her property. This property remained under the control of the tribunal until the case was settled. The term of imprisonment awaiting trial could be quite extensive, and during that time, the accused was denied the sacraments and, usually, contact with family members or legal counsel as well.[10]

In the course of the investigation, inquisitors asked the accused to consider the charges and to confess willingly before the formal proceedings began. If a confession was not offered, a formal trial was held, complete with witnesses and their testimony for both prosecution and defense. A finding of "not guilty" was rare if there was enough evidence or testimony (at times consisting only of witness statements) to convince the inquisitor and the tribunal that the accused was probably guilty. It was during the period of investigation prior to the formal trial, verdict and sentence that torture was used. The record is inconsistent. In some jurisdictions, inquisitors were careful to limit the use of extreme measures to only those cases they considered the most serious. In others, the system was abused.

Abuses of Interrogation Methods

One of the most infamous among early inquisitors was Conrad of Marburg, who in the 13th century was active in investigating heresy in Languedoc and later in the Rhineland. He was the first person to use the title "inquisitor of heretical depravity" (*Inquisitor hæreticæ Pravitatis*). Conrad may have been a Dominican, but many sources claim he was not. He, like so many members of the order, had built a reputation for himself of piety and self-denial, and was known to arrive in towns riding a donkey as an imitation of Jesus entering

Jerusalem. Citing "papal license" to investigate incidences of heresy, Conrad questioned the accused with exceptionally sadistic methods. The Archbishop of Mayence complained to the pope, stating that Conrad was exacting many false confessions with his methods, which included physical torture as well as threats of burning.[11]

The archbishop wrote:

> Whoever fell into his hands had only the choice between a ready confession for the sake of saving his life and a denial, whereupon he was speedily burnt. Every false witness was accepted, but no just defense granted — not even to people of prominence. The person arraigned had to confess that he was a heretic, that he had touched a toad, that he had kissed a pale man, or some monster. Many Catholics suffered themselves to be burnt innocently rather than confess to such vicious crimes, of which they knew they were not guilty. The weak ones, in order to save their lives, lied about themselves and other people, especially about such prominent ones whose names were suggested to them by Conrad. Thus brothers accused their brothers, wives their husbands, servants their masters. Many gave money to the clergy for good advice as to how to protect themselves, and the greatest confusion originated.[12]

Gregory IX was not convinced. He declared in his papal bull *Vox in Rama* (Voice on High) that Conrad was a champion of the Christian cause. He encouraged Conrad to continue his work against heretics and, expanding his mission, also against witches. Gregory considered the Inquisition to be "an integral part of pastoral care."[13]

Conrad was not only one of the most notorious of early inquisitors; he was also one of the most imaginative. He tied heretics to witchcraft and, specifically, to sexual depravity as well. This was a suitable fit for sadists like Conrad and inquisitors who followed him, whose victims

> were stripped down to undergarments or were wholly naked during torture; the display of bare flesh was essential to the work of the torturers while, at the same time, degrading and humiliating to the victims, but it is also true that the sight of naked flesh titillated at least some inquisitors and their henchmen as they watched the torturer at work. Indeed, the torture chamber was never a purely functional space like an operating room or a blacksmith's shop, although it resembled both in its equipage. Rather, it was a theater of pain in which the victim was put on display for the entertainment of his or her persecutors.[14]

No one was safe from Conrad's determination to wipe out heresy while making sexually based accusations, even the nobility.

Part of the reason for the zeal of Conrad and others was the rule that convicted heretics lost their property to the Church. Unless the local authorities took control over disposition of property seized from heretics, it usually went to the Church and to the inquisitors. The portion paid directly to inquisitors could be as much as one-third of the total value.[15]

In 1233, Conrad began an investigation of Count Henry II of Seyn. This was an unwise choice, since Henry was an exceptionally pious and highly esteemed man. He had endowed monasteries and churches and had even gone on a crusade. But Conrad had a witness who testified he had seen Henry riding on a huge crab on his way to an orgy. Henry, however, did not confess. Instead, he insisted on directly challenging the witness and the inquisitor. He demanded a trial before the king, archbishop and clergymen. In front of this tribunal, Conrad's witness admitted that he had testified falsely, under threat of being burned at the stake himself.

The archbishop convened a synod on July 25, 1233, to hear complaints against Conrad and his methods. The attending bishops and nobles agreed with the archbishop that Conrad went too far. Conrad immediately began an investigation of heresy among the nobles who had attended the synod, an early example of how the original mission of the Inquisition could easily be twisted into a personal vendetta. But before Conrad could go far with this new investigation his career came to an unexpected end. He was waylaid and murdered five days after the synod on his return journey to Marburg, on July 30.

While earlier inquisitions were designed to safeguard the innocent, this was not the case with Conrad's investigations. Pope Alexander III had many years earlier proclaimed that "it was better to pardon the guilty than to take the lives of the innocent." But Conrad had been unapologetic and zealous in his use of torture and even in executions of some innocent among the accused. He responded to complaints against him by saying, "We would gladly burn a hundred if just one among them were guilty."[16]

Dominicans and the Inquisition

The rules for Dominican-run tribunals were harsh, even with safeguards in place. For example, questioning of the accused required the presence of at least two witnesses; however, depending on the identity of the witness, this did not necessarily protect the rights of the accused heretic. There was ever present the assumption that someone accused of heresy was probably guilty, and that failing to confess meant that person was not worthy of God's grace. The extremes of torture to get confessions and the death sentence followed easily after the Dominican inquisitors convinced themselves that theirs was truly a mission from God.

The death penalty, seen as a cleansing of the soul of a misguided heretic, was also viewed within the Church as a positive outcome. It became such an important ritual that if an accused died in prison before the sentence could be carried out, the remains were burned. The process of burning at the stake was both punishment and symbolic salvation even for the lost soul of the heretic, and even after physical death. Whether a person found guilty was condemned to death or to life in prison, his property was confiscated and taken by the Church. This brings up the question of a financial motive.

Because in some instances witnesses were rewarded with the land and other assets of the person found guilty, many people accused of heresy were victims of their neighbors, enemies, or even strangers who wanted their land. The incentive among inquisitors in behalf of the Church to accuse the wealthy and find them guilty also created many innocent victims. As long as land and other property went to the Church, the landowner was actually more at risk for accusations of heresy; and the richer the person, the more likely a guilty verdict. This does not mean that the entire Inquisition became a method for seizing land, but that was one of the pitfalls in a system that rewarded the accusers when someone was found guilty.

In the decade of the 1230s, inquisitors were sent to France, Spain and Germany to investigate charges of heresy. Especially in France where the Cathar movement was quite influential, the Inquisition was very active. By 1255, all areas of Western and Central Europe had Inquisition tribunals and executions underway.

Ironically, involvement of the Dominican Order as the primary investigative arm for the Church was based not only on the education and training of Dominicans, but also on its primary mission: saving souls and preaching the word of God. The order's founding and purpose was expressed by Pope Honorious III (1216–27), who wrote in 1221:

> He who always makes His Church fruitful with new offspring, wanting to make these times measure up to former times, and to propagate the Catholic faith, inspired you with a holy desire by which, having embraced poverty and made profession of regular life, you have given yourselves to the proclamation of the Word of God, preaching the name of our Lord Jesus Christ throughout the world.[17]

This basic purpose became the foundation for even the most extreme methods for forcing confessions and then granting absolution or, failing that, "cleansing" the soul of the heretic through burning at the stake. This process was not seen as cruel, but as both pious and merciful in the eyes of the inquisitors. In the same document, the intent is further explained:

> We also undertake as sharers of the apostolic mission the life of the Apostles in the form conceived by St. Dominic, living with one mind the common life, faithful in the profession of the evangelical counsels, fervent in the common celebration of the liturgy, especially of the Eucharist and the divine office as well as other prayer, assiduous in study, and persevering in regular observance. All these practices contribute not only to the glory of God and our sanctification, but serve directly the salvation of mankind, since they prepare harmoniously for preaching, furnish its incentive, form its character, and in turn are influenced by it. These elements are closely interconnected and carefully balanced, mutually enriching one another, so that in their synthesis the proper life of the Order is established: a life in the fullest sense apostolic, in which preaching and teaching must proceed from an abundance of contemplation.[18]

The "salvation of mankind" has always been at the core of the Dominican Order's purpose, as witnessed by its many good works throughout history. However, this concept also justified the activities of the order and its inquisitors from the 13th to the 16th centuries. By turning over the guilty to the secular authorities to carry out sentences, the inquisitors freed themselves from responsibility for the outcome; in fact, it was the accused person's refusal to confess that led to extreme sentences being imposed. The inquisitors argued that they were only trying to save the soul and promote the salvation of mankind.

Even so, the extremes to which inquisitors went were controversial. Although the papacy lauded the Inquisition as the Holy Office (*Sanctum Officium*) and cited the good works being done in the name of God, it was ultimately necessary for the pope to exempt these same inquisitors from the jurisdiction of any and all secular authorities. This not only extended to avoiding interference in their acts, but also allowed inquisitors to excommunicate anyone who got in their way. Exemption from secular law was declared and reiterated by Popes Alexander IV in 1259 and Urban IV in 1262. Perhaps most troubling was the provision allowing inquisitors to absolve their agents (and each other) from any acts of violence imposed on accused heretics.

The inquisitors within the Dominican Order worked hand in hand with the secular authorities charged with carrying out sentences, although the official roles were kept separate. The initial aversion to imposition of death sentences led to a widespread trend toward life imprisonment for accused heretics. Lesser offenders might be granted freedom of movement within the prison walls (*murus largus*), while the worst heretics often were sentenced to solitary confinement (*murus strictus*), possibly in very small cells, for life. When heretics were sentenced, their homes were completely destroyed and their families forced into homelessness.

In various parts of Europe, confiscation of property was managed in different ways. In Venice, for example, property all passed to the State, increasing the incentive to find heretics, especially those heretics who also happened to own large estates. In the rest of Italy, property was to be divided between the State, the Holy Office of the Inquisition, and the Curia — again providing incentives to look for heretics among the larger landowners. The papacy and the tribunals actively encouraged citizens to turn in their heretical neighbors with the promise of a reward to be paid from the heretic's assets.

Even the dead were not exempt from accusation and punishment. Their bodies were exhumed and they were declared post mortem to have been heretics; a tribunal was held to declare them guilty; and their remains were burned as punishment. The abuses of torture during interrogation, expanded investigations and flimsy accusations, seizures of land and other assets, and even crimes against the dead demonstrate how excessively the zeal of inquisitors was applied to a helpless population. These excesses were not prevented by the intellect or pious lifestyles of Dominicans; in fact, these attributes made the Inquisition and its practices much worse.

The order's fervent belief in its mission and purpose prevented any well-meaning inquisitors from questioning the Inquisition on any level. In fact, at the Dominicans' first chapter meeting in Bologna in 1220, an announcement was made that the purpose of the order was a first priority and that no rules would be allowed to get in the way of the mission. The decision was made by Dominic at that chapter meeting that members of the order were to be granted complete freedom to pursue their mission of preaching and salvation, and required complete flexibility and initiative; this invited abuses that only worsened over the next two centuries.

Nor did freedom of action apply only in Catholic areas of Europe. Through the establishment of many schools and teaching missions in Eastern Europe and the Far East, the order spread both its ideals and the faith. Teachers (like Albertus Magnus and Thomas Aquinas) advanced the reputation of the Church and of the Dominican Order, and rightly so; furthermore, the example set by the lives of poverty led by Dominicans in spreading the gospel represented the best of Christianity. This meant preaching the word far and wide, even beyond the Christian world, in accordance with the Gospel of Matthew: "Go therefore to all nations and make them my disciples."[19]

The example of the Dominicans was used effectively against heretics. The many missions, convents and schools established by the Dominican Order gave credibility to the Inquisition, and the ideal of leading a sparse life and doing good works was based largely on Dominic's own experiences before the order had been founded. Dominic had noted that papal legates exhibited splendor and pomp in their travels, the height of hypocrisy. As Dominican inquisitors had dedicated their lives to poverty and Christian preaching, Pope Gregory reasoned that their motives were above reproach. As history has shown time and again, however, a combination of superior intellect and religious zeal does not always ensure that the individuals are also universally compassionate, especially when given unlimited power.

CHAPTER 4

The Cathars' End and Expanded Inquisitions

Punishment is meted according to the dignity of the person sinned against, so that a person who strikes one in authority receives a greater punishment than one who strikes anyone else. Now whoever sins mortally sins against God ... but God's majesty is infinite. Therefore, whoever sins mortally deserves infinite punishment; and consequently it seems just that for a mortal sin a man should be punished forever.
— Thomas Aquinas, *Summa Theologica*, 1265–74

The initial targets of the Dominican inquisitors were the Cathars. With the end to the lengthy crusade, the Church was determined to eliminate this enemy once and for all. The entire Church leadership became obsessed with the Cathars, fearing a resurgence of the movement. This sense of imminent threat caused a determined Church leadership to use the new Inquisition for its purposes, not only to attack heresy but also to do away with a movement it considered a direct threat to its singular authority. So the Dominicans and their Inquisition were sent into Southern France to root out the now weakened Cathar heretics and ensure that they would never again be able to rise up against the Church.

The Inquisition was established initially with this goal in mind, although it quickly expanded beyond the diminished Cathars to encompass many more varieties of heresy. To the Catholic Church, no movement that challenged the sacraments or defied the unlimited power and authority of the papacy could be allowed to go unpunished.

One of the first requirements placed on known members of the Cathar sect was that they wear a yellow cross as a means of identification, a requirement set forth as part of the initial Dominican mandate. The order stated that all Cathars

shall carry from now on and forever two yellow crosses on all their clothes except their shirts, and one arm shall be two palms long, while the other transversal arm shall be a palm and a half long and each shall be three digits wide with one to be worn in front on the chest, and the other between the shoulders.[1]

The rule further forbade Cathars from leaving their homes without the yellow cross in plain sight. The forced marking of the Church's perceived enemies was not a new idea, but an extension of one that had been tried before. The distinction had been applied to non–Christians for many years. A 1215 decree initiated by Pope Innocent III required that "Jews and Saracens of both sexes in every Christian province and at all times shall be marked off in the eyes of the public from other peoples through the character of their dress."[2] The idea was applied to the Cathars after the end of the Albigensian Crusade as a way to keep track of heretics and to follow their movements, based on fears of a renewed threat, both in doctrine and military terms.

The Treaty of Paris ended the crusade, or at least the military aspects of the Church dispute with the Cathars, but it also marked the beginning of the Inquisition. The Church faced an enormous problem in quelling this movement, since it was not only the Cathar clergy that brought such grief to the Church, but widespread public support and sympathy. The citizenry saw the Church as affluent and corrupt and the Cathars as sincere, spiritual and honest. The movement offered an alternative to the Church.

The Church's distrust of Cathars predated the formal Inquisition established by Gregory IX, and steps were taken, even in the extreme, to prevent Christians from getting information that could lead to questions aimed at Church dogma. This extended to the step of banning the reading of the Bible itself. The decree was passed down by the papacy that before lay people would be allowed to read the Bible, local priests and bishops must rule as to whether particular passages would be useful and allowed, or subversive and banned:

> In early times the Bible was read freely by the lay people.... New dangers came in during the Middle Ages.... To meet those evils, the Council of Toulouse (1229) and Tarragona (1234) forbade the laity to read the vernacular translations of the Bible. Pius IV required bishops to refuse lay persons leave to read even Catholic versions of Scripture unless their confessors or parish priests judged that such reading was likely to prove beneficial.[3]

The exact language from the Council of Toulouse is unmistakable, and demonstrates how threatened the Church was by allowing people to become too informed:

> We prohibit the permission of the books of the Old and New Testament to laymen, except perhaps they might desire to have the Psalter, or some Breviary for the divine service, or the Hours of the blessed Virgin Mary, for devotion; expressly forbidding their having the other parts of the Bible translated into the vulgar tongue.[4]

The threat was very real to the Church, as evidenced by the ruling coming out of this meeting. Out of 45 canons that came out of the council, 20 dealt specifically with procedures for finding heretics and bringing them to justice. In addition to the restriction on reading the Bible in Canon 14, two other canons laid down the base rules for the future Inquisition and were developed specifically to contend with the continuing threat from the Cathars:

> We appoint, therefore, that the archbishops and bishops shall swear in one priest, and two or three laymen of good report, or more if they think fit, in every parish, both in and out of cities, who shall diligently, faithfully, and frequently seek out the heretics in those parishes, by searching all houses and subterranean chambers which lie under suspicion. And looking out for appendages or outbuildings, in the roofs themselves, or any other kind of hiding places, all which we direct to be destroyed.[5]
>
> ... the house in which any heretic shall be found shall be destroyed.[6]

Harsh measures against heretical movements in general and the Cathars in particular were commonplace in the military portion of the Albigensian Crusade. As early as 1209, a complete disregard for the innocent civilians of areas under assault was evident and crusaders willingly slaughtered entire towns and villages without attempting to identify good Catholics from heretical Cathars. The combined lengthy warfare, which hardens people in all cases, and the indulgences granted to the crusaders by the pope made such an attitude understandable.

This tendency extended from the military to the tribunal forms of the fight against heresy. The Church treated this struggle as one of survival. The Dominicans did not directly order the killing of suspects but took steps to torture people into confessing or testifying against others. The desired outcome — eradication of Cathars and other heretics— was so important a task that any means justified the end, even if innocent people were punished and killed.

Inquisition Trends and the Cathars

By the time Gregory IX instituted the Inquisition, the ground rules were in place. By that time the papacy had faced more than 200 years of problems in determining how to punish heretics or suppress their heresy. This was one aspect of the ongoing power struggles between popes and emperors; and the papacy's desire to arrive at an appropriate formula was hampered by the recurring charges of heresy leveled by popes against disobedient or defiant emperors. It was difficult to expect support from monarchs for extreme measures against heretics when those same emperors had been the focus of the Church's wrath. This was not a new problem with the conflict between Gregory and Frederick; it went all the way back to the previous century.

In that time, a period when heretical movements were flourishing and expanding, a conflict arose between Pope Alexander III (1159–81) and Emperor Frederick Barbarossa. They reconciled in 1177, which was documented in the

Treaty of Venice. In that treaty, the emperor acknowledged both the spiritual and temporal powers of the pope over Rome, an important turning point. Previously, emperors had held that they had temporal powers and the pope had only spiritual powers. However, Frederick's concession did not bind future emperors to agree to the same principle although the Church may have assumed that it did.

After the treaty was signed, the papacy felt increasingly empowered to punish heresy and, on a more subtle level, to expand the definition of heresy to include insolence and defiance of the Church. This "crime of defiance" (*ad contumacia*) was considered as much a form of heresy as the spreading of anti–Church beliefs. By the end of the crusade against the Cathars, the Church had developed a broad range of authority to find and punish dissenters as well as their followers and supporters. After the Treaty of Paris ending the Albigensian Crusade, there was no peace for Cathars or even for non–Cathar citizens in the Languedoc region of France; as the Inquisition spread, citizens throughout Europe were subjected to the same expanded power to punish on the part of the Church and its powerful Dominican Order.

The crusade had gone on for more than two decades and as a consequence, a shift occurred within the Church. In previous accusations of heresy, the Church had been careful to ensure that a tribunal was held to hear the issues before judgment was passed down. But in the areas where Cathars had been strong, local inquisitors were willing to kill heretics without the benefit of any hearings; this was out of the control of the pope, as from a military point of view it had been expedient to rid the area of heretics rather than taking the time to initiate a legal process. When Gregory placed the Dominicans in charge of the Inquisition in Southern France, he wanted not only to expand the search for heretics, but to institutionalize the procedure for tribunals as well. The Albigensian Crusade had once and for all done away with the debate over Church jurisdiction in any area. The assumption of universal power over spiritual matters was expanded to include temporal jurisdiction, and as far as the Church was concerned, that jurisdiction included *all* Christian lands.

This change further led to a new approach to finding and punishing heresy. Since the time of Innocent III, the Church had preferred the policy of persuasion to convince heretics to seek absolution and return to the Church. Now, with the Dominicans going out into the countryside to actively seek out heretics and place them on trial, the trend moved away from persuasion and began to favor coercion. This was supported by lay authorities in local areas who were required by Church law to actively support the Inquisition. This support included not only helping to set up tribunals, but going the additional step of reporting suspected heretics to the Dominican inquisitors when they arrived on the scene. One consequence of the long military conflict between crusaders and Cathars was a growing trend in lynch mob reaction to real or perceived heretical movements. This drove heretics underground, with the unintended consequence that it became harder to identify them. The trend toward coercion, coinciding with the end of the days when Cathars preached their beliefs openly, only increased the Dominicans' zeal for punishing heretics, including expanded use of torture during interrogations:

> The slow movement from persuasion to coercion also increased the importance of investigation, of inquiry. And when no accusers came forward, or when synodal witnesses seemed unable to learn anything of heretics, those witnesses had to be given investigative powers, with new rules of evidence and a new legal procedure. The twelfth century had seen a revolution in legal procedure, and the new procedure for discovering and trying heretics borrowed much from it.[7]

Before this time, legal process required that the burden of proof rest on the accuser. If a case could not be made to the tribunal's satisfaction, the accuser faced possible legal reprisals. The historical legal process also relied on witness testimony, documentation, and judicial discretion. As inquisitional tribunals spread, a new approach developed. Accusations could be brought by the tribunal itself even without an outside accuser; and the requirement for witnesses or other evidence was not always heeded. The application of principles was inconsistent, with some inquisitors relying solely on the confessions of the accused, even when those confessions were obtained through torture or offered up in exchange for the promise of leniency. Many people confessed and became witnesses against others in order to avoid more extreme sentences.

The legal system outside of the Inquisition grew with the inquisitorial system and mirrored it in ways that the papacy had not anticipated. For example, as the number of legal cases grew, papal legates were appointed as judges. Many of these legates had no legal training but were versed in Church law, and so Church law was applied more and more in secular disputes. As the problems arising out of this system became evident, using members of the Dominican Order to run inquisitorial investigations seemed a perfect solution. The Dominicans were well trained in both Church and secular legal issues. And Dominic's familiarity with the Cathars was an added advantage in assigning his followers to investigate heresy not only in Southern France, but throughout Europe.

In fact, the application of inquisitorial methods against Cathars and other heretics exceeded any previously known secular punishments. Those found guilty of heresy risked losing not only their lives, but all of their property and the inheritance rights of their heirs. Their homes were destroyed and family members exiled as part of the punishment. A widespread attitude grew among both Church and secular authorities: heretics incurred a debt of hatred (*animadversion debita*) as one consequence of their heresy. This meant imposing whatever penalty the local authorities deemed appropriate. Once the Dominicans were placed in charge Gregory IX made it clear that *animadversion debita* meant the death penalty, and this was expected to be applied vigorously.

The trend was more than a change in legal process and rules of evidence used in inquisitorial tribunals; it also changed the secular legal system. A widespread fear of heresy among local populations (largely derived from the 21-year suffering during the crusade against the Cathars) increased the severity of punishments, expanded the use of the death penalty, and led to more cooperation between Church and secular courts. All of these changes, in turn, accelerated the Inquisition. In the past, heresy had been considered a crime of perception, strictly a spiritual matter between Christians and the Church; but the Inquisition criminalized heresy and placed it on the same criminal level as treason. To the Church (and especially the Dominican inquisitors) heresy was the worst of all crimes because it was committed knowingly by those who should remain faithful to the Church. It was thought of as a crime directly against God.

The well-organized Dominicans, aided by trained investigators and experts in theology, made the tribunal efficient and effective. By the middle of the 13th century, Pope Gregory had authorized secret courts and arrests without the need for warrants as part of the effort to control Cathars and prevent a resurgence of that movement and others. To prevent an organized Cathar problem, confessed members were forcibly relocated to cities and towns where heresy had never been a problem in the past. In any town where heresy was believed to have been wiped out, everyone was required to swear oaths against all heresy. But the promise of severe punishment even for those suspected of being Cathars only made it more difficult to find them. Harsh measures did not eliminate the threat; they had the opposite effect of sustaining underground Cathar cells. In 1229, the year the 21-year crusade ended, it appears that the Church thought the matter had been put to rest; its new, stricter rules were designed to prevent the Cathar movement from continuing. But the problem remained widespread in spite of severe penalties and increased tribunals aimed at the Cathars.

The Inquisitorial Cathar Problem

The Church legal system was constructed to ensure that there would never be a shortage of heretics. The accused had incentives to cooperate and to become a witness against others, in order to preserve family and property. The choice to resist resulted in loss of everything, including life and property; and as the inquisitorial system grew, defiance to the system became a form of heresy equally condemnable as actively denouncing the Church.

Even with the Church's nearly total control over the region where Cathars had thrived, it was not always smooth for the Dominican inquisitors. Even when Church efforts were bolstered with military support, the Cathars resisted actively and at times with violence. Cases came to light in which inquisitors were beaten or even murdered by locals who believed the tribunals were going too far. In response, inquisitors were known to excommunicate entire towns, a power they had been given by the Church to shore up their authority. Another form of resistance was refusal to appear in front of the tribunal, a defiance the inquisitors could not understand or tolerate. However, attempting to seek out the defiant accused person could be dangerous, especially if the entire population viewed the inquisitorial process with hostility. This increased the likelihood of violent reaction to enforcement measures.

It was not only distaste for inquisitorial methods that led to this resistance, but a growing awareness that many inquisitors and their assistants were corrupt. One opponent of the Dominicans, a vocal Franciscan named Bernard Délicieux, observed that no Christian, even the most devout, was safe from the Inquisition. He even stated that "if Peter and Paul themselves appeared before inquisitors they would be found guilty of heresy." Bernard further complained that the inquisitors, by their extreme measures, "decatholicized Catholics." Bernard was publicly critical of abuses by inquisitors, calling them butchers and worse: "The time has come about which it is written that there would come certain people dressed in the clothing of sheep, having within the hearts of wolves, eating and devouring people."[8]

These sentiments spread as inquisitors expanded their investigations. The growth of resistance to inquisitors and their tribunals expanded beyond the regions where Cathars had been active and soon included entire regions. The Church had assumed and hoped that heretics would want forgiveness and would abandon their Cathar beliefs, repent and return to the Church. The severity of threatened punishments was intended to create a logical and easy return to the fold. However, things did not proceed as the Church had expected. In fact, the more the tribunals spread and the more people suffered burning at the stake, the more resistance grew. In 1242, a team of inquisitors in the town of Avignonet near Toulouse was murdered with swords, lances and axes. The team was well known and the lead inquisitor, Dominican William Arnold, had been the most active inquisitor in the area. Far from ending the intrusion of the Inquisition, the murders led to an escalation of Inquisition activity in the area.[9]

The inquisitor who replaced Arnold was a Dominican named Ferrier. He was the most experienced inquisitor of the day and had a reputation for severity in investigation and sentencing. The escalation was met with an equally fierce response among the Cathars. The Cathars wanted to renew the war with the Church, and over the next decade localized revolts occurred. These were quelled by French forces cooperating with the Church. A concerted effort by the Church to root out Cathar leaders resulted in the execution of over 200 "perfected heretics" in March 1244. The Cathar leadership relocated to Lombardy in Northern Italy and established a Cathar church in exile. The situation in Languedoc had become untenable not only because of the escalated inquisitorial presence, but also because of the French military powers pitted against them and at the same time, the loss of support among the local population. By 1250, the number of Perfecti remaining was estimated at lower than 4,000, and 2,500 of these had relocated to Lombardy.[10]

Unlike the situation in the past, when Cathars were able to practice and preach openly, the movement had been driven underground. Lombardy was a safe refuge for the moment, but the leaders of the movement knew the Church was actively focused on them as primary targets of the Inquisition. By the middle of the 13th century, the Church attitude toward Cathars was so hostile that there was little chance a captured Cathar would be found innocent in a tribunal. However, the Cathars continued to spread and preach, but at great risk. Church investigations led to identification of leaders who were then arrested and tried; in 1278, dozens of Cathars were arrested and burned at the stake in Verona. As the Inquisition grew in Italy in response to the Cathar migration, it matched the organization of the Inquisition in Southern France. In Milan and Florence, Dominican inquisitor Peter of Verona organized militias to find and arrest heretics, bring them to trial and pass sentences.

The Church continued its battle against the Cathars and other accused heretics throughout the late 13th century. The Dominicans financed their work through seizures of property and expanded their operations by training and adding additional interrogators, both within the order and from the outside. The financial motive — the need to fund the growing activities of the Inquisition — was one incentive to pass guilty verdicts, especially when investigation and interrogation had used a lot of resources.

The rule that the Church was permitted to seize the property of anyone found guilty of heresy made wealthy citizens especially vulnerable to the Inquisition. The added incentive offered to accusers in the form of a share of money or property of those found guilty encouraged rivals and enemies to turn one another over to the Dominicans, and acting first was prudent, especially when enemies were involved.

Inquisitors preferred leaving the role of interrogation to lay underlings because the process, including torture, was unpleasant. The Dominicans believed earnestly in their mission, viewing heresy as "the worst sin" and both a social and political crime, not to mention a spiritual one. But the landscape was changing. Originally, the inquisitors told themselves they were trying to save souls and to correct the error of the heretic's ways; their purpose was benevolent. But as resistance grew and Cathars, among others, resorted to violence and even resisted torture while refusing to confess, the intent of the Inquisition became more punitive and less compassionate. The crime of defiance became, in many ways, *worse* than the spiritual crime of non-belief.

This evolving attitude is evident in literature produced by Dominican inquisitors and leaders of the Dominican Order. Raymond of Peñafort, head of the Dominicans from 1238 to 1240, wrote in his confessor's manual *Summa de penitentia* (1225–35) that his purpose was to help his fellow Dominicans when passing judgment on "souls in the penitential forum." Thus, the Dominican Order did not separate its functions as investigators and inquisitors from the role of priests and savers of souls. And so one of the requisites for a heretic to achieve redemption was completed penance and demonstrated contrition. The leap here is that accused heretics, notably devout Cathars, were not willing to admit that they had committed any sin, and so there was no wrong for which to atone. The Dominican inquisitors saw matters differently, insisting that a heretic had to come back to the Church by admitting the sin completely, based on what the Dominicans considered the standard for true atonement:

> If, within a specified time, [heretics] come voluntarily as penitents to tell the exact and full truth about themselves and about others. All those who presented themselves were to abjure all heresy and swear to take active steps to aid in the pursuit and seizure of other heretics.[11]

In other words, penance and contrition were not enough. To gain forgiveness, the heretic had to bring others to the Dominican tribunals as well.

The Dominican point of view required both a legal and sacramental form of contrition. If a person confessed but felt no contrition, the sin could not be forgiven. Just as any sin is confessed to achieve absolution, the sin of heresy was not satisfied through only a legal process, but also required a true return to the faith, in the view of the Dominican inquisitors. This high standard was at odds with the tendency of some inquisitors to become corrupted by their own power and to accumulate wealth in exchange for favors to accused heretics. It also held heretics to a higher standard than those committing other, more "secular" crimes.

This raised an interesting problem for the Church. Dominican inquisitors assumed to know when contrition was sincere and when it was not. Because repentance takes place within a person's mind and soul, it is never possible for someone else to know whether a confession is heartfelt or not. The Church separated the Dominicans from the accused heretics and presented a vast distinction in both spiritual and legal terms. Whereas heretics were in league with the Devil, the Dominicans were God's own representatives with the power not only to absolve sinners of sins, but also to decide whether contrition was sincere.

Bernard Gui and Dualism

In the same way that heresies of the first 1,000 years of Church history influenced both dogma and policy, the Cathar movement had great impact on 13th century Church legal issues and writings. One of the most prolific writers of the period was Bernard Gui, a Dominican inquisitor based in Toulouse. His guilty verdicts have been estimated at more than 900 over 15 years.

Gui's work as inquisitor and author was influenced by the Cathar movement as well as by past Christian authors. He published numerous books during the early 1300s including histories of the Church's struggle against heresies during the previous 100 years. These publications included histories of the

Augustinians in Limoges (*Traité sur l'histoire de l'abbaye de St. Augustin de Limoges*); the bishops of Toulouse (*Chronique des évêques de Toulouse*); and the Dominican Order (*Compilation historique sur l'ordre des Dominicains*). However, Gui's best-known book was *Conduct of the Inquisition into Heretical Wickedness* (*Pracuca officii inquisitionis heretice pravitatis*), which is widely known as the *Inquisitor's Manual*. In this work, Gui documented methods to be used by inquisitors in questioning accused heretics.

The infamous *Inquisitor's Manual* describes the problems inquisitors faced in investigating Cathars (whom Gui referred to as Manichaean heretics). Of these, Gui wrote that

> they usually say of themselves that they are good Christians, who do not swear, or lie, or speak evil of others; that they do not kill any man or animal, nor anything having the breath of life, and that they hold the faith of the Lord Jesus Christ and his gospel as the apostles taught.... [T]hey claim that confession made to the priests of the Roman Church is useless, and that, since the priests may be sinners, they cannot lose nor bind, and, being unclean in themselves, cannot make others clean. They assert, moreover, that the cross of Christ should not be adored or venerated, because, as they urge, no one would venerate or adore the gallows upon which a father, relative, or friend had been hung. They urge, further, that they who adore the cross ought, for similar reasons, to worship all thorns and lances, because as Christ's body was on the cross during the passion, so was the crown of thorns on his head and the soldier's lance in his side. They proclaim many other scandalous things in regard to the sacraments.[12]

Gui provided additional information and detailed advice on specifically how to question heretics, while explaining the theological basis for destroying the heretic's arguments. In the fifth and last section of the book, Gui analyzed the beliefs of the five heretical groups he considered most important: Cathars, Waldensians, pseudo–Apostles (false prophets), Beguins (radical members of the Franciscan Order), and others (Jews, sorcerers, and invokers of demons).

In the section "General Advice and Remarks," Gui explained the procedures for interrogation based on whether the accused arrived at his own free will or was brought unwillingly before the tribunal. Further distinctions were made between those accused directly of heresy and those accused of supporting or protecting other heretics. The individual was sworn in and asked to voluntarily admit any heretical activities. If the individual admitted to these, or if the tribunal accepted the accusations of other witnesses, a date was set to hold a formal hearing.

The hearing was based on testimony given by witnesses and statements given by the accused heretic. Anyone who openly disputed the authority of the Church or challenged specific doctrine could easily be found guilty of heresy, and the guilt was assumed in advance. This created a perverse assumption that any defense was proof of guilt. A guilty person would argue, proving his guilt; and an innocent person would argue, also proving his guilt. The only choice, in Gui's mind, was for the accused to confess. As Gui stated, one is presumed to be a heretic from the very fact of striving to defend error. But because modern heretics endeavor and seek covertly to disguise their errors rather than openly to confess them, even men versed in the Scriptures cannot prove their guilt, because they manage to escape by verbal trickery and carefully contrived subtleties.[13]

The inquisitor viewed heretics not as poor souls who had been misled by false arguments, but as crafty and well-versed, as intellectual opponents who could easily confuse even well-taught men, "slipping cleverly out of their hands by the sly cunning and tortuous ambiguity of their replies." Noting the difficulty in catching heretics when those heretics refused to admit their sin, Gui failed to also note how an accused person would be viewed as guilty merely for presenting a defense of his or her own thoughts. This obvious point escaped analysis and demonstrates the underlying assumption by the tribunals: If a person is accused, he must be guilty. Otherwise why offer an accusation?

The inquisitor's view of Cathars is revealing. The Church attitude, after struggling against the Cathars for so long, was that they were skilled adversaries, and this fact demanded equal skill on the part of inquisitors to see through the disguise. Gui recommends a series of questions to be asked to uncover the heretic or to trick him into slipping up, believing the crime would be revealed in the Cathars' answer. These questions included:

- Have you ever seen or known of a heretic, by name or reputation?
- When and how often have you seen them?
- Whose company were they in?
- Have you ever received a heretic in your home?
- What were their names and who brought them there?
- How long did they visit?
- Who else came to see those heretics while in your home?
- Did this heretic eat blessed bread and how was it blessed?
- Did you eat any of the blessed bread?
- Did you enter into any covenants with them or were you accepted into their faith?
- Did you see them salute anyone in a heretical manner? (bending the head to one side and then the other, and saying "Your blessing" three times)
- Have you attended a heretication of any person? (a blessing for those close to death)
- Who else was present and where did this take place?
- What have you heard preached by heretics against the Church?
- What have you heard heretics say about the Church sacraments?
- Have you heard heretics criticize veneration of the cross of Jesus?
- Do you believe that heretics known to you were good, truthful men?

- Do you believe heretics you knew were of good faith, in a good sect, and followed a good doctrine?
- Do you believe heretical sect members could be saved within their sect?
- How long have you shared in these beliefs?
- When did you first begin to accept these beliefs?
- Do you continue to accept these beliefs?
- Have you previously been summoned by another inquisitor?
- Have you previously confessed to any heresy?
- Have you ever rejected heresy before any inquisitor?
- Were you restored to communion of the Church or absolved?
- Since that time, have you been involved in any matter of heresy?
- Have you ever accompanied a heretic from place to place or had their books in your possession?[14]

It is easy to see how this line of questioning, with its many accusatory and leading questions or generalized inquiries, could easily lead to charges being brought and the accused being suspected of lying. This is especially the case when, unknown to accused heretics, other witnesses had already implicated them in a heretical activity, association or practice. The Church's obsession with (and fear of) the Cathars was expressed both in the overall tone of the Inquisition and in Gui's preoccupation with the Cathars as the greatest threat among heretics.

Other Heresies of the 14th Century

The Cathars were foremost in the minds of Gui and other Dominican inquisitors, as they were in the minds of the popes in this period. Gui also documented the activities and beliefs of other heretical sects, including the Beguins. This was a sect that branched off of the Franciscan Order, calling itself the Poor Brethren of Penitence. By 1315, according to Gui, this sect had begun to be "exposed in their erroneous opinions." Many were accused and convicted of heresy and burned at the stake.

The Beguins were accused of challenging the authority of the Roman Church and the pope. Gui wrote of this sect:

The Beguins live in villages and small towns, where some of them live together in little dwellings which, in the phraseology they affect, they call "houses of poverty." Both the occupants and those who dwell in their own private homes quite frequently gather together in these houses with associates and friends of the Beguins on feast days and Sundays. There they read or listen to the reading in the vernacular from the above-mentioned pamphlets or tracts, out of which they imbibe poison, although certain other things are also read there: the commandments, the articles of faith, legends of the saints, and a summa on vices and virtues. Thus the school of the devil, with its appearance of good, seems, in monkey fashion, to imitate the school of Christ in some ways.... [T]hese Beguins have certain patterns of overt behavior, in speech and other actions, by which one may distinguish them from other people. Their method of address or of returning a salutation is this: As they approach or enter a house, or meet on a journey or on the street, they say, "Blessed be Jesus Christ," or "Blessed be the name of Jesus Christ."[15]

The problem that Gui and other inquisitors had with the Beguins was that they questioned the pope's authority. The Beguins taught that the Rule of St. Francis (with its vows of obedience, chastity and poverty) was the same life Christ led, and that anyone who lived contrary to this rule was a heretic — which called into question the lack of poverty among the elite of the Church. The Beguins believed that if anyone, including the pope, tried to change the rule of St. Francis, he would be acting against the Gospels. The sect also taught that the pope lacked the authority to grant dispensation to those who had taken the three Franciscan vows, because the vows were made to God and not to the Church. This insistence on being answerable only to a higher power than the pope was seen as an outrageous heresy, and even though the Poor Brethren were more pious than most clergy of the day, they were brought before the inquisitorial tribunals. When they refused to abandon their beliefs, they were condemned and burned at the stake.

Just as Cathars thought of themselves as devout Christians, the Poor Brethren demonstrated exceptional devotion to their beliefs. But the Church took as a threat any movement that challenged the Church and the pope as the ultimate authority in all matters, spiritual and temporal. The experience in the Cathar conflict and the crusade of the previous century resulted in a belief among Church authorities that no dissent was acceptable, even among the most pious of mendicant orders or Christian sects. Even when a set of beliefs was based on loyalty to Christ and adherence to the Gospels, the Church saw any defiance as a form of heresy — especially if the authority of the pope was questioned as part of that belief.

Gui and his fellow inquisitors were also intent on arresting sorcerers and proving them heretics. The belief in witches predated Gui by several centuries, and the personage of "witch" and "sorcerer" were confused with one another. The Great Witch Hunt that was practiced in Europe from the 15th to the 18th centuries grew out of the Inquisition much later; during Gui's tenure as inquisitor, he included witches and sorcerers with Jews in a blanket condemnation of non–Christian, pagan, and other heretical practices. In this regard, the original definition of heresy, which was restricted to Christians abandoning or questioning doctrine, began to expand to those outside Christianity.

The Church obsession with witches was expressed as early as the 10th century in a document called the *Canon Episcopi*. The exact date of origin is not known. It was first documented by Regino of Prüm, a Benedictine abbot who died in 915. He wrote of the epistle in *Libri de synodalibus cuasis et disciplinas ecclesiasticis*. The document identified witchcraft with pagan beliefs. For example:

> Have you believed or have you shared a superstition to which some wicked women claim to have given themselves, instruments of Satan, fooled by diabolical phantasms? During the night, with Diana, the pagan goddess, in the company of a crowd of other women, they ride the backs of animals, traversing great distances during the silence of the deep night, obeying Diana's orders as their mistress and putting themselves at her service during certain specified nights. If only these sorceresses could die in their impiety without dragging many others into their loss. Fooled into error, many people believe that these rides of Diana really exist. Thus they leave the true faith and fall into pagan error in believing that a god or goddess can exist besides the only God.[16]

Superstitious beliefs grew through the years after this work was published. In the late 12th century, one book described a meeting of witches:

> A black cat of marvelous size climbs down a rope which hangs in their midst. On seeing it they put out the lights. They do not sing hymns or repeat them distinctly, but hum through clenched teeth and pantingly feel their way towards the place where they saw their lord. When they have found him they kiss him, each the more humbly as he is the more inflamed with frenzy, some the feet, more the tail, most the private parts.[17]

This reference to kissing of a cat's private parts may be the source for the later false accusation leveled by Alain de l'Isle toward the Cathars, claiming the practice was the source for the word "Cathar."

As lurid and "un–Christian" as witchcraft was alleged to be, it was not its actual practice that was treated as a form of heresy. A distinction was made between the practice of witchcraft as a non–Christian faith, and belief in the existence of witches on the part of Christians. It is that belief that constituted heresy, because it represented a departure from Christian doctrine. Inquisitor Gui also used the crime of sorcery (*maleficium*)—generally meaning magic or magical acts—as a form of heresy and a crime worthy of the inquisitorial tribunals.

During the reign of Pope Clement V (1305–14), accusations of sorcery were prominent in the tribunals of the Knights Templar. (The full name of this group was the Poor Fellow-Soldiers of Christ and of the Temple of Solomon, or *Pauperes commilitones Christi Templique Solomonici*.) On October 13, 1307, all known Knights Templar were arrested by French King Philip IV, and confessions were obtained under torture. Pope Clement V issued a papal bull, *Pastoralis Præeminentiæ*, on November 22, 1307, ordering all European rulers to arrest Templars and seize their property. Clement ordered through another bull, *Ad providam*, that all Templar property be given to another order of Knights, the Hospitallers.

Throughout the 13th and 14th centuries, the definition of heresy expanded.

Not only did "heresy," and thus the jurisdiction of the inquisitorial tribunal, extend to matters of disputed faith; it also encompassed witchcraft and sorcery and even non–Christian practices, including Judaism. The inclusion of Jews in the Inquisition arose as part of Bernard Gui's expanded role as a leading Dominican inquisitor of the 14th century.

Jews and Lepers

Including Jews in the tribunals became common practice and was well known later, during the infamous Spanish Inquisition. However, it began originally when Bernard Gui decided to persecute Europe's lepers as part of his mission to eradicate heresy. Gui argued that lepers were diseased not only in body, but also in soul. Lepers were brought before tribunals after Gui accused them of added leprosy-causing powder to drinking water as part of a massive conspiracy to destroy Christianity. Virtually every leper in France was killed as a result, most locked into houses which were then set on fire.

That was not enough, however. The rumor grew to include Jews as accomplices in the leper conspiracy. The alleged leprosy-causing concoction consisted of human blood, consecrated host and urine, according to the Church. Jews were accused of working with the Devil to destroy the Church, resulting in the conviction of many Jews and the exile of many more. Jewish wealth was seized by inquisitors and secular authorities. In 1320, groups of zealous youths (*Pastoureaux*) embarked on a crusade to the Holy Land with the purpose of forcefully baptizing and converting Jews. They traveled barefoot and dressed in rags, carrying crosses. In 1321, a series of trials resulted in convictions and executions of many lepers and Jews. By the 1340s the Inquisition had moved far from its original attack on heresy as a departure from Christian doctrine. Tens of thousands of Jews were killed in France and Germany.

As the Inquisition expanded its mandate and cast its net to catch many different types of heretics, opposition to the absolute authority of the Church was brewing in Europe. This growing movement would lead eventually to the Reformation a century later. It all began quietly with two leaders, an English theologian named John Wyclif and a Bohemian priest named John Hus, who dared to challenge the undisputed power and might of the Church.

CHAPTER 5

The Age of Wyclif and Hus

*We declare, we say, we defend and pronounce that to every human creature
it is absolutely necessary to salvation to be subject to the Roman pontiff.*
— Pope Boniface VIII, *Unam sanctam*,
November 18, 1302

In 1302, Pope Boniface VIII (1294–1303) declared that "to every human creature it is absolutely necessary to salvation to be subject to the Roman pontiff." This declaration, which came in the papal bull *Unam Sanctam* (One Church), defined the Church position for the 14th century and beyond. The declaration that Christians were expected to be literal subjects to the pope — the ultimate position of papal supremacy — itself led to increased instances of heresy. It was the distinct requirement of submission to the pope (not to Christ or to the Church) that troubled so many Christians at a time when enlightened views were growing. In the 14th century, a greater number of Europeans knew how to read. Furthermore, the excesses of the Church effort against the Cathars and the expanding Inquisition fueled heretical movements and accelerated the breakaways that led finally to the Reformation.

Boniface's policy made the Church inaccessible to any intellectual arguments not approved by the pope. It was one of Boniface's many failed initiatives. Although highly intelligent, he was inept as a politician. His many attempts at placing his opinion in the middle of European politics were not effective, and were made worse by the underlying assumption of his own power, prestige and God-given last word. Boniface

> constantly intervened on the international plane, but his policies all too often misfired because they were impulsively conceived, even more because his conception of the pope as universal arbiter was no longer palatable to the new political order.[1]

The Reformation movement was not originally intended as a breakaway from the Church. Rather, it was an attempt at discussing change within the Catholic Church — an attempt that was not only unsuccessful but treated with disdain and attacked as heresy. The problems faced by reformers can be traced back to the absolute requirements expressed in *Unam sanctam*. The position of the Church was not open for negotiation:

> The Bull [*Unam sanctam*] lays down dogmatic propositions on the unity of the Church, the necessity of belonging to it for the attainment of eternal salvation, the position of the Pope as supreme head of the Church, and the duty thence aris- ing of submission to the Pope in order to belong to the Church and thus to attain salvation.[2]

Beginning in the 14th century, several concurrent movements resisting both the Church position and the Inquisition developed and spread. These included two prominent challengers to the absolute authority of the Church, John Wyclif and John Hus.

A Changing Time in Church History

The population of Europe was growing quickly and a new fervor of learn- ing marked the beginning of the end of Church domination in medieval Europe. People learned to read, and universities were built and expanded. As people became better educated, they challenged old ideas including those of the Church. From the Church's point of view, education and knowledge properly remained exclusively within the clergy and most focused in the mendicant orders of Dominicans and Franciscans. The confrontation over the previous 100 years between the Church on one side and movements like the Waldensians and Cathars on the other was as much a struggle over knowledge as over spiritual dogma. The heretical movements interpreted scripture in their own ways and were at odds with the Church; no longer willing to simply trust in the clergy for information, people developed their own ideas and challenged traditional beliefs. The papacy wanted to retain its position as the sole authority on all spiritual matters, but the times were changing and people no longer accepted this premise.

Beginning in the 14th century, just when Boniface was trying to strengthen the power of the papacy, the concept of absolute supremacy of the Church began to fade and a shift occurred for the first time toward national identity and authority. The concept of independence of countries from the authority of the Church was in part a struggle against the Inquisition and its claimed universal authority to punish heretics. The idea of a nation as separate and apart from other nations and from the Church was new. The expansion of the definition of "heretic" itself only led to more challenges, and any acts of defiance to Dominican inquisitors were viewed as a serious form of heresy. A new intel- lectual freedom and a growing sense of spiritual freedom had arrived, and no matter how many people were condemned and burned at the stake, the Church could not stop this trend.

These panels by Wolfgang Sauber, date unknown, depict two pioneers of the Reformation, John Wyclif and John Hus. Both challenged papal supremacy through intellect and reason.

Adding to the problems the Church had in enforcing its supremacy through the Dominican-led Inquisition was the problem of Church governance. For the first three-quarters of the 14th century, the papacy had relocated from Rome to Avignon, France. In 1377 it returned to Rome, but between 1378 and 1415 — a period of a second Great Schism (the first being the split between Catholic and Orthodox Christian Churches) — rivals in Rome and Avignon separately claimed the papacy. Between the years 1409 and 1415, three different people claimed to be pope (the third in Pisa, Italy), a situation that caused great confusion and unrest.

While the Church was in disarray and still trying to exert its authority through proclamation and Inquisition, a movement was growing to recognize the rights of human beings both as citizens and under the law. The Inquisition's operation as a form of "thought police" was losing favor and losing steam. The growing dissatisfaction with the policies and abuses of the Church and the desire for greater rights was expressed by leading thinkers of the age, even as the Church condemned them as heretics.

The events that led up to the decline of the papacy and Church authority also explain how and why the traditional Church was becoming a thing of the past, and why the Reformation that happened 100 years later was even possible.

The transition between the medieval Church and the modern Church required not only that the unlimited power of the papacy give way, but also that the power and abuses of the Inquisition be unraveled. This took many decades to achieve, all beginning with the weakening of the papacy, essentially the end of the Church theocracy and the beginnings of applied common law and the rights of the individual. This contrasted with the period when the Inquisition was at its strongest, when the papacy determined virtually all matters of law in Christian countries.

The Church's insistence on its doctrine of infallibility and control over all spiritual and temporal life was contradicted by the corruption and extravagance of the papacy. The new nationalism that began to emerge in Europe was separate from the "Church nationalism" of the Christian empire. Rather than identifying themselves as Christians, people began to think of themselves as German, French, or Spanish. These changes were matched in development of new ideas in art, music and literature.

For the first time in Christianity, free debate of issues and policies began to occur, even though the Church continued to threaten the ultimate punishment for dissent, and even for questioning papal authority. The social changes that eventually led to the Reformation had begun, even during the time that the Inquisition threatened any and all dissent. And so, even as the Inquisition continued, and as the Church excommunicated and executed those who questioned its dogma and authority, the changes were occurring throughout Europe. In spite of the evolving social and artistic awareness in Europe, the Inquisition continued and also evolved, and took on even more ghastly aspects. In Germany especially, the definition of "heretic" was expanded to include witches, and tens of thousands of people were burned at the stake or otherwise tortured and murdered in the name of the Church; and toward the end of the 15th century (in 1478), the infamous Spanish Inquisition began, lasting until 1540. The Church's attempts to expand its authority over "heresy" broadened even as the population of Europe became increasingly enlightened. The Church, like so many powerful institutions before and since, was unable to evolve with the times, preferring to use the threat of force and accelerated torture and execution to try to force the continent back into the Dark Ages.

The Papacy in Complete Turmoil

The social reforms, including challenges to infallibility as a core principle of the Roman Church, were made possible by several events taking place at the same time. In the 1340s, the death of millions from Black Plague was widely explained as God's punishment for worldly sin. The catastrophe of the plague affected the European outlook on life for many decades to come. This included questioning the traditional institutions and values, most of which had been controlled by the Church. Even the most devout Christians, seeing entire regions falling to the illness, questioned why the "infallible" Church was powerless to put an end to the suffering.

Another theory was that the Black Plague was a Jewish conspiracy. This led to growing anti–Semitic sentiment throughout Europe and eventually to widespread persecution of the Jews 100 years later in Spain. In 1348, a Jew named Agimet admitted under torture that he had been given a package of poison and venom and told to distribute it among the wells and springs in and around Venice. This confession led to the arrest of more Jews, many of whom also confessed under torture to spreading the plague by poisoning wells throughout Italy and France. The hysteria aimed at Jews was intermixed with a growing fear of witchcraft. For French and German Christians, Jews and witches were seen as parts of a single, concerted anti-societal conspiracy of which anti–Christian poisonings were only one small part. The Jews were easy targets for fearful people who had seen a lot of death from the plague. The lower than average mortality among Jews from the plague only increased this suspicion, even though it was easily explained:

> Segregated in their own quarters (where the Jews lived as humble artisans except for a very small elite of bankers and rabbis), the Jews were cut off from the rodents on the wharves and the cattle in the countryside, the main carriers of infectious disease. In addition, rabbinical law prescribed personal cleanliness, good housekeeping, and highly selective diets. These conditions may well have isolated the Jews from the hot spots of plague and their practical quarantine aroused suspicion that they were responsible for the disease to which they themselves seemed immune. Of course only a general paranoid attitude to Jews among the populace could activate these suspicions into pogroms.[3]

This developing suspicion of Jews grew over time and easily enabled the Inquisition to expand its investigations from heretics to Jews.

Another major social change taking place was the disintegration of the papacy itself. Pope Boniface VIII is usually identified as the individual most responsible for a long period of decline in the papacy. Historians of the time summarized his reign thus: "He came in like a fox, he reigned like a lion, and he died like a dog" (*intravit ut vulpes, ragnavit ut leo, mortuus est sicut canis*). In contrast, Boniface's successor, Benedict XI (1303–4), was a more spiritual and less worldly man who tried to mend fences. When he died a year after becoming pope, an 11-month conclave ensued, finally ending with the election of Clement V (1303–14). Clement chose to set up his papacy in Avignon, and this began what has been called the "Avignon exile," the "Western Schism," or the "Babylonian captivity" of the papacy, a period of more than 70 years when the papacy operated from France. It saw seven men elected pope, all of whom were French.

This relocation of the papacy caused great turmoil throughout the Christian world. The split erased much of the reverence the Christian world had held for the papacy, now becoming a French institution rather than a Roman one. The period was also scandalized by corruption, with popes living in luxury and known for their sexual excesses. Nepotism was widely practiced in the organization of the papal court, and bribery and the selling of indulgences rose to previously unknown levels of abuse. The papal palace was overrun by money-making schemes and prostitution. Petrarch called the papal palace the "sink of every vice" and the French papal court a "fountain of afflictions, the refuge of wrath, the school of errors, a temple of lies, the awful prison hell on earth."[4]

It was not until 1377 that the papacy returned to Rome. However, the long period of abuse of the office and its consequent degeneration opened the door for many to question whether the institution of the Christian Church was in good hands. The excesses of the Inquisition throughout the 14th century gave way to the demand for greater freedom in the 15th. It was in this environment, following a period of confusion and years of concurrent popes and antipopes, that the modern era of the Church began. It had become clear that the leaders of the Church did not always know best; in fact, their dependence on the Inquisition to keep the people in line only sped up the movement toward the Renaissance and away from the ignorance of the past and from the exclusive control by the Church over all knowledge and education.

In this environment, after the devastation of the Black Plague, the corruption of the papacy and the ever-growing abuses of the Inquisition, revolutionary ideas were born. These ideas—as simple as the belief that the pope was not the supreme authority on earth—were called heresy by the Church, and with a desire to keep matters under control with the unquestioning repression of the past, the Church went after the revolutionary thinkers of the age with as much energy and resolve as ever. Primary among these thinkers were John Wyclif in England and John Hus in Bohemia.

John Wyclif

A great thinker of the 14th century was an English theologian named John Wyclif (alt. Wycliffe, Wycliff, or Wickliffe). As a lay preacher, he was an outsider to the Catholic clergy. The Church called his followers Lollards, a derogatory name referring to an individual lacking training or education. Over time, the word came to be used to describe any heretic, especially in England. Followers also took up the name of Poor Priests. Wyclif promoted a simple adherence to the teaching of Christ in contrast to the excesses and temporal wealth of the papacy and Church elders. Beyond the disputes over accumulation of wealth by the clergy, Wyclif also held controversial theological views. He believed in predestination and viewed the Christian Church as a "Church of the Saved" or a community of faithful believers. Many Lollard beliefs were similar to the Church's official doctrine, with one critical exception: Wyclif opposed the papacy's claim to authority over secular matters. He favored a system in which the Church would have authority only over spiritual matters. Wyclif's opinion of the pope went beyond a question of who held the ultimate right to secular power. He called the pope "the anti–Christ, the proud, worldly priest of Rome, and the most cursed of clippers and cut-purses."[5]

This defiance of Church authority marked Wyclif as a heretic in the view of the Church. In historical context, however, he has come to represent the first vocal step away from traditional and unquestioned Church authority, and the earliest voice in the Protestant Reformation that followed many years later (he is referred to as "The Morning Star of the Reformation").

Wyclif published *De civil dominio* in (1376–8) in which he expressed his belief that the clergy had no right to temporal political power and also promoted the idea of a return to the simple, apostolic life. This was a bold claim made during a period when the Inquisition remained in force in Europe and the mendicant orders continued to hold great power, even in England. While Church leaders condemned Wyclif's statements, he became popular as a lecturer throughout England. He published more books, including *Postilla super totam bibliam* in 1375–76, *On the Truth of Holy Scripture* in 1378, *The King's Duty* in 1379, and *The Pope's Power*, also in 1379.

His controversial challenges to Church doctrine led to a summons to appear before William Courtney, the Bishop of London, on February 19, 1377. The bishop demanded an explanation of the statements Wyclif had been making about the Church, its power and the pope. Wyclif was accompanied by several supporters, and a large crowd also appeared at the church. Nothing came of the meeting; apparently Wyclif's obvious popularity protected him.

Wyclif was not discouraged by the confrontation and continued to publish his views. He questioned many of the widely accepted Church sacraments. For example, he challenged the doctrine that the Eucharist created the actual presence of Christ. He also questioned the value of confession, the worship of the saints, the use of relics, and the concept of purgatory. He was especially critical of the clergy for its accumulation of property and wealth. These challenges not only to Church authority but to its basic doctrines raised important questions in the minds of Christians: Were priests even necessary if the sacraments of communion and confession were not valid? Could ordinary people communicate directly with God through prayer, making the priests' role unnecessary? And if there was no such place as purgatory, did people need to buy indulgences from priests or bishops? Wyclif wrote of these ideas in his published books, bringing attention to himself and creating a popular movement away from established Church doctrine.

Church leaders accused Wyclif of blasphemy and heresy. Among his most controversial opinions was that the mendicant orders (which operated the

Inquisition) should be controlled through secular authority. On May 22, 1377, Pope Gregory XI (1370–8) published a bull against Wyclif, demanding that he be imprisoned until his sentence was determined by a papal court. The vice chancellor of Oxford responded by remanding Wyclif to a sort of house arrest at Black Hall, which did not last long; it was surely less severe than what the pope had intended. Gregory wrote in his bull that "Wyclif was vomiting out of the filthy dungeon of his heart most wicked and damnable heresies, whereby he hoped to pollute the faithful and bring them to the precipice of perdition, overthrow the Church and subvert the secular estate."[6]

The bull criticized 19 articles from Wyclif's writings and demanded that he be investigated. The pope threatened to cut off Oxford University's funding if Wyclif was not punished for his positions. In 1382, a synod concluded that many of Wyclif's teachings were heretical or in error and dangerous to both the Church and the State, and he was forced to retire from his teaching position at Oxford. The popularity of his ideas and association with many powerful friends (notably John of Gaunt, First Duke of Lancaster and an influential nobleman) saved Wyclif from the Inquisition and excommunication. After retirement, he continued writing, producing *Trialogus* in 1382 and *Opus Evangelicum* in 1384.

Upon his death, the condemnation of Wyclif did not end. In the words of one historian:

> On the feast of the passion of St. Thomas of Canterbury, John de Wyclif, that instrument of the devil, that enemy of the Church, that author of confusion to the common people, that image of hypocrites, that idol of heretics, that author of schism, that sower of hatred, that coiner of lies, being struck with the horrible judgment of God, was smitten with palsy and continued to live till St. Sylvester's Day, on which he breathed out his malicious spirit into the abodes of darkness.[7]

Although Wyclif died at the end of 1384, he remained a problem for the Church for many years to follow. In 1401, an anti–Wyclif statute was extended to the Lollards by Parliament, condemning Wyclif and his followers. The statute, *De hæretico comburendo* (*The Burning of Heretics*), described the Lollards:

> And of such sect and wicked doctrine and opinions, they make unlawful conventicles and confederacies, they hold and exercise schools, they make and write books, they do wickedly instruct and inform people, and, as much as they may, excite and stir them to sedition and insurrection, and make great strife and division among the people, and do daily perpetrate and commit other enormities horrible to be heard, in subversion of the said Catholic faith and doctrine of the Holy Church, in diminution of God's honor, and also in destruction of the estate, rights, and liberties of the said English Church; by which sect and wicked and false preachings, doctrines, and opinions of the said false and perverse people, not only the greatest peril of souls, but also many more other hurts, slanders, and perils, which God forbid, might come to this realm....[8]

In 1408, the Constitutions of Oxford banned all of Wyclif's writings, especially his late-life translation of the Bible into English. The new law declared that English translation of the Bible was itself a form of heresy. Wyclif was posthumously named a heretic 29 years after his death by the Council of Constance (May 4, 1415), which declared "John Wyclif to have been a notorious heretic, and excommunicates him and condemns his memory as one who died an obstinate heretic."[9]

Under a ban of the Church, his books were ordered burned and his remains were exhumed. In 1427 his remains were dug up and burned, and his ashes were thrown into the River Swift. Thus the Church disposed of a heretic many years after his death. Nevertheless, his ideas persisted.

Wyclif had never intended to found the movement called the Lollards, although its members gathered around his statements and publications. Wyclif had only intended to question the contradiction he saw between the life of poverty and devotion he believed was encouraged by the Gospels, and the lifestyle of the pope and Church bishops. The substitution of papal infallibility for the more fundamental belief in God having a direct linkage with the faithful also disturbed Wyclif and, after his death, his followers.

In the decades after Wyclif's death, Lollards were brought before the tribunals of the Inquisition and an active crusade was initiated against them. Many recanted but many more were found guilty of heresy and executed. Heresy trials in England had been rare up until this time, but the Lollards were of special interest to the inquisitors. The movement had gained in popularity in spite of persecution. One writer of the day claimed that out of every two men encountered on the road, one was sure to be a Lollard.[10]

In 1401, Henry IV became King of England and under his rule a new policy was undertaken in dealing with the Lollards. Parliament passed an act the same year legalizing the burning of heretics, the first law of its kind in England, which led to executions of hundreds of accused heretics. This law outlawed preaching, teaching or publishing by Lollards; offenders were to be tried by courts of the local diocese and upon being found guilty, handed over to civil authorities and burned at the stake.[11]

John Hus

John Hus (alt. Jan Huss or John Huss) was a Bohemian Catholic priest. Born in 1372, he was a follower of Wyclif and his ideas and an important forefather of the Protestant Reformation.

Hus came to the attention of the Church when he spoke out against indulgences. He also believed that the papacy and clergy had to be reformed and wanted services to be conducted in both Latin and the local language of the congregation. His address *Quæstio magistri Johannis Hus de indulgentiis* was taken directly from Wyclif's book *De ecclesia* and from his treatise *De absolution a pena et culpa*. Hus agreed with Wyclif's view that no pope or bishop had the authority to go to war in the name of the Church, and that sins could be forgiven only through repentance and not through payment of money (indulgences).

Hus drew an immediate negative reaction from the Church. Pope Alexander V (antipope 1409–10) issued a bull in late 1409 authorizing the local archbishop to quell Hus and other followers of Wyclif. All books written by Wyclif were to be burned and preaching of his doctrines was banned. Hus appealed to the pope, arguing that it was absurd to burn books on non-theological topics such as logic or philosophy, a policy that would be likely to lead to banning of books by notables such as Aristotle; but nothing was changed. All manuscripts of Wyclif's writings were gathered and burned and Hus was warned to not continue repeating the ideas Wyclif had promoted. Hus protested his condemnation, writing to the archbishop:

> I am accused by my adversaries before your paternity's grace as if I were a scandalous and erroneous preacher, contrary to the Holy Mother Church, and thus wandering from the faith.... I wish to refute the scandalous accusations of my enemies.[12]

The pope declared Hus excommunicated in 1411. Throughout Bohemia, people rioted in support of Hus and against the Church position banning him from teaching Wyclif's ideas. The Prague government also agreed with Hus, who continued preaching in spite of the Church ban. Some of Hus' followers burned copies of the papal bull in defiance of the Church.

When followers of Hus expressed their view agreeing with Hus that indulgences were improper, they were beheaded, becoming the first martyrs in what came to be known as the Hussite Church. No amount of reasoned arguments swayed the Church from its position regarding Hus and his writings. The course of condemnation was already begun and there was no turning back:

> Hus was now caught in the familiar trap of medieval "heretics" and dissidents, from which he could escape neither by "proving his innocence" nor by "recantation." The more vigorously and publicly he defended himself and his orthodoxy the more insistent became the accusations.[13]

Papal legates tried to convince Hus to comply with the papal bull by giving up his message, without success. The conflict only escalated as Hus continued to preach his and Wyclif's ideas. The pope instructed Prague's cardinal of St. Angelo to take steps to silence Hus. The Church ordered his chapel destroyed and Hus responded defiantly, stating that Jesus Christ was his ultimate judge, not the pope. Czech King Wenceslaus forced Hus to depart Prague, but his absence did not quiet his followers. In 1412, the king suggested a synod to reconcile Hus with the Church, and it was held in the palace of Prague's archbishop. The synod did not accomplish its intended reconciliation.

Emperor Sigismund issued a letter to Hus promising him safe conduct (*salvo conductus*) if he would attend the Council of Constance. Hus traveled to Constance to try to persuade the Church elders to change their position. Meanwhile, Hus' enemies argued that the promise of safe conduct was not legally binding because Hus had been declared a heretic. The authorities agreed. Going back on their word, they ordered Hus arrested. On December 8, 1414, he was placed in a dungeon at a local Dominican monastery. In the same month, Pope John XXIII (antipope in Pisa, 1410–15) had appointed a council of three bishops to investigate and try Hus. Under the prevailing inquisitorial rules, the prosecution was able to produce witnesses but Hus was not allowed to present a defense or employ an advocate to argue his side. He was placed under control of the archbishop of Constance and moved to his castle, where he was kept in chains. He was fed poorly on a starvation diet, and became diseased in these conditions.

On June 5, 1415, the tribunal began. Hus, still relying on his promise of safe conduct, apparently assumed that if he could explain himself the matter would come to an end. He told the tribunal that he would recant if his error could be proven by citations from the Bible. He was told he had to agree with four conclusions: first, that he was in error in stating his theses; second, that he now renounced his previous beliefs; third, that he now recanted; and fourth, that he agreed to the opposite of what he had previously believed.

Even though Hus attended in good faith, the matter had already been decided. At his tribunal, whenever Hus tried to speak to defend himself, he was shouted down by the attendees, a collection of cardinals, bishops and theologians. The tribunal was determined to burn Hus at the stake even if he did recant. This was confirmed by a record kept of the trial by Peter of Mladovice. Hus refused to recant, however, even under aggressive questioning. Hus was interrogated at his tribunal by Didachus, a Minorite friar from Spain who was known for his skill in posing trick questions at trial.[14]

Hus was found guilty on July 6, 1415. He was read the charges, and then refused the opportunity to respond. He was sentenced to death with the words:

> The holy council, having God only before its eye, condemns John Hus to have been and to be a true, real and open heretic, the disciple not of Christ but of John Wyclif, one who in the University of Prague and before the clergy and people declared Wyclif to be a Catholic and an evangelical doctor — *vie catholicis et doctor evangelicus*.[15]

Still refusing to recant, Hus asked God to forgive his enemies.

The ritual continued; a paper hat was placed on his head with the inscription *Hæresiarcha* (leader of a heresy) and a drawing of the devil. He was then delivered under guard to the local secular authorities with the order, "Take him and do to him as a heretic." When the suggestion was made that Hus should be provided with a confessor, a nearby priest replied that a heretic did not deserve the sacraments even before death. Hus responded, "There is no need of one. I have no mortal sin." He was bound by ropes and chains to a stake, and asked once more to recant. Hus replied, "God is my witness that I have never taught that of which I have by false witnesses been accused. In the truth of the Gospel which I have written, taught, and preached, I will die today with gladness." Then the fire was lit.

Hus was immediately considered a national hero and martyr, and his memory fueled the rebellion against the Church for the next 100 years, leading up to the Reformation that defied Church authority and swept across Europe. The combined influence of Wyclif and Hus was a key ingredient in this movement. It was not until more than 500 years had passed that Pope John Paul II (1978–2005) expressed (in 1999) "profound regret for the cruel death inflicted on John Hus." The pope even said that an inquiry should be held to decide whether Hus could be cleared of the crime of heresy.[16]

Jerome of Prague

The legacy of Wyclif and Hus was their contribution to the Reformation the following century. At the time of their defiance, the Church was still considered all-powerful, even in England and Prague; so their willingness to face the wrath under a period when the Inquisition remained a powerful legal force was remarkable.

Furthermore, their influence did not end with their deaths; in fact, it spread. The Lollard and Hussite movements expanded and were considered in later years to be among the very first of many Protestant faiths.

A year after Hus died, a friend and follower named Jerome of Prague was condemned by the same council that tried Hus, and Jerome was burned at the stake. He left no writings, but between 1398 and 1406 he studied at Prague, Oxford, Paris, Cologne and Heidelberg universities.

In 1410, Jerome had spoken publicly in favor of Wyclif's views, and this was brought up by the Council of Constance four years later. Jerome was excommunicated by the bishop of Krakow and returned to Prague, where he spoke in support of Hus and his ideas. He went to Constance to support Hus but was persuaded to leave since he was under threat of arrest. However, on his return trip he was arrested and imprisoned and later returned to Constance. He was charged with leaving the area while under a summons even though that summons had been issued after he left. He freely admitted his support for Hus and was imprisoned to await trial. He became very ill during his imprisonment and recanted his beliefs at a public hearing. On May 23, 1416, Jerome was tried, and on the second day he reversed his previous recantation. The council concluded that Jerome was a follower of both Wyclif and Hus, and called him a rotten and withered branch (*palmitem putridum et aridum*) of their heresy. He was found guilty on May 30.

Jerome was led from the cathedral wearing the heretic's hat, which was adorned with paintings of red devils. He was burned at the stake at the same spot where Hus had died the year before.

The period in which Wyclif and Hus lived marks the end of total domination by the Church over both spiritual and temporal thought. These pioneers demonstrated that the Church was not necessarily supreme, nor was it the last word in religious belief. This suggestion grew and became a full-blown revolution within the Church; and 100 years later, when Luther attempted to reform the Church, it was the Church that rejected the suggestion. As a result, the Reformation became a full schism that split the Roman Church into many different groups. The seemingly minor differences in theology, blown out of proportion by the Church and the papacy, only strengthened the desire for a different approach that included the right of people to worship as they wished without fear of the Inquisition, and the ability to question the right of the Church to accumulate wealth while forbidding dissent of any kind.

During this period, the early 15th century, another development began to take hold throughout Europe and especially in Germany and France. The Church expanded the definition of heresy to include anyone who practiced witchcraft. Prior to this time, anyone who believed in witchcraft was called a heretic; but from the middle of the 15th century, the accusation that someone was a witch came under the jurisdiction of the Inquisition. The next chapter chronicles how this movement spread in Western Europe.

CHAPTER 6

The Great Witch Hunt

It has indeed lately come to Our ears, not without afflicting Us with bitter sorrow, that in some parts of Northern Germany ... many persons of both sexes, unmindful of their own salvation and straying from the Catholic Faith, have abandoned themselves to devils, incubi and succubi, and by their incantations, spells, conjurations, and other accursed charms and crafts, enormities and horrid offences, have slain infants yet in the mother's womb, as also the offspring of cattle.

—Pope Innocent VIII, papal bull *Summis desiderantes affectibus*, December 5, 1484

Beginning in the middle of the 15th century, a panic spread across Germany and eventually France as well, where accused witches became the targets of the Inquisition. In 1484, Pope Innocent VIII (1484–92) published his infamous bull authorizing inquisitors to take any action they deemed necessary to find, try, and destroy witches. This took the inquisitorial methods of interrogation to new heights of cruelty and led to tens of thousands of deaths under unimaginable conditions.

In heretical investigations before the time of the Great Witch Hunt, inquisitors were likely to use intellectual arguments to try and convert accused heretics, before torture was used. But the efforts to convert witches through reason were not to be used; gaining confessions by any means and then executing the witch was the singular goal. The "heretic" took on a new and expanded meaning. No longer was a heretic simply a person who had strayed from the true tenets of the Church. Now a heretic was actually evil and a worshipper of the devil, who used spells and hexes to harm good Christians. The transition had been completed: from efforts to redirect misguided Christians, to panic over actual evil beings living among innocent people and posing a real threat to their physical and spiritual health.

With the expanded definition of the heretic, the Inquisition expanded as well. In the past, Dominican inquisitors had convinced themselves that the use of torture was necessary to gain confessions in many instances (some speculate that torture was used sparingly). But now the inquisitors were given full authority to use extreme measures on accused as well as witnesses to gain as many confessions as possible. The hysteria fed on itself and grew as a new feature of the Inquisition. The initial intention of quelling breakaway Christian movements was quickly replaced with a focus on destroying witches and wizards.

The Origins of Witchcraft

The belief in witchcraft can be traced back to the Celts as long ago as 700 B.C. Witches worshipped a god of nature, a life source or divine creator. Many current-day celebrations and calendar dates (including Christmas, Halloween, May Day, spring and fall equinox, and winter and summer solstice) are at least partially traceable to many non–Christian sources including older pagan religions and witchcraft. The Celts had their own priests, the druids, who were also teachers and healers. The nature-based origins of witchcraft also tie in to the Celts, who worshipped trees.

Paganism (including witchcraft) is also traced to Celts. The word *pagan* means "country dweller" and encompasses the Celtic worship of many natural things and, over time, the evolution of using potions with healing qualities. Eventually, this practice grew into the concept of casting spells to make others fall ill or even to fall in love. The range of practices involving natural worship and the use of spells are the basis for witchcraft. Witches have also been believed to hold the power of telling the future.

The medieval association of witches with demon worship or devil worship was an invention of the Church. The papal bull issued by Pope Innocent VIII in 1484 documents this association between witches and worship of the devil, making witchcraft not a separate religion but an act of heresy against all of Christianity.

Association with magic through rituals was a further expansion of what the Church perceived as using dark powers instead of relying on God. Anyone who chose witchcraft and dark powers was a heretic. Magic could be "black" (intended to do harm to others), "green" (getting into harmony with nature), or "white" (healing others or improving their prosperity or living conditions). In modern times, some forms of magic (collectively called folk magic) have evolved into herbalism, faith healing, candle magic, mind-reading and clairvoyance. The Church position beginning in the 15th century and continuing to the modern day is that all forms of magic are based on witchcraft and are heretical. Even if the intention is to perform good works, the Church position is that magic violates Christian doctrine.

What some would perceive as a legitimate religion, an alternative to Christianity, was viewed by the Church as a form of heresy and a direct threat to

human bodies and souls. The Church made a specific effort to demonstrate that witches were intent on harming Christians through human sacrifice, imposing spells and disease, and corrupting the innocent (especially young girls) through sexual seduction. To justify bringing witches under the jurisdiction of inquisitors, the argument also had to be put forth that the choice to use witchcraft as an evil power was made by Christians, meaning it was not just an alternative religion but a form of heresy. Anyone believing these arguments was without doubt terrified by witches and supported efforts by inquisitors to root out the evil and destroy it.

The medieval Church used accusations of witchcraft against heretical sects like the Waldensians and Cathars as a way to turn people against them. The image of a witch flying on a broomstick at night and dressed in black clothes with a distinctive hat originated centuries before Christianity as a part of harvest rites; but the Church encouraged and advanced the image in its attempt to frighten people away from heretical sects. In 1440, a document called *The Waldensian*

Stained-glass window in Saint Walburge Church, Xertigny (France), by Gabriel Loire after World War II when the church was rebuilt. Joan was convicted of heresy and witchcraft, but she never recanted her belief in hearing the voices of God and angels, and never admitted attending rituals with witches.

Idolatry (*Valdenses ydolatræ*) "accused the Waldenses with having intercourse with demons and riding through the air on sticks, oiled with a secret unguent."[1]

The fact that women were the primary targets of the witch hunts suggests an additional motivation for the Inquisition's pursuit of witches. The anti-female attitude among the Dominicans especially included a belief that women were inherently weak and prone to sin, were easily tempted, and would abandon God upon being tempted, if only to have sex with the devil or to pursue their own pleasures. The Church's perception of women as a threat came from its aversion to the variety of witchcraft called *Wicca*, which worshipped a female deity. The origins of Wicca include worship of a goddess or both god and goddess (similar to Eastern beliefs in yin and yang).

Herein lies the problem the Church found in Wicca: Any worship of a goddess was a direct challenge to the masculine version of God promoted by the Church. Central to Wicca belief is the idea that a female deity is the generator of all life, a parallel between human birthing and spiritual matters. The Church distorted Wicca's generally benign belief system and focused on Wiccan beliefs in magic, as proof of witchcraft and sorcery — in other words, as an *evil* force. This point enabled the Church to emphasize witchcraft as a single force opposed to the "good" and as a threat to Christians.[2]

The merging of witchcraft and heresy into a single phenomenon began in earnest with Pope Eugene IV (1431–47). He had condemned Joan of Arc as a "witch and heretic," and she was burned at the stake on May 30, 1431. Eugene issued a decree in 1437 instructing all inquisitors to seek out devil worshippers as part of their investigation of heretics. And in 1440, Eugene issued a bull, *Ad perpetua rei memoriam*, identifying witches as Waldensians. The desire on the part of the Church to equate witches with heretics accomplished two goals. First, it provided new targets for the Inquisition in a period of turmoil, in the hope that post-plague Europe would continue to accept the Church and the papacy as leaders. Second, it further consigned major heretical sects to the side of evil.

Nevertheless, the persecution of witches as heretics did not accomplish the goal of solidifying the population behind the Church. A new social order had begun. In post–Cathar, post-plague Europe, a spirit was emerging, a desire for freedom of thought, liberty, and the end of Church dominance. For the first time, people had the power to make such demands; the plague had killed an estimated one-third of Europe's population and now even basic labor was highly valued. Following the plague years, it would take many decades to repopulate farms and factories, and workers were in demand. This demographic catastrophe created a new era that ended both feudalism and Church domination. The individual now had value, and the mysticism and spiritual power of the Church were no longer accepted. The Church recognized the new era but was not able to adapt to it, so instead the Church invented a new enemy. The witch, as a new type of heretic, became the Inquisition's focus. The past non–Christian pagan witch had not previously been thought of as a heretic. In earlier Church opinion, only a Christian could become a heretic by knowingly straying from established doctrine. Now heretic and witch became indistinguishable. Under the new definition, a heretic was anyone the Dominican inquisitors decided to investigate, and the victim of this attention was usually female.

The association of witches and heretics was formalized in the 15th century, but it was not a new idea. The threat of witchcraft was found much earlier in Roman law, when the Church and Rome formed their partnership in the 4th century. Roman law mandated burning at the stake for anyone convicted of worshipping demons, and also called for enslavement for witches. In 825, bishops in attendance at the Council of Paris recommended that secular authorities punish witches and others who practiced pagan rituals. In 873, French king Charles the Bald issued laws instructing authorities to hunt down and execute witches and sorcerers. The same sentiment was expressed by Alfred the Great who ordered death, exile or fines for witches and diviners. When Pope Innocent IV (1243–54) approved of torture to uncover heresy in his bull of May 15, 1252, *Ad extirpanda* (For the elimination), he also called for punishment of heretics "as if they were sorcerers."[3]

Even before Innocent IV's bull, trials and executions of witches had been carried out throughout Europe. In the early 12th century, German judges had ordered witches and wizards burned at the stake. By the middle of the 12th century, the "water test" of witches had been devised. Accused witches were thrown into deep water. If they floated and lived, that proved that they were witches and they were then burned at the stake. If they sank and drowned, it proved they had been innocent. A recurring theme in both drowning and burning of witches is that accusers were likely to be awarded the property of the person who was found guilty, providing an incentive for expanding accusations. Eventually, however, burning at the stake became the most popular remedy for witches in Germany, Italy, and England. In Germany in the 13th century, "heretics, enchanters and sorcerers" were ordered burned.

Witch Trials in Spain

In Spain in the mid-period of the Great Witch Hunt, Inquisition tribunals were far more lenient than in the rest of Europe. This may seem to contradict the history of the Inquisition's harshness against other groups, notably converted Jews and Lutherans. In Spain, as elsewhere, accused witches told fantastic tales of their supernatural exploits, stories brought out under torture or the threat of it. But the inquisitor in Saragossa, Pedro Ciruelo, had an explanation. He believed that the stories inquisitors were hearing came from pacts entered with the devil, but that people entered these pacts as the result of ignorance and superstition. Ciruelo urged leniency toward accused witches.

Still, there were exceptions to this relatively lenient approach. In 1427, Franciscan missionary and preacher Bernardino da Siena campaigned against baby killers and witches, whom he termed "devilish women" (*femmine indiavolate*). He encouraged his listeners to denounce witchcraft and to show no sympathy for witches, asking how they would feel if a witch had murdered one of *their* children. He asked that anyone who suspected another of being a witch report them at once to the Inquisition. The denunciations soon began in large numbers. A trend began, in which those accused of the most fantastic crimes were most likely to be found guilty and burned at the stake. The possibility that accusations had been exaggerated or entirely fabricated was rarely considered.

In 1525 in the Roncesvalles region in northern Spain, the witch hunt accelerated for a short time. In that year

sorcerers were accused of causing the deaths of children, poisoning people by serving them a "green soup" made from toads and children's hearts, and smearing their own bodies with an ointment before attending nocturnal meetings in the course of which they would kiss a black cat.[4]

Painting by Rossello di Jacopo, 15th century. A Franciscan preacher, San Bernardino was a zealot who accused witches of kidnapping and killing babies, and told anyone who suspected a neighbor of witchcraft to report them to the Inquisition. Large numbers of accusations followed, resulting in many victims' being accused of fantastic acts of witchcraft and condemned before the Inquisition. (In the Refectory of the Basilica of Santa Croce, Florence, Italy.)

Following these rumors, dozens of people were arrested. A court-appointed expert was allowed to examine suspects' left eyes where the devil was alleged to have left his mark.

In May 1525, the Council of Navarre disputed inquisitors' claims concerning prosecution of witches. The Spanish inquisitors argued that only they were qualified to judge witches. A decision was reached in 1526 in which inquisitors were granted full authority. However, in Aragon a different standard prevailed. There secular authorities wanted to limit the Inquisition to cases of heresy and exclude witchcraft from the jurisdiction of the tribunals. Both the local magistrates and the inquisitors claimed to have jurisdiction, and the matter often came down to who was able to try a case first. The dispute continued until the early 17th century without resolution.

The guiding authority concerning guilt or innocence of witches came from the Supreme Council of the Inquisition, which had issued guidelines to secular courts as early as 1537. The courts were instructed to ascertain whether the accused had connection with any disappearances or deaths. They were also to ask whether harvests had failed, and if so, from what causes. Inquisitor Martín de Castañega suggested that people should be tried only when the facts of a case could not be explained by natural causes. He also recommended leniency on the grounds that women were weak and simple-minded and could be made to confess to anything. Inquisitors tended to prefer educating ignorant people who had fallen into witchcraft, rather than sending them to prison or condemning them to death. In the few cases resulting in guilty verdicts for witchcraft or the practice of magic, most of the convicted were given penances or lashes. Some were paraded in public riding on mules and forced to wear a cap of shame while onlookers threw onions at them. When death sentences were imposed, they were likely to be overturned by local bishops.

Some of the accusations were farfetched, even by standards of the day. For example, accused witches were suspected not only of entering pacts with demons, but also of predicting the future, curing the sick or concocting potions to make others fall in love. By 1610 the trials of witches had fallen off considerably, with a notable exception in Logroño, to the northeast of Madrid and near the Bay of Biscay. In a trial that year accusing 29 people, it was said that a newly recruited sorcerer was

> made to fly to the spot where the Sabbath was celebrated. Here, the devil presided, seated on a kind of throne. His appearance was that of a black man with shining horns that illuminated the scene. The newcomer renounced the Christian faith, recognized the devil as his god and lord, and worshipped him, kissing his left hand, his mouth, his chest and his private parts. The devil then turned round and presented his backside, which the sorcerer also had to kiss.[5]

Based on this testimony, six of the accused were sentenced to burning at the stake and another six died while imprisoned. The remaining accused sorcerers were acquitted of the charges. At the time this sentence was considered severe even given the imaginative description of the crime they were accused of committing. In Spain, the usual course of events was much more lenient, and compared to trials in Germany where witches were far more likely to be punished harshly, this incident was exceptional in Spain.

Innocent VIII and Witchcraft

In the growing fervor to find witches and bring them to the Inquisition, many areas of Europe went into a panic, believing that witches were everywhere. The more people who were arrested and burned at the stake, the worse the panic became. By 1484, it had reached a height and Pope Innocent VIII issued his infamous bull *Summis desiderantes affectibus* (Desiring with Supreme Ardor).

Besides the stark accusation that many people in northern Germany and other regions had abandoned themselves to "devils, incubi and succubi" and were committing ghastly acts against unborn children, the papal bull contained the names of local inquisitors, noting that until that time they had had no authority to "punish, imprison, and penalize" criminals other than for specific instances of heresy. Now, "being desirous of removing all hindrances and obstacles by which the good work of the inquisitors may be let," Innocent decreed "that the aforesaid inquisitors be empowered to proceed to the just correction, imprisonment, and punishment of any persons" and extended the power to excommunicate, suspend, or impose "yet more terrible penalties, censures, and punishments ... without any right of appeal" to both accused witches and anyone who supported or defended them.[6]

This was an extraordinary extension of inquisitorial powers. It not only folded accused witches and sorcerers into the definition of heretics, but did away with any right of appeal. Anyone who might have tried to defend an accused witch or offer arguments or testimony contrary to the accusation was likely to be accused of the same crime, convicted and executed. It was clearly more prudent to step out of the way of the Inquisition than to stand up and challenge the unlimited authority of the Dominican inquisitors. The pope had granted them complete power to arrest, interrogate, torture, and execute anyone suspected of practicing witchcraft or offering support to a witch. Practically the only protests against the expanding witch hunts came from the victims themselves. Even later in the 200-year witch hunt era, reformers like Martin Luther and John Calvin supported the policies against witches and professed a strong belief in their existence.

In the original creation and definition of the Inquisition, there had been no mention of witchcraft or sorcery. Legal policy regarding punishment of witchcraft as one form of *maleficium* (a term covering any demonic activity) belonged in the secular realm, and at the time the Church had focused solely on heretical activities. By the middle of the 13th century, however, the involvement of the devil in heresy itself came to the attention of inquisitors. Women reportedly escaped from priests by flying through the air. Under torture, women confessed to many things; one "confessed she had indulged in sexual intercourse with a demon for many years and given birth to a monster, part wolf and part serpent, which for two years she had fed on murdered children."[7]

Past methods for interrogating, trying and executing accused witches had been sporadic and inconsistent. But from the middle of the 15th century onward, policies were clarified and made consistent by the Church. As witches were now to be classified as a special brand of heretics, the office of the Inquisition was given total and exclusive authorization to find, interrogate and execute witches.

Taking advantage of the panic it helped to create, the Church used the fear of witches and demonic power to enforce its hold over Christians. The panic itself is not easily understood except in this context. The Church relied on people's fears to hold onto their spiritual allegiance. Without the protection of the Church, individuals would be at the mercy of witches and the demons they served. The 14th century plague had radically changed how Europeans saw themselves and their security, and it became clear that even the power of the Church could not save people from death. That loss of prestige had to be replaced, and the widespread hysteria about witches was a perfect solution. The development of the new "burning times" of witchcraft trials was the culmination of several ideas. The Inquisition itself, previously focused on heresy, was expanded to encompass witchcraft as an outgrowth of numerous and persistent conspiracy theories. The witch, conspiring with demons to murder children for sacrifice, was only the latest aspect of previous beliefs that Jews intentionally caused leprosy and had spread the plague by poisoning wells. Witches, who became known as "plague spreaders," were likely to be tied in to Jewish communities as part of the panic that developed first in Germany and then throughout Western Europe. The blame for witch hunts has been leveled at sects of the Reformation, since the majority of trials were held at the height of the Protestant movement and many of its leaders supported persecutions. However, even though Protestant beliefs included a strong fear of witches and resulted in many persecutions, the origins of the witch hunts were in the papacy and the Inquisition. Just as heretics of the past had been turned over to secular authorities for execution, condemned witches were also turned over to local authorities, whether under Catholic or Protestant control, to be burned or hanged.

The Hammer of Witches

At the same time that Innocent VIII expanded the authority of the Inquisition to include witches, he appointed regional inquisitors to carry out investigations. Two of the best known of these inquisitors were Heinrich Kraemer and Johann Sprenger, both German Dominicans who authored the authoritative witch hunter's manual, *The Hammer of Witches* (*Malleus Maleficarum* or, in German, *Hexenhammer*). The book was written in 1486 and was published in Germany in 1487. Its purpose was to dispel arguments against the existence of witchcraft and to provide detailed instructions on identifying, interrogating and convicting witches.

The book has three parts. In Part I, a series of questions and answers is intended as proof of the existence of witchcraft. The second part describes how witchcraft manifests itself in the world. The third part provides procedures for detection and prosecution. The descriptions of how witches are bound to the devil and how the devil appears to them (as a cat, goat, bull, dog, or black man, for example) are very detailed. The authors exhibit the common preoccupation with sexual matters, a trait seen in many writings about Inquisition methods. They explain "the several methods by which Devils through witches entice and allure the innocent to the increase of that horrid craft and company," noting that while "honest matrons ... are little given to carnal vices but concerned for worldly profit," young women are "more given to bodily lusts and pleasures," and for this reason the Devil works with young women "through their carnal desires and the pleasures of the flesh."[8]

The manual is filled with highly detailed descriptions of how demons take the shape of animals, transport from place to place, kill babies and the unborn and even eat their bodies, hold orgies, defile the sacraments, and entice innocent young girls through seduction in various forms. It is especially preoccupied with the exact process of sexual intercourse that takes place between the devil and the witch; for example, one detailed discussion (in Part II, Question 1, Chapter IV) is on the topic, "How in Modern Time Witches perform the Carnal Act with Incubus Devils, and how they are Multiplied by this Means." The debased sexual condemnation is universal, the book stating that "it is common to all sorcerers and witches to practice carnal lust with demons."

In the section dealing with how witches are to be prosecuted, the manual identifies rumor as a sufficient cause for indictment, stating that an investigation can begin "when there is no accuser or informer, but a general report that there are witches in some town or place; and then the Judge must proceed, not at the instance of any party, but simply by the virtue of his office."[9]

Again showing an obsession with sexual practice, the book instructs that as a first step, the accused is to have all hair removed, especially the hair of the private parts, "for in order to preserve their power of silence they are in the habit of hiding some superstitious object in their clothes or in their hair, or even in the most secret parts of their bodies which must not be named."[10]

Explanations causally mention torture as an effective means of gaining confessions, observing that witches are known to be unable to cry, but cautioning inquisitors that some crafty demons may allow the witch to cry under torture to deceive the judge. Clearly, no matter how the accused responded — with tears, or without — guilt was assumed, and a confession was invariably gained with enough torture of one kind or another. And because the subject was accused of witchcraft and not of a more esoteric form of heresy, saving the accused, or bringing them around to reject witchcraft or sorcery, was not seen as a practical outcome. The book also advises that anyone who zealously defends an accused witch should be suspected. The defense itself may serve as proof that the defender is also a witch.

Although the *Malleus Maleficarum* was intended as a guide for judges, inquisitors and interrogators, it betrays the depravity of the inquisitors themselves. Certainly the book provides no limitations for the activities of inquisitors. On the contrary, it provides many general routes for arriving at the desired conviction while spending a good deal of time on sexuality, including not only sexual practices of witches and demons, but "proper" methods for discovering hidden charms or imps in the pubic hairs of the accused or tricks used by witches during torture.

The sexual focus of this text was embarrassing even to the Church, which rejected it as an "official" manual for inquisitors. Even so, the manual was used widely by secular courts.

There had been a history of discomfort on the part of the Church in delving too deeply into charges of witchcraft, not only because they had long been viewed as secular crimes, but also because of the inevitable sexual details that came out during the investigations.

Misogyny as a Factor

The Church found women to be easy targets for accusations of witchcraft. The depravity of individual inquisitors, not always documented as clearly as in the perverse details of the *Malleus Maleficarum*, was a recurring problem that crossed over the line into sadism. Inquisitors argued that they needed to search the bodies of the accused for a *witch's mark* or *witch's teat*. This was a permanent mark consisting of a scar or colored brand, usually hidden from view somewhere on the woman's body. The witch's teat was believed to be used to feed milk or blood to imps or the devil himself. After such feedings, inquisitors argued, the devil impregnated the woman and the offspring, a *cambion*, immediately grew to adulthood and began performing evil deeds.

To look for the witch's teat, of course, the inquisitor was required to thoroughly examine the accused woman's body. Birthmarks, moles and natural blemishes were cited as witch's marks. A commonly held belief that witch's marks did not bleed when pricked led to the ritual known as "pricking a witch," in which inquisitors — usually working before large crowds — stuck pins into scars and other marks. Even in cases where no visible marks were seen, inquisitors argued that the devil was capable of leaving invisible marks; in such cases, pins were stuck into various parts of the body anyhow. If inquisitors were not convinced they had found the witch's teat, they resorted to torture. They applied hot fat to the eyes, underarms, or thighs, often resulting in infection and death.

Obviously, many of these "trials" were nothing but lewd spectacles and sadistic sexual brutality. That such monstrous abuses were possible reflects not only the depravity of inquisitors and of the Church itself, but of the low social status of women in those times:

> Having a female body was the factor most likely to render one vulnerable to being called a witch. The sexual connotations and the explicit sexual violence utilized in many of the trials make this fact clear. Just which women were targeted and under what circumstances reveals much more about the status of women in early modern Europe.[11]

The most likely women to be accused were poor or elderly, and a majority were unmarried. (There were financial incentives, however, to accuse widows in control of property, since upon conviction their property was turned over to the inquisitors, the court, and the Church.) An accused witch was likely to be seen by neighbors as somehow different and was usually disliked. One author reported that the accused were "women which be commonly old, lame, bleare-eyed, pale, fowle, and full of wrinkles."[12] Other observers called witches "damnable vermin" and "hideous bitches" among other description, demonstrating that likely victims were most likely to be elderly and unattractive, not to mention powerless in 14th and 15th century society. The record shows, however, that girls as young as eight were also accused of witchcraft, as well as the occasional man or boy.

The Church, with its long-established male-dominated hierarchy and its clergy sworn to celibacy, seemed to find women suitable targets for the lurid and imaginative accusations that were typical of the period. Accusations could include not only consorting with the devil, but murdering children and animals and even causing hailstorms. Nevertheless, many women accused of even the most fantastic offenses confessed "upon kindly questioning and also torture," as one account stated. A recurring theme of torture-driven confessions was admission to riding on broomsticks and pitchforks and having sex with the devil.

Typically, execution of a condemned witch was exceptionally cruel. In Germany the accused, who had already been tortured into confession, was burned with hot irons on the breasts and arms, her right hand cut off, her body burned at the stake, and her ashes thrown into the closest river.

The likelihood of a male witch being executed was far less. Both Church and secular law favored men. For example, women were banned from offering legal testimony even in their own defense, whereas men were allowed to speak at their own trials. Men were also more likely to be allowed to appeal sentences to higher courts or even to governing bodies, and the papal restriction on appeals was applied almost exclusively to convicted female witches. In many instances, accused couples were treated differently. The man was more likely to be released after paying money or using influence, while the woman was more likely to be found guilty and burned at the stake.

The reasons for these outcomes are complex. Beyond the strong misogyny among inquisitors and the Church at large, social realities were also at play. After the plague, with such widespread death, a chronic labor shortage led to increased rights for workers, especially in non-farm occupations, which were dominated by men. Meanwhile, the Church viewed women as more disposable, weaker and more easily tempted, and also as inherently evil beings. From the Church view, a lot of this attitude is based on the Christian assignment of blame to Eve for tempting Adam, "proving" that women were evil, thus adding a rationale supporting the witch hunts focusing on women. Early Church writer Tertullian (ca. 160 —ca. 220)* addressed women as follows:

> Do you not know that you are Eve? The judgment of God upon this sex lives on in this age; therefore, necessarily the guilt should live on also. You are the gateway of the devil; you are the one who unseals the curse of that tree, and you are the first one to turn your back on the divine law; you are the one who persuaded him whom the devil was not capable of corrupting; you easily destroyed the image of God, Adam. Because of what you deserve, that is, death, even the Son of God had to die.[13]

Clearly, the social stigmatization of women as evil, weak, and less deserving than men fit perfectly with attitudes within the Church. The Dominican inquisitors were not the exception in the Church, but the rule.

The tendency among inquisitors to so easily condemn women under the guise of religious piety parallels the historical treatment of Jews:

> The medieval conception of women shares much with the corresponding medieval conception of Jews. In both cases, a perennial attribution of secret, bountiful, malicious "power" is made. Women are anathematized and cast as witches because of the enduring grotesque fears they generate in respect of their putative abilities to control men and thereby coerce, for their own ends, male-dominated Christian society. Whatever the social and psychological determinants operative in this abiding obsession, there can be no denying the consequential reality of such anxiety in medieval Christendom. Linked to theological traditions of Eve and Lilith, women are perceived as embodiments of inexhaustible negativity. Though not quite quasi-literal incarnations of the Devil as were Jews, women are, rather, their ontological "first cousins" who, like the Jews, emerge from the "left" or sinister side of being.[14]

The inclusion of Lilith as a figure in the development of witchcraft as a *Jewish* conspiracy against Christians is important. Lilith was originally the name given to a storm demon whose name is also given as *Lilitu*, known as an entity who spread disease and death. This legend goes back to 4000 B.C. as part of

---

*Tertullian (full name Quintus Septimius Florens Tertullianus) was one of the earliest Christian scholars and was fiercely opposed to heresy. He also advanced Christian theology and invented the term "trinity" (*trinitas*) to define the nature of God.

The Witch, from Ardern Holt, ***Fancy Dresses Described; or, What to Wear at Fancy Balls,*** 1896. The image of a witch eventually merged with the images of popular figures like Old Mother Hubbard and the fairy godmother. But even up to the 19th century, the image of the witch included many of the symbols seen in this lithograph: the broom for night airborne travel, a serpent twisting around the hat, the owl atop the hat, the black cat curled around her neck.

Sumerian mythology. In Jewish folklore, Lilith is variously described as a demon or as Adam's first wife. The sole biblical reference to Lilith is in Isaiah and included in a description of "God's day of vengeance" from Isaiah 34:8. The list of prophecies that follow include one that "wildcats shall meet with hyenas, goat-demons shall call to each other; and there too Lilith shall repose, and find a place to rest."[15]

As a she-demon from Jewish mythology, Lilith fit two Church concepts of evil: First was the pagan worship of a female deity as opposed to God as a masculine figure, and second was an evil force using dark powers (i.e. witchcraft) to harm Christians. The single biblical reference was not the only source of this belief, however. Lilith also appeared in the Dead Sea Scrolls:

> And I, the Instructor, proclaim His glorious splendor so as to frighten and to terrify all the spirits of the destroying angels, spirits of the bastards, demons, Lilith, howlers, and desert dwellers ... and those which fall upon men without warning to lead them astray from a spirit of understanding and to make their heart ... desolate during the present dominion of wickedness and predetermined time of humiliations for the sons of light, by the guilt of the ages of those smitten by iniquity — not for eternal destruction, but for an era of humiliation for transgression.[16]

This mention of Lilith further reinforces the mythological belief in Lilith as an evil force associated with "destroying angels" and "demons," which fit well into the Church's portrayal of witches as evil forces. Additional references to Lilith are found in the Talmud as well, such as references to "unclean" children having the likeness of Lilith (*Niddah* 24b), "making water like a beast" (*Erubin* 100b), and with a notable reference to depraved sexually and sexual temptation, the statement that "whoever sleeps in a house alone is seized by Lilith" (*Shabbath* 151b).

These references to Lilith as she-demon, bearer of disease, and seductress all conform to the Church concept of a "witch" as a temptress of good Christians, and as a woman easily tempted into evil by satanic forces. The belief in witches was not solely an outgrowth of the Lilith story, but that story surely confirmed what Dominican inquisitors preferred to believe about women as weak, sexual, and evil beings.

The image of a witch gradually evolved into more of a mythological figure than a creature living among the people of Europe. By the 19th century, the image of the witch had merged with the fairy tale and the children's nursery rhyme. The well-known figures of Old Mother Hubbard and the fairy godmother all were elaborations on magical powers of bewitched women. In artwork in England especially, the figures of witches and these nursery rhyme characters are even pictured in the same outfit and symbols: a quilted petticoat, chintz tunic, muslin apron, velvet bodice, ruffled sleeves, spectacles, mittens and stick, a lace cap, high-heeled shoes with rosettes, and a pointed hat with a peacock feather.[17]

The witch hunts continued for 200 years, finally ending as suddenly as they had begun in the middle of the 17th century. Meanwhile, as the Church's power and influence declined through the period and the Inquisition faded as the Reformation developed, a new interest in paganism arose as part of the Renaissance.

The Birth of Humanism

During the same period that women were being hunted and killed in the witch hunts of the Inquisition, a period of growing enlightenment also began in Europe. This movement — Humanism — was based largely on increasing doubts about the moral superiority claimed by the Church. It was also part of a Renaissance that included a growing admiration and acceptance of paganism, coupled with increasing doubts of Church power and authority. The development of technology enabling mass production of books furthered this changing social condition, and once and for all did away with the once exclusive domination of the Church over literature and reading.

The Church and the Humanists were clearly enemies. The scholarly monks and mendicants of the past had been the primary sources of knowledge in the past and the Church wanted to keep this old order. Writers of the day not only posed a challenge to the Church, but actively criticized and even ridiculed it. These writers charged monks with hypocrisy and a lack of chastity. Authors such as Machiavelli (among many others) seemed to believe they were immune from the Inquisition, a sign that activities against old-style heretics were waning even as witches were being tried and killed. A growing movement to "follow nature" (*sequere naturam*) defied the Church requirement that mankind follow God and obey the Church.

The corruption and nepotism within the papacy made Humanism stronger and weakened the Inquisition even during the height of the Great Witch Hunt. For example, Pope Sixtus IV (1471–84) appointed two of his nephews as cardinals soon after being elected pope, immediately granting them generous allowances. This was followed by appointments of dozens of other relatives, also granted financial benefits by the new pope. Sixtus created a tax on houses of prostitution, legalizing them in order to create a source of revenue. At the time, there were an estimated 6,800 prostitutes operating in Rome, and a majority of priests and bishops had at least one concubine. On top of the corruption and nepotism, relatives of the popes were accused of numerous other crimes including pederasty.

For the first time, cases of open heresy and criticism of the papacy were leveled without consequence. Abuses were so many and so well known that the popes did not move against writers, artists and other Humanists vocalizing their charges. The conditions of decline in the papacy made paganism and Humanism widely appealing and beliefs like astrology had a rebirth. Many popes of the period had their own astrologers employed in their palaces, even though past popes had condemned astrology as a form of heresy.

The invention of the printing press, occurring about the same time that the Great Witch Hunt began, enabled criticisms of the papacy and the Church to gain a larger audience than ever before. The Humanist belief system grew to define the idea that although God created the universe, humans had developed it and created industry and the arts. So "Humanist studies" (*Studia Humanitatis*) included courses in philosophy, music, poetry, history and literature, quickly replacing the monk or priest as the sole source for education. The movement could not be easily called a heresy because it did not deny God's role in Christianity; it only expanded the role of mankind within that creation. One great challenge to Church educators and thinkers was the Humanist emphasis on the study of primary sources rather than simply accepting the teachings of others (such as priests). The movement's motto was "to the sources" (*ad fonts*).

Not relying on Church thinkers alone, Humanists translated and published the works of classical Greece and Rome, which they considered the height of human literature and intellect. Eventually, a conflict developed between religion and science. Meanwhile, the artistic aspects of the Renaissance were leading people away from Christianity toward a devotion to virtue *outside* of Christian faith. Culture, in other words, was replacing Christianity as the dominant force in Christian countries.

At the same time, however, the Inquisition was revived and became more active than ever before. A focus on a new enemy, the Spanish Jews, gave birth to the infamous Spanish Inquisition.

Stage Two:
The Spanish Inquisition

CHAPTER 7

The Jews and Conversos of Spain

We order that each and every Jew of both sexes in our temporal dominion [Church States], and in all the cities, lands, places and baronies subject to them, shall depart completely out of the confines therein within the space of three months after these letters shall have been made public.

— Pope Pius V, *Hebræorum gens*, February 26, 1569

Pope Sixtus IV (1471–84), best known for commissioning the Sistine Chapel, issued an obscure papal bull in 1478 called *Exigit sinceras devotionis affectus*, which authorized an investigation into questions of whether converted Jews were legitimate Christians or were secretly continuing to practice Jewish rites. Thus began the period of the Spanish Inquisition, which exceeded the abuses of past periods, even the Great Witch Hunt.

The Spanish Inquisition is the best-known and most infamous chapter in Church history. The first stage of the Inquisition had been designed to wipe out Cathars and Waldensians, and the targets had quickly expanded to additional forms of heretical action and thought. By the middle of the 15th century, witchcraft was also a target. In Spain, the Inquisition went even farther, and tribunals were created to find and eliminate *Conversos*, Jews who had converted to Christianity but were continually under suspicion for secretly practicing Jewish rites.

The fact that practicing a religion other than Christianity was criminalized by the Spanish Inquisition demonstrated that by this time, the Church recognized no bounds to its authority and mission. This was justified by the argument that Conversos were claiming to be Christians while secretly practicing another religion; but the underlying motive was to eliminate Jewish influence in Spanish culture. In the view of the monarch and the inquisitors involved, Conversos would always be under suspicion.

The expanded use of torture and the broadened definition of heresy found a new expression in the persecution of Spanish Jewry. The Dominicans, who continued to serve as primary managers of the Inquisition, dropped any pretense of desiring to correct heretical error, and any converted Jewish man, woman or child suspected or secretly continuing to practice Jewish rites was likely to be tortured and burned at the stake. The crime of heresy moved away from a strictly defined Christian error and became a different type of crime: practicing the wrong faith. The specific criminalization was defined as converting to Christianity as a pretense but not sincerely accepting the doctrines of the Church.

Papal Decrees against the Jews

The history of the Church demonstrates a long-standing distrust and dislike of Jews. The Spanish Inquisition was not a spontaneous or new idea, but the culmination of centuries of papal denunciations of Jews and their ability to function within Christian society. Numerous formal papal bulls and declarations were issued over the 400 years before the Spanish Inquisition.

On April 29, 1221, Pope Honorius III published *Ad nostrum noveritis audientiam*, requiring Jews to wear badges when in public and banning them from holding public offices. On March 5, 1233, Gregory IX wrote *Sufficere debuerat perfidioe judoerum perfidia*, forbidding Jews from hiring Christian servants. (This last clause was strengthened in 1244 when Innocent IV wrote in *Impia judoerum perfidia* that Jews could not hire Christian nurses.) Popes Clement IV (in 1267), Gregory X (in 1274), and Nicholas IV (in 1288) issued bulls, all titled *Turbato corde*, declaring that Christians were legally barred from converting to Judaism.

In the 14th century, Pope John XXII issued two bulls regarding Jews. First was *Ex parte vestra* (August 12, 1317), dealing with the treatment of relapsed converts. Second was *Cum sit absurdum* (June 19, 1320), ruling that as long as Jews converted to Christianity, they did not need to be despoiled.

In the 15th century, Pope Martin V, in *Sedes apostolic* (June 3, 1425), reinstituted the requirement that Jews wear distinctive badges in public. On August 4, 1442, Pope Eugene IV stated in *Dudum ad nostrum audientiam* that Jews were not allowed to live in the same houses with Christians, and also could not hold public office. Pope Sixtus IV published *Exigit sinceras devotionis affectus* on November 1, 1478, authorizing King Ferdinand of Spain to investigate instances in which Jews converted to Christianity might be secretly continuing to practice as Jews. In 1482, Sixtus decreed in *Numquam dubitavimus* that Ferdinand was to appoint inquisitors to continue with this investigation.

Even after the Spanish Inquisition had begun, popes continued to issue decrees against Jews. Throughout the 16th century, these continued. Pope Paul IV stated in *Cum nimis absurdum* (July 14, 1555) that Jews were forbidden to live with Christians, or to take employment in any industry. Pius V expanded this restriction with *Cum nos nuper* (January 9, 1567) banning Jews from owning real estate; and in *Hebræorum gens* ("The Jewish Race," issued February 26, 1569) he expelled Jews from the Church States. This was the most specific and extraordinary bulls of Pius V. He concluded:

> The Jewish people fell from the heights because of their faithlessness and condemned their Redeemer to a shameful death. Their godlessness has assumed such forms that, for the salvation of our own people, it becomes necessary to prevent their disease. Besides usury, through which Jews everywhere have sucked dry the property of impoverished Christians, they are accomplices of thieves and robbers; and the most damaging aspect of the matter is that they allure the unsuspecting through magical incantations, superstition, and witchcraft to the Synagogue of Satan and boast of being able to predict the future. We have carefully investigated how this revolting sect abuses the name of Christ and how harmful they are to those whose life is threatened by their deceit.[1]

This denunciation was followed by the order expelling Jews from Church-controlled states. Although by that date the Spanish Inquisition had practically run its course, the papal distrust of Jews did not end. In 1592, Clement VIII wrote *Cum sæpe accidere* banning Jews from selling goods in public. And the following year, he penned *Cæca et obdurate* restricting areas where Jews were allowed to live. Later the same year, he published *Cum Hæbræorum militia* making reading the Talmud a crime.

The declarations did not stop. As late as 1727, Pope Benedict XIII wrote *Emanavit numer*, laying down conditions in which Jews could be forcibly baptized. Two years later, in *Alias emanarunt*, Benedict forbade selling of goods by Jews. Benedict XIV wrote *Singulari nolbis consoldtioni* in 1749 on the topic of Christians and Jews marrying; and in 1751, he published *Elapso proxime anno* concerning Jewish heresy (which by traditional definition is contradictory, since a heretic had to be Christian to commit the sin) and *Probe te meminisse* setting down rules for baptizing Jewish children.

Benedict XIV also published the *Beatus Andreas* (1755), in which a child named Andreas von Rinn was alleged to have been murdered by Jews some 300 years before, in 1462. This decree beatified the child based on the allegation that he had been the victim of a ritual murder conducted by Jews. The pope declared that such ritual murders were fact and were part of Jewish practice, not exceptions. The presumed general guilt of all Jews in such practices became a primary justification for anti–Semitic practices within the Inquisition. Even in modern times, stories have been told of Jews practicing child crucifixion and Kabbalistic black magic. Even today, small groups of Catholics continue to accept these stories as true. For example, some still believe that St. Simon of Trent (patron saint of torture victims, who was canonized by the Church, but whose sainthood was revoked in 1965) was murdered by Jews, in spite of a complete lack of evidence. An Internet site declares:

> Little St Simon of Trent was mercilessly martyred in the 15th century in Italy by Ashkanazi Jews. This two-year old child from the Italian town of Trent was kid-

napped by a few Ashkenazi Jews from his home on the eve of Passover 1475 AD. At night, the kidnappers murdered the child; drew his blood, pierced his flesh with needles, crucified him head down calling "So may all Christians by land and sea perish," and thus they celebrated their Passover, an archaic ritual of outpouring blood and killed babies, in the most literal form, without usual metaphoric "blood-wine" shift.[2]

Similar lurid accounts were particularly common during World War II, when atrocities were allegedly committed against Christian children, and innocent young girls were said to have been seduced by lecherous older Jewish men. Such tales were cited by Nazi Germany to justify removing Jews from occupied territories. Using the anti–Semitic newspaper *Der Stürmer* ("The Attacker"), Nazis spread the myths throughout German society.

The Nazis also employed a policy called *Sippenhaft*, which means blood guilt, based on the charge that guilt for a crime was hereditary due to diseased blood. The doctrine, also known by the phrase "kith and kin," was used as a basis for the anti–Semitic Nazi philosophy, based on a claim that Jews were responsible for every ill that had ever befallen Germany and the Christian world. This was the ultimate expression of blood guilt.

In the context of the Spanish Inquisition, the long history of blood guilt allowed the Church and inquisitors to place blame on Jews for any and all heretical threats, especially the physical and spiritual dangers they posed. The history of anti–Jewish proclamations from a long line of popes made the Spanish Inquisition respectable and justified, even reasonable and necessary, in the view of members of the Spanish clergy.

The Spanish Inquisition began with the order from the papacy to the Spanish king, authorizing the establishment of new Inquisitional tribunals to investigate the Conversos and the charges being made against them. It led to more extreme measures against the Spanish Jews including torture, exile, property seizures and murder.

The Background of Jews in Spain

Large numbers of Jews had converted to Christianity between 1391 and 1417, a period in which many persecutions of Jews led to the problems between Conversos and "Old Christians" in Spain. To understand how the Spanish Inquisition came into being, the history of Spanish Jewry has to be examined briefly.

Anti-Semitism was by no means a purely Christian invention. Instances of ill-treatment of Jews predate Christianity; but the conflicts between Jews and Christians have always had a special flavor of their own based on the origins of Christianity itself as a *departure* from established Jewish society. This conflict extended to the holy books, expressed even as denial of Jewish rights to lay claim to the Old Testament, with a recurring theme that

Pope Clement VIII issued bulls banning Jews from selling goods and restricting where they would be allowed to live. He even outlawed reading the Talmud. (Statue from Clement's tomb in the Borghese Chapel of the Basilica di Santa Maria Maggiore, Rome.)

Jews are the worst people, the most godless and God-forsaken, of all the nations upon earth, the devil's own people ... stamped by their crucifixion of the Lord.... Such an injustice as that inflicted by the Gentile church on Judaism is almost unprecedented in the annals of history. The Gentile Church stripped it of everything, she took away its sacred book; herself but a transformation of Judaism, she cut off all connection with the parent religion. The daughter first robbed her mother, and then repudiated her.[3]

During the first few centuries of Christianity, numerous Christian scholars argued that the new faith should be properly considered a branch of Judaism, and this belief persisted, including the argument that Christians should respect and observe Jewish rites. During these times, other Christian writers repeatedly distanced the faith from Jewish roots, but only when the Church aligned with Rome and became the *Roman* Church was the Church clearly departed from Judaism. The resulting official Church

aimed not only at the reinterpretation of the Bible; it aimed also at the expurgation from Christianity of any Jewish trait, notion or custom affecting any part of its religious life — i.e., its dogma, its form of worship and, above all, its conception of God. It is indeed by the effort of so many Christian thinkers to shake off from Christianity anything "Jewish" that one may best gauge the depth of their antipathy toward Judaism and the Jewish people.[4]

This early Christian attitude and antagonism toward Jews and everything Jewish set the scene for centuries of suspicion and distrust from the papacy, Church leaders and Christian society.

Jews had settled in Spain long before the 15th century, partly to avoid the disruptions common to Western European life from endless invasions of territory by many groups, including Franks, Visigoths, Vandals, Huns, Saxons, and Ostrogoths. The turmoil and chaos caused the relocation of European populations many times while also creating definitive national consciousness for the first time. This was true in Spain as elsewhere in Europe, where citizens identified themselves as Spanish rather than as descendants of a particular tribe or racial group. A notable exception was the Jews, who had a long history of identity as a separate group of people (both racially and religiously) by this time. Their distinct religious and social customs set them apart from society wherever they settled. Anti-Semitism in Spain appeared as early as the 4th century, when the Council of Elvira convened (ca. 303–314). This gathering resulted in the issuing of several canons, including the requirement of Christians to remain separate from Jews; in fact, its decree lumped together "Jews, pagans and heretics."

During the 4th and 5th centuries, anti–Jewish writings and laws appeared throughout the Christian and Roman empires. John Chrysostom accused Jews of every imaginable evil. St. Jerome described Jews encircling Christians and tearing them limb from limb. Jerome claimed that Jews loved money above all else and complained that their population multiplied "like vermin." Other

Christian writers of the day, including Augustine, Eusebius, Ambrose, Gregory of Nyssa and Cyril of Alexander, also expressed anti–Jewish opinions. The Church was known to stir up mobs to pillage and burn synagogues and Jewish cemeteries, followed by pressure on secular authorities to forgive or ignore anti–Jewish crimes. Laws aimed at Jews were enacted throughout Christian lands, mostly in order to keep Jews and Christians apart. Such laws forbade Jewish property ownership, inter-marriage with Christians, economic exchange, and participation in the law and government. They even included a prohibition on Jews' making accusations against Christians or testifying against them in civil or criminal trials.

Conversions of Jews in Early Spanish History

In this developing system of exclusion and separation, Jews were tolerated within Christian society but were kept poor and apart from opportunities to prosper. In Spain, the Visigoths had settled the Iberian Peninsula by the 6th century, and a conflict arose between two competing faiths, Visigoth Arianism and Roman Catholicism. In the interest of uniting the area as a single nation, these two primary groups compromised. The population was both ethnically and spiritually united, although dogmatic conflicts between them continued for many years. In 612, a new Visigoth ruler named Sisebut took the throne and immediately passed several laws against Jews living in the region. In the attempt to reconcile Catholic and Arian sects, the continuing presence of Jews troubled the ruler, who preferred that Jews convert to Christianity rather than continuing to practice their separate faith. The refusal of a majority of Jews to convert angered Sisebut, who issued a new order in 616 ordering Jews to convert or leave the kingdom; failure to make this decision was punishable by death. Large numbers of Jews, unable to afford to leave or unwilling to uproot their families, underwent the forced conversion and became *Conversos*, Jews converted to Christianity.

The origin of suppression of Judaism in Spain was based in the monarchy and not in the clergy and in those early centuries, the Church opposed forced conversions. The official Church position on the matter was that anyone forced to become Christian could not be considered a true Christian, and that only a willing conversion would be recognized by God (and the Church) as a genuine decision. However, Church distrust and dislike of Jews was evident in centuries of papal bulls and synods. The development of legal mandates by Spanish monarchs was more political than theological, however. In agreement with the papal position on Jewish culture and religious practice, Spanish monarchs attempted to control the influence of Jewish culture in Christian society.

This was certainly the case when Sisebut wanted to unite the Arians and Romans; the existence of a large portion of the population in the kingdom consisting of Jews made this more of a problem and Jews became the common enemy. As a political move, Sisebut overlooked a requirement of the time, to call a Council to decide the matter. Sisebut did not want to have the matter fall within the jurisdiction of the Church; he only wanted to unite the entire kingdom to a single version of one religion. Consequently, Jews would have to go along with this plan or leave. Sisebut had no intention of leaving the final decision up to the Church, knowing that the Jewish conversion would be viewed as forced.

When Sisebut died in 621, his successor, Swinthila, relaxed the rules, and forced conversions came to an end. Many of the Jews who had migrated to Gaul and other regions were allowed to return and practice their faith without restriction. The laws restricting Jewish rights were repealed or ignored under the new monarch. However, the respite did not last. Swinthila's reign was followed by the reign of Sisenaud, who passed new legislation requiring that Jews give up their faith. An even more draconian law was enacted by Sisenaud at the Fourth Council of Toledo in 633. He ordered that Jewish children be taken from their parents and given to Christian families to raise. All Jews who had been baptized but continued to practice Jewish rites were to be sold as slaves. And no Jews would be allowed to remain in Spain. Finally, the law required that every future king take an oath to proceed sternly against relapsed Jewish converts.

The next king, Chintila, declared at the Sixth Council of Toledo (638) that no non–Catholics would be allowed to live in Spain under any circumstances. Chintila was followed by Receswinth (reigned 653–72). He claimed at the Eighth Council of Toledo (653) that all heresies in Spain had been eliminated with the exception of Judaism, which he said still "defiles the soil of the Kingdom." Under prevailing Church laws, forced conversion was not allowed. However, Receswinth got around this by issuing his own codes declaring it illegal for Jews to practice their faith, celebrate Passover, observe the Sabbath, follow their dietary laws, circumcise their children, or marry under Jewish tradition. Receswinth ordered that any violations of his new laws would result in execution "under the most ingenious and excruciating torture."[5]

Whether or not the Church supported attempts by various kings to rid the empire of Jews, the Spanish Catholic community continued to treat Jews as an unwelcome foreign sect and not as a part of the community of the nation. The Church, in comparison, saw Jews in the same way it saw all non–Christians and heretical Christian sects: not as a foreign minority but as enemies of the Christian faith. As Jews continued to compete socially and economically within the Spanish kingdom, earlier resentment quickly turned into hatred, on both an economic and a theological basis. While much of the early distrust centered on Jews who had converted as required under the law but continued to practice Jewish rites in secret, the lines between converted Jews and practicing Jews became blurred. The Church managed the issue of forced conversions by referring to them as Christians in every sense, and subject to the rules of Christianity. So once an individual had become Christian, regardless of the circumstances, the rules of Christianity applied. A distinction was made between the banned practice of forcing conversion, and the rules regarding those who had already been converted no matter the conditions of that conversion. The Church stated that because these converts had "received the divine sacraments, the grace of baptism, were anointed by the chrism, and partook in the body and blood of the Lord, it is proper that they should keep the faith."[6]

Although the Church insisted it did not approve of forced conversions, it did rule that Jewish husbands could be forcibly removed from their Christian wives unless they converted to Christianity[7]; and that Jewish children could be removed from Jewish converts who had reverted to Judaism to save those children from exposure to Jewish beliefs.[8] The Church was suspicious of any converted Jews and viewed circumcision as barbaric:

> Very many of the Jews who, some time ago, were promoted to the Christian faith, are now not only known to blaspheme Christ and perform Jewish rites; they are also presumed to practice the abominable circumcisions.[9]

Whether relapsed converts were common or rare, the Church of the 7th century saw this problem as a serious one. So even those not known to have relapsed were held under continual suspicion and forced to practice a downgraded version of Christianity in which their social rights were limited by the law, the Church or both. And so the converted Jew was not allowed to practice the Jewish faith or to fully realize life as a Christian. All were suspect. Legal restrictions were designed not only to keep practicing Jews out of public office, prevent them from intermarrying with Christians, and exclude them from other social benefits, but to restrict the rights of their children as well. Laws passed to restrict Jewish rights named Jews and "those who are of the Jews," meaning their children, whether parents were labeled as Christian or Jew.

The issue became even more complex when Jewish merchants, in order to ensure protection of their social situation, donated large sums of cash to Spanish nobles. There were two choices available: First, the Jews could be forced to convert, meaning they would no longer need to pay for protection. This choice proved impractical since the Church took steps to ensure that even converted Jews remained under suspicion and were not to be treated in the same manner as non–Jewish Christians. The alternative was to take steps to impoverish the Jews so that they could not afford to pay for protection. King Receswinth attempted to accomplish this by imposing penalties of confiscation of property on Jews for virtually every infraction of law, even minor ones.

Jews in Spanish Society

From 680 to 687, a ruler named Erwig for the first time entrusted Church bishops with enforcement of anti–Jewish laws. Among Erwig's new application of previous laws was a restriction on exiled Jews' returning to Spain. He asked the bishops at the Twelfth Council of Toledo (681) to help "eradicate the Jewish pest, root and branch" from the kingdom.[10]

A majority of Jews remained in Spain and coped with increasingly punitive laws. Many converted and abandoned Judaism, while many more secretly continued to practice their religion, and a widespread Converso community survived through for centuries. By the middle of the 8th century, there were almost no Jews living in Spain. Many Conversos remained, but they were hidden from the authority of the government and of the Church.

In the period of 711–14, the Moors conquered the Iberian Peninsula, leaving a greatly reduced geographic northern area of Christian-controlled Spain. The small pockets of Jewish communities remaining under Christian control endured while the struggle between Christian and Moorish Spain continued. This placed Jewish communities in an even less tenable position. Neither Christian nor Moslem segments of the country welcomed Jews. Ironically, as persecution of Jews in Moorish Spain worsened, many returned to Christian Spain as refugees. The Jewish community in Spain once again began to grow and flourish.

When the Moors conquered the area, Jews initially saw them as liberators. The Spanish monarchy and Church had combined to make Jewish life intolerable, so this reaction to a new regime was understandable. They not only welcomed the conquerors but aided them whenever possible as they battled with Spanish Christian forces. "They tied their destiny to Moslem domination and stood by it loyally in all areas of life."[11]

In the first century of Moslem rule in Granada, Jews and other minorities were well treated and accepted into society. However, by the 11th century sentiment once again turned against the Jews. Moslem rulers began demanding that both Jews and Christians convert to Islam or face death. In 1066, Jews were expelled from Granada and any who refused to leave risked being killed. Jews emigrated, many to the more tolerant region in and around Toledo, which was reconquered by Christian forces in 1085.

As the Christian reconquest of Spain continued, the Christian monarch actively encouraged Jews to return. Under the Moors, Jewish life had improved to the extent that Jews were able to operate as successful traders, and as the land became increasingly Christian, Jewish traders and Christian merchants formed alliances and relationships improved. Repopulating cities taken by Christian forces as the Moors were gradually expelled included welcoming returning Jews into Christian Spanish life. While the Moors had once considered Jewish refugees to be allies, they now distrusted them and suspected them of forming alliances with Christians. Moslem raids against Christian areas involved armed conflict with Jews fighting for the Christian side when they had resettled in those areas.

By the middle of the 13th century, Jews had gained a level of social influence in Christian Spain, notably in finance, government, and trade outside of Spain. They were for the first time able to defend themselves against measures by the government to curtail their rights. Spanish Jews lived in Christian Spain under the protection of a series of monarchs who prevented attacks on them. The many valuable services provided by Jewish merchants and bankers were of great value to the monarchy, even though opposition to Jewish presence also grew, notably among the Church bishops. Opposition in the larger cities was especially strong, based on distrust of Jewish influence with the monarchy.

The transition of Jewish fortunes began when Castilian King Alfonso XI died of the plague in 1350. Plague had taken its greatest toll in the cities, where people lived a more congested life. Rumors that the Jews had intentionally spread the plague among Christians once again led to suspicion and fear. The death of Alfonso led to renewed calls for segregation of Jews from the rest of society. Anti-Jewish sentiment grew not only among the peasant class of Spanish Christians but also within the Church. The plague had brought on severe economic hardships throughout Europe and so Jews were easily targets. Economic problems were blamed on "Jewish usury," lending money and charging interest. Anti-Jewish sentiment was on the rise even though the monarchy officially continued to protect Jewish civil rights.

The Campaigns of Ferrán Martínez

Between 1367 and 1417, large numbers of Jews converted to Christianity to avoid persecution and expulsion. Following a period of great influence of Jews on the Spanish monarchy, the trend began to reverse, and public as well as government and Church favor toward Jews once again declined. In 1391, the Spanish Jewish community was the world's largest; within three years, it lost one-third of its population to mass killings ordered by King Enrique III (1379–1406). In 1378, the archdeacon of Écija, Ferrán Martínez, had begun a campaign against Spanish Jews, calling on King Enrique II (1369–1379) to continue the mass killings he had ordered his troops to commit earlier. Martínez also instructed bishops within his archbishopric to expel all Jews from their towns and avoid even speaking with them. He warned that failing to follow these orders would result in the bishops' excommunication.

Martínez was not only archdeacon; he also had been appointed as diocesan judge by the archbishop of Seville, a position in which he claimed the right to hear cases in which Jews were involved. The Church had long favored placing bishops in the position of judges, although the Spanish monarchy opposed the arrangement. The king's preference prevailed, meaning that Martínez was breaking the law by hearing such cases. Nevertheless, Martínez petitioned for special permission to hear cases of dispute between Christians and Jews, and permission was granted to him. With this, Martínez expanded his jurisdiction and imposed obviously biased rulings in the cases over which he presided. In response, Jews appealed to a higher court, and this chaos within the court system forced the king to make a ruling. In 1378, King Enrique II wrote to Martínez and ordered him, "Do not dare to interfere in judging any dispute which involves any Jew in any manner."[12]

Ignoring the king's order, Martínez expanded his vendetta, sending letters to Church officials in his diocese and ordering them to deny rights of residence to Jews, once again instructing them to eject all Jews or face excommunication. The king repeated his order and further decreed that any Jews summoned by Martínez were not to appear before him. Martínez at last took the king's order seriously and retreated from his order to have Jews expelled.

When Enrique died in 1379, he was succeeded by Juan I. The following year, under Juan, a ruling was made denying Jews the long-established right to run their own criminal courts. They were also banned from serving in the monarchy's administration. Martínez now found it easier to operate, and he resumed his involvement in legal disputes involving Jews. The new king, however, repeated his predecessor's warning that Martínez was not to engage in these activities. Juan further ordered that cases involving disputes between Christians and Jews were not to be adjudicated with involvement from Martínez.

Although Martínez ceased his involvement with court cases involving Jewish parties, he began campaigning for conversions of Moorish slaves owned by Jews in Seville. The reasoning was that since Jews were legally barred from owning Christian slaves, conversion would require that their slaves be freed. Martínez also increased his inflammatory preaching, stating that Christians who killed Jews should not be punished under the law. He guaranteed that no Christian would be punished for such a deed. A subsequent royal order forbade Martínez from attempting to convert Moorish slaves and from encouraging the murder of Jews by Christians. The strongly worded order quieted Martínez from public statements for the moment, but his message ushered in a new era of anti–Jewish sentiment. In 1383, the monarchy cancelled one-third of debts owed by Christians to Jews and the remaining debts were placed on a 15-month repayment moratorium.

Martínez emerged again, making more inflammatory statements. He demanded complete separation of Jews from Christian society as well as the destruction of all synagogues built in his archbishopric. He ultimately destroyed his own campaign by claiming that he and he alone was the ultimate authority on everything related to Jewish rights. He even boasted that the pope had no authority to issue papal bulls allowing Jews to build new synagogues. The archbishop of Seville, Pedro Gómez Barroso, finally took action. He appointed a committee of lay and clerical experts to investigate Martínez and his statements, notably his claim of authority over local matters above the pope. The committee began by asking him if it was true that he had claimed the pope had no rights regarding Jews in Spain. Martínez, a true zealot in his own cause, confirmed this to be true, and refused to reverse his position, insisting it was his right to ban construction of synagogues, and not the pope's. The archbishop ordered Martínez to cease preaching immediately, stating that he would be a "suspect of heresy" if he defied the order.

The following year, the archbishop died, and three months later, Juan I also died. Martínez assumed control within his region, and on December 8, 1390, he issued orders to all towns to destroy synagogues in their areas. Many towns quickly obeyed, and for the Jews of Seville, there was no authority to whom they could appeal. An urgent complaint was filed with the regency that ruled after Juan's death. Noting that Martínez remained under suspicion of heresy, the regency called on the Church to place Martínez under ecclesiastic censure, fine him, and threaten further penalties if Martínez did not reimburse Jews for their losses.

Even though both the monarchy and the Church had warned Martínez to stop his actions, the events of the day accelerated anti–Jewish sentiment in Seville. Rioting mobs grew in size and the anti–Jewish movement spread throughout Castile. Martínez had capitalized on a popular hatred of Jews and the incidences of property damage and personal harm expanded. Not only was violence on the rise; the monarchy gradually gave way as well to the rising tide of anti–Jewish expression. As the level of violence grew, Martínez, knowing that the Church would not allow him to order outright killings of Jews, called on mobs to demand conversions of Jews if they desired to live. He placed himself in the position of piously trying to save the Jews from death by converting them and saving their souls. Faced with violence from an angry and hate-filled mob, Jews who did convert were promised immediate safety; the violence would stop as soon as they consented to baptism.

Contradicting the Church and monarchy's position on forced conversions, Martínez insisted that forced converts were indistinguishable from voluntary converts. The position Martínez offered soon spread to the middle classes where it gained popular acceptance. In Valencia alone, the level of violence was so severe that entire Jewish-populated areas converted to bring an end to the destruction. City leaders began appealing to the king and asking him to encourage Jews to convert to put an end to the violence, leading to the belief among many that somehow the Jews, by refusing to convert, were responsible for the violence.

The Church's unwillingness to put an end to Martínez' anti–Jewish activities or to enforce its threat of excommunication, was based on its agreement that Jewish conversion was a desirable way to resolve the dispute and end the violence. Even though Jews who refused to convert were frequently murdered on the spot, the Church turned a blind eye to the violence and allowed Martínez to continue spreading his message.

The year 1391, when the worst violence against Spanish Jews occurred under the leadership of Ferrán Martínez, was a turning point for the Jews of Spain.

Forced conversions created the underground society of the Conversos, those Jews who became Christians under the threat of death. This may have seemed an initial triumph for Spanish Christianity over Judaism, but it created a long-term problem that would not be addressed by the Church until nearly 100 years later, when the Spanish Inquisition was initiated.

CHAPTER 8

Conversos in the Fifteenth Century

By its own admission, if also to its regret, the Inquisition enjoyed no jurisdiction over professing Jews.... [I]nquisitors were authorized to arrest and
punish only Christians who had converted to Judaism, and Jews who had
converted to Christianity but continued to practice their old faith — that is,
Jews who "return to the vomit of Judaism."

— Jonathan Kirsch, *The Grand Inquisitor's Manual*, 2008,
quoting language from the Council of Basel, 1435

Following the large-scale rioting and destruction of 1391, efforts to convert Jews to Christianity and to root out Jewish influence accelerated. One of
the most active people in this effort was Solomon ha-Levi (also known as Paul
of Burgos), chief rabbi of Burgos, a city in North Central Spain.

Paul was well educated not only in Jewish literature but also in Latin. This
provided him with a connection to local Christian authors and clergy and to
their anti–Jewish arguments and rationale. At first, he presented counter-argu-
ments in defense of Jews, but he eventually became convinced that Christianity was a force that could not be stopped. This logic led him to argue that there
was no point in sacrificing property and even life when Christianity was going
to win out in the end. With this rationale, Paul and many of his relatives converted to Christianity on July 21, 1391, only weeks before the large-scale riots
brought about by Ferrán Martínez. Many others in northern Spain converted
after the riots to avoid danger to themselves and their families. Paul found himself detested by those Jews who had resisted and not converted, probably contributing to his decision to leave the area and study in Paris.

At the University of Paris, Paul met Pedro de Luna, influential cardinal of
Aragon who in 1394 won election in Avignon as Pope Benedict XIII (antipope,
1394–1423). That same year, King Charles VI of France expelled all Jews from
all areas of France except Avignon, where they were relocated and forced to live
in crowded conditions. Paul of Burgos encouraged Benedict to expel the Jews

from Avignon unless they converted to Christianity. His association with Benedict and efforts to have the Jews further exiled made it clear that Paul was an enemy to both French and Spanish Jews. In 1398, Benedict sent Paul back to Spain as archdeacon of Treviño in the diocese of Burgos. In 1403, Benedict named Paul bishop of Cartegena. In this capacity and as official ambassador from Benedict to the Spanish court, Paul became a close friend of King Enrique III. Paul was influential on Enrique and on his successor in creating new taxes and new legal restrictions on Jewish money lending.

Pope Benedict was intent on eliminating all Jewish influence in Europe and believed that accomplishing this would bring him acclaim as a great spiritual leader. The trend toward expulsions or conversion (forced or voluntary) could not be reversed. The most severe laws were published in 1412.

The Laws of Catalina

In 1412, a series of new laws known as the Laws of Catalina were passed. Their intention was to reduce all influence of Jews in Spain; to ensure that Jews lived in poverty and lacked any power or influence; and further, to deprive Jews of the means of livelihood.

The laws required all non–Christians (both Jews and Moors) to live apart from Christian society. Failure to move to a designated area within eight days would result in loss of property and criminal punishment. Jews and Moors were also forbidden from having any public warehouses, shops, or other areas where they could sell their goods, again including severe penalties for non-compliance. Even within the areas where Jews were consigned to live, they were not allowed to set up shop in any form to sell merchandise to Christians.

Historians have long debated the origin of these laws. Some believe they were initiated by the monarchy, and others believe the Church instigated them. The actual source for these laws was Paul of Burgos, who was zealous in his desire to please Benedict and the Spanish monarchy by working to bring about Jewish conversions to Christianity. Paul was at this time a permanent fixture in the court. He wrote that the crimes of Jews were worse than those of the residents of Sodom, and that Jews "deserved a prolonged chastisement and agony to make their punishment heavier, and hence their long exile and the tortures it entails."[1]

With Paul's own conversion from rabbi to anti–Jewish spokesman complete, his influence with the Spanish monarchy led to passage of the Laws of Catalina. Under these laws, Jews were no longer allowed to work in the medical profession in any capacity, or even to visit Christians with medical problems. They could not attend Christian weddings or funerals. Jewish men were no longer allowed to shave or to cut their hair, but were legally required to let their hair and beards grow naturally, which ensured that Jews would be easily recognized, so that Christians would not accidentally associate with them. Collectively, the new laws were intended not only to exclude Jews from Spanish commerce and trade, but also to ensure that they were completely segregated from Spanish society in every possible way. The combined social and economic restrictions on Jews made it virtually impossible for the segregated Jewish community to survive. A justification for the laws was "the need to prevent the faithful from falling into the errors that converse with the infidels might occasion."[2]

With Jewish society unable to contribute anything productive to Spanish society, it would seem the motive for these laws was to force Jews to emigrate. However, part of the Catalina laws forbade Jews from leaving their neighborhoods and forbade Christians from offering them shelter. Leaving the country was specifically declared illegal as well. Thus, without being able to support their families or take part in society in any manner and not even being able to leave, only one course remained for survival: conversion to Christianity. Circumventing the widespread aversion to forced conversion, these restrictive laws gave Jews no other choice but to turn to Christianity "voluntarily."

The only options left — wealthy Jews becoming poor and poor Jews starving to death — made conversion a logical choice. Predictably, once these laws were enacted, large numbers of Jews did convert to Christianity. Entire communities converted en masse, a spectacle that was applauded by the Church as a sign of the success of Christ's message and the defeat of Judaism in Spain. Benedict sanctioned the laws, recognizing that they were solely responsible for the massive Jewish conversions that were taking place throughout Spain. The official Church view was that the conversions were entirely voluntary — just as heretics confessed "voluntarily" under torture.

Thus the ex-rabbi Paul of Burgos created a legacy for himself, not as the educated and intellectual Jewish scholar of his youth but as one of the most prominent figures in the effort by Spain's monarchy and the Church to destroy all remnants of a successful Jewish community in northern Spain. His efforts, however, had an unforeseen consequence: the migration of large numbers of converted Jews into urban centers throughout Spain. Once restrictions were lifted on Jews who had converted, ex–Jews began competing with Christians in many occupations.

The resilience of converted Jews was demonstrated by their rapid adjustment to life as Christians within Spanish society. Whereas in the past the Christian and Jewish segments of Spanish society had coexisted even when the Church preferred restrictions on Jewish activities (both economic and social), the distinctions no longer existed, at least not legally. But recovery was not easy for the Jews. Upon returning to their previous homes, many found their property had been destroyed by rioting Christians. Jewish money lenders, now Christian, discovered that their written contracts were invalidated and collateral was no longer held under lien. As a consequence of these changes, most converted Jews reentered Spanish society with little or no wealth.

The decimated Jewish communities could not rebuild their own business enterprises, since they had been scattered and forced into restricted communities and legally barred from even preserving their business assets. So the enterprising Jewish business owners were forced to compete with their Christian neighbors. In spite of the lifting of legal restrictions on their activities, these Jewish business owners quickly discovered that Christians did not let go of their prejudices easily. Many businesses would not employ converted Jews or do business with companies formed by them. Furthermore, the Jews had to adjust to Christian religious practices. Newly converted Jews had to work even on their Jewish Sabbath and holidays, while avoiding work on Sundays and Christian holidays or special festivals. They had to change all of their religious activities, including taking part in Sunday mass and participating in the sacraments.

In this repressive environment, it did not take long for many Jews to begin practicing their Jewish rites in secret. The Converso community recited Jewish prayers before going to mass, and held small meetings in homes. Many ex–Jews adjusted to lives as Christians, however, and abandoned Judaism as a practical matter. Constant fear of being caught practicing Judaism, as well as reluctance or inability to spend the time required to lead a double life, resulted in the decline of practicing Conversos over the years.

The Council of Basel

By the middle of the 15th century, Christian hatred of the Conversos had grown to the breaking point, and those who supported Jewish conversion discovered that the outcome of such conversions was far from peaceful. No one can know with certainty the expectations of those who engineered the conversions earlier in the period. The fact that Jews were cut off economically and socially and at the same time forbidden to leave the country leads to the conclusion that a smooth transition into Christian society was expected by both Church and monarchy. Judaism in Spain was expected to completely disappear as Conversos replaced Jewish traditions with Christian rites. This did not occur; in fact, even those Jews who willingly and completely embraced Christianity continued to be treated as second-class citizens, were excluded from many economic opportunities, and were viewed with suspicion, distrust and even hatred.

The actual number of Conversos who continued to secretly practice Jewish rites is also impossible to know. The Church may have exaggerated the problem, and the Spanish monarch concurred with the Church's assessment. Whatever the reality, as the Conversos became successful in the Spanish economy, especially in urban areas, the perception also grew that Conversos were deceiving Christian society. A widespread view was that Converso deception needed to be managed and resolved in some manner.

Some historians have viewed the period prior to 1449 as a time of peace and harmony between "New Christians" (*Cristianos nuevos*) and "Old Christians." But the social distrust between the two groups continued and was expressed in many forms of discrimination. Growth in the suspicion that Conversos were not truly Christian paralleled growth of Converso influence and participation in the Spanish economy. Eventually the relationship between "Old" and "New" came to a boiling point. By 1449, it was not only the established local Conversos that presented problems for Christians in Spain, but increasing numbers of new arrivals that were showing up in Spanish cities. It is ironic that in an effort to rid Spain of Jews by requiring conversion, both monarchy and Church actually created a larger population of Conversos in the country, and the Converso community was thriving economically as well as socially. By the 1430s the Church tried to curb the expansion of Conversos with a series of new laws and regulations aimed at ensuring that Conversos became true Christians.

In Basel, Switzerland, in 1431, an Ecumenical Council was convened by Pope Martin V (1417–31) to address a series of pressing Church issues. In its 20th session in 1435, the Council of Basel passed a regulation requiring local bishops to take steps aimed specifically at making sure Conversos were taught correctly to become true Christians. The Council requirements concerned converts to the faith and read:

> Let the priests who baptize them and those who receive them from the sacred font carefully instruct them, both before and after their baptism, in the articles of the faith and the precepts of the new law and the ceremonies of the Catholic Church. Both they and the bishops should strive that, at least for a long time, they do not mingle much with Jews or infidels lest, as occurs with convalescents from illness, a small occasion may make them fall back into their former perdition. Since experience shows that social communication between converts renders them weaker in our faith, and has been found to damage much their salvation, this holy synod exhorts local ordinaries to exercise care and zeal that they are married to born–Christians, in so far as this seems to promote an increase of the faith. Converts should be forbidden, under pain of severe penalties, to bury the dead according to the Jewish custom or to observe in any way the Sabbath and other solemnities and rites of their old sect. Rather, they should frequent our churches and sermons, like other Catholics, and conform themselves in everything to Christian customs. Those who show contempt for the above should be delated [conveyed, referred] to the diocesan bishops or inquisitors of heresy by their parish priests, or by others who are entrusted by law or ancient custom with inquiring into such matters, or by anyone else at all. Let them be so punished, with the aid of the secular arm if need be, as to give an example to others.... There should be careful inquiry into all these things in provincial councils and synods, and an opportune remedy should be applied not only to negligent bishops and priests but also to converts and infidels who scorn the above. If anyone, of whatever rank or status, shall encourage or defend such converts against being

compelled to observe the Christian rite or anything else mentioned above, he
shall incur the penalties promulgated against abettors of heretics. If converts fail
to correct themselves after a canonical warning, and as Judaizers are found to
have returned to their vomit, let proceedings be taken against them as against
perfidious heretics in conformity with the enactments of the sacred canons. If
there have been granted to Jews or infidels, or perhaps shall be granted to them
in the future, any indults or privileges by any ecclesiastics or secular persons, of
whatever status or dignity, even papal or imperial, which tend in any way to the
detriment of the catholic faith, the Christian name or anything mentioned above,
this holy synod decrees them quashed and annulled; the apostolic and synodal
decrees and constitutions enacted about the above remaining in force. In order
that the memory of this holy constitution may be perpetually retained and
that nobody may be able to claim ignorance of it, the Holy Synod orders that
it should be promulgated at least once a year during divine service in all cathedral
and college churches and other holy places where the faithful gather in large
numbers.[3]

These rules were aimed at making sure that Jews were not able to convert
in name only. But this measure did not address the growing resentment among
Old Christians in Spain, who charged that Jews had converted only to save their
property from seizure under the law and that the Conversos were using their
wealth to secure their influence and power in the country. The common belief
that Jewish wealth had been accumulated through usury (which was illegal) led
to growing calls to return that wealth to the original Christian borrowers by
cancellation of debts.

The Council's rulings were in response to this developing conflict between
Old Christians and New Christians. The anti–Jewish Christians pointed to the
lack of participation among many Conversos in established Christian rituals.
The Conversos responded that their lack of knowledge about Christian rituals
was responsible for their less than full commitment to the faith. And so the
Council's ruling stipulated that even after baptism, bishops were to ensure that
converted Christians be fully trained in the requirements and rites of their new
faith. The Council had ensured the rights of Conversos while also threatening
punishment for violation by way of the Inquisition. The end result was that the
Church ruling made it more difficult to bring charges against Conversos
specifically because they were not Christian since birth. If the intention of the
Church through these decrees was to merge Conversos and Christians and eliminate the hostility, it did not succeed. Neither side was fully satisfied with what
the Church considered to be a sensible compromise.

The matter was hardly put to rest. Controversy about the rights of Conversos intensified over the next decade and ten years later, in 1444, King Juan
II issued a *cedula* (letter) to the councils of all major Spanish cities. He ordering that Conversos were to be treated "as if they were born Christians" and were
legally entitled to all rights of citizenship.[4]

If King Juan II hoped his ruling would end the conflict that was growing
in Spanish society, he was as mistaken as the Church had been a decade earlier.

The Toledo Riots of 1449

The struggle between Christians and Conversos erupted in Toledo. This city had at one time been ruled by the Moors, and Christians living there had a deep hatred toward both Muslims and Jews, based not only on the repressive rule of the past, but on the perception that non–Christians could not be trusted. When Toledo was reconquered by Spanish Christians, the majority of Moors had left the area; but the Jewish residents of the city had remained for the most part and the city became a center of Jewish commerce in Spain. By 1449, under protection of the monarchy, local nobility, and the Church, Jews were thriving in Toledo even under the growing resentment of Christian-born citizens. Thus, Toledo became both the center of Jewish life and economic activity, and a primary center of anti–Jewish resentment among Spanish Christians.

A nobleman, Pero Sarmiento, had been loyal to the monarchy up until 1449, and had been well known for his loyalty and past service. In 1446, in Sarmiento's sixteenth year of service, he was appointed by King Juan II as governor of Toledo. However, he was unhappy with his position. Two years earlier the king had revoked his appointment as chief magistrate (*alcalde mayor*) in the Court of Appeals and awarded the position to Pero López de Ayala, the former chief magistrate. Disputes over the proper holder of the judgeship went on for two years and were resolved in 1448 with Sarmiento prevailing in one respect: the king demoted Ayala to a post on a lower court. However, at the same time, the king denied Sarmiento control over the city that was usually given over to its governor. The king, apparently concerned that Sarmiento might use the city's military forces against him, restricted his access to military strongholds around the city and that led to the riots that followed, with Sarmiento leading the revolt.

The power struggle between Ayala and Sarmiento was based partly on Sarmiento's insult at having his post revoked by the king as well as the limitation on exercise of his powers as governor. But Sarmiento also knew that in the Castilian court, having a powerful enemy like Ayala could lead to sudden arrest and removal to a remote prison. Sarmiento was not as well connected politically as his enemy, but he knew that his future was at risk. In May of 1448, Sarmiento's concerns were made even worse when several noblemen were arrested without explanation and their properties confiscated. It appeared to Sarmiento that the king was removing anyone he perceived to be an enemy or potential enemy. He thought he was probably on the list of wanted men and, given the reduction of control over local military forces, he concluded that he had only one choice: to rebel against the monarchy and seize power.

In January 1449, Sarmiento's dispute with the monarchy turned violent. He could not rely on local politicians or nobles for support in a rebellion, but he allied himself with Marcos García de Mora, a Toledo native and notorious criminal. Most important to the interests of Sarmiento and his intentions to create a revolt, García hated Conversos passionately. Like Sarmiento, García resented the local nobility and the monarchy of Spain. The two together concluded that the best way to fuel the spirit of rebellion was to stir up local anti–Converso sentiments. Stirring up the *común* (laborers and workers) would enable them to gather enough manpower to make a revolt successful. Rumors were spread about the self-interest of tax collectors and the monarchy, a convenient target since Alonso Cota, Toledo's treasurer and a Converso, had recently approved a loan to the monarchy (which also required levying an additional tax).

On January 27, an angry crowd had gathered in response to claims that Cota was in a conspiracy with the monarchy to defraud the city. The crowd went to Cota's house and set it on fire. The poorer citizens, most burdened by the newly imposed tax, easily directed their rage against Conversos; the antagonism between Old Christians and Conversos had been brewing for decades, and it did not take much to tip the protest into acts of violence. But what may have looked like a spontaneous outbreak and tax protest was actually the result of careful planning by Sarmiento and García. Aiding them were local Church officials, although their roles were limited to inciting the crowd with speeches. Many houses were burned, mostly those owned by Conversos. The rioters also seized the military strongholds in and around the city to prevent retaliation. The efficiency with which the military strongholds were overpowered indicates that a lot of planning was involved in these "spontaneous" riots.

After taking over the city's military strongholds, the crowd installed their own leaders, a further sign of organization and planning. An "angry mob" tends to not be organized enough to appoint leaders or to efficiently accomplish strategic goals. In this instance, three of the four important gates of the city were taken swiftly; only the Tower of San Martín put up resistance, and only for a brief time. The plan was clearly not as spontaneous as it might have appeared. Once the strongholds were captured

> [t]he insurgents then put the gates and bridges under the command of their own men. Could these appointments have been made by a rabble that lacked leadership and planning? One would not expect such actions of a mob that had burst into a spontaneous outbreak. Such a mob, having spent its fury, tends to disperse and disappear. In Toledo the attackers behaved differently. The captains entrusted with guarding the gates, the bridges and other strategic outposts were no doubt chosen before the outbreak, with a view to securing these positions once they were captured by the rebels.[5]

Sarmiento, having secured the city, demanded cancellation of the new loan and ensuing tax. The authorities complied at once and Sarmiento declared himself the head of the city's political and military arms. The local authorities agreed.

Toledo Under Sarmiento

The reign of Sarmiento, aided by García, was harsh. Conversos were the primary targets of the new Toledo administration. Sarmiento was ambitious and saw his new role as an opportunity to solidify his political base and to gain wealth. For this, he required more than the support of the *común* class; he also wanted to gain ground among the Toledo nobility and wealthy upper classes. To this end, he needed to convert the passive Converso community into what would be seen as active opposition to the new regime. Sarmiento needed to portray Conversos as a threat to the security of wealthy Toledo residents. And so he ordered the leading Conversos arrested. The wealthy Converso leaders were despised more than anyone by the *común* so these arrests were popular. Under torture, these leaders confessed to taking part in a conspiracy against the newly formed city government.

Not only did Sarmiento have the support of the *común* in this initiative; the upper classes were supportive of this effort as well, at least partially for financial motives. Since the wealthy Conversos had been judged guilty, Sarmiento was able under the law to confiscate their property. The valuables were divided among the city (which needed funds badly), the local nobles, and Sarmiento, who became wealthy at the expense of the Conversos. The blood-lust against Conversos was heightened by the arrests, and to further please the *común*, the wealthy Conversos were cruelly executed; Sarmiento ordered his executioners to "cut them to pieces."[6]

The Conversos resisted briefly and armed clashes broke out. Small groups of armed Conversos, led by Juan de la Cibdad, took place sporadically. Cibdad was killed in a skirmish and hanged upside down in La Plaza de Zocodover, a main square of Toledo. This ended the attempt at armed resistance by the Conversos. Sarmiento promised that if the Conversos stopped resisting by force of arms, he would protect them from retaliation. The Conversos had little choice, so they agreed and surrendered. However, in spite of his word, Sarmiento embarked on a reign of terror including random arrests, torture and execution. Property was taken over by the city as each Converso was taken into custody. Sarmiento prevented mob sackings of Converso neighborhoods and destruction of property; he preferred to acquire the properties intact to enrich himself, his friends and the city. So the dismantling of Converso wealth and community was accomplished in an orderly and systematic matter.

At this point, the Church became involved, resulting in a shift away from politics and toward religion. The vicar of the cathedral church in Toledo, Pero Lope Galvez, was in charge of the local Church judicial system while the archbishop was away. The charge that Conversos were in a conspiracy with the monarchy to overthrow Sarmiento's regime was a difficult one to sustain, given the fact that his forces were in charge of the city and its military. But a charge of religious crimes did not require a conspiracy and could be made against the whole community. The Church authorities, working with Sarmiento, began describing Conversos as not only secret Jews but also as heretics and traitors. This offense extended not only through the city, but all of Spain and, in fact, throughout the Christian world. Sarmiento ordered formation of a commission to investigate the new charges of religious crimes. The description of "secret Jews" or *Marranos* included potentially anyone forced to convert to Christianity, suspected of secretly adhering to Jewish rites and beliefs. In Spanish, the word *Marrano* translates to "filthy" and was also a reference to swine and the Jewish prohibition from eating pork. Many Spanish Christians referred to Conversos as Marranos, although the generalization was supposed to be limited only to those who did not truly embrace Christianity. Another term that developed during this period was *judíos escondidos* (hidden Jews), also called Crypto-Jews.

In addition to the Marranos, some Conversos were also classified as "temporary" Conversos, those who having agreed to become Christian by force or without any other choice did not have their children baptized. In those cases where baptism was demanded or forced on the so-called temporary Conversos, they washed the child's head upon returning home to "remove" the act of baptism. This group also ate no pork, continued to observe important Jewish holidays such as Passover, and acted as Christians only to the minimum requirements imposed on them.

No one knew how many Conversos actually continued to practice Jewish rites in secret. Even so, the Sarmiento-operated commission found that the Conversos were guilty of the widespread secret practice of Jewish rites. The government used these findings to appoint a special tribunal to hear cases against Conversos and invited Christians to offer testimony of such crimes. Although the ensuing trials and executions were not ordered by the pope or even the local archbishop, they were met with enthusiasm, especially by the *común*.

In May 1449, only four months after the initial revolt in Toledo, King Juan II and his army had begun approaching Toledo with the aim of retaking it from Sarmiento. Recognizing the threat, Sarmiento negotiated with the monarchy. He invited the king to enter the city with only a small force; he also asked for assurances that he would not be removed from power; and he demanded that he be exempted from any charges resulting from the revolt or its aftermath. The king rejected all of these demands but did not enter the city either. However, Sarmiento knew that he would not be able to keep his power for much longer. A compromise was reached allowing Sarmiento to keep the wealth he had taken from the Conversos along with promises that he would not be prosecuted. Even so, Sarmiento was not willing to let matters with the Conversos rest.

On June 5, 1449, Sarmiento presided over a meeting in Toledo to announce a new law. The *Sentencia-Estatuto* (Judgment and Statute) specified that Jews were guilty of crimes that could not be resolved merely by conversion to Christianity (the judgment). Accordingly, Conversos were banned from holding any office or testifying in court (the statute). The statute not only included a ban on serving as witnesses, but effectively forbade Conversos from suing as well. The provisions were also to be imposed on all Converso offspring into the future. In spite of the previous attempt at resolving differences between Old and New Christians through conversion, the new law set up a form of social privilege and advantage of Old Christians over New or converted Christians.

The negotiated change in Toledo's government included both enactment of this law and replacement of Sarmiento with the Castilian heir apparent, Prince Don Enrique. The settlement included a promised end to persecutions of Conversos; but the new law had demoted them en masse to second class citizens with no legal rights and no ability to take part in politics or to gain protection under the law. The arrival of the prince as the new ruler of Toledo was accompanied by uncertainty about the future of the Conversos. The arrests, executions, and property seizures were over, but under the new law Conversos—like their predecessors the unconverted Jews—were left with no social or economic standing. The new laws against the Conversos quickly spread to other regions of Spain. In spite of the promised end to violence, rioters burned the homes of Conversos and wounded or killed their residents. The new laws did nothing to protect Conversos from danger; if anything, they simply prevented Conversos from being able to appeal to the courts for protection.

The End of Sarmiento's Reign

A delegation of Church authorities tried to have the *Sentencia-Estatuto* annulled. The Church had been invested for decades in the conversion approach to the Jewish question, and had worked to ensure that Conversos were treated as equal Christians. Cardinal Juan de Torquemada, uncle of the Dominican inquisitor Tomás de Torquemada who would rise to infamy later, asked Pope Nicholas V (1447–55) to intervene. Responding to the cardinal's request, Nicholas wrote in his 1449 bull *Humani generis inimicus* that "all Catholics are one body in Christ according to the teaching of our faith." The pope excommunicated the drafters of the decree in Toledo and King Juan II supported the pope's position.

However, the pope's bull qualified his condemnation of anti–Converso legislation, including the language:

> But if it is found that some of these people, after having been baptized, do not savor the Christian religion, or fall for the errors of the Jews or the gentiles, or do not guard the precepts of the Christian faith, either because of malice or of ignorance, in this case there should enter into force what was established by the Toledan Councils in the chapter *Constituit* as well as in another place, wherein it is stated that apostates of this kind should not be admitted to such honors on a par with other Christians.[7]

This clause meant that it remained possible to persecute Conversos in Spain, as long as it could be claimed that they were not practicing Christianity sincerely.

When the prince took control of Toledo, one of the first challenges he faced was from the Christian nobles. They favored getting rid of the rebels and restoring the previous order in the city, but they also wanted the conditions of *Sentencia-Estatuto* to be kept in force. But as the new ruler of the city, the prince deftly enlisted the support of the *común*. This came about when García and a small group of supporters positioned themselves in the tower of the city's cathedral church. García had once counted on Sarmiento as a loyal supporter, but now with the prince in command, Sarmiento wanted no connection to him under any conditions. The prince asked the *común* to join his forces in overcoming García even though he did not need the help, wanting to establish them as his allies. García was captured and placed on trial, found guilty and sentenced to be drawn and quartered. This was a ritualistic method of execution, involving being hanged until almost dead, disemboweled, emasculated (with entrails and genitalia burned in view of the condemned), cutting of the body into four parts, and finally, beheading. So it was that the life of García came to an end. The *común*, who gladly followed him in the murder of Conversos, just as enthusiastically watched his demise.

Sarmiento was first asked and then ordered to leave Toledo for good. He agreed to comply on the condition that he would be allowed to take with him the possessions he had acquired from the Conversos. He left in February 1450 in the middle of the night.

Even with the end of the rebellion and the pope's condemnation of the *Sentencia-Estatuto*, the Old Christians of Toledo continued to believe in the intention of the law. Contrary to the official Church position, the old antagonism toward Jews remained alive but was aimed now at Conversos. The rationale was partly based on the law; the view among many Christians in Toledo was that the law was justified because Conversos were criminals, based on a reading of both civil and canon law, both of which stated:

> Converts of Jewish descent, because they are suspect in the faith of Christ, in which they often vomit while they readily Judaize, should not be allowed to hold offices or benefices, either public or private, by means of which they may injure, offend and mistreat the Old Christians; nor can their testimony against these Christians be of any validity.[8]

The reference in canon law was to the Fourth Council of Toledo, in which canon 65 stated that Jews (or those who are "of Jews") should be kept from public office. This canon was interpreted to mean that Conversos (being of Jews) were to be included in the ban. However, no known civil law confirmed or supported such a ban in spite of the arguments presented. The less than exact phrase "suspect in the faith" kept the door open so that any Converso thus accused could be considered exempt from the mandate that all Christians were to be treated equally. A religious-based argument resulting in the charge that Conversos were criminals concerns the fact of conversion itself. A non–Christian could not be charged with heresy under long-established definitions. But once a Jew was baptized, voluntarily or not, the laws of heresy applied immediately; so secretly practicing Jewish rites became heresy under that definition.

In addition to the civil and criminal rationale for continuing to persecute Conversos, there remained the long-standing social prejudice against them. In the text of the *Sentencia-Estatuto* was the charge that Conversos

> having stolen large and innumerable quantities of maravedis [gold coins] and silver from the King our Lord and from his revenues, taxes and tributes ... have oppressed, destroyed, robbed and depraved most of the old houses and estates of the Old Christians of this city, its territory and jurisdiction.[9]

Cardinal Juan de Torquemada

During the debate between the authors of the *Sentencia-Estatuto* and the papacy, one of the more vocal defenders of Converso rights was Cardinal Juan de Torquemada. His father was Alvar Fernández de Torquemada and his mother, whose name has not been preserved for history, was rumored to be a New Christian (Converso). The fact that Cardinal Torquemada might have had Jewish blood is ironic given the legacy of his infamous nephew.

Juan started his career in the Dominican Order, rising to the rank of cardinal and eventually named to the important position of political emissary. He was an expert in canon law and theology like so many other Dominicans, and he had written on many topics including papal rights (his best-known work was *Summa de Ecclesia*, thought to be the most important work on the topic of papal supremacy), forgiveness of sins, the Virgin Mary and the Eucharist. He published more than 40 books and tracts.

In 1434, he had been appointed by Pope Eugene IV (1431–47) to serve as Master of the Sacred Palace, making him the curia's official theologian. He was given many additional honors by subsequent popes, including being named "Defender of the Faith and Protector of the Church" by both Eugene IV in 1439 and Pius II in 1458. Following the death of Pius II, he was even considered for the post of pope, which he declined due to poor health.

The 1449 Toledo revolt broke out at the same time that Juan de Torquemada's reputation was reaching its height within the Church. Picking Torquemada to represent the papacy and to investigate the matter was a logical choice for Pope Nicholas. He possessed both the theological and political skills as well as having connections within the Spanish court. He wrote a famous tract concerning the conflict in Toledo called *Tractatus*. In this work, Torquemada stated what so many had thought but few in Spain had ever expressed: that the deep-seated hatred of the Conversos was not truly based on any religious crimes, real or perceived. Rather, the hatred was based on the success of the Conversos in adherence to Christian doctrine and way of life. He believed that a majority of Conversos had converted completely and successfully and were treated as lesser Christians primarily due to that success. He referred to the Conversos as Christ's faithful (*fideles Christi*); he saw the uprising against the Conversos not as a Christian movement against Jews, but as a movement that threatened Christianity itself; and he referred to the claims made by Old Christians during the riots as a form of heresy, calling the followers of Sarmiento agents of the devil, practicing a form of heresy that "spreads slowly like a cancer."[10]

Tractatus was a strong condemnation of the *Sentencia-Estatuto*, effectively combining moral arguments with scholarly and legal refutation of the law's assumptions. He questioned the motives of accusers in trials of Conversos and even criticized the judges who sat on tribunals. He also pointed out the unreliability of tribunals in which the accused were not allowed to offer a defense, and in which confessions were the result of torture. Torquemada's harsh criticism of the anti–Converso laws and tribunals could just as easily have been leveled against the Inquisition, past and future, and its methods throughout Europe. He concluded that the motives of anti–Conversos in bringing criminal charges was to seize property for their own enrichment, after which "to give their crimes some semblance of virtue, they decided to stage a trial over invented heresies."[11]

Torquemada's influence led to Pope Nicholas' excommunication of the drafters of *Sentencia-Estatuto*, and supported the monarchy's removal of the rebels from Toledo. His findings also pointed out the lack of validity in claims by the rebels that Toledo Conversos were involved in a conspiracy to kill Old Christians, a charge that led to many deaths and injuries, much destruction and confiscation of property, and widespread loss of public offices previously held by Conversos. But the Church position opposing the actions of the rebels and the *Sentencia-Estatuto* did not end the debate. The Church had hoped that by taking steps that led to conversion, the ex–Jews of Spain would simply disappear into Christian Spanish society. Two factors prevented this: the separate identity and nature of Jewish culture (which the Church seemed not to understand) and the deeply held fear and distrust among Old Christians toward Jews, including those who had converted. The defense presented so often, that many Jews had embraced Christianity and abandoned Judaism, did not ring true among many Old Christians. They suspected that the secret continuation of Jewish rites was widespread and conspiratorial, even though Cardinal Torquemada argued there was no evidence to support this theory.

Before his death, Marcos García de Mora had written an explanation of the events that took place in Toledo, and Cardinal Torquemada referred to this work in his rebuttal of the entire incident. In this document (called the *Memorial* because it was widely circulated after García's death), the pope's conclusions and Torquemada's opinion of the events that took place during the revolt were challenged. García rebutted the charges leveled at the rebels and summarized the primary attitude of anti–Converso thought:

> All converts who belong to the Jewish race or who have descended from it — that is, who were born as Jews, or are sons, grandsons, great-grandsons, or great-great-grandsons of Jews who were baptized, including those who descended newly and recently from that most evil and damned stock, are presumed, according to the testimonies of Scriptures, to be infidels and suspect of the faith. From which follows that the vice of infidelity is not presumed to be purged until the fourth generation.[12]

Although quite detailed the *Memorial* cannot be treated as a reliable source for the history of the 1449 riots and rebellion. García's deep hatred of all Jews and Conversos is clear in its tone, justifications and rationale. Whether or not he believed his own exaggerations cannot be known, but he was a witness to and participant in the events and certainly knew that he was distorting fact. For example, he could not have possibly believed that he and his fellow rebels armed themselves for protection against a Converso-led conspiracy to do harm to Old Christians; even so, he insisted that this was the motivation for the incident. He assumed that any and all Jewish conversions were insincere and that Jews were inherently evil. He went beyond the religious arguments against Jews, making the distinction racial as well as religious. However, the *Memorial* was an interesting document insofar as it provided a view into the distorted mindset of the instigators of the Toledo events, including García's proposed solution: the extermination of all Conversos in Spain.

Even with the papacy's condemnation of the events of 1449, persistent anti–Converso sentiment led the Church to further action. For years, Old Christians had complained that Conversos were not having their children baptized and were continuing to observe Jewish holidays while quietly ignoring Christian rites and observances. In 1451, King Juan II asked the papacy to appoint a special commission to look into these charges. The rhetoric of the time included charges brought by members of the clergy to incite anti–Converso sentiment. Franciscan Friar Alfonso de Espina was instrumental in escalating anti–Converso feelings in Spain; he wrote in *Fortalicium fidei* (Fortification of the Faith) that Jews were known to murder children, and claimed that the Church had an obligation to force the baptism of Jewish children.[13]

Espina's hatred for Jews and Conversos included the claim that the Conversos posed the greatest threat to Christianity of all times. In Espina's view, the fact that most of Spanish Jewry had been converted did not mean the conversion program had succeeded — only that the underlying problem had become less visible. This occurred as Enrique IV took the throne in 1454; his reign was a relatively peaceful period for the Conversos. Even so, Espina's campaign included labeling Conversos as religious criminals. As a consequence, a movement began to expel Jews from several territories and towns. The subsequent robberies and seizures of synagogues were widespread and on May 28, 1455, the monarchy warned all local authorities to stop anti–Jewish and anti–Converso steps.

Espina continued preaching against Jews and Conversos even though the monarchy had halted his actions. Among Espina's charges was the repeated claim that Conversos were heretics. His message led to deeper divisions and distrust between Old and New Christians.

In 1461, Enrique recognized that simply forbidding the destruction and robbery of Converso properties was not going to end the conflict. He instructed his emissary to the papacy to submit a formal request for a new Inquisition, to determine whether there were any serious incidences of any heresy in Castile, with the idea that if these threats were uncovered and resolved, peace would be established once again. The king proposed appointment of four inquisitors to oversee the investigation with the final selection of candidates to be left to the king. This was the first step in establishing what would later grow into the Spanish Inquisition, in which centuries of hatred toward Jews and Conversos would explode in vengeance aimed at resolving the issue once and for all.

CHAPTER 9

The Age of Torquemada, the Grand Inquisitor

> From the 1440s, resentment against Conversos began to change the charac-
> ter of Castilian anti–Semitism.... [B]y this time the Conversos were also
> accused of being false Christians, either continuing to Judaize or being out-
> right atheists. Increasingly, the baptism of Conversos came to be regarded
> by many Christians as invalid, or at least not sufficient to remove from Con-
> versos the taint of Judaism or atheism. As Christians, the Conversos also
> faced a new kind of risk, for they (unlike Jews and Muslims) were now sub-
> ject to ecclesiastical discipline, particularly to an inquisitor, if they were also
> suspected of heresy.
>   — Edward Peters, *Inquisition*, 1989

Two years after Spain's King Enrique IV requested that the pope establish a new Inquisition, Pope Pius II (1458–64) complied. The overall purpose of this new Inquisition was to investigate instances of heresy among the Conversos of Spain. The two-year gap between request and decision was due to conflicts in both Spanish and papal politics. Enrique insisted on having the new Inquisition operated by Dominicans, and wanted the Franciscan Alfonso de Espina to be kept out of the process. Enrique knew that Espina was a fanatic and would use a new Inquisition to abuse the rights of Conversos, an outcome the king wanted to avoid.

Enrique had promised the Franciscans in Spain that he would request approval for a new Inquisition. Wanting complete control over how the tribunals would be formed, Enrique included in his petition to the pope a provision granting the king exclusive right to appoint inquisitors himself. The king did not want the Conversos completely destroyed, but he believed he needed to respond to pressure from the Franciscans to take action against them. The negotiations continued until March 1462, when Pius issued a bull setting up the new Inquisition.

The bull, *Dum fidei catholicæ*, was issued on March 15, 1462. It authorized the establishment of an Inquisition in Castile according to the outline Enrique had proposed. But the problem in Castile was not with Conversos secretly practicing Judaism, but with Old Christians and their unwillingness to accept Conversos as equals. This reality was acknowledged widely among both secular and clerical authorities in Castile, and establishment of the new Inquisition may have been as much to quiet down the voices of suspicion as to seek out any actual heresy among Conversos. The wrongdoing among Old Christians in spreading false rumors and inciting suspicions made the rift between Conversos and the rest of Christian society more a social problem than a religious one. The king had requested approval for the new Inquisition as a political move, not to investigate actual instances of heresy.

The year after the bull was published the fanatical anti–Semite Espina pressured Enrique to put the Inquisition into full effect, without success. Espina was instrumental in keeping anti–Converso sentiments high among Old Christians, including the continuation of older anti–Jewish suspicions. Now, more and more, Conversos were being called *false* Christians and even atheists. Enrique tried to quell the unrest by appointing a panel of bishops to operate the Inquisition; but Enrique had no interest in a full-scale operation involving arrests, public trials and executions.

In 1463, Espina publicly accused Conversos of a great heresy, and demanded that Enrique put a full-scale Inquisition into motion. He claimed that Conversos were continuing to secretly practice Judaic rites, including circumcising their children. One of his supporters, a Franciscan named Fernando de la Plaza, made an extraordinary claim in one sermon, that he had in his possession the foreskins of hundreds of Converso children who had been illegally circumcised by their parents. The claim caused a sensation and King Enrique challenged the claim. He summoned Fernando to appear before him and ordered him to produce the foreskins. Fernando reported with a modified claim, that he did not have the actual foreskins in his possession as previously claimed but that the incident was reported to him by others. However, he refused to divulge the names. The incident turned out to be a great embarrassment to the Franciscans and to Espina.[1]

The period from 1463 to 1474, the last decade of Enrique's rule, was one of turmoil and was characterized by a standoff: the Old Christian and Franciscan camp, desiring a new Inquisition, versus the king's court. But the resentments did not go away; they were only deferred. As soon as Enrique died in 1474, a tide of anti–Semitism rose up throughout Castile. This year also marked the beginning of the reign of Queen Isabella.

Ferdinand and Isabella

Born in 1451, Isabella was only 23 when she became queen in 1474. She had married Ferdinand, son of John II of Aragon, on October 19, 1469. This marriage resulted 10 years later in the unification of the monarchies of Aragon and Castile, and the couple's great-grandson Philip II became the monarch of the kingdom of Spain, for the first time creating a single Spanish kingdom on the Iberian Peninsula.

As soon as their reign began, Isabella and Ferdinand were beset by growing demands for an accelerated Inquisition to root out Conversos and identify them as heretics. From 1477 to 1478, Isabella was in Seville, where Dominican inquisitor Alonso de Hojeda claimed he had discovered a ring of judaizing Conversos. He convinced Isabella that this discovery required an Inquisition since the problem was sure to have spread throughout Castille. His claim was supported by a report written by the archbishop of Seville, Pedro González de Mondoza, and Dominican friar Tomás de Torquemada, the nephew of Cardinal Juan de Torquemada.

In 1478, after repeated requests from Hojeda and other anti–Conversos, Isabella and Ferdinand asked Pope Sixtus IV (1471–84) to issue a papal bull to establish a new Inquisition. On November 1, 1478, Sixtus issued his bull, *Exigit sinceras devotionis affectus,* creating the new Inquisition to be based in Castile. Terms of this new Inquisition included a ruling that three priests were to be appointed to a tribunal, with their selection left up to the royal couple as Ferdinand and Isabella had insisted. In 1480, the first tribunal was established, consisting of royal appointees of two Dominicans, Juan de San Martín and Miguel de Morillo, as well as Juan Ruiz de Medina as adviser. Allegations of Converso plots to arm and assault or assassinate the inquisitors led to numerous arrests and the convictions of many among the accused. On February 6, 1481, six Conversos were found guilty of heresy and condemned to be burned at the stake. The Spanish Inquisition had begun after years of consideration, debate and negotiation.

The urgency of the inquisitors' efforts convinced the papacy to mandate the appointment of an additional seven inquisitors. More tribunals were set up in Córdoba in 1482 and in Ciudad Real and Jaen in 1483. Among the newly appointed inquisitors was Tomás de Torquemada. But even with the power of the monarchy behind it, expanding the Inquisition to Aragon proved more difficult than the monarch had hoped. Aragon was Ferdinand's home, and the people of Aragon did not want anything to do with the Inquisition in their region. The people appealed to Pope Sixtus IV, who issued a bull prohibiting the Inquisition from establishing a tribunal in the region. The bull responded to claims made in the request and was exceptionally critical of the Inquisition and its procedures, noting that

> many true and faithful Christians, because of the testimony of enemies, rivals, slaves and other low people — and still less appropriate — without tests of any kind, have been locked up in secular prisons, tortured and condemned like relapsed heretics, deprived of their goods and properties, and given over to the secular arm to be executed, at great danger to their souls, giving a pernicious example and causing scandal to many.[7]

In response, Ferdinand and Isabella complained to the pope. Sixtus yielded to them, publishing a suspension of his previous bull. Sixtus went even farther in an effort to placate Ferdinand and Isabella, issuing another bull on October 17, 1483, in which Tomás de Torquemada was named to the post of inquisitor general for Aragon, Valencia and Catalonia. The successor to Sixtus, Pope Innocent VIII (1484–92), believed the death sentences of the Inquisition were overly harsh, and proposed allowing appeals to Rome for anyone convicted by the tribunals.

Challenging the pope, Ferdinand issued a very strongly worded ruling in December 1484. He decreed that anyone attempting to appeal sentences passed by tribunals of the Inquisition without prior permission from the crown was to be put to death and their property confiscated. This decision set up the Inquisition as the sole institution with authority throughout Spain to pass final sentences and overrule the process of appeal, overruling even the pope in jurisdiction of the tribunals and those accused under its procedures. The public in Aragon continued to oppose the Inquisition even after the papal bull allowing it was published, but in September 1485 an inquisitor named Pedro Arbués was murdered in Zaragoza, and public opinion immediately turned against the Conversos and in favor the of the Inquisition.

Over the next decade, the activities and locations of the new Inquisition's tribunals spread rapidly. In 1492, the Spanish army defeated the Moors and retook Grenada after a 10-year war, ending the period called the *Reconquista* (reconquest). The same year, Ferdinand and Isabella issued an order expelling all Jews from the country.

The Treaty of Grenada was signed on November 25, 1491, between Ferdinand and Isabella and the Muslim ruler Abu-abdallah Muhammad XII (known in Spain as Boabdil). The treaty ensured the safety of Moors living in Spain and promised religious freedom in exchange for the kingdom's surrender and the end of armed conflict. However, the importance of the Inquisition took precedence over the political intentions of the monarchs. Ferdinand and Isabella first ordered Jews to be relocated into separate communities. They then expelled all Jews from Spain.

The order against the Jews was published on March 31, 1492, and was called the Alhambra Decree. Also known as the Edict of Expulsion, it ordered that all Jews were to leave the kingdom by July 31. About 200,000 complied and left, but the remaining Conversos became the focus of the Inquisition. Also under threat were the remaining Muslims. (A forced expulsion of Muslims took place later, in 1502, with the choice given to leave or convert.)

From the Church perspective, Ferdinand and Isabella were valued for their efforts at bringing all of Spain under Christianity. This was accomplished by expulsion of non–Christians as well as through trials within the now institutionalized offices of the Inquisition. The title *los Reyes Católicos* (the Catholic Monarchs) was given to Ferdinand and Isabella by Pope Alexander VI (1492–1503).

In the later years of their reign, Ferdinand and Isabella tried to cement relations between their monarchy and other rulers in Europe. Their children were married to various rulers; their famous daughter Catherine of Aragon was the first wife of King Henry VIII and mother of English Queen Mary I.

Although famously remembered for supporting Columbus in his voyages to the New World, Ferdinand and Isabella also supported and promoted the Spanish Inquisition, which was equally important as a critical phase in development of the early modern history of Europe.

The Expansion of the Inquisition

The legacy of Ferdinand and Isabella can be defined as a successful unification of the country into a single kingdom, and as an equally successful ecclesiastical unification of an entire nation under a single faith. The Inquisition may have been based on the sincere beliefs of the monarchs in the Church; but the underlying motives went back many decades and were at least as rooted in a deep-set social prejudice as in a desire for spiritual unity. The social and economic success of the Conversos created enemies among the Old Christian community, as well as among both Dominican and Franciscan inquisitors. Although the official Church policy had always been opposed to forced conversions, the elimination of Jewish influence was seen as a positive step — even if achieved through the Inquisition and its extremes.

In fact, the Church had been committed for many decades to the idea that accepting conversions from Jews would cause the Jewish presence in Spain to disappear. This assumption proved incorrect, and the Church worried a great deal about the problem, real or perceived, of Conversos continuing to practice Judaism in secret. But a far greater problem was the growing anti–Converso movement in Spain. This movement saw the Inquisition as a welcome opportunity to eradicate Jews from Spain completely, even if that required killing thousands based on the excuse of hunting down heretics. Conversion, even when coerced, enabled the Church to justify arrests. Even though opposed to forcing Jews to convert, the Church policy was that once Jews became Christians, the rules of the Church took jurisdiction over their actions.

The problem faced by the Church and those Church members who wanted to be rid of Jews and Conversos was jurisdictional even with this rationale. It was long established that the Inquisition was only empowered to oversee the activities of baptized Christians, whereas non–Christians could not be punished under canon law. The hundred-year effort to convert Spanish Jews was, in this respect, an opportunity for the anti–Semitic and anti–Converso forces. Just as the definition of *heresy* was expanded in Germany and France to encompass witches, the definition of *heresy* in Spain included Conversos on the suspicion that they remained Jewish in secret. Now that the individuals under suspicion were Christian, they were subject to the Inquisition.

This interpretation of jurisdictional rights of the inquisitors did away with the potential problem of bringing non–Christians before tribunals (including those forced to convert). As a result, the Spanish Inquisition is best remembered for its persecution of Conversos. But in addition, Muslims who had converted to Christianity were also investigated and for the same reasons. Those suspected of secretly practicing Islam after conversion were called *Moriscos* (meaning Moor-like), and the majority of these Moriscos resided in Granada, Aragon and Valencia. By law, all Muslims living in Castile were legally required to convert in 1502. Muslims in Aragon and Valencia were not legally required to convert until 1526, although the majority had undergone forced conversions during the Revolt of the Brotherhoods (1519–23).

The revolt (in Spanish, *Rebelión de las Germanías*) was directed against King Charles I in Valencia. It began when, in 1519, an outbreak of plague hit the region. Many believed the plague was punishment for immorality, with Muslims and homosexuals the target of most of the anger.

The rioting *Germanías* (members of artisan guilds or unions) replaced the royal government and set up a "Council of Thirteen" with one representative from each of 13 unions. The council gave the power to its members to keep a monopoly of their professions and to exclude anyone who was not a member. This anti-feudal initiative was the precursor of modern-day unionist movements. However, one of the actions was to move against Muslim citizens — called *mudéjars* — and force them to convert to Christianity. Once converted, the New Christians who were previously Muslims were labeled as *Moriscos*. The nobles in the area had been employing Muslims for low-paying manual jobs, leading to resentment among Christians who believed this low pay policy held down their own wages.

The suspicion and resentment between Old Christians and New Christians (in this instance the Moriscos) mirrored the problems experienced over many decades in Castile between Old Christians and Conversos. Many of the New Christians were suspected of continuing to practice Islam in secret. They were also accused of secretly aiding the Barbary pirates who regularly raided shipping on Spain's Mediterranean coast. Since those pirates were Muslims, the now converted Spanish Muslims were viewed with suspicion by Old Christians. Eventually, the Spanish Inquisition shifted its emphasis from Conversos to Moriscos, who represented a majority of those appearing before tribunals after 1570.

The Inquisition had originally been focused against heresy, but in Spain (as in other parts of Europe at the same time) the scope of tribunals grew. In Spain, inquisitors arrested, tortured and executed thousands of "heretics" under a range of definitions, including Judaizers (Conversos secretly practicing Judaism), Moriscos, Lutherans (by this time the Protestant Reformation was well under way), the superstitious (witches and sorcerers), those guilty of heretical propositions (verbal offenses, blasphemy, statements of religious beliefs, charges of sexual immorality, and sins among the clergy), bigamists, those committing acts against the office of the Inquisition, and alumbrados (meaning "illuminated," a Gnostic sect in Spain that although peaceful and unorganized was viewed as a form of heresy deserving to be punished). The Inquisition expanded because the Church authorities (specifically the inquisitors) saw enemies everywhere they looked, and with their unlimited power, inquisitors could try anyone they thought insufficiently Christian. Even the sin of *simple fornication*, or having sex without the purpose of procreation, could result in charges before the Inquisition. Expanding this broad definition farther, anyone charged with homosexuality, rape, or bestiality faced the death penalty. Even though many of these expanded varieties of crimes within the Inquisition were in conflict with the jurisdiction of the secular courts, inquisitors did not feel bound to respect that limit. In other words, the Inquisition in Spain took on a new definition, with a crime defined as anything the inquisitors named as guilty of a form of heresy, under an expanded definition of behavior of which the inquisitors disapproved.

This debate was especially strong in Seville. In 1506, the local Inquisition looked into charges of sodomy and made many arrests. After a hearing, 12 people were condemned and burned. Three years later and after investigating the incident, the Council of the Suprema (full title: *Consejo de la Suprema y General Inquisición,* or Council of the Supreme and General Inquisition) in Castile ruled that the crime was not within the Inquisition's jurisdiction, arguing that unless the crime could be shown to be connected to a separate incidence of heresy, it belonged in the secular courts. The inquisitors argued that it was an appropriate crime for the Inquisition based on the claim that sodomy had been first introduced in Spain by the Moors, making the commission of the sin a form of heresy. In spite of local clerical resistance, in 1524 the Spanish ambassador received a decision from Pope Clement VII (1523–5) limiting the scope of the Inquisition to heresy only, and demanding respect for local laws and local jurisdiction.

In spite of the pope's specific ruling to the contrary, the Inquisition tribunals continued to bring charges for rape, sodomy, bestiality, sexual abuse of children and other sexual and moral wrongs, with the justification based on liberal definitions of heresy. Many of the confessions, like those of previous heretics, were gained under torture. The justification of inquisitors for expanding their activities beyond heresy and into such crimes included the argument that sexual crimes were heretical and were crimes against nature; that by their commissions, the crimes were themselves acts of heresy; or simply that the inquisitors believed they had the power to try anyone they wanted, regardless of secular law in the area.

Although the Inquisition may have been conducted under different names, it continued to exert influence. As late as the 19th century, even Spanish men suspected of being Freemasons could be tried and convicted for heresy, on the argument that the Freemasons were either atheists or heretics, or both.

The Procedures of the Inquisition

In addition to its original conception as a court for religious inquiry, the Spanish Inquisition worked cooperatively with the monarchy. The king was authorized to appoint inquisitors, and of course also held the power to replace inquisitors at will. The Suprema supervised the activities of the local inquisitors under this politically-controlled system. Inquisitors general reported directly to the Suprema, whose power grew through the history of the Inquisition.

Membership was between six and 10 individuals and the Council met every day except holidays. Morning sessions dealt with cases involving sodomy, bigamy, and witchcraft. Afternoon sessions reviewed or heard all other cases. As the scope of the Inquisition expanded, the widespread tribunals were centralized more and more. The cases were heard by actual tribunals which reported to the Council; and these tribunals included two inquisitors and other court officials, bailiffs and a prosecutor. Most inquisitors were members of the clergy and were educated in both canon law and secular law. The inquisitors' knowledge of Church law was deemed of greater value than knowledge of prevailing secular law or the rules of due process.

An accusation was brought by a prosecutor, who also investigated the case and interrogated witnesses. Court theologians (*calificadores*) were given the task of determining whether a defendant's conduct constituted a punishable act of heresy. The tribunal also employed a notary of property (*notario de secuestros*), who made an inventory of properties owned by the defendant; a notary of the secreto (*notario del secreto*), who recorded the defendant's testimony; and a general notary (*escribano general*), who recorded the tribunal's formal proceedings and judgment.

The *alguacil* detained and jailed the accused. The *nuncio* sent out official notices and summons. The *alcaide* was a jailer who oversaw and fed prisoners during their investigation and trial. Lay "consultants" (*familiares*) were permanent fixtures and either added testimony or advised the tribunal on procedure. The entire process was financed not by the Church or other outside sources, but through confiscation of property previously belonging to those found guilty by the tribunal. This glaring conflict of interest explains why so many of those accused of heresy during the Spanish Inquisition were among the wealthiest Converso citizens. It also points to the problem that as the activities of the Inquisition spread and became more complex, more people had to be paid; thus, more people of means had to be brought before the tribunal and found guilty to pay for its expenses. The problem was summarized well by the words of a convicted Converso from Toledo in a letter sent to Charles I:

> Your Majesty must provide, before all else, that the expenses of the Holy Office do not come from the properties of the condemned, because if that is the case, if they do not burn they do not eat.[3]

The procedures of the Inquisition, while obviously biased, were not disorderly. Specific procedures were developed by the Inquisitors General, notably Torquemada, who was an accomplished organizer. The entire process included several distinct and separate parts:

1. *Arrival ceremony.* If a team of inquisitors was sent out to smaller towns surrounding a base of operations, a ceremony was held upon their arrival. This began with holding a mass and then issuing an edict of grace, a plea for all those knowing themselves to be heretics to come forward and confess. After the call for voluntary confessions, the tribunal made accusations of its own, based on witness reports or responding to complaints from local priests or bishops. The advantage to confessing within the edict of grace was the possibility of surviving the following Inquisition. A repentant heretic who became a witness against others could escape with a penance or other light sentence. Or, if found guilty, they were strangled before being burned at the stake, a more merciful end than the alternative — being burned without first being strangled.

2. *Accusation.* For anyone faced with an inquisitional tribunal, a light sentence or an unpleasant death were the only outcomes available; once accused, the chances for a heretic to be found not guilty were slim. These terrifying choices caused many people to come forward in order to place themselves in a favorable position, especially if they had enemies. Even those not confessing would be anxious to offer witness statements to avoid facing accusations themselves. The process of Inquisition, in which *anyone* could bring an accusation or testimony, practically guaranteed that any tribunal the inquisitors set up would result in convictions. Even if no one volunteered to confess or offer testimony, the tribunal itself could bring charges against anyone it decided to define as a heretic. Within the Converso community of Spain, there were plenty of targets; and those families with wealth were especially desirable for charges of heresy. Anyone found guilty faced confiscation of their property; inquisitors depended on such confiscations to support their work. It was not only the loss of property that led to many preemptive confessions; upon being found guilty, heirs were also denied inheritance when the inquisitors seized the family estate and all of its wealth.

Simply coming forward and confessing was not enough to gain forgiveness or to ensure a light sentence. The confessed heretic also was required to name all of his accomplices. As a result there was never a shortage of witnesses and accusations; inquisitors found themselves surrounded by heretics, and the more they inquired, the more they found. Eventually, the edict of grace was replaced by an edict of faith, which was a series of instructions on how to spot heretics. Anyone coming forward to denounce a neighbor as a heretic was able to do so anonymously and the accused was never informed of the source of accusations, allowed to cross-examine the witness, or even given the chance to offer a defense.

3. *Detention.* The accused person was taken into custody as soon as denunciations were made. Incarceration could be lengthy, especially in instances where many were charged with heresy in a single community. While the accused was held under detention, his property was seized and held pending the outcome of a tribunal. Property could be sold to pay for the costs of detention, meaning that families of accused heretics ended up homeless and without income. This situation could go on for many months before the tribunal was held. During detention, the accused were not allowed access to the sacraments and were not informed of the nature of charges against them. Their families were not informed either; so an individual could be incarcerated for many months and the family put out of their home, with no information provided about why the person was detained and his property seized.

4. *Interrogation.* Before the Spanish Inquisition, the process of interrogation was focused mainly on dialogue, at least as a first step. This was especially true during the period when Cathars were the primary targets of Dominican inquisitors and the belief prevailed that a fallen Christian could be reasoned with and saved. However, in Spain the Conversos were not only hated; they were also distrusted. The inquisitors had no interest in convincing the accused of their error, and only wanted to gain confessions and pass sentence. This goal was achieved in a majority of cases.

Interrogation involved three methods. The *garrucha* (also known as the *strappado*) was a system of suspension using ropes and pulleys, augmented by weights attached to the ankles. The arms were tied behind the victim's back, and the victim was first hoisted into the air, then dropped violently, dislocating arms and causing great pain. The *toca* (also called *tortura del agua*) was a form of waterboarding. A cloth was placed over the accused person's mouth and water poured over the cloth, so that the person thought he was drowning. Finally, the *potro* was a rack, and a favorite method of inquisitors. The person was placed on the device and arms and legs slowly stretched, causing tearing of the muscles and dislocations.

The canon law overseeing Inquisition tribunals recognized that confessions obtained by torture were not admissible. As a result, tribunals made sure that those accused confessed freely *after* the period of torture had ended. The expression *confessionem esse veram, non factam vi tormentorum* (the confession was given freely and not resulting from torture) was attached to virtually all confessions automatically, regardless of what had actually taken place.

5. *Hearings and trial.* The trial was based on the testimony of witnesses and the accused. The accused was provided with an advocate, who usually was a member of the tribunal and whose role was limited to encouraging the accused person to tell the truth. The procedure was quite detailed and a complete transcript of each trial was maintained in the permanent record. Accused persons, having already given a confession, had only two ways to escape conviction. First, they could find witnesses to testify for them, which was difficult given the distinct possibility that such a witness might also face an accusation of heresy. Second, the accused could prove that witnesses were not telling the truth. Because the accused was incarcerated throughout this procedure, this was not an easy task; and others, even knowing the accusations to be false, feared getting involved in this process.

After the trial, inquisitors met with a team of *consultores*, experts in canon law, to determine the outcome. Because a "voluntary" confession was in hand, pleas of not guilty were rare. Inquisitors did not take part in interrogations as a matter of procedure but relied on others, insulating themselves from the unpleasant details of how confessions were obtained. So they were able to maintain their piety and to convince themselves that these confessions had been voluntary. As in past periods, inquisitors also wanted nothing to do with torture directly, in order to maintain the illusion that they were sincerely trying to eliminate evil.

6. *Sentence.* Acquittals of accused heretics were rare during the Spanish Inquisition. There were several other possible outcomes. First, the proceedings could be suspended. Defendants were released but remained under suspicion, and the trial could be resumed at any time. This was a variation of acquittal without a need to issue an admission that the accusation was found to be not true. Second, a guilty verdict could result in a requirement of public penance. Such penance could include exile, fines, imprisonment, or other acts aimed at paying for the crime of heresy. A third possibility was reconciliation. In this process, the defendant was forgiven, but only after loss of all property and a jail sentence (at times a long one). The fourth possible outcome was a guilty verdict, after which the accused was delivered to the secular authorities for public execution. The favored method was burning at the stake.

The burnings were staged to attract large crowds and were festive events. When many accused were to be burned the event could last all day. The ritual began with a mass and then a public procession of the guilty heretics. Their sentences were read to the crowd. Although torture was not supposed to be part of the carrying out of the burnings, the secular authorities were free to make the spectacle go quickly or slowly. There were instances in which the condemned were taken from the stake when near death to prolong their pain, and then returned and finally killed.

The ritual of burning at the stake was even applied to those who had died in prison while awaiting trial or who died under torture. In these cases, the tribunal was held and those found guilty were burned in effigy. Although the Spanish Inquisition is defined as lasting into the 16th century but not beyond, instances of condemnation for heresy and burning at the stake continued into the late 18th century, finally ending during the reign of Charles IV (1788–1808).

Tomás de Torquemada

The most infamous figure of the Spanish Inquisition was the Dominican Tomás de Torquemada, who served as an inquisitor from 1483 to 1498 and was the first inquisitor general. Sebastián de Olmedo, historian and chronicler of the day, described Torquemada as "the hammer of heretics, the light of Spain, the savior of his country, the honor of his order."[4]

He was a zealot known for accusing, trying and executing Jews and Muslims in Spain and a supporter of the Alhambra Decree of 1492 mandating the expulsion of all Jews from Spain. Under Torquemada's direction, every Spanish Christian over the age of 14 (for boys) or 12 (for girls) was subject to the oversight and investigation of the Inquisition. The forced conversions of thousands of Jews and Muslims expanded the Inquisition's jurisdiction while keeping those converts under suspicion of the newly-expanded crime of heresy. As grand inquisitor, Torquemada was hated and feared, and knowing this, he traveled with a bodyguard of 300 men. In spite of Church rationale that the extremes of torture and burning at the stake were unusual for the times, the reputation of Torquemada as a fanatical inquisitor has endured. As the ultimate authority and manager of the Spanish Inquisition, he appointed other inquisitors and tribunal officials to work under him, and his power to define the tribunals and their procedures was unlimited.

Even though Torquemada is remembered as the personification of abuses during the Spanish Inquisition, he was a complex figure. He worked to eliminate corruption within the tribunal system and to reduce the incidence of false charges. However, complimenting Torquemada for these reform measures does not offset the realities of the Inquisition and its abuse of its victims. Torquemada enthusiastically supported the use of torture during interrogations and accepted the premise that confessions, even coerced confessions, were adequate evidence for conviction and referral to secular authorities for execution. He labored to improve the workings of the system, but the system itself abused thousands of victims.

As nephew of the well regarded cardinal and theologian Juan de Torquemada, Tomás shared a partial Jewish descent (his grandmother was a Converso). Even so, in his role as a Dominican and inquisitor, he exploited Ferdinand and Isabella's desire to unify Spain under a single religion by encouraging the 1492 mass expulsions of Jews and continuing the work of placing Conversos on trial and having them executed on charges of heresy. The Alhambra Decree, of which Torquemada was a major supporter, expelled Jews on the rationale that

> there are certain bad Christians that judaised and committed apostasy against our Holy Catholic faith, much of it the cause of communications between Jews and Christians. Therefore, in the year 1480, we ordered that the Jews be separated from the cities and towns of our domains and that they be given separate quarters, hoping that by such separation the situation would be remedied. And we ordered that an Inquisition be established in such domains; and in the twelve years it has functioned, the Inquisition has found many guilty persons.... Furthermore, we are informed by the Inquisition and others that the great harm done to the Christians persists, and it continues because of the conversations and communications that they have with the Jews, such Jews trying by whatever manner to subvert our holy Catholic faith and trying to draw faithful Christians away from their beliefs.... All of which then is clear that, on the basis of confessions from such Jews as well as those perverted by them, that it has resulted in great damage and detriment of our holy Catholic faith.... Therefore, with the council and advice of the eminent men and cavaliers of our reign, and of other persons of knowledge and conscience of our Supreme Council, after much deliberation, it is agreed and resolved that all Jews and Jewesses be ordered to leave our kingdoms, and that they never be allowed to return.[5]

As a result of the Inquisition and the Alhambra Decree, a majority of Conversos did leave the country, relocating in North Africa and Eastern Europe. The majority, however, went to Portugal. The Inquisition soon followed them there.

The Portuguese Inquisition

The expulsion of Jews from Spain in 1492 created a mass exodus to other countries, notably Portugal. King João II expelled Jews from Portugal in 1496, four years after Spain issued a similar decree, and in 1497, he decreed the forced conversion of any remaining Jews. Unlike the Spanish Conversos, the Portuguese *Cristãos novos* (New Christians) did not live under suspicion as they did in Spain, and were allowed to retain a separate culture and identity even as Christians within Portuguese society.

Trouble began for the Cristãos novos in 1506 when many were massacred in Lisbon. Although the monarchy forbade exclusionary laws and prevented social discrimination against this group, incidents recurred. In 1531, the Cristãos novos community was blamed for a severe earthquake in Lisbon, renewing new calls for steps against the community by either the monarchy or the Church. João III, who had ascended to the throne in 1521, decided to ask Pope Paul III (1534–49) for a new Inquisition, and in 1536 Paul issued the order.

The first grand inquisitor in Portugal was named by João III. He chose his younger brother, Henry, who later became a cardinal and eventually, the successor king. The Portuguese Inquisition is significant not only because it mirrored the Spanish Inquisition, but also because it exported investigations to many of its colonies. These included Brazil, Cape Verde, and Goa in the Indian colony. In Goa, the themes of anti–Semitism and anti–Islamism were expanded to include new "heretics," crypto–Hindus and crypto–Buddhists, converts from those faiths to Christianity who were accused of continuing to practice their original religion in secret. Investigations of the Portuguese Inquisition also involved accusations of witchcraft, divination, bigamy, and sexual crimes (especially sodomy). The offices of the Inquisition also became involved in censorship of books considered unacceptable or heretical to Catholics.[6]

Inquisition trials continued in Portugal and its colonies until 1821. Many Portuguese Jews had also emigrated to Mexico, where a new Inquisition in the 16th–17th centuries focused on converted Jews from Portugal, as well as on the crime of blasphemy and other forms of immorality.

The Later Inquisition in Spain

As the Inquisition in Spain progressed, it also changed its scope. The Conversos had been forced from Spain from 1492 onward, so the primary objects of the Inquisition no longer could be found in great numbers. The focus of inquisitors shifted to political reformers and Humanists. Although the Inquisition lost its impetus to a large degree after the 15th century, it continued to exist as an institution into the 19th century, and retained its power to hold tribunals and to punish anyone found guilty of a range of sins loosely defined as heresy.

The Conversos who had been at the center of the early Spanish Inquisition may have been as naïve as the Church. By converting to Christianity, Spanish Jews may have assumed that discrimination against them would stop — that as they became integrated into Christian society, the distinction between Christian and Jew would become invisible. Even the sincerely converted, however, quickly discovered that they could not exist in Spain as religiously Christian but of Jewish ancestry. The distinction between Old Christians and New Christians would always keep them apart and prevent full acceptance within Christian Spain. In fact, the act of conversion itself compounded suspicion and distrust among Old Christians.

Even when the Spanish Inquisition was demonstrably abusive toward its victims, the monarchy felt helpless to affect its course, and often did not desire to have any effect. The Inquisition became a racially-motivated initiative against Jews and everyone knew it. Ferdinand, however, had wanted matters to work for him in both ways: punishing those Conversos guilty of heresy, while expecting the remaining Converso community to continue contributing to the Spanish economy. The king could not fail to realize that in openly taking a stand against the racists, he was treading on shaky ground. He did not wish to appear as defender of the Conversos, which would spoil his image as their oppressor and persecutor — the image he had acquired through this sponsorship of the Inquisition — and preferred to avoid direct action against the racists....[7]

This problem prevented Ferdinand from taking any steps to curtail the abuses that occurred under the office of the Spanish Inquisition. He opposed the *limpieza de sangre* (blood guilt) theory that characterized so much of the anti–Converso sentiment in Spain during his reign, even tolerating *limpieza* sentiments held by powerful Christian political interests. He managed to prevent passage of any anti–Converso *limpieza* laws during his lifetime; but after Ferdinand's death in 1516, anti–Converso sentiments accelerated. Statutes were adopted to impose *limpieza* rules on Conversos, even those judged by the Inquisition to be reconciled with the Church. Conversos were not allowed to practice as doctors, druggists, or notaries. In 1522, the Inquisition issued a decree forbidding universities of Salamanca, Valladolid and Toledo to grant any degrees to Conversos.[8]

From this time forward and through to the end of the Spanish Inquisition in the 18th century, the movement served a dual purpose, as a religious and racial movement.

Anti-Semitic Measures of Silicco

The Inquisition did nothing to quell the anti–Semitic feelings among Spanish Christians. If anything, the success of the Inquisition, if measured by its conviction rate, confirmed the belief among Old Christians in a widespread Jewish conspiracy. This sentiment was encouraged in the middle of the 16th century by a Spanish cardinal, Juan Martínez Pedernales, better remembered by the name Siliceo. In 1546, while archbishop of Toledo, Siliceo stirred up anti–Jewish and anti–Converso feelings once again. He announced that in addition to being banned from Spanish military, universities, and medicine, Conversos would not be allowed to enter the priesthood either.

This ruling required approval from the pope, who was reluctant to agree with Siliceo's ruling. Siliceo told the pope that he had copies of numerous letters written between Spanish Conversos and Jews in Constantinople. He claimed that the letters suggested that Spanish Conversos train their children in finance with the goal of stealing wealth from Spanish Christians; oppressing Christians by gaining political office; and entering the priesthood to destroy Christianity from within. The instructions, according to Siliceo, also included the suggestion that Conversos enter the medical field so they could kill Christian patients, and that they feign conversion to gain an advantage over Christians.

Siliceo forwarded copies of these letters to the pope as proof of a world wide Jewish conspiracy, and asked the pope to approve his anti–Converso statute. The obvious forgeries make a point that the continuing anti–Converso sentiment in Spain was more racial than religious, but zealots like Siliceo continued to characterize the Conversos as a direct threat to the Church. Quoting the words of Franciscan Alfonso de Espina nearly 100 years earlier, Siliceo wrote to the pope that Converso doctors "took their offices for no other purpose than killing the Old Christians."[9]

While the extraordinary claims made by Siliceo did not convince Pope Julius III (1550–5) of the need for the *limpieza* statute, they did mark a change in Inquisition focus, away from the search for heretics into a clearly racial theme. In this expanded theme, inquisitors focused on the four primary areas thought to be of interest to Conversos: commerce, politics, medicine and the priesthood. The conspiracy theory was promoted by racists like Siliceo. The transition into a primarily racial movement solidified from Siliceo's time onward. In the post–Ferdinand era the

> Inquisition was essentially a child of the racist movement, and in both its thinking and feeling it tended toward the racist point of view. Under Ferdinand this tendency was curbed, and the Inquisition had to act, at least formally, within the limits of a strictly religious persecution. But under his successors it was given greater freedom ... and in the days of Siliceo its racist language was plain and unmistakable.[10]

The origins of the Spanish Inquisition, that "child of the racist movement," explain only a part of the historical context of the movement. Not only within Spanish society but as part of the larger Inquisition that preceded it, the Spanish Inquisition is most interesting in the degree that it wandered so far from the original religious motivations led by the Church. In practice, the Spanish Inquisition was generated by Ferdinand and Isabella and strictly controlled by them. After the deaths of Torquemada and both monarchs, the Inquisition changed in its zeal and scope. That is the single characteristic that made the Spanish Inquisition unique in the history of Inquisitions before and after this period.

CHAPTER 10

The Spanish Inquisition
After Torquemada

To make a man or woman confess to the crime of false belief—and especially when it is a crime that he or she did not commit—torture is sometimes a practical necessity. Or so the Inquisition discovered, not only to the
sorrow of its victims but also as an object lesson to authoritarian regimes
down through the ages.
— Jonathan Kirsch, *The Grand Inquisitor's Manual*, 2008

Tomás de Torquemada died on September 16, 1498, in Ávila and was followed by several new inquisitors in the years after. Changes also occurred within
the monarchy. Queen Isabella died in 1504 and King Ferdinand in 1516. All of
these events affected the course of the Spanish Inquisition.

The next grand inquisitor was the Dominican Diego de Deza. He distrusted
and disliked Conversos as much as Torquemada. He was known for his zealous approach to the post and for his cruelty to those under suspicion. In 1507,
Pope Julius II (1503–13) ordered Deza to tone down his methods. At the same
time, Deza came under suspicion of enriching himself by taking property of
accused heretics for himself and even of taking advantage of female prisoners
during interrogation. Like his predecessor, Deza was of Jewish descent on his
mother's side, which led his enemies to accuse him of secretly being a practicing Jew. The controversy surrounding Deza and recurring suspicions about his
methods and integrity led to his forced resignation in 1507.

Torquemada had been known for his unyielding hatred of Conversos, but
his reputation was clean. He was not accused of any dishonesty or scandals during his reign as grand inquisitor; in fact, he worked to ensure that inquisitors
were above charges of scandal. After Torquemada's death, the reputation of
various inquisitors and of the Inquisition itself deteriorated as the scope of
investigations expanded.

Diego Rodríguez Lucero was the inquisitor in Cordova between 1499 and

1508. He was also reputed to be zealous and aggressive in persecuting Conversos, including the sister and nephews of Hernando de Talavera, archbishop of Grenada. Talavera, a confidant of Isabella, was also threatened with arrest shortly after Isabella's death. These excesses led to a revolt in 1506 against the Inquisition, and during the chaos prisoners were set free. Lucero fled but was arrested in 1508 and forced to retire.

The Political Aspects of the Inquisition

During this period after Ferdinand and Isabella, it was not certain whether the Inquisition was an office of the monarchy or of the Church. Although there were instances of cooperation between the two, there were also conflicts. Ferdinand and Isabella had willingly initiated the Spanish Inquisition for their own political motives, specifically the unification of Spain under a single government. This required, in their view, a country also unified by a single religion. The persecution of Conversos came about as a result of many political, social and religious pressures on the monarchy. After the deaths of Ferdinand and Isabella, the role of the monarchy was greatly reduced, and two changes occurred. First, the Church took a more active role in the search for heretics as a primary activity of the Inquisition. Second, with the majority of Conversos and Moriscos gone from Spain, the Inquisition was running out of victims, so the scope of investigations and the definition of heretics expanded.

Historian Henry Lea disputes the claims that the Inquisition was primarily instituted and controlled by the monarchy. Lea says this belief was promoted by Catholic scholars to "relieve the Church from the responsibility" for the Inquisition. He suggests that "writers of the faith no longer seek to apologize for the Inquisition and to put forward royal predominance to relieve it from responsibility."[1]

The scholars to who Lea refers usually expressed the opinion that Ferdinand and Isabella were devout Catholics and that the Inquisition was created by them as a form of religious duty. The Spanish Inquisition was quite different from previous Inquisitions because of the political interests that motivated it and also because of its expanded definition of heresy. The persecution of Conversos was motivated by racial distrust and hatred more than by any spiritual interest in eliminating heretics. The thousands of victims who confessed under torture and were as often as not accused of committing crimes of thought or perception rather than overt actions or statements complicated any religious intent and gave way to political, social, economic and cultural motives in Spain at the time. Politically, the monarchs were responding to pressure to rid the country of non–Christians; and even though Conversos were by Church mandate to be treated as full Christians, this mandate was consistently ignored by inquisitors. The Church did little to remedy the situation, convinced that ridding Spain of Conversos and Moriscos achieved the aim of creating a completely Catholic Spain.

In the frequent disputes between the monarchy and the papacy, Spanish rulers wanted to control the Inquisition in many ways, from picking inquisitors to determining how and where tribunals were to be held; at the same time, they sought to identify the Inquisition as a holy office under the Church, operated by Dominican holy men devoutly intent on finding and eradicating heresy against the *Church*, never specifically to find and punish crimes against the *State*. Early on in the history of the Inquisition, the pope discovered that criticism of the monarchy's operations met with strong resistance; and the monarchy discovered that the pope quickly backed down.

An example of the papacy's acquiescence to the monarchy occurred when Sixtus IV forbade establishment of an Inquisition in Aragon. Sixtus strongly criticized the imprisonment, torture, and confiscation of properties taking place in the name of the Church and with the involvement of the Spanish clergy. Nevertheless, when Ferdinand complained strongly about the pope's interest and challenged his criticism, Sixtus immediately withdrew his objections and even issued a contradictory bull approving of the new Inquisition, not only in Aragon, but also in Valencia and Catalonia. The pope also named Tomás de Torquemada as first inquisitor general in the new bull. All of these adjustments in Church policy pleased the monarchs. When successor Pope Innocent VIII recommended allowing appeals of convictions in Spain to the papacy, Ferdinand again raised a challenge, declaring that anyone filing an appeal without *prior* consent from the crown would be put to death and their property confiscated. The papacy again backed down. It was clear to everyone, including Ferdinand and Isabella during the initial phase of the Spanish Inquisition, that the pope would not risk losing the allegiance of the Spanish crown.

Ferdinand and Isabella had clear control over operation of the Inquisition in every regard, even though the Dominican inquisitors also hid behind the veil of holy purpose. Ferdinand was never daunted by the papacy when they challenged him:

> While publicly he swore reverently of papal authority and presented himself as the pope's loyal servant, he actually held the popes in contempt, defied their instructions when they displeased him and vehemently demanded that they be revoked and that the popes do his bidding. He viewed the papacy as a political tool which could be useful to him in attaining his ends, and he could hardly contain his wrath and impatience when it did not live up to his expectations.[2]

The days when popes threatened excommunication of monarchs as a means for controlling their behavior and gaining their obedience were over for the most part, at least during the years of the Spanish Inquisition. The popes of this period never threatened Ferdinand or Isabella or their successors with any direct punishment for defying their authority. The only threat of "further measures"— possibly meaning excommunication — advanced to Ferdinand was made by

Julius II, and Ferdinand replied by threatening the loss of allegiance to the papacy from both Castile and Aragon. The pope retreated from his position, making a political decision to allow Ferdinand to retain state control of the Inquisition as he saw fit.

Once Ferdinand and Isabella had both died, the Inquisition lost not only its high level of activity but its political support as well. The majority of Conversos had left the country or been victimized or silenced and forced underground by the Inquisition by this time, and it was difficult for inquisitors in Spain to maintain their zeal. A change was inevitable. At this point, inquisitors turned their interest from Conversos to other heretics in Spain.

Lutherans as New Targets

Conversos remained under suspicion, believed to be importing anti–Christian ideas to Spain, even when they were no longer in Spain. For example, by the 1520s, Spanish authorities thought that many Conversos who had left the country were sending Lutheran literature into the country. The spread of the Reformation in Europe was a major problem not only for the Church, but specifically for the Inquisition. Not only was Lutheranism a new form of heresy; it was spreading rapidly and was widely popular.

Luther's defiance of the Church and its authority had by this time begun a widespread movement in parts of Europe, and so the Spanish Inquisition turned its attention to a different brand of heresy. This did not mean Conversos were forgotten; only that they were believed to be the instigators of the Reformation and its influence in Spain.

Literacy itself, augmented by the widespread capability of spreading printed material, spelled doom for the Inquisition. The Church had always relied on its control of information to maintain power. For both the Spanish monarchy and its tribunals of inquisitors, new points of view and religious alternatives were finding their way into the country. Meanwhile, the question had come up: Was the Inquisition still necessary? By this time the need to exist had become the Inquisition's chief motive. As inquisitors were forced to expand their self-justification, their targets had to be expanded as well. The lack of an easily recognizable target had reduced the popularity of the Spanish Inquisition. It became apparent that spiritual authority (once assumed, as long as inquisitors were focused on Conversos) was in question. As the availability of information outside of Church control increased, the authority of the Inquisition decreased.

A problem for Spanish authorities was that printing presses had been around for more than 70 years by the 1520s and literature was easily and cheaply mass-produced. No longer did the Church have the corner on production of books or on literacy. The spread of printing was accompanied by a spread in literacy, and the Church monopoly on information unraveled. The suspicion about Lutheran literature being smuggled into Spain was not altogether unfounded. Many ships arriving in Valencia and other ports were found to include as cargo barrels of Lutheran literature. Crews were arrested and cargo (along with the ships themselves) was burned. Literature deemed to be subversive was not limited to Lutheran theology. In 1542, inquisitors uncovered a plan to import several hundred copies of a book published in Antwerp, called *The Institution of the Christian Religion* by Francisco de Encinas (using the pen name Francisco de Elao), a Spanish Protestant. This book consisted mainly of translations of Calvin's *Catechism* and Luther's *A Treatise on Christian Liberty*. Encinas also published the first complete Spanish edition of the New Testament. Encinas never returned to Spain; he had hoped with Spanish-language works that Spanish Christians would embrace the evangelical movement. The office of the Inquisition was too powerful, however, and the Protestant movement would not take hold there. Spain remained a primarily Catholic country.

The role of literacy in dispelling long-held dependence on the Church was only one of many factors that reduced Church power over time. It had been true in the past that the majority of citizens were entirely dependent on the Church for education, spiritual guidance and even salvation. But as literacy spread, so did a growing sense of nationalism and individual identity. This conflicted with the Church's traditional position that "identity" for Christians meant accepting (without question) the doctrine of the Church. The fact that heretical movements continually arose was beyond the understanding of many Church leaders. Why would anyone risk salvation and question what the Church told them? The Spanish Inquisition defined the changing landscape in all of Europe and the transition was stronger in Spain than elsewhere. Just as people began objecting to Church corruption, materialism and abuse of power, the Inquisition was attempting to *increase* its hold over people. It is ironic that one of the guiding forces behind the Spanish Inquisition was the desire by the monarchy to unify Spain as a single country with a single religion. It was the sense of nationalism that gave citizens an alternative identity to that of "Christian" within Europe. The alternatives included not only nationalistic stirrings brought on by the increasing power of monarchs, but the Reformation led by notable personalities like Luther and Calvin and the defiance of monarchs and their attitude toward the Church. It was no longer fair to assume that the Church held the last word in either temporal or spiritual matters.

Illuminism in Spain

During the same period, Desiderius Erasmus Roterodamus (born Gerrit Gerritszoon) began a movement that was a much greater threat to the Catholic

Church and of greater interest to the Inquisition. Erasmus was a Dutch Catholic theologian and prolific scholar. He had many disputes with Luther, but he also criticized the Church, especially for abuses by the clergy. He also believed that reform could occur from within the Church rather than through Reformation movements. He had first entered the priesthood as an Augustinian canon, but soon received from Pope Leo X (1513–21) dispensation to pursue his writing.

He believed that men had free will, an idea that Lutherans disputed. But he also believed that the Church needed to relax its strict dogmatic beliefs, which he thought were superstitious. Erasmus favored a faith based strictly on the Gospels and less on the power of the papacy and Church hierarchy. This Humanist theory is variously called Erasmism and Illuminism.

Under the theory of Illuminism, believers claim to develop individual spiritual enlightenment. The fact that this blessing came *outside* of the Church and apart from the control of the Catholic priesthood made it an especially alarming challenge to Church authority. The followers of this movement were called the *Illuminati*, a name that today tends to signify a conspiratorial or secret group, especially a shadow government wielding the real power behind the current ruler of a country. However, when related to Erasmus, the term refers to enlightened spirituality. Erasmus has been called "Prince of the Humanists" and "the crowning glory of the Christian humanists."[3]

Erasmus published a book entitled *Enchiridion* on the topic of spiritual Christianity and it was translated into Spanish by 1525. This book was widely read and its ideas accepted by intellectuals but not by the clergy. In 1527, Alfonso Manrique, grand inquisitor and archbishop of Seville, convened a commission in Valladolid to determine whether Erasmus' book was a danger to the faith. Manrique, who was sympathetic to Erasmus, hoped the commission would settle the question. The commission did not come to any conclusions, so the publications promoting Erasmus' ideas continued to spread throughout Spain.

Although the question remained unsettled, Spanish clergy and inquisitors were intent on bringing Erasmus' followers to trial. The fervor for persecution was never as strong as it had been against Conversos, but even so, the Inquisition needed fresh victims. Attention turned to the Humanist tendencies of Erasmus and also to the followers of Illuminism. Like Erasmus, followers of this idea believed that the Church had become too strict in its beliefs. However, while many Catholics of the day confused Erasmus' followers with Illuminists, they were not the same. Erasmus desired reform from inside the Church, and Illuminism rejected Church authority. The new focus of the Spanish Inquisition became the Illuminist movement.

As one branch of Illuminism, the *Alumbrados* (Spanish for "The Illuminated") believed they were divinely inspired by the Gospels and the love of God, placing them *above* the authority of the Church and the pope (and the Inquisition). Ignatius of Loyola, noted Catholic scholar and founder of the Society of Jesus (the Jesuits), was brought in front of an inquisitorial panel in 1527 and charged with being sympathetic to the Alumbrados. He was released with a warning. Others were not so fortunate, although in comparison to the Conversos, relatively few Alumbrados were executed. Many received lengthy prison sentences or were given penances.

To the Inquisition, distinctions between Erasmists and Illuminists were not important. Both were part of a disturbing trend away from strict Catholic loyalty to the pope, and toward a humanist ideal of free thought. Because the Inquisition continued to arrest and try anyone opposed to strict adherence to Catholic principles, many humanists moved to Italy where they were freer to practice their beliefs and express their ideas. This remained true until later in the 16th century when the Roman Inquisition began cracking down on religious freedom and anti–Church expression.

The Inquisition was most active against Protestants in the 1550s and 1560s. In 1558, inquisitors in Valladolid and Seville arrested many accused of practicing Lutheranism or sympathizing with the movement. Arrests included many members of the clergy and nobility. In some instances, simply failing to take a position against Protestants was reason enough for arrest. Bartolomé Carranza, archbishop of Toledo, a well-respected scholar and Dominican, was criticized by inquisitors and arrested in 1559 for not naming names of Lutherans who had confided in him (this was viewed as not only a sin, but specifically a crime). Carranza had also published a catechism containing statements the inquisitors did not like. For example, the book included recommendations to clergy for resisting bad advice. The Inquisition was intent on prosecution and did not appreciate advice aimed at avoiding it. In an atmosphere where inquisitors suspected Lutherans of being everywhere, Carranza was under suspicion as a heretic at worst, or of committing serious errors at least.

Carranza challenged the jurisdiction of inquisitors, stating that because he was an archbishop, only the pope had the right to pass judgment on him. Pope Pius IV (1559–65) agreed and demand that inquisitors transfer the archbishop to Rome for trial. The matter turned into a political crisis when King Philip II (1556–98) said the pope should stay out of Spanish affairs, even claiming that matters of heresy belonged within Spain and were under the jurisdiction of the Spanish Inquisition and not the papacy. The controversy, one of the first times a ruler had directly defied the pope, continued until 1567, when Pius IV's successor Pope Pius V (1566–72) threatened to excommunicate not only the king but the entire kingdom. Philip finally transferred Carranza to Rome where a lengthy trial was held, lasting nine years. In 1576, after being imprisoned for over 17 years, Carranza was released with a warning to amend his errors. He died a few weeks later.

The year 1559, when Carranza had first been accused and arrested, was a turning point in the history of the Spanish Inquisition. Arrests were of such volume that the prisons were quickly filled and there were not enough inquisitors to hold tribunals. On May 21, 1559, fourteen accused heretics were sentenced to death, including some already dead who were exhumed and their remains burned at the stake. In Seville on September 24 of the same year, more than one hundred more were condemned, with twenty-one receiving death penalties. In December 1560, seventeen more were burned at the stake. Most of the condemned in these trials were from the clergy and nobility. Their heresy was being Protestant, which inquisitors easily defined as a form of "error" or being knowingly heretical. An outcome of this sudden inquisitorial fervor against Lutherans was the beginning of anti–Inquisition expression. Pamphlets and books appeared around Europe protesting the punishments of Lutherans in Spain. After 1560, the instances of trials of Lutherans and other Protestants died away.

A distinction was not always made during this late period between Lutherans and Illuminists. Many were accused of being both, and both were considered equally suspicious in the minds of inquisitors. The Illuminist movement, influenced largely by Erasmus and Humanist ideas, moved from Spain into France by the early 17th century under the name *Illuminés* and later to the United Kingdom where they were known as "French Prophets."

The Spanish Witch Hunts

During the same period as the late Inquisition, the infamous Great Witch Hunt was under way in other parts of Europe, notably in Germany and France. This hunt also moved to Spain briefly and many accused witches were victims of the late Spanish Inquisition.

The witch hysteria was not as severe in Spain as it was elsewhere. Spanish inquisitors had their hands full with Conversos and then Lutherans and Illuminists. In 1525, sorcerers were brought to tribunals and accused of killing Christian children, poisoning others with soup made from toads and children's hearts, and kissing black cats. A tribunal in the Roncesvalles region employed experts to examine the left eye of those accused, to find the devil's mark left on the guilty. A conflict arose between inquisitors, who claimed sole jurisdiction over matters of witchcraft as a form of heresy, and the Council of Navarre, which wanted to remove witchcraft as a crime within the jurisdiction of inquisitors. The following year, a mixed commission met in Granada and determined that the inquisitors had the sole task of trying witches. Even so, the issue remained in conflict and in many parts of Spain, secular authorities challenged the inquisitors' right to try witches or to define witchcraft as a form of heresy. In Aragon, secular authorities defined inquisitors' jurisdiction as limited solely to matters of heresy. Inquisitors claimed the limitation did not extend to witches; they cited their rights under emergency procedures (*judicio sumarísimo*) to hold trials and noted that the procedure did not allow any appeals. By the time local magistrates tried to intervene, the accused witches had often already been tried, convicted and executed.

The question of whether secular authorities would have been more or less harsh cannot be answered. Execution of witches was rare in Spain and some secular judges criticized inquisitors for their leniency. However, if inquisitors interpreted charges of witchcraft as a form of heresy, sentences were likely to be more severe. The confusion as to how to treat accused witches under the Inquisition was somewhat resolved in 1530.

That year, Pedro Ciruelo, inquisitor in Saragossa and a professor in the city of Alcalá, wrote guidelines used by other inquisitors in the treatment of accused witches. Acknowledging that some practices in the realm of witchcraft involved pacts with the devil, he urged inquisitors to be tolerant of superstitious behavior among the accused. From this point forward, a majority of inquisitors appear to have favored a more lenient treatment of witches, with punishments seldom including death sentences. In 1537, the Supreme Council of the Inquisition (*Suprema*) published more formal guidelines. Before an individual could be charged with witchcraft, a series of facts had to be investigated. Had anyone died or disappeared? Were harvests destroyed? Were any other suspicious events (such as unexplained diseases) attributed to the accused person?

Jurist Fernando de Valdéz was appointed grand inquisitor in 1547 and the trend toward leniency continued. He believed confessions were being coerced and ruled that accused witches should simply be released and sent home. In 1550, an inquisitor in Barcelona named Sarmiento lost his position for sentencing six witches to death with no proof of a crime. Other verdicts were revoked in the following years, a sign that the Spanish Inquisition had lost its impetus and that the once undisputed office (with full support of the monarchy) was gradually losing out.

Even in cases where convictions were passed down, death sentences were rare. Lighter sentences were more likely and the extremes seen elsewhere in Europe never occurred in Spain when it came to the trials of witches. For example, in 1664, four women in Cordova were sentenced as magicians. They were "paraded, riding on mules, naked to the waist and wearing caps of infamy; and the spectators pelted them with onions."[4]

Closely associated with witchcraft and sorcery was astrology, a practice deemed heretical by inquisitors (even though many popes had their own astrologers in their employ at various times). The *Index Librorum Prohibitorum* (Index of Prohibited Books) published in 1559 under the direction of Pope Paul IV (1555–9) included over 550 authors and their works (including Erasmus), and books of astrology or other books assumed to predict the future were high on the list of banned texts. In some isolated cases, inquisitors brought astrologers before their tribunals. In 1585, Pope Sixtus V (1585–90) issued a bull, *Coeli et terræ*, calling astrology a form of superstition and calling on inquisitors to suppress it.

The End of the Spanish Inquisition

As inquisitors ran out of Conversos and other heretics, they sought new subjects. Even more obscure than witchcraft, sorcery, magic, and astrology was the accusation that "unseemly talk" (*palabras deshonestas*) was punishable as heresy. The stern Dominicans, unaccustomed to any challenge of their authority, expanded the definition of punishable offenses and a debate arose over the question of critical thought and speech. Was this behavior the result of ignorance about dogma, or a deliberate form of heresy? Such generalized wrongs as blasphemy or failing to respect the Ten Commandments were viewed as heresy even among many peasants who did not even know the definition of the sacraments and were barely familiar with rites of the Church.

"Unseemly talk" included blasphemy, gossip, and even jokes about the faith or members of the clergy. Most of those found guilty were given warnings and penance, meaning reciting prayers or paying light fines. Many examples of unseemly talk were quite innocent. One person summoned before the tribunal was Francisco Martínez Berralo of Ocaña, who had been heard saying that if a particular person died and went to heaven, his donkey would accompany him, complete with harness. He was summoned before the Toledo inquisitorial tribunal in 1555 and given a stern warning about such utterances concerning the afterlife.[5]

Secular challenges to the Inquisition led to its gradual decline. By the 1570s, the primary goal of the Spanish Inquisition — removal of all Jews from Spain — had been more or less met. Efforts to expand the tribunals to witches and other heretics never caught on. Yet the danger to anyone speaking against the Church or questioning its dogma remained. Inquisitors now turned their eye on fellow clergymen and effectively prevented any and all dissent or political opposition to the authority of the Church. The Spanish monarchy continued to rely on the Inquisition as a means for preventing any political dissent, so the tribunals served a dual purpose as they had from their beginnings. Torture became rarer during interrogations, and the infrequent cases of execution for heresy, which had once been public spectacles, became more discreet and took place quietly without much publicity.

As a state institution, the Inquisition remained a useful tool of the Spanish monarchy for repressing dissent and keeping political thought under wraps. The idea of eliminating the Inquisition as a permanent state institution did not come from any internal reform, but from Napoleon Bonaparte. In 1808, his brother Joseph was forced to leave Madrid. When Napoleon's *Grand Armée* invaded Spain to restore his brother to the throne, he signed several decrees doing away with many Spanish institutions—including the office of the Inquisition. This presented a dilemma for the Spanish elite, who wanted independence but had never seriously thought the Inquisition could be undone.

Under a new constitution drawn up by the Cortes (national assembly) in

Cádiz in 1813, Spain was reorganized with a new parliament and the monarchy was left with only limited powers. The new constitution also limited the power of the nobility and the Church and ended the Inquisition. Jurisdiction on matters of religion was given to bishops as it had been in medieval times. Secular courts were granted the power to punish heretics, so even with elimination of the Inquisition, procedures were left in place for ecclesiastical courts to denounce heretics and refer them to secular courts for punishment. The most significant change, even with procedures left in place to punish heretics, was that the power to investigate such charges was taken from inquisitors and given to bishops.

In 1814, when King Ferdinand VII was returned to the throne, the Inquisition was reinstated. The king called the Inquisition the most effective office for ensuring domestic peace. Gone were Conversos and witches; the "new" Inquisition focused on Freemasonry as the latest type of heresy. This reinstated office did not last long. In 1820, the liberals again took control and put the constitution back in place.

When Ferdinand VII again took back control of the country, he recognized the unpopularity of the Inquisition and did not try to reinstitute it. In its place he put a so-called series of Faith Commissions (*Juntas da fé*) in each diocese, presided over by local bishops. These commissions generally had little legal or enforcement power. These offices were disbanded once and for all after the death of Ferdinand VII, on July 15, 1834, by the regent María-Cristina. The Spanish writer Mariano José de Larra wrote the epitaph for the period: "Here lies the Inquisition, the daughter of faith and fanaticism. She died of old age."[6]

Stage Three:
The Reformation and
the Roman Inquisition

CHAPTER 11

Martin Luther

Reason is the greatest enemy that faith has; it never comes to the aid of spiritual things, but — more frequently than not — struggles against the Divine Word, treating with contempt all that emanates from God.

— Martin Luther, *Table Talk* (from Preserved Smith, *Luther's Table Talk: A Critical Study*, 1907)

The third stage of the Inquisition was the *Roman* Inquisition, which was initiated to keep the rapidly expanding Reformation movement out of Italy. The Reformation began with defiance of the Church and the papacy on the part of a priest, teacher and Augustinian monk, Martin Luther.

The Reformation turned into a completely new form of Christianity, although it originated as a dispute within the Catholic Church over well-known corruption and abuse. As a change in political, social, and cultural attitudes the mood of reform began in the 15th century with the teachings of Wyclif and Hus, two figures recognized as the earliest philosophical leaders of the movement that successfully challenged Church supremacy.

The Legacy of Wyclif and Hus

The Church believed that it settled the debate over the teachings of Wyclif and Hus with its condemnation of both men. Wyclif had died in 1384, but even after death the Church believed it was necessary to exhume his remains and burn them at the stake. Hus was summoned before the Council of Constance and given assurances that he would not be harmed. Going back on this promise, the Council ordered a trial for heresy, and Hus was burned at the stake.

The legacy of Wyclif and Hus reminds us that Martin Luther's positions were part of an evolving challenge to the Church and the papacy. Wyclif has been called "The Morning Star of the Reformation," and his teachings led to many later expansions of his initial challenges, especially concerning corrup-

tion in the clergy and the papacy. At the Council of Constance, held from 1414
to 1418, the condemnation, trial and execution of Hus was only one of the
significant outcomes. At the same gathering, the Church restated and even
expanded its claim to dominance over all things on earth, including ruling monarchs. In its session of April 6, 1415, the Council issued the *Hæc sancta*, declaring that because the Council was

> legitimately assembled in the holy Spirit, constituting a general council and
> representing the Catholic church militant, it has power immediately from Christ;
> and that everyone of whatever state or dignity, even papal, is bound to obey it in
> those matters which pertain to the faith, the eradication of the said schism and the
> general reform of the said church of God in head and members.[1]

Yet the idea that the Council and the Church were endowed with such
sweeping powers was quickly going out of style. At this period, the advent of
enlightenment across European society was evolving into a direct challenge to
the power of the Church. Besides the stirrings of the Reformation, the Humanism movement was under way and for the first time, people were able to buy
and read books, no longer having to rely on priests and bishops for information or education. These forces made the Reformation inevitable. Even those
(including Luther) who preferred reforming the Church from within were fighting a losing battle.

During this early period of Reformation, the Inquisition was a useful office
for quelling dissent. As one of many definitions of heresy, *any* statement of dissent was punishable by death. Even pointing out Church corruption in matters such as selling indulgences and other abuses was not tolerated. Early
Reformation leaders were condemned as heretics within the prevailing rules of
the Church and tribunal authority of the Inquisition.

The whole matter of indulgences was devised by Pope Clement VI (1342–52),
who wrote in his bull *Unigenitus* that God wished that deserving persons

> might have an infinite treasure, and those who avail themselves thereof are made
> partakers of God's friendship. Now this treasure is not hidden in a napkin or
> buried in a field, but he entrusted it to be healthfully dispensed — through blessed
> Peter, bearer of Heaven's keys, and his successors as vicars on earth — to the faith-
> ful, for fitting and reasonable causes, now for total, now for partial remission of
> punishment due for temporal sins ... and to be applied in mercy to them that are
> truly penitent and have confessed.[2]

This mandate led to many abuses among the clergy, enriching themselves
and the papacy by selling forgiveness, and ultimately providing the fuel for
Luther's primary objections. The Reformation became a movement starting
from Luther's desire for the Church to recognize and correct the excesses
involved with selling indulgences. Luther's "crime" was not based on errors of
theology as had been the case when Dominicans debated Cathars. Now the
Church attacked dissenters and the Inquisition became an institution to control utterances and criticism, even when the criticism was completely justified

by the facts. As with old-style heretics disputing the doctrine of the Church, critics like Luther came under threat of punishment to include condemnation, excommunication and even death.

The dispute between the Church and Reformation leaders was not a matter limited to theology, by any means. As Reformation leaders pointed out, the Church had become corrupt after centuries of control over the population and the wealth the Church had acquired for itself. The clergy, living in palaces and enjoying a lavish lifestyle far better than that of the average citizen, became a symbol of this corruption. The moral attitudes among the same clergy, many of whom had live-in mistresses and concubines and who raised fortunes for themselves, were insensitive to the growing dissatisfaction with this situation. The Church, rather than trying to reform itself, chose instead to silence dissenters, using the Inquisition as its primary enforcement arm.

The Reformation was made possible by the growing distance between the Church and the people, and was accelerated by the economic and social changes that developed after the Black Plague. With such massive loss of life throughout Europe, skilled labor was at a shortage and people suddenly had their own economic power outside of the rights or privileges granted to them by the Church. The Black Plague demonstrated, in fact, how out of touch the Church was with society. Not only was the pope powerless to stop the widespread pestilence; society was beginning to see that papal infallibility and supreme power had no valid basis. The revolution in religious thought was not limited to the Reformation, although the movement was the most effective expression of the changing economic and social change of the day. The revolution in thought was also occurring in the economic changes of the day, with increased rights of workers, improved and expanded competition for business, growing literacy and education among common citizens, and the removal of restrictions on commerce throughout Europe. In these sweeping changes, the Church with its medieval point of view and continued reliance on superstitions was left behind.

This was the legacy of Wyclif and Hus. In their time, they promoted dialogue not so much about matters of theology as the political position of the Church. Wyclif challenged the Church's right to hold temporal power, and because he was widely published, his ideas were not limited to the Oxford campus where he taught, but spread quickly throughout Europe. Predictably, the claim led to charges of blasphemy and heresy and after his death, Wyclif's books (and his remains) were burned in an effort to rid the world of his ideas. His followers, the Lollards, were punished in later years by the Inquisition and many were condemned and burned at the stake. Hus, who was a follower of Wyclif, spoke against selling of indulgences and also proposed that the mass be given in both Latin and the language of the congregation. These revolutionary ideas led to his condemnation as well. But killing the people speaking these thoughts and even burning their writings did not silence their voices. With public dissemination of books possible for the first time, new ideas and challenges were conveyed easily to many people and the Church could not control or ban the ideas that Wyclif, Hus and others shared. Even the most effective weapons of the Church, excommunication, Inquisition, and execution, could not silence the voices of change.

The movement failed to die off even with burning of books and condemnation of heretics. In fact, the demand for reform and greater freedom only expanded over time. The Church used the Inquisition to hold down the voice of dissent to a degree, at least until the social revolution that was started by Martin Luther.

Luther's Life

Luther originally wanted to study law, but quite suddenly he changed his mind and decided to enter the monastery and join the Augustinian order. He sold his books and property, dropped out of school, and to his father's dismay, took his vows in 1506. He was ordained the following year.

He was sent to the newly founded University of Wittenberg to teach theology and moral philosophy. In 1510, Luther traveled to Rome to further his theological studies. But outside of his academic life, Luther discovered that the clergy in Rome were living a life of leisure and worldly pleasures, far from the ideals of poverty and piety Luther had envisioned for himself as a devout Catholic. Cynicism and lack of concern with religious matters were the status quo among the Roman clergy. For example, the term "good Christian" (*buon Christiano*) was used by Roman priests to refer to a person as a fool. Disillusioned, Luther returned to Wittenberg.

A visit to that city by papal emissary and Dominican friar Johann Tetzel changed Luther completely. Tetzel was there to sell indulgences. He was a shameless salesman offering salvation to those willing to pay for forgiveness of their sins, no matter how serious. Tetzel cited authority granted directly by the pope for forgiveness in return for cash. Luther wrote of Tetzel and his message as both extreme and offensive: "He had grace and power from the Pope to offer forgiveness even if someone had slept with the Holy Virgin Mother of God, as long as a contribution would be put into the coffer."[3]

Luther also was offended by Tetzel's claim that even Saint Peter, if he were present, would have no greater power than he (Tetzel) had, claiming in addition that he had saved more souls that Peter. Tetzel even boasted that if someone paid for a soul currently in purgatory, that soul would be released the moment the coin was placed into the coffer. Tetzel preached that God was bound by acts of the pope. So if the pope forgave a sin, God had to forgive it as well. His argument was that God had delegated his powers to the pope and no longer held them Himself; all divine power now rested in the papacy. Anyone who disputed or challenged this claim, Tetzel pointed out, was at risk of being brought before the Inquisition and charged with heresy. Even more radical was Tetzel's claim that a payment of cash was all that was needed for forgiveness of sins, and that there was no additional need for remorse or penance. He stated that indulgences could be paid for forgiveness of *future* sins as well as for past sins.[4]

According to Luther, one event demonstrated how outrageous it was to sell indulgences; the ironic outcome of the incident is worth noting. A nobleman, Luther wrote, was intrigued with the concept of forgiveness for future sins, and asked Tetzel if he could be given a letter of indulgence. Tetzel replied that this was possible, but only if payment were made immediately. The nobleman paid a large sum and received the letter complete with Tetzel's seal. But when Tetzel left the area on his way home, the same nobleman attacked him, beat him, and took all of his cash. He told Tetzel that this was his future sin, for which he had bought forgiveness. The local duke, upon seeing the evidence, decided not to press charges against the nobleman, who under the law was blameless and had been forgiven in advance.[5]

Whether the story was true or anecdotal is not important; it made Luther's point. His exposure to Tetzel was the last straw, and he published a complaint about the selling of indulgences. He wrote his *Disputation of Martin Luther on the Power and Efficacy of Indulgences*, which has become better known as the document that started the Reformation, Luther's *95 Theses*. The ideas in Luther's dissertation were intended as the starting point for internal reform, and not as a confrontation or challenge to the Church. He sent this document in a letter of October 31, 1517, to Albrecht, archbishop of Mainz and Magdeburg, and to Wittenberg's own bishop, Hieronymus Scultetus.

Luther also took the dramatic step of posting his *95 Theses* on the door of the Wittenberg church-castle; this was done at high noon on October 31, 1517, a day celebrated in Germany as the birth of the Reformation. As he posted his *95 Theses*, Luther invited public discussion of his points. Although no one showed up to have the discussion, copies of the *95 Theses* were made and widely distributed within a matter of weeks. In those times, there were no formalized book sellers and the method of distribution was hand to hand.

The *95 Theses* was a direct retort to the practice of granting indulgences, and specifically refuted the claims made by Tetzel. Among the most controversial of Luther's *95 Theses* were:

6. The pope has no power to remit any guilt, except by declaring and warranting it to have been remitted by God....

10. Those priests act unlearnedly and wrongly, who, in the case of the dying, reserve the canonical penances for purgatory.

13. The dying pay all penalties by death, and are already dead to the canon laws, and are by right relieved from them.

21. ... those preachers of indulgences are in error who say that, by the indulgences of the pope, a man is loosed and saved from all punishment.

28. It is certain that when the money rattles in the chest, avarice and gain may be increased, but the suffrage of the Church depends on the will of God alone.

32. Those who believe that, through letters of pardon, they are made sure of their own salvation, will be eternally damned along with their teachers.

35. They preach no Christian doctrine, who teach that contrition is not necessary for those who buy souls out of purgatory, or buy confessional licenses.

37. Every true Christian, whether living or dead, has a share in all the benefits of Christ and of the Church, given him by God, even without letters of pardon.

45. ... he who sees anyone in need and, passing him by, gives money for pardons, is not purchasing for himself the indulgence of the pope, but the anger of God.

48. ... the pope, in granting pardons, has both more need and more desire that devout prayer should be made for him, than that money should be readily paid.

52. Vain is the hope of salvation through letters of pardon, even if a commissary — nay, the pope himself — were to pledge his own soul for them.

66. The treasures of indulgences are nets, wherewith they now fish for the riches of men.

75. To think that papal pardons have such power that they could absolve a man even if — by an impossibility — he had violated the Mother of God, is madness.

77. The saying that, even if St. Peter were now pope, he could grant no greater grace, is blasphemy against St. Peter and the pope.

82. ... Why does not the pope empty purgatory for the sake of most holy charity ... if he redeems an infinite number of souls for the sake of that most fatal thing, money, to be spent on building a basilica ...? [the reference was to Pope Leo X raising money to build St. Peter's Basilica through the sale of indulgences]

86. ... Why does not the pope, whose riches are at this day more ample than those of the wealthiest of the wealthy, build the one Basilica of St. Peter with his own money, rather than with that of poor believers?[6]

The *95 Theses* led to the Reformation, but they were not originally intended as an attack on the Church or on the papacy, but only as a condemnation of the abuses done in the Church's name through selling of indulgences. But the debate over this publication represented a turning point. Not only did publication of the *95 Theses* begin the Reformation in earnest; it also marked the moment when overt dissent from the Church was finally possible without immediate arrest and trial. The threat of the Inquisition was certainly a possibility and Luther, thinking his publication would result in a movement within the Church to right the wrongs he highlighted, probably also realized that he was in danger, especially as the papacy and clergy responded to his words.

The entire document was deemed blasphemous because it questioned the practice of indulgences and laid blame squarely on the pope. Leo X (1513–21) was an extravagant and worldly pope whose nepotism and excessive use of indulgences were well known. But the direct challenge, especially accusing the pope of using money raised in the manner of Tetzel, was not acceptable and made Luther guilty, in the eyes of the Church, of both blasphemy and heresy.

Debate Between Luther and Church Officials

Clerical reaction throughout Germany, including among monastic orders and especially Dominicans, was almost universally negative. Luther had at first been deeply troubled by the widespread negative response. Predictably, the Dominican Tetzel was among the major writers against Luther. However, Tetzel and other critics could cite no examples of where Luther had erred in his claims; nor could they cite support for indulgences in Scripture or canonical law. Critics attempted to dispute Luther by citing papal infallibility, but this principle itself was being debated within the Church at the time, so this was an unconvincing argument.

Luther had three years between publication and response from the pope to judge how the rest of the clergy reacted to his complaints. During this time, he overcame his initial fears about possible arrest and punishment. He began preaching and writing and found his voice, in the process gathering a growing number of supporters to his cause. He argued against the concept of papal authority and said he had made no heretical statements. He had hoped during these three years to receive a favorable response from the pope so that dialogue and reform could be undertaken. This was not to be.

Later gave one of his most important sermons in 1518 while addressing an assembly of Augustinian monks at Heidelberg. Several of the monks in attendance were impressed with Luther's arguments and ended up working later as reformers on their own. Not aware of the growing movement in favor of Luther, the pope took three years to reply in the mistaken belief that if ignored, the matter would die away on its own. Taking a quasi-inquisitorial approach, Leo appointed a commission to investigate Luther's theses in March 1518. The leader of this commission was a Dominican and professor of theology named Silvester Mazzolini. Within a few months, the commission concluded that Luther "was an ignorant and blasphemous arch-heretic." Luther, now emboldened by public support, responded by advising Mazzolini not to make himself more ridiculous by writing books.[7]

This was another example of a bold departure from the tradition of the clergy, known for its obedience to the pope and to his commissions. The next step was predictable. On August 7, 1518, Luther was summoned to Rome and ordered to appear within 60 days to recant and admit his errors. On August 23, the pope ordered Frederick III, elector of Saxony (known as Frederick the Wise), to detain Luther and turn him over to the local papal legate. The pope in this correspondence referred to Luther as a "child of the Devil." However, Frederick supported Luther and arranged a meeting for him with the papal legate with assurances of a safe return.

The meeting took place between Luther and the legate, Cardinal Cajetan, on October 12–14. The cardinal promised his friendship to Luther but demanded a retraction of Luther's errors, along with unquestioning submission to the pope. Luther refused, stating that he was required to obey God and not man. The cardinal threatened excommunication; the meeting ended with the cardinal refusing to have any further discussions with that "deep-eyed German beast filled with strange speculations."[8]

It was clear to Luther that the promised safe passage was doubtful, so he arranged an escape from the castle with the aid of friends, leaving on October 20. Luther wrote to the pope on November 28 asking for a general council and hoping to avoid excommunication. He expressed a fear to friends that Pope Leo X was the Anti-Christ. By now he realized that the Church was not interested in reform, only obedience.

In 1519, the pope sent his nuncio, Karl von Miltitz, to meet with Frederick III and also to negotiate directly with Luther. Miltitz met with Luther and admitted that much of the blame for the dispute belonged to Tetzel (by now deceased). On Miltitz' suggestion, Luther wrote to Leo X on March 3, 1519, expressing humility and citing devotion to the Church. He also, however, refused to retract his beliefs.

Knowing a bull of excommunication was going to be issued, Luther concluded that the papacy itself was an anti–Christian institution and even referred to papal power as a stronghold of Satan. In his works "Address to the German Nobility," "Babylonian Captivity of the Church," and "Freedom of a Christian Man," all published early in 1520, Luther severely criticized the papacy, often using incendiary language. He set down many ideas that formed the central concepts of the Reformation to follow. He preached that Christians could communicate directly with God, questioning the need for the pope and for priests. Clearly, such questioning was an act of heresy. By denying the exclusive privilege of priests to mediate between humankind and God, Luther aggressively attacked the very assumption that priests were necessary in the practice of Christianity.

Response of Pope Leo X

There was no doubt on the part of Pope Leo X that Luther was a heretic and that his writings and statements after publication of the *95 Theses* were evidence of the growing problem. Luther was not quietly fading away but gathering support and becoming even more bold. The state of the papacy and of the Church in 1520 is obvious in its approval of Tetzel's extraordinary claims and shameless money-raising efforts, but disapproval of Luther's challenges to Tetzel. Within three years from the posting of the *95 Theses* on the door of the church in Wittenberg, the pope reacted. On June 15, 1520, he published his bull of excommunication, *Exsurge Domine* (Arise O Lord), also entitled "Condemning the Errors of Martin Luther."

Referring to Luther's dissent and to past Inquisitions (including tribunals against witches and other heretics) the pope noted that Germans

> have always been the bitterest opponents of heresies, as witnessed by those commendable constitutions of the German emperors in behalf of the Church's independence, freedom, and the expulsion and extermination of all heretics from Germany. Those constitutions formerly issued, and then confirmed by our predecessors, were issued under the greatest penalties even of loss of lands and dominions against anyone sheltering or not expelling them. If they were observed today both we and they would obviously be free of this disturbance.[9]

Leo then summarizes Luther's arguments and follows with a very clear denial of each and every point Luther raised, closing the door to further discussion or negotiation and expressing no interest in reforming any Church practices. Leo wrote:

> No one of sound mind is ignorant how destructive, pernicious, scandalous, and seductive to pious and simple minds these various errors are, how opposed they are to all charity and reverence for the holy Roman Church who is the mother of all the faithful and teacher of the faith; how destructive they are of the vigor of ecclesiastical discipline, namely obedience.... [W]e condemn, reprobate, and reject completely each of these theses or errors as either heretical, scandalous, false, offensive to pious ears or seductive of simple minds, and against Catholic truth. By listing them, we decree and declare that all the faithful of both sexes must regard them as condemned, reprobated, and rejected.... We restrain all in the virtue of holy obedience and under the penalty of an automatic major excommunication.... [F]rom our heart we exhort and beseech that he cease to disturb the peace, unity, and truth of the Church for which the Savior prayed so earnestly to the Father. Let him abstain from his pernicious errors that he may come back to us. If they really will obey, and certify to us by legal documents that they have obeyed, they will find in us the affection of a father's love, the opening of the font of the effects of paternal charity, and opening of the font of mercy and clemency.... We enjoin, however, on Martin that in the meantime he cease from all preaching or the office of preacher....[10]

Quite clear in Leo's bull was the threat of excommunication for any of Luther's followers and for anyone who was found reading Luther's writings. By this time, three years after Luther's *95 Theses* were published, his following had grown considerably, a point the pope seems not to have understood. The threat in Leo's bull included references to past enforcement of Church laws in Germany, even citing the "greatest penalties" imposed on heretics of the recent past. The threat of Inquisition to Luther and his followers was clear, though the German Church had questionable support to actually arrest and try Luther without public protest.

The Life of Martin Luther, printed by H. Schile, ca. 1874. Luther defied papal authority after the Church refused to consider his suggested reforms or to end practices such
as selling indulgences. At center, the print shows Luther burning the papal bull of
excommunication. Vignettes around the edges show scenes from Luther's life and por-
traits of Hus, Wyclif, and other "heroes of the Reformation."

The pope was not alone in condemning Luther. In 1521, Luther was ordered
to appear before Emperor Charles V at the Diet of Worms.

The Edict of Worms

In the age of Wyclif and Hus, Luther would have been arrested immediately and brought to the Inquisition, where he would have been pronounced
guilty and burned at the stake. But things had changed. The public had gotten
word of Luther's challenge, and a popular agreement with his points made the
entire matter very public. In addition, Germany, unlike other parts of Europe,
was ruled by more than 300 independent city-states and lacked a central government other than the occasional gatherings of the heads of imperial states
under the authority of the Roman Emperor. As a formal institution, the Inqui-

sition had less direct power in the region that would become Germany than in other sections of Europe, notably Italy, Spain and France. Even as inquisitors were able to organize and set up tribunals for witches in Germany, inquisitions for heretics such as Luther were not as easy to establish. To many of the local rulers, Church-run Inquisitions were not always welcome. So the Church solution to Luther's defiance relied on local political agreement to create an appropriate punishment and take the matter to the secular authorities.

For this reason, the Church relied on Roman emperor Charles V. While Luther was a well educated priest and widely respected theologian, Charles was only 17 at the time. Even so, the emperor was assigned the responsibility of representing the interest of the Church. The emperor convened a general assembly called the Diet ("Diet" is a forum of legislators of the Roman Empire, or in Germany a Reichstag). The assembly met in the town of Worms located on the Rhine River, and took place from January 28 to May 25, 1521.

Luther spoke in his own defense. Once a timid speaker, Luther was emboldened now, in part because a large crowd of supporters had appeared at the meeting. He described his writings as belonging in three categories: works that had been well received by friend and foes, which he refused to reject; books attacking abuses and lies within Christianity and the papacy, which Luther believed he could not reject without allowing the papal tyranny to continue; and other writings including attacks on individuals, for which Luther apologized for his harsh tone but not for content. He concluded by saying that if he could be provided with proof of any error based on the Scriptures, he would reject those writings.

The Diet of Worms issued an edict (*Wormser Edikt*), which ruled on Luther and his *95 Theses*. The assembly demanded that Luther reverse his heretical positions and called for his arrest. It included the language:

> we forbid anyone from this time forward to dare, either by words or by deeds, to receive, defend, sustain, or favor the said Martin Luther. On the contrary, we want him to be apprehended and punished as a notorious heretic, as he deserves, to be brought personally before us, or to be securely guarded until those who have captured him inform us, whereupon we will order the appropriate manner of proceeding against the said Luther. Those who will help in his capture will be rewarded generously for their good work.[11]

Luther recalled that the same promise of safe passage had been made to Hus and then violated. In the Hus case, the justification for not keeping the promise of safe passage was that it wasn't enforceable since Hus had been judged a heretic. Luther found himself in the same position, with the Diet of Worms calling him a heretic in agreement with Leo X and banning all of his books.

Luther quickly left the assembly to return home. He was on the verge of being arrested and subjected to either an Inquisition or a secular punishment based on his refusal to reverse his positions. He did not return home but was hidden for his safety in Wartburg Castle. His ally and protector, Frederick III, hid Luther to protect him from inquisitors. During his time in this protective custody, Luther started work on his German translation of the Bible. After he reemerged, the Edict of Worms was never enforced; by this time, Luther's ideas had become so popular that both secular and Church officials were fearful of his public support.

The Inquisition in other areas was enforced against Lutherans, as Luther's followers were soon to be called. In Belgium and Holland, several followers were arrested and placed on trial. Among Augustinians in Antwerp in 1521, Jacob Probst, prior of the local monastery, was forced to publicly recant and deny Luther's ideas. Two other monks—Johannes van Esschen and Hendrik Voss—were burned at the stake on July 1, 1523, after refusing to repudiate Luther's teachings.

The Protestant Movement as Heresy

Church reaction to the writings and statements of Luther demonstrates how ill-prepared the pope and Church leaders were to deal with any outspoken and direct defiance. No one expected the boldness in the face of possible penalties and at the time the Inquisition remained powerful and posed a very real threat. The great debate surrounding these events was whether or not the Church had the power to silence Luther or his followers. The dispute came down to a question of whether or not the pope could keep his claim to power over all things:

> Luther had broken the laws of the Church. He had taught doctrines which the Pope had declared to be false. Would or would he not retract? ... [H]e replied briefly that he would retract when his doctrines were not declared to be false merely but were proved to be false. Then but not till then. This was his answer, and his last word. There ... the heart of the matter indeed rested. In those words lay the whole meaning of the Reformation. Were men to go on forever saying that this or that was true, because the Pope affirmed it? Or were the Pope's decrees thenceforward to be tried like the words of other men, by ordinary laws of evidence?[12]

For centuries, anyone who challenged the papacy or the Church had lost; the Church always won the arguments and with the Inquisition in full force and with its unquestioned power, it was dangerous for anyone to raise questions without great risk. But Luther was emboldened by widespread support among the people; and at the same time, the Church had become utterly corrupt and worldly. Leo X had turned the papacy into his own family business and enriched many of his relatives, financing his own lifestyle with the indulgences that emissaries like Tetzel were selling. So complete was the Church's power that the pope initially did not take Luther seriously. Could he possibly succeed against the power and might of the Church? It was doubtful.

However, Luther's questions about the infallibility of the pope and the rights of the papacy over the people were not new ideas. They had been growing and circulating for many years, but usually in silence. While preaching chastity, the papacy indulged itself in unabashed sexuality. While preaching poverty, the pope, cardinals and bishops lived in luxurious castles and led lives of leisure. While making claims to representing God on earth, clerics acted in the most ungodly manner. Luther was not the only person to realize this; but he was the first to criticize it so publicly. That is why Luther has come to be known as the leading voice of the Reformation.

Other social and cultural changes were under way at the same time, which helped move the Reformation forward. In Germany, the decentralized governments wanted to be freed from Church control, and as the Reformation grew in size, many among the nobility adopted these new ideas as a means to break free from Church control and to seize Church-owned land for themselves. For nobles and commoners alike, the new movement was viewed as a way to gain greater freedom from the authoritarian rule of the pope and his inquisitors.

On a social and political basis, the Reformation was viewed as a way not only to improve conditions, but also to break from the Inquisition and its long-standing ability to repress citizens and seize property from the condemned. The Church, its bishops, and inquisitors had enriched themselves by seizing lands and properties and taking inheritances from the remaining family, who often were simply evicted from their homes without any means of income and sent away to suffer in poverty, even with no charges of heresy brought against them. The crimes of the accused justified seizures like this at the expense of families, and the practice was widespread. When the Reformation began and people realized that they could break from the Church without being dragged before an Inquisition's tribunal, they were happy to join in the movement.

The Church did not give up without a fight. It continued to declare that the Reformation was a form of heresy and a serious one. The Counter-Reformation of the Church was meant to reinstitute the Inquisition and bring the citizens of Germany back into compliance with Church rules. As part of this movement, the Church attempted internal reform. The Council of Trent was an ecumenical council convened to provide these reforms while also defining the Reformation movement as heresy. The council took place over three periods: 1545–49, 1551–52 and 1562–63. Among the council's determinations was a clear definition of the Protestant movement as a form of heresy. While Protestant leaders had hoped for a toned-down conclusion and continued dialogue, the council made it clear that there would be no compromise. Leading Protestants were invited to attend and take part in the council, but they were denied any voting rights. This decision put an end to all Protestant cooperation.

The reforms the council undertook were aimed at ending corruption or, more to the point, at countering *perceptions* of corruption among the Christian lay population. They did abolish some of the more extreme abuses such as selling of indulgences but did little to stem the growing Reformation movement, which had been one of the original purposes. Church leaders demonstrated themselves to be inflexible in holding on to final authority in all spiritual matters. For example, they concluded that Church's biblical interpretation was final and not subject to further debate. Anyone who offered a different interpretation would be charged with heresy. In a move away from progressive thought, the council strengthened its opposition to many developments in Renaissance-era art and music. Rather than reconciling Church policy with a rich and growing discovery of new expression through art, the Church ruled, for example, that polyphonic music was not acceptable. The council explained this decision:

> All things should indeed be so ordered that the masses, whether they be celebrated with or without singing, may reach tranquilly into the ears and hearts of those who hear them, when everything is executed clearly and at the correct speed. In the case of those masses which are celebrated with singing and with organ, let nothing profane be intermingled, but only hymns and divine praises. The whole plan of singing should be constituted not to give empty pleasure to the ear, but in such a way that the words be clearly understood by all. And thus the hearts of listeners be drawn to desire of heavenly harmonies in the contemplation of the joys of the Blessed. They shall also banish from church all music that contains whether in the singing or in the organ playing things that are lascivious or impure.[13]

The example of control over music reinforced the Church and its adherence to tradition, even while the Reformation challenged long-standing assumptions. The council reaffirmed its highly criticized veneration of the Virgin Mary, saints, and relics. Views to the contrary, specifically Protestant views, were ruled void with the conclusion *anathema sit* ("let it be anathema").

The inability of the Church to find compromise with Protestants defined the progress of the Reformation. If anything, the Council of Trent attempted to move policy backward to a more traditional, Church-controlled time. Artistic developments like polyphonic music and Renaissance art could not be turned back and continued forward concurrently with the Reformation itself. Luther's bold challenge to the supremacy of the pope and questioning of widespread Church corruption ended centuries of Church domination throughout Europe. His success in making this challenge and his continued defiance of the pope even under threat of excommunication and arrest also changed forever the way that the people of Europe viewed the Inquisition. Once all-powerful and able to move freely and create tribunals for even the most minor offenses, the entire structure of the Inquisition (like the Church overall) was for the first time seen as vulnerable, as an institution that could be challenged and defied without fear of arrest, torture and execution.

CHAPTER 12

Anglicanism and Calvinism

We thought that the clergy of our realm had been our subjects wholly, but now we have well perceived that they be but half our subjects, yea, and scarce our subjects: for all the prelates at their consecration make an oath to the pope, clean contrary to the oath that they make to us, so that they seem to be his subjects, and not ours.

— King Henry VIII, speech to Parliament, May 11, 1532

Two significant changes furthered the development of the Reformation in the 16th century. First was a conflict between King Henry VIII and the papacy, leading to a schism between the Roman and English churches and resulting in the growth of Anglicanism. Second was a development in Europe expanding Luther's initial dispute with the Roman Church, leading to yet another movement, Calvinism.

The Inquisition made its way to England briefly during the reign of Mary I (queen of England and queen of Ireland), to suppress activities of Wyclif's followers, the Lollards. Compared to the process elsewhere in Europe, notably in Spain, the Inquisition in England was mild and served a greater political than religious purpose.

Queen Mary ruled from 1553 until 1558, and during her reign over 300 dissenters were burned at the stake. The "Marian Persecutions" earned the queen the name "Bloody Mary." She was intent on ensuring that England remained a Catholic country. Later, during the reign of Mary's half-sister Elizabeth, this trend was reversed and England became known as the center of Anglicanism. King Henry VIII (Mary's and Elizabeth's father) entered into conflict with the pope over the issue of divorce and the question of who had the final word (pope or king); this conflict led to the religious schism in England. The sole attempt at reversing this trend on a religious premise was made by Mary I; on a political basis, the pope encouraged Spain to go to war with England during Elizabeth's reign with the intention of overthrowing her and restoring Mary to the throne.

The politics of this struggle cannot be separated from the religious elements, since both were aspects of the same power struggle. The teachings of Wyclif and development of the Lollard movement were the starting point for religious developments in England.

The Lollards

Although the Lollard movement began when John Wyclif was alive, the movement was never formalized as a sect and did not develop a central doctrine of its own. Lollards did not follow any one authority. Their common ground was a dislike of the clergy as a corrupt institution and an equal dislike of the Catholic belief in divine appointment of the pope. Lollards criticized widespread corruption in the Church, and their beliefs relied entirely on what was said in the Scriptures. Lollards promoted translation of the Bible into English so that even the poorly educated could read it for themselves. This idea — making the Bible available to everyone — was treated as a serious form of heresy when it was proposed by Wyclif in the 14th century.

Near the end of the 14th century in 1394, a group of Lollards presented a document to the English Parliament called *The Twelve Conclusions of the Lollards*. This document criticized the Roman Church and cited evils that had grown out of the Church's ownership of property, forced celibacy, image worship, and indulgences, as well as the assumption of Christ's presence in the Eucharist. Predating Luther's complaints about corruption and indulgences, the Lollards came to the attention of English authorities with this document, a revolutionary idea in a time when the Catholic doctrine was the only acceptable form of belief. Under the reign of Henry IV, Parliament passed the legislation in 1401 that for the first time authorized burning heretics at the stake. The new law, *De hæretico comburendo* (*The Burning of Heretics*), also forbade Lollards to preach, to teach or to publish their beliefs.

Another important ban in this law was ownership or publication of a translation of the Bible. This was aimed specifically at the Wyclif translation, also called Wyclif's Bible. The law said that any biblical translation was an act of heresy.

This ban reappeared 150 years later. In the 1550s Bishop Cuthbert of London associated Lollards with Lutheranism. He wrote in a license to Sir Thomas More that owning English translations was heretical:

> Since of late, after the Church of God throughout Germany has been infested with heretics, there have been some sons of iniquity who are trying to introduce into this country of ours the old and accursed Wycliffite heresy and its foster-child the Lutheran heresy, by translating into our mother tongue some of the most subversive of their pamphlets, and printing them in great quantity. They are, indeed, striving with all their might to defile and infect this country with these pestilential doctrines, which are most repugnant to the truth of the Catholic faith. It is greatly

to be feared, therefore, that Catholic faith may be greatly imperiled if good and learned men do not strenuously resist the wickedness of the aforesaid persons....[1]

Even though the 1401 law had specifically created the means for a new Inquisition and authorized Church bishops to condemn heretics, many did not consider it enough. In 1409, the archbishop of Canterbury, Thomas Arundel, created the *Constitutions of Oxford*, intended to strengthen provisions against English heretics, especially the Lollards. Arundel's *Constitutions* reclaimed authority for the Church in all spiritual matters, including punishment of heretics. The 1401 law had authorized bishops to arrest, imprison and interrogate those accused of heresy. At the 1407 Synod of Bishops presided over by Arundel, lengthy discussion formed the basis for the *Constitutions* which not only added weight to the law but condemned 267 propositions found in Wyclif's writings.

The English Inquisition, in spite of the law and support of the clergy, never gained the momentum it held elsewhere. Executions were rare and the Lollards evolved into a political force. This occurred even with the 1401 law and its formally established procedures, bolstered by the support of Arundel in his *Constitutions*. Elsewhere legal and Church-based documentation had been used to accelerate the pace of Inquisition; in England these changes came late in the history of Inquisition, and lacked the enthusiasm seen in France, Germany, Italy and Spain.

The 1401 law mirrored similar laws passed previously in other parts of Europe. It created an inquisitorial court operated by bishops, but upon condemnation, a guilty person was to be turned over to the local sheriff and a sentence carried out. After many were condemned and many more recanted, the Lollard movement virtually disappeared in England's cities, although it continued in rural areas into the 16th century. In 1559, the anti–Lollard law was repealed by Parliament as part of its Supremacy Act.

The Lollard movement promoted many beliefs that were important in the evolution of the Reformation. A central tenet of the Lollards later became an important point of dispute between Reformation leaders and the Church. The Lollards challenged the Church's assumption that it was the one true Church. Citing the corruption of the clergy and the papacy, Lollards stated that the Church had wandered from the true intention of Christianity. Another revolutionary idea was their support for a form of lay priesthood. Lollards denied that priests held any special authority, most importantly forgiveness of sins. Lollards preferred direct prayer to obtain forgiveness. They thought that Catholic rites had become overly ceremonial and had lost touch with the Christian population.

The Lollards had a mix of beliefs and no one series of beliefs represented all of the Lollard theology. One group called the pope the Anti-Christ and preached that the end times were near. The claims of this sect brought attention to the movement, and all Lollards were accused of heresy from the time of the legislation of 1401 through the end of the reign of Mary I in 1558.

To many, the Lollards deserve little more than a footnote in the history of the Reformation. However, their challenges to Church supremacy and their criticism of indulgences and Church corruption were the centerpieces of the Reformation itself.

King Henry VIII and the Counter-Inquisition

The issue of papal supremacy came to a head in a direct conflict between King Henry VIII and the pope. The king asked the pope to grant a divorce from Catherine of Aragon after she had failed to produce a male heir. Pope Clement VII (1523–34) refused this request, but Henry secretly married Anne Boleyn in 1533 and had Thomas Cranmer, archbishop of Canterbury, nullify Henry's former marriage. Clement countered the decision and declared Henry's divorce and remarriage void, and also excommunicated the king.* Henry broke with the Church and declared himself the head of the Church of England, also known as the Anglican Church.

Henry was declared the supreme head of the Church of England by the Convocations.† The position by the Church of England was further legalized by the statute known as the Supremacy Act of 1534, in which Parliament also declared Henry the head of the Church. This law read in part:

> be it enacted by authority of this present Parliament, that the king of our sovereign land, his heirs and successors, kings of this realm, shall be taken, accepted, and reputed the only supreme head in earth of the Church of England, called *Anglica Ecclesia*; and shall have and enjoy, annexed and united to the imperial crown of this realm, as well as the title and style thereof, as all honors, dignities, pre-eminences, jurisdictions, privileges, authorities, immunities, profits and commodities to the said dignity of supreme head of the same Church....[2]

On March 31, 1534, the king's representatives posed a question to the Church of England's Convocations. The question was "Whether the Roman pontiff has any greater jurisdiction bestowed on him by God in the Holy Scriptures in this realm of England, than any other foreign bishop?" The Convocation of Canterbury overwhelmingly voted in the negative (34 nay, 1 doubtful and 4 ayes). The Convocation of York considered the same issue and on June 2 wrote to the king, "The Bishop of Rome has not, in Scripture, any greater jurisdiction in the kingdom of England than any other foreign bishop."[3]

So the course had been set: the English monarch was granted full authority, replacing the pope as the supreme head of the Church. Even so, the Church of England did not consider this to be a clean break from Catholicism. Its doctrine is a hybrid, both Catholic and Reformed. It is described as part of the universal Church established by Christ and based on the Anglican version of the Apostle's Creed:

---

*Clement's order of excommunication was suspended, but was replaced by a new bull of excommunication by Pope Paul III two years later.

†The "Convocations" are the two assemblies of the Church of England, representing the provinces of Canterbury and York.

I BELIEVE in God the Father Almighty, Maker of heaven and earth: And in Jesus Christ his only Son our Lord, Who was conceived by the Holy Ghost, Born of the Virgin Mary, Suffered under Pontius Pilate, Was crucified, dead, and buried: He descended into hell; The third day he rose again from the dead; He ascended into heaven, And sitteth on the right hand of God the Father Almighty; From thence he shall come to judge the quick and the dead. I believe in the Holy Ghost; The holy Catholic Church; The Communion of Saints; The Forgiveness of sins; The Resurrection of the body, And the Life everlasting. Amen.[4]

The Church of England had always been a separate unit of the Church, partly because of geography and partly because of a demand for a degree of independence in the British Isles from the central authority of Rome. Britain had been Christian since the early days of Christianity, and Church fathers like Tertullian wrote of a well-organized Church community in the third century. The Church of England as an entity was formally created by the so-called Gregorian Mission, an effort started by Pope Gregory I in the year 596 with the intention of converting all Anglo-Saxons to Christianity.

Even with the widespread success of the Gregorian Mission to Britain, the natives maintained a strong identity independent of Roman control. As early as 664, the Synod of Whitby convened to settle disputes between the central Church and Britain. At the synod, the Christian Church in Britain was reorganized under two archbishops (Canterbury and York) and the development of a local monastic system. The pope was recognized as the ultimate authority and the archbishops had control only locally.

There were two distinct liturgical forms of Christianity in Britain at the time. First was the well-known Roman version and second was the Ionan. In the latter organization, also known as *Celtic Christianity*, Irish monks living in a monastery on the isle of Iona differed in the determination of when Easter was to be celebrated. So the Roman Easter and Ionan Easter were celebrated at different times and became a symbol of differences between the two versions of Christianity. The synod created uniformity throughout Christianity for the celebration of Easter but to many at the time, the dominance of Rome was viewed as in intrusion. Advocates of the Roman position had the last word, arguing that the Roman authority — specifically the pope — had the final word on all matters. Ionan supporters resisted what they perceived as the Romanizing of Celtic Christianity.

Many centuries later during the Reformation, old arguments were reintroduced and used as examples of Rome's attempt to subjugate the British Church. Distinctions between Roman and Ionan Christianity and the liturgical practices of Rome and Britain created a virtually permanent antagonism. While the Church of England became part of the breakaway from Rome during the Reformation, it continued to think of itself as "Catholic" in many ways. Even so, the influence of Reformation ideas also plays a key role in the more recent evolution of the Church of England and its distinction and separation from the traditions of the Roman Church.

The reform aspects of the Church of England included many Protestant innovations developed in 1563, after Henry's lifetime and during the reign of his daughter, Elizabeth I. The *Thirty-Nine Articles of Religion* defined the Anglican beliefs, many of which were viewed as heretical by the pope; but the Church was unable to stop the tide of the Reformation and in England, even the law against the Lollards had been repealed and the Catholic Church was not able to exert its power any longer.

During Henry's lifetime, activities against the Church were direct and severe. After Henry declared himself head of the Anglican Church and broke with the pope, Parliament dissolved all monastic and religious orders within England, Ireland and Wales. This was a form of Counter-Inquisition. It included seizures of income and property held by Catholic groups and their members.

On August 30, 1535, Pope Paul III (1534–49) excommunicated Henry. (The bull of excommunication, however, was not published until December 17, 1538.) Paul, in *Eius qui immobilis*, proclaimed

> that King Henry has incurred the penalty of deprivation of his kingdom and [has] been sundered forever from all faithful Christians and their goods. And if meanwhile he depart from this life we decree and declare ... that he ought to be deprived of Church burial. And we smite [him] with the sword of anathema, malediction and eternal damnation.... We decree and declare that all the sons of King Henry ... born or to be born, and the rest of their descendants ... are deprived of all dignities and honors whatsoever.... And all the subjects of the same King Henry we do absolve and utterly release from their oath of fidelity, from their allegiance and from all kind of subjection to the King.... Commanding them nevertheless, on pain of excommunication that they utterly and entirely withdraw themselves from obedience to the said King Henry....[5]

The dispute did not end there. Henry was determined to audit, seize property from, and close many of the Catholic monasteries in England. The state of Catholic religious orders in England had been on the decline for many years, and many monasteries and convents had only half the numbers desired to maintain a self-sustaining lifestyle. At the start of the 14th century, approximately 5,000 friars were active in England; by the 16th century, the number was lower than 1,000 and the majority lived outside of the friaries. Many supported themselves with outside employment and many owned property in spite of vows of poverty.

The decline of Catholic religious orders in England did not deter Henry from his measures. The anti–Catholic decisions he and Parliament reached were retaliatory after the pope's excommunication order. Before the First Suppression Act was passed, Parliament had sent Thomas Cromwell, Henry's chief minister, to visit all of the English monasteries. He was instructed to inform the members of these monasteries that their first duty was to the king and not to the pope. Cromwell also began compiling an inventory of assets and income of all Catholic monasteries in England and Wales. Henry drafted authorization for Cromwell, including the mandate and order that the dean, parsons, vicars, and others having cure of souls anywhere within this deanery, shall faithfully keep and observe ... statutes and laws of this realm made for the abolishing and extirpation of the Bishop of Rome's pretensed and usurped power and jurisdiction within this realm, and for the establishment and confirmation of the king's authority and jurisdiction within the same, as of the supreme head of the Church of England....[6]

Cromwell next sent his representatives around to examine the "quality of religious life" in the various monasteries, looking for "superstitious activities" and "moral laxity" (meaning sexual activities). As a result of this investigation, 243 monasteries were dissolved and others forced to pay fines to the crown. The dissolved monasteries' property was invariably seized by the crown, and Cromwell was put in charge of a new agency to oversee this property, called the Court of Augmentations. Just as older Inquisitions had seized property of condemned heretics, in Henry's Counter-Inquisition, Catholic monasteries were closed and assets seized. In those instances, monks and nuns were given the choice of a secular retirement with a cash settlement, or transfer to a larger monastery or convent within the same order. In at least two cases (those of the Norton Priory in Cheshire and the Hexham Abbey in Northumberland) resident monks resisted with force, actions Henry deemed treasonous. The Norton monks were imprisoned for several months, and the Hexham monks were executed. Like the crime of "heresy" in Dominican-run Inquisitions elsewhere, the crime of "treason" was treated swiftly and brutally in Henry's Counter-Inquisition. So the circle was completed, with the Counter-Inquisition treating Catholic clerics to the same disfavor as "heretics" had been receiving from Catholic inquisitors for many years.

Continued resistance in isolated areas led to hangings of abbots in a small number of cases. However, by 1539, when Parliament passed a new law allowing voluntary surrender of Church-owned property, most monasteries were already dissolved in England, Wales and Ireland. Many previously monastic-owned Churches survived because they had been used for worship by both Catholic and Protestant groups. Other buildings were converted to barns or stables. Cromwell's campaign created a new market for the sale of Catholic items including relics, choir stalls, and stained glass windows.

Henry's crown gained approximately £150,000 per year from seizures of property and income from the monasteries, one-third of which was promised in monastic pensions. After 1540, much of the property was sold to fund Henry's wars with France and Scotland, and this led to an additional profit of £1.4 million by 1547.

England as a Protestant Country

After Henry's death in 1547, Edward VI reigned for six years. During his reign, England officially adopted Protestantism as its official religion and replaced the Latin mass with its own English service. This was reversed during the brief reign of Mary I, 1553–58, when Lollards were once again persecuted and burned at the stake under an attempted renewal of the English version of the Inquisition. Although the Protestant movement had not been universally popular in England, Mary's decision to condemn heretics to burning at the stake turned popular sentiment against the Catholic Church. At Mary's death in 1558, Elizabeth I became the new ruler and after years of conflict between Catholics and Protestants, England emerged with a Protestant majority.

Relations between the two Christian sects were harmonious until 1570. Until that time, Catholics and Protestants had worshipped together and tolerated each other's beliefs. But then Pope Pius V (1570–2), a strong supporter of the Inquisition, tried to undo the entire Protestant movement in England. Pius had constructed a palace in Rome specifically to house inquisitorial tribunals and attended many trials in person. His goal was to keep Protestantism out of Italy but in this effort, he also was determined to stop the movement elsewhere. In 1570, Pius issued a bull, *Regnans in excelsis* (Ruling from on high), forbidding Catholics to worship with non–Catholics, declaring Elizabeth not the rightful queen of England, and declaring her to be excommunicated. He referred to Elizabeth in the bull as "Elizabeth, the pretended Queen of England and the servant of crime," and stated that she had "removed the royal Council, composed of the nobility of England, and ... filled it with obscure men, being heretics."[7]

The conflict between Elizabeth and the papacy created political tension as the pope encouraged England's enemies to go to war and replace Elizabeth with the Catholic Mary, Queen of Scots, cousin of Philip II of Spain (and husband of the late Queen Mary I of England). Philip agreed with the pope that Elizabeth was a heretic. But after Mary plotted against Elizabeth, she was taken from house arrest and executed in 1587 for plotting against the crown. Pope Sixtus V (1585–90) promised a large payment to Philip if he would invade England, declaring the planned invasion a crusade. In 1588, the Spanish Armada was defeated by English forces and after the defeat the pope declined to make the promised payment.

This defeat has gained fame as one of the greatest naval upsets in history, but it also defied the pope's plans to use the military might of Spain to punish the defiant English. The failure of this effort was as great a loss to the papacy as it was to Spain. The Spanish Armada, also called *Grande y Felicísima Armada* (Great and Most Fortunate Navy) and also termed *Armada Invencible* (The Invincible Navy), contained 130 ships, 8,000 sailors and 18,000 soldiers. The Armada sailed from Lisbon on May 28, 1588, ready to face the much smaller English fleet, with only 34 royal vessels (plus many smaller ships and privateer-owned ships). After some minor skirmishes, the Armada arranged itself in a tightly formed defensive crescent formation. At midnight on July 28, the English lit up eight "fire ships" with pitch and gunpowder and sent them downwind into the Spanish formation. Most of the Spanish fleet cut their anchor cables and fled. They were not able to recover an advantageous position, and the English navy was victorious. For Spain and its "invincible" navy, it was a humiliating defeat. For the pope and his "infallible" stance, it meant the end to attempts at overthrowing Queen Elizabeth and eliminating the Church of England. For English members of the clergy, the outcome was more direct and ominous.

The Church, never able to impose an Inquisition on England as long as the country was ruled by a Protestant monarch, had worked with the Spanish monarch to invade and defeat the country and put a Catholic monarch in Elizabeth's place. Had this succeeded, the likelihood of a renewed Inquisition was in little doubt. However, Elizabeth reacted to the pope's conspiracy with the Spanish king with a Counter-Inquisition of her own. After the failed invasion, Elizabeth declared that all priests were guilty of treason, including anyone who protected or sheltered priests. Many English Catholics were executed under Elizabeth's orders.

The persecution of Catholics in England continued into the reign of James I from 1603 to 1625 and was heightened by the Gunpowder Conspiracy of 1605. This was an assassination plot by English Catholics against the king, with the plan including the killing of James, his family, and the Protestant aristocracy. Assuming all of these dignitaries would be in attendance for opening ceremonies of the Houses of Parliament on November 6, 1605, the plan was to blow up the building with everyone inside. Guy Fawkes, an explosives expert, was recruited to make the bomb consisting of 36 barrels of gunpowder in the basement of Parliament. The plot failed, but it led to renewed persecution of Catholics. Fawkes has become a representative of a simplified version of these events and the connection to a conflict between Protestant rulers and Catholic citizens is rarely highlighted as part of the Gunpowder Conspiracy. Nevertheless, the events dramatically affected the history of England and of relations between the two Christian sects.

Today, "bonfire night" is celebrated in England on November 5, when Guy Fawkes is burned in effigy and fireworks are set off. Children display effigies before burning and ask strangers for "a penny for the guy" as part of the tradition. (Fawkes' first name is also the origin of the term "guy" to refer to any male.) Another tradition grew from this important event. To this day, when the king or queen of England enters Parliament on opening day (the only time the monarch appears in that chamber) the Yeomen of the Guard search Westminster Palace's cellars to ensure that no explosives are there. A nursery rhyme also honors the day:

> Remember, remember the Fifth of November,
> The Gunpowder Treason and Plot,
> I know of no reason
> Why Gunpowder Treason
> Should ever be forgot.

The Gunpowder Plot defined the religious conflict of the day, even though its significance has been largely lost over time. The events in England during the period of the Reformation marked the end of the Inquisition as it had been practiced in preceding centuries. The reasons for the Church's loss of power include distance between Rome and London, the Reformation taking place during these decades in Germany and other parts of Europe, and a growing sentiment against the Church as supreme authority and temporal power. Wyclif and the Lollards were essential in furthering this trend; in the years since Wyclif's death the Lollards quietly questioned Church authority in theological and political matters. Once the English monarchy also directly defied the pope, the once all-powerful Inquisition was a thing of the past, at least in England. (During the same time, the Spanish Inquisition continued as a powerful institution, and the European Great Witch Hunt was under way as well.) The Church came to realize that the once feared act of excommunication no longer held sway over kings and queens. Neither Henry VIII nor his daughter Elizabeth I was affected in decision-making by papal excommunication or challenge. The acts of the papacy to conspire with England's enemies led to swift retaliation against Catholicism through England, rather than forcing the monarch to submit to papal authority.

John Calvin

Social and religious trends in the Anglican Church were confined to England. The rest of the Reformation was spreading throughout the remainder of the Christian world after Luther's bold break with Rome. In Switzerland, yet another movement gained popular support after 1530, led by the French theologian John Calvin.

He had been trained as a lawyer and left France after a violent uprising in France against Protestants. In Basel, Switzerland, Calvin published *Institutes of the Christian Religion* (*Institutio Christianæ Religionis*) in 1536. This book became the central expression of Calvin's beliefs that formed his movement of Protestant theology. Topics included doctrine, the sacraments, and Christian liberty. Calvin described himself as devoted before he broke with the Roman Church. He did not consider his ideas to be the foundation for a new form of Christianity, but rather part of a reform movement aimed at corruption within the Catholic Church. His original intention in writing the book was to present a defense of French Protestants (the *Huguenots*) who were under assault by French Catholics at the time.*

Calvin had undergone an unexpected religious conversion while studying law at the University of Bourges. Part of this change included his break with

---

*The word "Huguenot" is derived from the German *Eidgenossen* which means "Confederates," and mispronounced in French as "Eignots," eventually becoming the nickname for French Protestants.

Roman Catholicism and activism in the French Protestant movement. He was influenced by a reformer, Nicholas Cop, rector of the university. Cop gave an address on November 1, 1533, in which he spoke about the need for reform within the Church. He was denounced as a heretic by the university faculty and fled to Basel, Switzerland. Calvin was implicated in the charge of heresy as a close friend of Cop and went into hiding for the next year.

An incident occurred on October 17, 1534, that forced Calvin to leave France once and for all. The Affair of the Placards (*Affaire des Placards*) was so named when blasphemous anti–Catholic posters appeared around Paris, Blois, Rouen, Tours and Orléans. Reaction was violent and Calvin realized that he could no longer stay in France with the threat of arrest or imprisonment.

Calvin's fears were justified. Orders were put out for the arrest of all Protestant suspects and the prisons were quickly filled. On January 29, 1535, six Protestants were burned in a spectacle at Notre Dame. They were suspended by ropes and slowly lowered into the flames. Dozens more were later burned in other cities, had their tongues cut out, or were fined, imprisoned, tortured, and exiled.

Calvin, among those who fled from France, spent three years moving from place to place under assumed names, finally settling in Geneva. There Calvin took the title of "pastor" in 1537 and, for the first time, began pastoral duties including presiding at weddings and church services. This was an important step because Calvin had received no consecration or ordination. Without the approval of the Catholic Church, he was not "legally" permitted to serve as a pastor, but this step away from the Catholic requirements of consecration set a precedent in the Reform Church. The less formal ordination of Protestant ministers was a break from the rigid requirements imposed on those entering the priesthood.

By 1541, the Geneva City Council, supporting Calvin's reform ideas, passed a series of Ecclesiastical Ordinances (*Ordonnances ecclésiastiques*) on November 20, 1541. These ordinances defined four areas of ministry. These were *pastors* who were to administer sacraments; *doctors* to instruct congregations in matters of Christian faith; *elders* who provided structure and discipline within the congregation and Church hierarchy; and a court, or "Consistory" (*Consistoire*), made up of lay members of the congregation. This court was empowered to rule on ecclesiastical issues but not on civil ones. It was allowed to impose sentences including excommunication, but this power was withdrawn in 1543 and reverted to the secular courts.

During this period, Calvin made contact with Michael Servetus, a Spaniard who was a fugitive from the Spanish Inquisition, which had ordered his arrest. Having rejected the doctrine of the Trinity, Servetus first wrote to Calvin in 1546, but Calvin became impatient with his requests to visit in Geneva. Calvin refused to ensure his safe conduct. Servetus was arrested in 1553 and brought before Cardinal Tournon, archbishop of Lyons and the French inquisitor general, where his letters to Calvin were presented to the tribunal as proof of heresy.

Although Tournon was a fierce persecutor of Protestants, Calvin cooperated with his investigation by having copies of his letters from Servetus delivered to the tribunal. Assisting Tournon in this investigation was a second inquisitor, Matthias Ory. The evidence was enough to find Servetus guilty of heresy. However, Servetus escaped before sentence was passed down. Sentenced *in absentia* for heresy, violating royal ordinances, and escaping from prison he was condemned to the gruesome punishment of slow burning.

Servetus arrived in Geneva and attended one of Calvin's sermons. Calvin turned him over to the authorities and wrote a list of charges against him. Servetus was sentenced to death and was burned at the stake on October 27, 1546. Even though Calvin worked to reform corruption within the Church, he was not above using the power of Church and State for his own purposes. The irony in the condemnation of Servetus is that the original charge of heresy was based on his letters to Calvin.

Clearly, Calvin considered Servetus a theological foe. Many of the basic beliefs of the two men were in conflict, and Calvin had not welcomed Servetus to Geneva, viewing him as an embarrassment and, after his arrest on charges of heresy, a potential liability. Calvin did not want to be caught in the Inquisition along with Servetus, so he provided copies of letters Servetus had sent to him as part of the evidence that led to his condemnation. Calvin's role in the execution of Servetus was seen negatively by fellow reform leaders for many years.

Critics accused Calvin of being a new pope and inquisitor for his part in the sentencing and execution of Servetus. Many feared that the act would encourage Catholic inquisitors to accelerate persecutions against Protestants throughout Europe; others called Calvin a hypocrite for taking the same stance as the Catholic Church, which he had criticized for the same abuses. But Calvin insisted that it was the duty of every Christian judge to punish heretics with death.

The criticisms were often made against Calvin anonymously, in fear of his power and influence both as a religious and political leader. In addition to pamphlets, books were published anonymously appealing for religious tolerance and liberty. Calvin interpreted these publications as attempts at justifying heresy and sparing heretics from just punishment. But Calvin, among other Protestant leaders, viewed a movement for increased religious freedom as a dangerous heresy. An aide to Calvin, Theodore Beza, wrote in 1554 in defense of Calvin's position that

> the toleration of error is indifference to truth.... [I]t destroys all order and discipline in the Church. Even the enforced unity of the papacy is much better than anarchy. Heresy is much worse than murder, because it destroys the soul. The spiritual power has nothing to do with temporal punishments; but it is the right and duty of the civil government, which is God's servant, to see to it that he receives his full honor in the community.[8]

The irony of this position is sharp when compared to past justifications by pontiffs for their own Inquisitions and condemnation of heresy. The pro–Catholic forces seized on Calvin's position to point out his hypocrisy and to condemn him for his support of the death penalty in light of his criticisms of the Church.

Servetus was the first person to be tried and burned at the stake on the authority of a Reformed church, specifically one influenced and to a degree controlled by Calvin. Both Calvin and Luther criticized the Church Inquisition in its many forms while also acknowledging the right of the Church to execute heretics. This led to widespread criticism of reformers by Catholics, pointing to the execution as an example of Reform hypocrisy. Among both Protestant and Catholic leaders, a debate and dialogue followed in which the right of Church and State to hold Inquisitions was questioned. In contrast to Spain, where at this time no religious dissent was tolerated in any circumstances, the dialogue evolving in central Europe occurred at a time when Protestant variations of Inquisition were under way in Switzerland and elsewhere in Europe.

Calvin and the Inquisition

The development of the Swiss Church led by Calvin was clearly anti–Catholic and a departure from accepted doctrine. Calvin's lack of ordination made his sermons and services "illegal" under Church rules. In 1544, Calvin attempted to open a dialogue with Pope Paul III (1534–49), in a document entitled *Admonitio paterna Pauli III*. In this letter, Calvin complained that the Church had refused to leave any avenue for reformers for discussions with Rome. The response was a series of decrees against Protestant leaders, issued through the Council of Trent.

Calvin wrote another letter in 1547 responding to the decrees, entitled *Acta synodi Tridentinae cum Antidoto*. And in 1549, he published a treatise called *Vera christiannæ pacificationis et Ecclesiae reformandæ ratio*, listing and explaining Reform doctrines he believed should be upheld and supported. This attempt at reasoning with the pope did nothing to soften the Catholic position. Reform leaders, including Calvin, were judged guilty of heresy.

Calvin and other reformers had at first given little thought to the "heresy" of Wyclif and the Lollards, or to Hus and other pioneers in what became the Reformation movement. The focus within the movement was on the pope as the enemy, criticizing the Church for assuming powers to which it and the pope had no right. The focus of this antagonism rested on a hatred of the Dominican Order as the Church's enforcement arm and the group singularly running the Inquisition, not only in Spain but throughout the rest of Europe.

The extent of Dominican involvement in past Inquisitions was not widely known at the time. In Spain, the culprit was identified as the monarchy that directly controlled the Inquisition. Elsewhere in Europe, blame fell to the pope. As Calvinism grew, this began to change:

> Although early Protestant thinkers did not particularly condemn St. Dominic and his order, after the mid-sixteenth century anti–Dominican feelings ran high, and the retrieval of medieval source materials indicated how closely the Dominicans had been associated with the inquisitions and particularly with the literature of heresiology, both in theological tracts and handbooks for inquisitors.[9]

As the Protestant movement rediscovered the true history of the Inquisition, an anti–Dominican movement grew. And so Dominicans became known among Protestants as those responsible for deluding popes and kings in order to further persecutions of their enemies. It was at least partially due to the excesses of the Spanish Inquisition that Protestant leaders were not subjected to the wrath of the dreaded Dominican inquisitors. Many Protestants were condemned and burned at the stake, but the wrath shown toward previous heretics (notably toward the Conversos and Jews of Spain) would never be matched in the later trials of Protestants.

This disparity may be blamed partially on a racial component. The anti–Semitic aspects of the Spanish Inquisition, resulting from decades of discrimination, distrust and conflict in Spain, have been well documented. Now, however, with the advent of the Protestant movement, a new variety of racial association with the Inquisition came about, in which the Spanish nation was cast as the force of repression, brutality and intolerance. This image, known as the Black Legend (*la layenda negra*), was exploited by Protestant leaders to portray Spanish brutality and racial policies as the "worst of the Church" with its Dominican Inquisition. Even though every country in Europe had to struggle with its own cultural and social issues involving Catholic versus Protestant, including dissent and repression leading to many variations on the Inquisition theme, the acceptance of the Black Legend identifying Spanish evils allowed people to set them apart as a special case. The "Christian" Protestants in Europe distinguished themselves not only from the Catholic movement controlled in Rome but more so from the Dominican-controlled evils of the Spanish Inquisition and the cultural Black Legend that it encompassed. The connection between the characterization of the Spanish Inquisition with the Dominicans, also known as the Black Friars, gives the term Black Legend an ironic double meaning.

The Reformation was based on a struggle against abuses by the Church, among which the Inquisition is certainly the most obvious. But once Protestants accomplished the religious freedom they desired, they turned on Catholic minorities, not only in England under the Anglican Church but elsewhere as well. In Germany and Switzerland, properties owned by Catholic orders were seized and their occupants banished, sent to prison, or murdered. In Sweden, Norway and Denmark, only Lutheran services were allowed; all other worship was outlawed. Under the penal codes of Queen Elizabeth I, the practice of any religion except Anglicanism was declared a crime. The power had shifted, but the punishments remained:

> The Reformers were ambitious of succeeding tyrants whom they had dethroned. They imposed with equal rigor their creeds and confessions; they asserted the right of the magistrate to punish heretics with death. The nature of the tiger was the same, but he was gradually deprived of his teeth and fangs.[10]

Just as earlier Catholic popes and cardinals attacked heretics out of fear that heresy would destroy the Church, the new Protestant leaders attacked their "heretics" (Catholics and Protestants putting forth heretical views) with equal ferocity and for the same reasons. Just as the Catholic Inquisition led to abuses, so too did the Protestant versions of "cleansing" in the name of God. To the Protestant leaders, the greatest heresy was denial of the Trinity, just as to the Catholic Inquisition the greatest heresy was any challenge to the trinity of God, pope and inquisitor.

In spite of the controversy surrounding Calvin and other leaders concerning their treatment of dissenters, the Reformation had begun and could not be stopped. The Church, desiring to prevent the movement from reaching Italy, initiated a new Inquisition to keep the Reformation away from Italian soil.

CHAPTER 13

The Roman Inquisition

> We should always be disposed to believe that which appears white is really black, if the hierarchy of the Church so decides.
>
> — Ignatius of Loyola, *Spiritual Exercises*, 1522–1524

The rapid spread of the Reformation in Europe was a clear signal to the Roman Church that it no longer had the power to control behavior. In the past, the threat of Inquisition silenced many heretics and other dissenters. In Spain, the Inquisition was effective in almost completely eradicating Jewish life through the justification of the Converso threat to "good Christians." However, in the 16th century, the Church could only protect what it controlled in its immediate vicinity. The distances between Rome and London or Paris were too great; and so the final version of the Inquisition was confined to Rome and the Italian Peninsula. The Roman Inquisition was originated to prevent the Reformation from completely destroying the Church by spreading into Italy.

The Church held onto the belief, now rapidly becoming unpopular, that the papacy held supreme power in both spiritual and temporal matters. This idea had been disproven by the English by converting a once–Catholic country into a nearly completely Anglican one. The threat of Inquisition faced by Luther and Calvin was quite real but easily avoidable. Reformation leaders were able to escape imprisonment and worse even in areas where Inquisition tribunals continued to hold great power. For example, in Paris and other cities in France, anti–Protestant initiatives resulted in many public executions, and in Germany the Great Witch Hunt continued to express its superstition through Dominican-run tribunals, cruel interrogations, and burning of witches. In Spain as well, the worst of the inquisitorial period was over by the closing decades of the 16th century; but the Church, with less temporal power than it had held in past centuries, believed it was under assault by the forces of the Reformation.

Although Roman Inquisition began primarily to stem the spread of the Reformation, like so many past expressions of anti-heretical activity it quickly branched out to include tribunals against an array of heretics beyond its original targets. Eventually, victims of the Roman Inquisition would include many scientists and artists, newly defined as heretical simply by contradicting the oldest beliefs of Christianity. Even with proof, a scientific idea could be condemned under the tribunals of the Roman Inquisition; and even artistic expressions, if taken as critical of the Church, were easily rolled into the newly expanded definition of the "heretic" as an enemy of the Church.

Creation of the Roman Inquisition

Pope Paul III (1534–49) created the Roman Inquisition and announced it in his bull of June 21, 1542, entitled *Licet ab initio*. The new Inquisition was officially called the "Congregation of the Inquisition" or simply the "Holy Office" (*Sanctum Officium*). Paul appointed Cardinal Giovanni Caraffa as grand inquisitor. Caraffa, who would later become known as Pope Paul IV (1555–9), defined his mission as grand inquisitor: "No man must debase himself by showing toleration toward heretics of any kind, above all toward Calvinists."[1]

A true zealot in the anti-heretical nature of the Roman Inquisition, Caraffa was not afraid to go after anyone he suspected of heresy. He once said, "Even if my own father was a heretic, I would gather the wood to burn him."[2]

Later, in the office of pope, Caraffa expanded the role and mission of the Roman Inquisition and in 1559, published the first Index of Forbidden Books (*Index librorum prohibitorum*). Also called the Pauline Index, this was the first of 42 indexes in all, in which the works of hundreds of authors were banned. The index was later confirmed in January 1562 by the Council of Trent. Prominent on this first version of the list were Reformation writers including Luther, Calvin and others. Manuscripts that were acceptable to Church censors carried the words *nihil obstat* (nothing forbidden) or *imprimatur* (let it be printed) on the title page.

The last index in this long series was published in 1948; and the index remained in force until it was suppressed by the Vatican in 1966, although the full meaning of that decision remains in doubt even today.

The suppression of the index in 1966 was not a specific ban on application of the index. On June 14, 1966, Pope Paul VI (1963–78) published a notification abolishing the index and removing its legal force. While the Inquisition's office (whose name was changed the year before to the Sacred Congregation for the Doctrine of the Faith) cited the pope's notification in describing the index as still retaining "its moral force (*suum vigorem morale*)," Catholic theologians continue to debate whether the index has a continuing existence and whether faithful Catholics have a moral obligation to not read or circulate forbidden books. In fact, contradicting the cessation order of the pope, the statement was issued by the head of the office on the same date as the pope's notification that

This Congregation for Doctrine of Faith ... reaffirms that its Index retains its moral value ... in the sense that it is appealing to the conscience of the faithful ... to be on their guard against written materials that can put faith and good conduct in danger.[3]

The influence and power of the Sacred Congregation for the Doctrine of the Faith remained strong even into the late 20th century. In 1985, Cardinal Joseph Ratzinger, the future Pope Benedict XVI (2005–), himself Prefect of the Congregation for the Doctrine of the Faith from 1981 through 2005, wrote his opinion that the index retained its moral value "for the more unprepared faithful."[4]

Benedict was by no means the first pope who had previously served as head of the Holy Office. The lineage of inquisitors becoming popes began with Caraffa's reign as Paul IV and continued. In 1556, Paul IV appointed Michele Ghislieri as grand inquisitor, and Ghislieri later reigned as Pope Pius V (1566–72). Under Pius V, the use of torture in interrogation once again was authorized after its ban earlier for use in the Roman Inquisition. In the first year of his papacy, Pius sponsored the first of many *auto-da-fés* in which many heretics were either burned at the stake or beheaded.

The primary characteristic of this new Inquisition that set it apart from previous ones was its Church-managed central authority to find and try heretics. In the Spanish Inquisition, the well organized series of tribunals was run by a grand inquisitor but completely controlled by the monarchy. In the European Inquisition controlled and run by Dominicans, there was no central control; the Inquisition was authorized by the pope but all authority was delegated to appointed Dominican inquisitors. In the Roman Inquisition, local tribunals, operated by either Dominican or Franciscan inquisitors, were intricate and organized but completely controlled from the central authority in Rome under the papacy itself.

The original targets of these tribunals were Protestants but in a very brief span of time, the focus was expanded to include apostasy (loss or abandonment of faith), bigamy, blasphemy, witchcraft, sorcery, alchemy, Judaizing, and many lesser infractions. Like previous variations of the Inquisition, the tribunals had considerable power to bring accused offenders before them, subject only to supervision from Rome. The closely organized tribunals caused confusion and in-fighting between inquisitorial tribunals and separate Episcopal courts (which were set up to administer spiritual law disputes, but were not part of the Inquisition), and with secular judges and courts. Ultimately, with the blessing and support of the pope, the Inquisition tribunals won disagreements on matters of jurisdiction.

The tribunals were organized with an inquisitor, a vicar, a notary, and lesser officials of "external vicars" (*vicari foranei*). The tribunals also consulted with legal and theological experts on matters of Church law. A bishop or other higher Church official, serving as an Episcopal vicar, was also required as part of the tribunal if and when the inquisitor wanted to approve the use of torture to interrogate an accused heretic or to pass a sentence of death. In previous Inquisitions, Dominicans had nearly complete autonomy and the ability to enter verdicts or approve the use of torture of either the accused or witnesses. The Roman Inquisition was more formal and included more safeguards for the accused, including the appointment of a bishop to approve sentences before they could be imposed. In fact, final sentencing was not usually announced until approved by the Supreme Congregation in Rome. The Congregation's decision was final and binding.

The Roman Inquisition held tribunals throughout the Italian peninsula but excluded Sicily, which was under the jurisdiction of the Spanish Inquisition. In some areas, jurisdiction was limited. For example, in Naples, which was a part of the Spanish empire, the Inquisition was conducted within the Episcopal courts. In many of the city-states in Italy at the time, inquisitors had to obtain approval from local rulers before arresting, interrogating, trying, sentencing and executing accused heretics. In those areas, secular legal experts were attached to the tribunals of the Inquisition to ensure proper procedures.

In Venice, the process was closely controlled by the local secular courts. Venice had built provisions into its secular laws against the crime of heresy and had a tradition of enforcing them rigorously. In Venice, cooperation between Roman inquisitors and Venetian secular courts was focused equally on the crimes of usury and heresy. In this city, heretics were not treated as Christian wrongdoers only, but also as criminals under the law. Venice was a special case, however, due to its unique geography and the political rivalry between its leadership and the papacy. Rome, still treated as the center of spiritual leadership of the Venetian Church, had been pressuring Venice to take steps to expel or try Protestants living in Venice.

In 1547, Venice instituted a tribunal of three lay judges, which was termed *Tre Savii sopra eresia* (The three wise men who know heresy). This tribunal worked directly with secular authorities, the papal nuncio and the local Franciscan inquisitor. Rome did not approve of the tribunal's supremacy over the accused heretics, and the tribunal was reduced in 1551 to the role of observers only.

When Pope Paul IV (1555–59) and Pope Pius IV (1559–65) reigned, the Roman Inquisition attempted to export its jurisdiction outside of the Papal States. Over time, the papacy exerted more and more control over Venetian and other tribunals, including taking over the right to appoint inquisitors of its own choosing. A Jewish community, or ghetto, was active in Venice and by definition, as non–Christians they were exempt from the Inquisition. But numbers of Spanish and Portuguese Conversos had migrated to Venice, and came under the suspicion that they continued to Judaize in secret. Some trials of Conversos took place in Venice, but the volume of cases and severity of punishments were nowhere near the levels of the Spanish Inquisition.

Tribunal Procedures

The Roman Inquisition was required to follow prevailing rule and court procedures, not only subject to approval from Rome but also in compliance with secular rules of court. Departing from the days when Dominican inquisitors roamed throughout France and Germany and set up tribunals wherever they wished, the Roman Inquisition relied on centrally regulated procedures and safeguards. There were more steps required in determining and approving the appropriate outcome for the tribunal.

Some changes provided accused heretics with a better chance at building a defense and even winning an acquittal. Witnesses and accusers were required to give depositions under oath for the first time. The accused was allowed to have an attorney, and written transcripts of the tribunal proceedings were given to the accused for review, with time allowed to prepare rebuttal testimony. The use of torture was also changed from previous practices. In the past, interrogators used torture to obtain confessions as part of the initial interrogation. In the Roman Inquisition, torture was allowed only *after* the defense had presented its case and only when evidence of guilt was strong, in the opinion of the inquisitor. A first offender was likely to get a lighter sentence than a repeat offender. "Life in prison" (*carcere perpetuo*) normally meant the guilty person would be paroled after three years, for example. Many prison sentences consisted of home arrest since Rome had few secure prisons.

One of the most interesting changes in tribunal practices was in the determination of sentences on the part of the Supreme Congregation in Rome. Any implausible confessions were thrown out if they were contradicted by the defendant's testimony during the trial. This prevented indictment on torture-induced confessions of the most bizarre crimes, notably in trials for witchcraft. In other parts of Europe, many were burned at the stake after confessing to the most unlikely of supernatural crimes; in the Roman Inquisition, this was mitigated with oversight by Rome, even with the most zealous inquisitors operating tribunals.

Prison and death sentences were in the minority, with lesser penalties prevailing. These included penance in several forms including wearing a penitential garment (the *sanbenito*) and cap (*coroza*), public readings on the steps of a local Church, fines, and recitals of prayers. The sentence of burning at the stake was applied in cases where an accused was "obstinate" or "unrepentant" and refused to admit error or reconcile with the Church. Repeat offenders and those accused of especially severe heretical crimes (such as denying the virgin birth of Mary of the divinity of Christ) also faced the possibility of a death sentence.

The procedures of interrogation and trial during the Roman Inquisition were well organized and records were kept of every phase. The purpose of keeping records and recording everything was twofold: to provide evidence and to find additional defendants. The written record (kept by the notary) became a document presented to the tribunal as evidence. So during interrogation, the notary recorded every question and answer given during questioning and torture. The procedure was kept secret, however and for good reason. Under interrogation, the accused was expected to name accomplices; torture was applied to get additional names, and when others were named the Holy Office wanted to quickly arrest them and subject them to the same treatment as the original defendant. And so, as in past Inquisitions, the arrest rates were impressively high. The process, because torture was used, was highly successful and there was no shortage of heretics.

One difference between this stage and previous ones, however, was that the rate of executions was far lower than before. For the first time, the tribunals were cautious about applying the death penalty and preferred to create acts of contrition among those accused, resulting in their returning to the Church and its good graces. It was also possible for accused heretics to clear themselves of charges if evidence was not strong enough, or if the defendant's attorney was able to impeach witness testimony in cross examination. The accused heretic was also allowed to produce his own witnesses to contradict the testimony of prosecution witnesses. Torture was usually applied only in cases of repeat offenders, extreme offenses, or those who would not name accomplices.

Controls over the use of coercion were also strictly enforced. The tribunal's inquisitor was allowed to authorize torture only if evidence was strong, and only after the defense had concluded its case. The inquisitor also needed approval from an advisory council representing the Holy Office. If torture was authorized, procedures issued by Rome had to be followed. If a defendant did not change his testimony even under torture, the evidence was thrown out and the accused person absolved. This was rare, and inquisitors had considerable leeway to determine the duration and severity of torture aimed at obtaining a confession and the names of others as part of the desired outcome.

For the first time in Inquisition history, a defendant had the legal right to an attorney to provide a defense; and a person who could not afford an attorney was provided one without charge. But an important distinction has to be drawn between the tribunal of the Roman Inquisition and today's "right to an attorney." If during the procedure the accused's attorney concluded that his client was guilty but not willing to admit his error and repent, the attorney was obligated to abandon his defense. The consequence of not abandoning a defendant who seemed to be guilty was that the attorney could also be accused of heresy, ending up as a defendant himself.

However, even if the lawyer thought his client was guilty, he had alternatives to quitting the defense. If he could make a case that the accused person had been insane or drunk, for example, pleading extenuating circumstances could affect the trial's outcome. The lawyer also had the right to ask for postponements, to bring doubt on the reliability of witnesses, or to point to inconsistency in testimony against his client. No longer were Inquisition tribunals stacked so that virtually every defendant entered the proceedings already presumed guilty.

Defendants could bring witness testimony into doubt if a defendant could show that the witness had ulterior motives. Now that testimony had to be given under oath, perjury became a serious offense. If the tribunal concluded that witness testimony was false, changes of perjury were brought and witnesses were imprisoned and placed on trial. The Holy Office acknowledged that in previous tribunals, numerous guilty verdicts had been entered based on false testimony; the new procedures were designed to improve the quality and reliability of evidence.

Sentences rarely included a death penalty. Imprisonment was more common, and many were sentenced to confinement in monasteries. Some were kept in cells within the monastery, and others were allowed freedom of movement within the monastic grounds. An even more reduced version of imprisonment, house arrest or limited movement within a town or village, was another version of punishment. The relatively rare death sentences were carried out by way of the traditional method, burning at the stake. A majority of those pronounced guilty were sentenced to public humiliation involving wearing of penitential clothing or performing public penance. The *auto-da-fé* was a public ceremony concluding with reconciliation between the heretic and the Church. "Reconciliation" involved applying punishment at the conclusion of the public announcement of a verdict, performing a mass, and reading of other statements.

Jesuits and the Roman Inquisition

At approximately the same time that Pope Paul III created the new Roman Inquisition, another force emerged in the Church, a new order of priests that answered directly to the pope. The Society of Jesus (the Jesuits) was created in 1540 with the approval of the pope, who instructed that no one could intervene in or supervise Jesuit activities except the pope. The Jesuits became the papacy's primary enforcement arm throughout Europe for fighting heresy, with a particular emphasis on Protestant heretics.

The Jesuits were fanatical intellectuals who followed guidelines set by the order's founder, Ignatius of Loyola (1491–1556), a Spanish knight who was named by the pope as the first superior general of the new order. Ignatius wrote the Jesuit Constitution, which stressed unquestioning loyalty directly to the pope and included the requirement of strict discipline, termed *perinde ac cadaver* ("the discipline of a corpse"). The motto of the Jesuit order was *Ad maiorem Dei gloriam* (for the greater glory of God).

The Jesuits were active throughout Europe but were a factor in the formation of the Roman Inquisition. Unlike the Dominicans of past Inquisitions who emphasized tribunals and punishment, Jesuits focused on education and conversion and created active missions and schools outside of Europe. The original intention of this order was to create both missionary and hospital centers in Jerusalem and to take a vow of absolute loyalty to the pope. Ignatius originally named his group the Friends of the Lord (*Amigos en el Señor*), or the Company of Jesus, referring to the military "company." Ignatius, himself a retired soldier, organized the Jesuits under a military structure.

Jesuits formed an important office of the Roman Inquisition. Ignatius first traveled to Rome in 1537 to ask Paul III to allow his followers to become ordained priests. On June 24, 1537, the first Jesuits were ordained in Venice. The ongoing war between Roman emperor Charles V and the Ottoman Empire prevented the Jesuits from pursuing their original goal of a pilgrimage to Jerusalem. So the Jesuits remained for the next three years in Italy. On September 27, 1540, Paul III created the order with his bull *Regimini militantis ecclesiæ* (To the government of the Church Militant).

The first purpose expressed by Ignatius in his *Formula of the Institute* was conformity among members to the conversion of non–Catholics. One historian wrote that this initial purpose was "the fundamental charter of the order, of which all subsequent documents were elaborations and to which they had to conform." Ignatius expected absolute obedience from members of his order. In his *Formula*, he wrote in the opening statement:

> Whoever desires to serve as a soldier of God beneath the banner of the cross in our Society, which we desire to be designated by the name of Jesus, and to serve the Lord alone and the Church his Spouse, under the Roman pontiff, the vicar of Christ on earth, should [agree to] ... a vow of perpetual chastity, poverty, and obedience....[5]

Beyond setting up schools in all parts of Europe, the Jesuits undertook the mission of converting non–Christians to Catholicism, and especially returning Protestants to the Church. The order, which zealously fought to counter the Reformation wherever it established missions, has been referred to as the pope's elite troops and soldiers. The Jesuit movement was effective at curtailing the spread of Protestantism and in converting many to Catholicism.

By the time the Roman Inquisition began, the Church's ability to enforce its doctrines was limited to the areas it ruled directly, known as the Papal States. Its political power in the remainder of Europe was largely gone and even while inquisitorial tribunals continued to work in cooperation with secular courts to carry out sentences, the simple authority to conduct Inquisitions on a large scale was coming to an end. The claim and restating of the Church's universal power, published during the Council of Trent (1545–63), carried with it no enforcement powers. When Pope Pius IV issued his ratifying bull *Benedictus Deus* (the Blessing of God) on January 26, 1564, he clarified that Catholics were required to strictly obey the Church under threat of excommunication. The pope also appointed a commission of cardinals to help him in enforcing his and the Council's decrees.

Development and Expansion of the Roman Inquisition

The Roman Inquisition was intended as an office to curtail the Reformation in Italy in its initial formation. During the same period, attempts were undertaken to reconcile Catholicism and Lutheranism, without success. The Diet of Regensburg in 1541 tried to reach agreement on matters of Church authority, discipline and definition of the sacraments, but by that time Lutheranism had taken hold in Europe and no compromise was possible. What had started out as an attempt by Luther to reform the Church from within had evolved into a movement with its own inertia. It was the beginning of a new schism in which the Roman Church would be broken into two major segments, Catholic and Protestant.

The Roman Inquisition successfully prevented Lutheranism from spreading in Italy. But elsewhere, with very little legal authority or enforcement power, its primary effort was the Jesuit-led educational and conversion-based efforts to bolster Catholic doctrine. Past Inquisitions had relied on Dominicans as inquisitors to enforce Church doctrine by publicly trying and executing heretics, at times for even minor offenses, including testifying as to the good character of someone accused of heresy. But in the Roman Inquisition, the Church took a different approach. Under the Jesuits, emphasis was placed on education, prevention of breakaway trends, and conversion. At the same time, even while the strategy became more intellectual and less punitive, the Roman Inquisition relied on censorship of literature and art, and eventually spread its definition of heresy into other realms.

Among these was a new jurisdiction, over behavior among the clergy. This evolved into the modern-day functions of the Church and its oversight of priests and nuns. In its beginnings, which were formulated at the Council of Trent, the activities of "Regulars" (priests) were to be supervised by the Church in the future:

> The holy Synod forbids, that any Regular, under the pretext of preaching, or lecturing, or of any other pious work, place himself at the service of any prelate, prince, university, community, or of any other person, or place, whatsoever, without permission from his own Superior; nor shall any privilege or faculty, obtained from others in regard hereof avail him anything. But should any one act contrary hereto, he shall be punished as disobedient, at the discretion of his Superior. Nor shall it be lawful for Regulars to withdraw from their own convents, even under the pretext of repairing to their own Superiors; unless they have been sent, or summoned, by them. And whoever shall be found to be without the order aforesaid in writing, shall be punished as a deserter from his Institute by the Ordinaries of the places. As to those who are sent to the universities for the sake of their studies, they shall dwell in convents only; otherwise they shall be proceeded against by the Ordinaries.[6]

The Inquisition gradually moved away from its infamous trials of heretics (who included Conversos, Lutherans, witches, sorcerers, alchemists, magicians, and blasphemers, to name a few) and became an office with power only in the geographically limited Papal States, and limited also to wrongdoing among the clergy. So prevention and punishment of clerical morality and censorship of published materials became the major efforts of the Inquisition. The office of the Roman Inquisition was briefly abolished in 1799 when France annexed the Roman Republic that had been formed the year before. In 1814, papal rule was restored in Rome and the Papal States and the Inquisition were quickly reinstated as well. But the papacy would never again hold the level of power it had in earlier centuries.

Before the duties of Roman Inquisition were limited to clerical oversight and censorship, a final chapter took place in Italy during the 17th century. In this period, the Roman Inquisition turned its attention to science and the arts. One famous victim defined this era with his scientific claims and later conflict with the Roman Church and its Inquisition. His name was Galileo Galilei.

CHAPTER 14

Galileo and the Center of the Universe

> I, Galileo Galilei ... abandon the false opinion that the Sun was the center of the universe and immoveable, and that the Earth was not the center of the same and that it moved ... [and] detest the said errors and heresies, and generally all and every error and sect contrary to the Holy Catholic Church.
>
> — Galileo, recantation to the tribunal of the Inquisition, 1633

During the 17th century, the Church was confronting modern times on many levels. The traditional Inquisition was becoming outdated as nations formed out of older feudal city-states and the Renaissance brought innovations in art, music and science. This revolutionary change across social and cultural lines increased the power of monarchs while reducing the power and influence of the Church. It was developments in the sciences that kept the Inquisition alive during this time, with very fundamental problems between what the Church believed and what science could prove.

On an equally important scale, social revolutions were accompanied by enlightened ideas on many topics beyond science. Artists and writers for the first time were free to express ideas, even those ideas that were not popular with the Church. The Index of Forbidden Books was an attempt by the Church to control the spread of such ideas, and to prevent heretical writings or art from reaching the masses. But the Church could not prevent people from learning about these changes.

Censorship was as much a reaction to the invention of movable type as it was to new scientific ideas. Publication of books meant that the Church could not control the dissemination of literature. The Reformation had created a literate revolution as growing numbers of people challenged Catholicism as the sole representation of Christian belief. This challenge also brought into question the authority of the pope and his claim to be the vicar of Christ on earth.

The Index of Forbidden Books (also called the Pauline Index for its founder, Pope Paul IV) included the works of nearly 600 authors, but the Church would discover that with each subsequent revision it needed to add a growing number of new authors and their books. The index censored existing books but did not prevent the generation of new ones.

The Council of Trent elaborated on the idea of the index, and issued its own Tridentine Index in 1564. The procedure for placing works on the index was complex and involved three steps. First, the Congregation of the Index, a special body created at the Council of Trent, met to decide which works would be called heretical. Second, a proposed list was sent to the inquisitor for review. Third, the inquisitor approved the list and then distributed it to all booksellers and publishers. These distributors were required to sign pledges to not publish or sell any of the books on the list. Failure to agree to these terms could result in booksellers' being charged with heresy and brought before the Inquisition.

Censors invariably assume that banning books will prevent ideas from spreading and will also prevent any similar disapproved writings from following. However, ideas cannot be stopped through censorship. Even though the Index of Forbidden Books became the papacy's main weapon for preventing the spread of science in the 17th century, the effort failed.

The Great Debate Between Church and Science

The Church identified many ideas as heresies, and the Roman Inquisition was originally focused on the Reformation forces and keeping them out of Italy. But this quickly changed and a major target of the Inquisition became scientific theory that contradicted Church doctrine. The most serious threat was the heliocentric theory, the belief that the earth revolves around the sun, and not the other way around. To the Church, this was heresy because it contradicted the Bible. If the words in the Scriptures were true, it meant that God created the universe to benefit the earth; therefore, the belief that the earth was not the center of the universe must be heresy.

The belief that the earth was the center of all things was based not only on biblical passages, but also on the long-accepted writings of Aristotle. The Church accepted Aristotle's version of science as the truth, and the Dominican Order made efforts to conform science and theology. The famous Dominican writer and theologian Thomas Aquinas wrote in his best-known book, *Summa Theologica*, that faith and reason were both necessary and existed with one another in harmony. Aquinas stated that God revealed Himself through nature, and based his theology on Aristotle's conception of the earth as stationary. This theology became one of the core beliefs of the Dominican Order; so anyone who

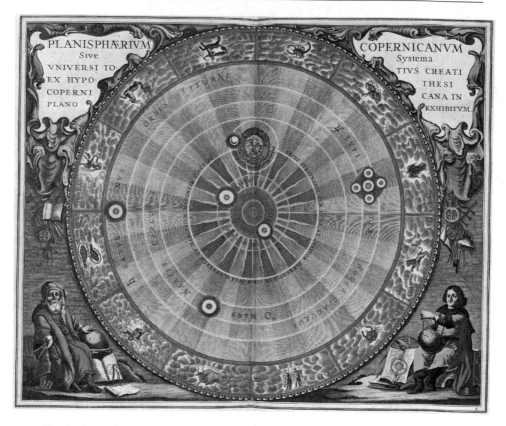

Planisphere of Copernicus, the system of the entire created universe according to the hypothesis of Copernicus, exhibited in a planar view. (Andreas Cellarius, 1646.) This work demonstrates the heliocentric theory, the idea — revolutionary in the 17th century — that the earth revolves around the sun rather than vice-versa.

questioned the belief in the earth as the center of the universe (the *geocentric model*) must be wrong.

Support for the accepted beliefs came from biblical passages and even from the major Reformation leaders. Martin Luther cited the book of Joshua and called the heliocentric theory "the over-witty notions of a fool."[1] Luther's reference was to Joshua 10:12:

> Joshua spoke with the Lord, and in the presence of Israel said: "Stand still, you sun, at Gibeon; you moon, at the vale of Aijalon."[2]

John Calvin also disputed the scientific challenge to Church doctrine, referring to the Bible and to simple logic. He asked:

> How could the earth hang suspended in the air were it not upheld by God's hand? By what means could it maintain itself unmoved, while the heavens above are in constant rapid motion, did not its Divine Maker fix and establish it?[3]

Calvin also criticized Nicolaus Copernicus, who originated the heliocentric theory, saying, "The earth is set firmly in place and cannot be moved. Who will dare to place the authority of this man Copernicus above the Holy Scriptures?"[4]

There was plenty of authority to cite in support of the prevailing wisdom on this topic. In addition to theologians and scientists of the day, and most notably the Dominicans, all adopting the theories of Aristotle as the last word, the Scriptures also offered ample evidence that the earth, not the sun, resided at the center of the universe. Among the citations favoring the geocentric belief were:

> The Lord has become King, clothed with majesty; the Lord is robed, girded with might. The earth is established immovably [Psalms 93:1].

> Declare among the nations, "The Lord is King; the world is established immovably" [Psalms 96:10].

> Tremble before him, all the earth. He has established the earth immovably [I Chronicles 16:30].

> You have spread out the heavens like a tent, and laid the beams of your dwelling on the waters; you take the clouds for your chariot, riding on the wings of the wind; you make the winds your messengers, flames of fire your servants; you fixed the earth on its foundation so that it will never be moved [Psalms 104:2–5].

> The sun rises and the sun goes down; and then it speeds to its place and rises there again [Ecclesiastes 1:5].

> God made two great lights, the greater to govern the day and the lesser to govern the night; he also made the stars. God put these lights in the vault of the heavens to give light on earth [Genesis 1:16–17].

> [God] made the earth and fashioned it, and by himself fixed it firmly [Isaiah 45:18].[5]

The earliest known expression of the heliocentric theory predated Christianity itself. The Greek scientist Archimedes introduced this idea in *The Sand Reckoner*, a paper of approximately eight pages written ca. 215 B.C., intended to express large numbers. Archimedes referred to an earlier work published by Aristarchus of Samos (ca. 200 B.C.), who wrote of the sun as the center of the known universe.

The Copernicus Dispute

The purpose Archimedes had for citing the heliocentric theory posed by Aristarchus was not to challenge the geocentric beliefs of others, but to create a mathematical model for estimating the distance of the stars and thus the approximate the size of the universe. The only model Archimedes could envision for this was based on an estimation of the distance the earth traveled in one orbit of the sun. This idea was ignored by scientists, including Aristotle, for centuries. His geocentric model fit perfectly with the core belief among Christians: The sun was created to make night and day on earth, and the earth was the center of the universe. The first serious challenge to this theory came from the Polish astronomer Nicolaus Copernicus (1473–1543).

Copernicus was not only a scientist, physician and lawyer, but also a church administrator. Astronomy was merely a hobby for him. His landmark publication was *On the Revolutions of the Celestial Orbs* (*De Revolutionibus Orbium Coelestium*), published one year after his death. He stated that the earth rotated on its axis once per day and orbited around the sun once per year. At first very little controversy was raised by the book, which Copernicus dedicated to Pope Paul III. In his preface Copernicus explained to the pope:

> Holy Father, some who discover that I here ascribe certain motions to the terrestrial globe will shout that I must be immediately repudiated. But a philosopher's ideas are not subject to the judgment of ordinary persons, because he endeavors to seek the truth in all things, to the extent permitted to human reason by God.

> Therefore I long debated whether to publish this volume, or, like the Pythagoreans, to reserve philosophy's secrets for kinsmen and friends.[6]

The theory expressed in Copernicus' text was that the sun could be proven mathematically to be the center of the universe (in his day, Copernicus was only able to observe movement of the closest planets, so the "universe" was also restricted to the sun-centered solar system to which earth belongs). He also observed that the earth orbited around the sun in an annual orbit, and he defined the order of the planets.

In his first chapter, Copernicus posited that the universe is spherical. In Chapter 2 he argued the case for a spherical earth:

> The waters also press down into the surface of the sphere, as sailors

Portrait of Nicolaus Copernicus, unknown artist, 16th century. Copernicus created new science by concluding after observations that the planets seemed to revolve around the sun. This defied Church teachings and the belief in the earth as the center of the universe.

know, since land which is not seen from a ship is visible from the top of its mast. Likewise, if a light is attached to the top of the mast, as the ship draws away from land, those who remain ashore see the light drop down gradually until it finally disappears, as though setting.[7]

In Chapter 10 ("The Order of the Heavenly Spheres"), Copernicus summarized the most controversial aspect of his theory:

I feel no shame in asserting that the moon and the earth traverse a grand circle amid the rest of the planets in an annual revolution around the sun. Moreover, since the sun remains stationary, whatever appears as a motion of the sun is really due rather to the motion of the earth.[8]

Most scientists in the 16th century rejected the Copernican theory. But it was tested mathematically and proven to provide more accurate navigational tables. So astronomers gradually accepted the heliocentric point of view. In 1576, Thomas Digges, an English astronomer and mathematician, translated *De Revolutionibus* into English and published *A Perfit Description of the Coelestiall Orbes* which furthered the Copernican point of view and supported the concept with mathematical proofs.

Around 1610, Paolo Antonio Foscarini, a theologian in Naples, published a book called *Lettera ... sopra l'opinione ... del Copernico*, an attempt to show that Copernican theories were not in conflict with biblical verses. This brought Copernicus' *De Revolutionibus* to the attention of the Church, and the book was placed on the Index of Forbidden Books. It remained under ban until 1835.

Giordano Bruno

A Dominican friar in Naples named Giordano Bruno (1548–1600) was held in high esteem for his knowledge of the philosophy of Aristotle. He was drawn to the debate over geocentric and heliocentric theories and gradually was convinced that there was something to the idea of the sun as center of the universe. This brought Bruno attention from the Naples office of the Inquisition.

In 1576, Bruno left Naples to avoid arrest. However, in Rome the same problem recurred and the Roman office wanted to persecute him for holding views opposed to those of the Church. He fled once again, and also left the Dominican Order. He relocated in France where he spent the next seven years lecturing on the topic of astronomy. Bruno wrote several books during this period. These included two books published in 1584: *Cena de le Ceneri* (The Ash Wednesday Supper) and *De l'Infinito, Universo e Mondi* (On the Infinite Universe and Worlds). Bruno stated in the latter work that the universe was infinite in size and contained an infinite number of stars and planets, with many planets inhabited by intelligent life. This progressive view of the universe led to trouble between Bruno and the office of the Inquisition.

His controversial beliefs forced Bruno to move several times through the

The Trial of Giordano Bruno by the Roman Inquisition. **Bronze relief by Ettore Ferrari (1845–1929). Copernicus was never tried by the Inquisition, and Galileo later escaped execution. Bruno, however, was imprisoned for eight years before being burned at the stake in 1600 for heresy. (Campo de' Fiord, Rome.)**

following decade until in 1591 he relocated to Venice. He was arrested and placed on trial. Recanting his previous statements and writings, he was sent to Rome for yet another trial the following year. He was kept imprisoned for the next eight years and interrogated several times about his beliefs. The Inquisition's tribunal concluded that Bruno was a heretic for making statements about the nature of the universe that did not conform to Scripture or to Church doctrine. He was burned at the stake in 1600.*

Bruno was a visionary, one of the first scientists to speculate about the scope of the universe and the possibility of alien life. For the Church of 1600, such ideas were utterly unacceptable; the entire Christian doctrine was based on the geocentric model and on God's creation of the entire universe for the purpose of serving earth's needs and sustaining life. If there were other planets and suns and other intelligent life, it brought into question the entire basis of the religion, going back to the book of Genesis.

Whether Bruno was condemned for agreeing with Copernicus, for declaring the universe to be infinite, or for speculating that intelligent life existed elsewhere, is not known. Any one of these beliefs was considered blasphemous

*In 1976, a geologist named Jack Hartung proposed that a lunar impact crater on the moon be named after Bruno. From that date onward, this crater has been known as the Giordano Bruno crater.

and could have resulted in a death sentence. Although death sentences were rare during the Roman Inquisition, it was clear that in the climate at the beginning of the 18th century, the risk of capital punishment was very real. At this time, Galileo was beginning to develop ideas of his own about the nature of the universe and he was surely aware of the risks he faced in defying Church beliefs.

Bruno's trial and execution represent an expansion of the Roman Inquisition. From its original purpose — preventing the Reformation from spreading to Italy — its focus had shifted to the heresy of scientific expression. Any scientist who published ideas that were contrary to the Church's geocentric beliefs was at risk. The most famous scientist who came to the attention of the Inquisition was Galileo.

Galileo and the Scientific Revolution

One of the most prominent scientists of the modern age was Galileo (1564–1642).[*] He played a prominent role both in the Inquisition and in a trend in history known as the scientific revolution. This revolution was characterized by several changes in how the natural world was viewed. Most important among these changes was the idea, based on Copernican writings, that the sun is the center of the universe, and not the earth. Another important attribute of this theory was the replacement of Aristotle's belief that matter consisted of five elements (earth, water, air, fire and ether).[9]

Galileo also contributed to the scientific revolution through the proposal of what is today called the scientific method. He wrote that physics

> is written in this grand book — I mean the universe — which stands continually open to our gaze, but it cannot be understood unless one first learns to comprehend the language and interpret the characters in which it is written. It is written in the language of mathematics, and its characters are triangles, circles, and other geometrical figures, without which it is humanly impossible to understand a single word of it; without these, one is wandering around in a dark labyrinth.[10]

In the same book, Galileo referred to mathematics as the language of God. His ideas were revolutionary and he is attributed with leading the world into the modern scientific era with his ideas concerning mathematics, physics and astronomy. One of his greatest accomplishments was the development of telescope design that vastly improved astronomical observation. With his improved telescope, Galileo was able to see and write about sunspots, to document the phases of Venus and to discover the four largest moons of Jupiter: Io, Europa, Callisto and Ganymede. He called this group of four "starlets," as he termed them, the Medicean planets to honor the influential Medici family of Italy.†

---

[*]Full name: Galileo di Vincenzo Bonaiuti de' Galilei.

†These four are today called the Galilean moons in honor of their discoverer.

During Galileo's life, most scientists accepted the geocentric beliefs advanced by the Church and supported by Aristotle's theories of the universe. From 1610 onward, Galileo publicly disputed these beliefs and theories and promoted the alternate heliocentric theory. This theory was controversial not only among scientists, but also among clerics.

In 1611, a Dominican friar, Niccolo Lorini, wrote a complaint to the Inquisition concerning Galileo's beliefs. Galileo responded with a defense written to Monsignor Piero Dini, a powerful Vatican official. His arguments were based on scientific observation and at this point the Inquisition was not prepared to challenge Galileo directly.

On December 20, 1614, another Dominican, Tommaso Caccini, gave a sermon in Florence denouncing Galileo. He stated that science and mathematics were contrary to the Scriptures and heretical. To support this belief, Caccini quoted the biblical passage, "There stood before them two men robed in white, who said, 'Men of Galilee, why stand there looking up in the sky?'"[11]

Caccini wanted the Inquisition to place Galileo on trial for heresy, but his sermon was not met with universally positive reaction. The Church rejected his arguments for the most part, agreeing only that Galileo's beliefs about sunspots (documented through his work *Letter on Sunspots*) was heretical. Based on this letter, the Inquisition again investigated Galileo, and announced on February 26, 1616, that he was banned from teaching, speaking in public, or writing any more about the theory that the earth orbited around the sun. The tribunal announced that the heliocentric theory was absurd and heretical, calling it "false and contrary to scripture."[12]

Pope Paul V (1605–21) ordered Jesuit Robert Cardinal Bellarmine, an esteemed scholar of the day and author of *Disputations About the Controversies of the Christian Faith Against the Heretics of This Time* (*Disputationes de Controversiis Christianae Fidei Adversus Hujus Temporis Haereticos* [1586–1593]), to issue a stern warning to Galileo. Bellarmine told Galileo that he was permanently banned from making any oral or written statement about the Copernican theory.

Galileo reacted to the stern warning by reversing his support of Copernican belief. This would have ended the matter, but in 1624, Pope Urban VIII (1623–44), a friend and patron, gave Galileo permission to write about Copernican theories on the condition that he treat the idea as a mathematical concept only, and not as fact.

With this assurance from the highest Church authority, Galileo embarked on another project. He published his best-known work in 1632, *Dialogue Concerning the Two Chief World Systems* (*Dialogo sopra i due massimi sistemi del mondo*). His original title had been *Dialogue on the Tides* because in the book he attempted to explain the earth's movement and used the changing ocean tides as proof that it did, in fact, move. But when he presented it to the office of the Inquisition for approval, he was ordered to remove all references to the tides from the title of the book as well as any claims in support of the earth's movement.

Even though he changed the title as instructed, Galileo's book presented the belief that the earth did move and that it orbited the sun, a direct contradiction to Church doctrine and accepted science of the day. He was described by the tribunal as under "grave suspicion of heresy" and forced to recant his statements publicly. He was sentenced to spend the remainder of his life under house arrest. His famous *Dialogue* was placed on the Index of Forbidden Books, where it remained until 1835. Galileo's sentence was not officially overturned until October 31, 1992, when Pope John Paul II (1978–2005) expressed regret on behalf of the Church about how Galileo had been treated. The pope officially conceded the point that the earth was not unmovable but orbited around the sun. This conclusion, the pope said, was based on a study conducted by the Pontifical Council for Culture.*

Galileo and the Inquisition

The problem Galileo faced was twofold. In any age, scientists who propose ideas contrary to current belief will meet resistance

Galileo Galilei, engraving taken from a watercolor portrait by Domenico Passignano. The best-known victim of the Roman Inquisition, Galileo created the modern scientific revolution with his theories. His support of Copernicus and the heliocentric theory brought Galileo to the attention of the Inquisition, even though he was a good friend of Pope Urban VIII. (Wallace Wood, *The Hundred Greatest Men*, 1885.)

*The Pontifical Council for Culture (*Pontificium Consilium de Cultura*) is a Church council created to oversee relationships between the Church and different cultures. It was founded by John Paul II on May 20, 1982. On March 25, 1993, the pope merged the Council with the Pontifical Council for Dialogue with Nonbelievers.

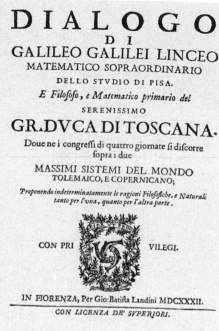

Title page from Galileo's most famous and controversial work, which presented the heliocentric theory as science and not just theory, leading the Inquisition to charge him with heresy. He was sentenced to life under house arrest.

and even ridicule from scientific peers. This was only part of the issue in the 17th century. Galileo also faced the threat of the Inquisition. So his ideas were considered not only scientifically false, but also heretical.

The Church had quietly tolerated the scientific dispute while continuing to describe Copernican theories as utterly false and heretical. But Galileo forced the issue to the front and the Inquisition was compelled to respond. The process had begun in 1611 when the Inquisition first studied Galileo's beliefs and cleared him, while also declaring that the heliocentric concept was heretical. However, Galileo's name was known to the Inquisition and it set him up for further inquiry. In the mindset of the Roman Inquisition, any subsequent actions contradicting Church doctrine defined Galileo as a recidivist, and that was a serious matter. It had always been a precept of the Inquisition that a heretic who had been given the chance to reverse his beliefs was accepted back by the Church, either with or without punishment. However, if that person later returned to a heretical belief, it was a far more serious form of heresy.

Galileo was cleared a second time in 1625 when accused of heresy after publishing *The Assayer* (*Il Saggiatore*). The charge was brought that the atomic theory Galileo presented in that book contradicted the belief in the Eucharist, in which bread and wine are transubstantiated into Christ's flesh and blood. It was rare for someone to be investigated twice by the Inquisition and cleared both times; Galileo was the exception to this, but the third time he was not so fortunate. After publishing *Dialogue* in 1632, Pope Urban VIII, who had previously granted Galileo permission to continue his writings, banned publication of the latest book. This was followed by Galileo's third tribunal before the Inquisition, in which he was interrogated for 18 days. The trial resulted in his sentence of house arrest and forced public recantation of his heliocentric beliefs at the Church of Santa Maria Sofia Minerva. His recantation was a requirement in order to avoid a more serious outcome. He stated:

> I, Galileo Galilei, son of the late Vincenzio Galilei of Florence, aged 70 years, tried personally by this court, and kneeling before You, the most Eminent and reverend Lord Cardinals, Inquisitors-General throughout the Christian Republic against heretical depravity, having before my eyes the Most Holy Gospels, and laying on them my own hands; I swear that I have always believed, I believe now, and with God's help I will in future believe all which the Holy Catholic and Apostolic Church doth hold, preach, and teach. But since I, after having been admonished by this Holy Office entirely to abandon the false opinion that the Sun was the center of the universe and immoveable, and that the Earth was not the center of the same and that it moved, and that I was neither to hold, defend, nor teach in any manner whatever, either orally or in writing, the said false doctrine; and after having received a notification that the said doctrine is contrary to Holy Writ, I did write and cause to be printed a book in which I treat of the said already condemned doctrine, and bring forward arguments of much efficacy in its favor, without arriving at any solution: I have been judged vehemently suspected of heresy, that is, of having held and believed that the Sun is the center of the universe and immoveable, and that the Earth is not the center of the same, and that it does move. Nevertheless, wishing to remove from the minds of your Eminences and all faithful Christians this vehement suspicion reasonably conceived against me, I abjure with sincere heart and unfeigned faith, I curse and detest the said errors and heresies, and generally all and every error and sect contrary to the Holy Catholic Church. And I swear that for the future I will neither say nor assert in speaking or writing such things as may bring upon me similar suspicion; and if I know any heretic, or one suspected of heresy, I will denounce him to this Holy Office, or to the Inquisitor and Ordinary of the place in which I may be....[13]

The Galileo controversy was, however, far more than a simple disagreement of either theology or science. It represents a turning point in both camps. For science, Galileo's observations and ideas were the start of the modern scientific revolution. For the Inquisition, it was an all too public attempt by the Church to silence opposition views to its doctrine. But in that attempt, the obvious flaws in Church doctrine became glaringly obvious. The Church had to either reconcile its doctrines to what was provable by science, or continue to ban books and threaten dissenters with burning at the stake. No longer could the Inquisition continue as it had in the past, by silencing "heresy" with burning at the stake or house arrest.

Galileo was vocal, widely published, and well known. This probably explains why he was able to escape the Inquisition on two occasions before his final appearance. The three portions of his punishment upon being declared a heretic (house arrest, public recanting of his previous statements, and banning of his books and further publication) were severe, but not as severe as his sentence could have been. He was originally sentenced to life in prison but due to his ailing health, this was reduced to house arrest. During his entire trial, however, Galileo was aware that a more dire outcome was possible. Had he insisted on retaining his scientific beliefs without contrition, there was a good chance that he would have sentenced to burning at the stake.

Galileo's Later Years

Even under threat, however, the truth of Galileo's science couldn't be kept quiet. He was allowed to return to his villa near Florence where he eventually went blind. While serving his sentence of house arrest, he wrote yet another book in 1638, *Discourses and Mathematical Demonstrations Relating to Two New Sciences* (*Discorsi e dimostrazioni matematiche, intorno a due nuove scienze*). This book summarized Galileo's work in physics throughout his lifetime and, unlike the controversial claims in his previous works, *Two New Sciences* was relatively uncontroversial. Even though the Inquisition had banned Galileo from publishing any further works, he was able to find a publisher in Leiden, The Netherlands (Elsevier).*

Two New Sciences presented "the science of materials" and "the law of falling bodies." In the science of materials, Galileo examined the strength of materials and the motion of objects. In the law of falling bodies, he presented experiments to demonstrate that rolling balls of different weight fell at the same rate of speed. This idea was revolutionary for its time, leading in part to Isaac Newton's later explanation of the laws of motion. Galileo explained his experiment based on use of an inclined ramp and bronze balls of different sizes and weights. He described how the time of travel for the balls was measured using a water clock, "a large vessel of water placed in an elevated position; to the bottom of this vessel was soldered a pipe of small diameter giving a thin jet of water, which we collected in a small glass during the time of each descent, whether for the whole length of the channel or for a part of its length; the water thus collected was weighed, after each descent, on a very accurate balance; the differences and ratios of these weights gave us the differences and ratios of the times, and this with such accuracy that although the operation was repeated many, many times, there was no appreciable discrepancy in the results."[14]

Whether Galileo's ideas as expressed in *Two New Sciences* would have been

*Elsevier continues to publish today, and is the world's largest source of scientific and medical books.

treated as heretical by the Inquisition is not known. He was not summoned before another tribunal. However, publication of this important book violated two important "rules" under the Inquisition. First, he was instructed to refrain from any further publishing. Second, he published without prior permission from the Congregation of the Index as an office of the Inquisition.

Upon his death, Ferdinand II, Grand Duke of Tuscany, wanted him buried at the Basilica of Santa Croce next to the tombs of his father and other ancestors; the Grand Duke also wanted to erect a statue honoring Galileo. Both plans were overruled by Urban VIII. Galileo was buried in a small room away from the main portion of the Basilica in a modest grave, and was reburied in the main Basilica nearly a century later in 1737. A monument honoring Galileo was also erected in the Basilica.

In 1718, the ban on publishing Galileo's work was lifted but excluded the most important of his works, the *Dialogue*. In 1741, Pope Benedict XIV (1740–58) allowed publication of Galileo's complete works with some censorship of the *Dialogue* and excluded some letters and lesser known papers.[15]

In 1758, the Church lifted its general prohibition in the Index of Prohibited Books on works promoting heliocentric theory, but the ban on uncensored editions of Galileo's *Dialogue* and Copernicus' *De Revolutionibus* remained in place. This ban was dropped in 1835.

In 1939, Pope Pius XII (1939–58) said in a speech that Galileo was among the "most audacious heroes of research" who had not been "afraid of the stumbling blocks and the risks on the way."[16]

In 1990, Joseph Cardinal Ratzinger (later Pope Benedict XVI) appeared to retreat from the past admiration of Galileo when he wrote that modern views on the topic formed "a symptomatic case that permits us to see how deep the self-doubt of the modern age, of science and technology goes today." Ratzinger also quoted the words of Paul Feyerabend:

> The church at the time of Galileo was much more faithful to reason than Galileo himself, and also took into consideration the ethical and social consequences of Galileo's doctrine. Its verdict against Galileo was rational and just, and revisionism can be legitimized solely for motives of political opportunism.[17]

These pronouncements led up to the 1992 apology by Pope John Paul II, but the topic remained controversial. Galileo was one of the most famous victims of the Inquisition, and his works are part of the foundation of modern science and physics. To the Church and the Inquisition, however, his ideas presented a problem because even though scientifically sound, they challenged their basic doctrines. Dominicans especially feared Galileo's ideas as their entire theology was based on Aquinas and his acceptance of Aristotle's beliefs concerning the universe. The controversy would not go away even with Galileo silenced. Finally, in March 2008 the Vatican decided to build a statue of Galileo within its own grounds, a decision that would have amazed Galileo as well as the Inquisition tribunals of the 17th century.

Stage Four:
The Modern Inquisition

CHAPTER 15

The End of Inquisitions

Ecclesiastical visions of papal monarchy, the church as universal community, negotiations of lay religiosity and autonomy, the mendicant enterprise, and new economics of exterior body and interior soul all interacted with genuine dissent and debate over the nature of the Christian faith, producing a precisely Christian conception of violent persecution.... The souls and bodies of Christians were brought under a control that was understood and presented as divine and earthly....
— Christine Caldwell Ames, *Righteous Persecution*, 2009

The *traditional* Inquisition in its many forms— based on formal tribunals and leading to punishments that included death sentences— gradually faded as the Church lost political power. The "papal monarchy" of the Middle Ages was replaced by a weaker form of Church leadership as countries formed from feudal states of the past, and as governments organized their own autonomous powers, laws, courts, and penal systems. The once unlimited power of the Church, based on a claimed spiritual mandate, was replaced by temporal powers.

Many events and political shifts added to this change in the power structure of the Church. The Protestant Reformation demonstrated that the papacy could be challenged, and figures such as Luther, Calvin and Henry VII all defied the Church in ways that created permanent, new, and distinctly separate Christian sects. Other forces were at work as well. The enlightened European population discovered during the Renaissance that self-expression and Humanist yearnings could provide alternatives to the Church itself. In the 16th and 17th centuries, the Church reacted to the growing Reformation with its own Counter-Reformation.

This movement evolved through several phases. First, the Church held onto the office of the Inquisition to examine and control beliefs and behavior wherever the Church still had the power of enforcement. At the same time, internal reforms focused on returning to a more fundamental expression of spirituality, improving education of clerics and setting examples through piety and good works. This initiative was expressed through the formation of many new religious orders. Third, a concerted effort was made to censor artistic expression through the Inquisition tribunals, and even to control how sacred music was composed. Finally, a new Holy War devastated Europe as Catholics and Protestants wrestled for control. The Thirty Years' War was one of the most devastating and expensive conflicts in European history.

All of these aspects of the Counter-Reformation grew from the age of all-powerful Inquisitions and abuse of power by Church leaders. Nepotism, the selling of indulgences, blatant sexual excess by popes and cardinals, and accumulation by cardinals and bishops of great wealth, all destroyed the reputation of the Church among its own followers.

The Counter-Reformation's Primary Thrust: New Religious Orders

The Counter-Reformation cannot be separated from the evolution of the Inquisition. It was a part of the changing political and spiritual landscape of the Church at the time. The establishment of the Roman Inquisition was the first phase of the Catholic Counter-Reformation (also called the Catholic Revival). The period began in about 1545 with the Council of Trent, and intention was put into action with the Roman Inquisition established in 1560 under the reign of Pius IV. The Counter-Reformation lasted until the end of the Thirty Years' War in 1648.

The Counter-Reformation relied at first on the Inquisition to enforce Church doctrine. As the movement evolved, the effectiveness of the Inquisition lessened due to political changes throughout Europe. In addition, challenging science was a fatal error of the Inquisition because, in spite of the accusation that expressing ideas about the universe contradicted doctrine and Scripture, the facts were easily proven; and educated scientists knew that the Copernican heliocentric theory was true. Other changes that diminished the Inquisition's power were the development of modern autonomous political states and the consolidation of courts and the law into country-specific jurisdictions apart from the Church. As these changes occurred, the Church tried to reform itself from within. The next phase in this movement was the creation of new religious orders and seminaries to train new priests. The Inquisition continued to operate in Spain and Italy, and to a lesser degree throughout Europe. However, no longer could Dominican inquisitors summon, try and execute anyone under suspicion. Local courts insisted on determining whether or not Inquisition tribunals were welcome in their communities.

One of the problems the Church attempted to correct at the beginning of the Counter-Reformation was the growing distance between clergy and lay members of the Church. The initial complaints of Protestant Reformers included the comparison between priests and bishops living in lavish palaces and the common people suffering in poverty. At the Council of Trent, the Church was forced to acknowledge that these complaints had merit. Rather than negotiate with Protestant leaders, however, the Church focused on improving education of its priests, publication of accessible writings such as the missal, and reform of some practices like selling indulgences to finance projects.

The Church put a stop to appointment of bishops in exchange for cash payments or for political purposes, and granted increased power to local bishops over religious life within their dioceses. Within this internal mood of reform, past Inquisition practices fell out of favor as the Church worked to develop new religious orders. These served a dual purpose: to promote Church doctrine throughout the Christian world (and especially among Protestants), and to strengthen parishes through education, piety, and reduced corruption. Among these new orders were the Jesuits, Capuchins, Ursulines, Discalced Carmelites, Theatines, and Barnibites. The newly formed religious orders were part of the Church's effort to combat Protestantism and also became a part of the Counter-Reformation with internal reforms aimed at returning the Church to its fundamentals.

The Jesuit Order, formally the Society of Jesus (*Societas Jesu*), was formed by Ignatius of Loyola in 1534 to prevent the further spread of Lutheranism in Europe; to create educational centers; and to report directly to the pope as a primary enforcement arm in the rapidly changing form of the Inquisition. Organized along military lines, the Jesuits were known for their zeal, unwavering discipline, and extensive training. They were prominent in missions to the Americas and Asia, and aggressively battled Protestant expansion. The order focused on education and conversion rather than the traditional Dominican-led tribunals. The Jesuit Order is today the largest order of males in the Church, with over 19,000 members.[1]

The Capuchin Order, officially called the Order of Friars Minor Capuchin (OFM), was created as a sub-group of the Franciscan Order, originated in 1520 by Matteo de Bascio. He wanted to return to the simple roots of solitude and penance as practiced by St. Francis. At first the Church tried to suppress this new order and attempted to arrest its members and try them through the Inquisition, so they went into hiding. They were accused of abandoning their vows, but in time the Church accepted them as part of the Counter-Reformation. The order established missions overseas and battled Protestant influence in the Americas and Asia.

The Ursulines was an order for the education of girls, founded in Italy by Saint Angela de Merici in 1535. The founder spent 17 years as leader of the Company of St. Ursula (patron saint of the Ursulines). With the purpose of caring for the sick and performing acts of mercy, they were formally recognized in 1544 by Pope Paul III. The ideal of attaining salvation through faith and good works was a repudiation of the concept of *sola scriptura* (by Scripture alone) emphasized by Protestant sects, especially Lutherans.

The Discalced Carmelites (OCD, or Barefoot Carmelites) was a mendicant order established in 1593 as part of a reform movement within the Carmelite Order, led by Spanish saints Teresa of Ávila and John of the Cross.

The Theatines, officially the Congregation of Clerks Regular of the Divine Providence (designated C.R.), was founded by Gaetano dei Conti di Tiene (St. Cajetan), Paolo Consiglieri, Bonifacio da Colle and Giovanni Pietro Carafe (later Pope Paul IV). This order vowed to promote virtue among the clergy and to combat the teachings of Luther. This order also devoted itself to preventing the spread of heresy (including Protestantism) and regenerating the clergy.

The Barnabites (designated B, fully named Clerics Regular of Saint Paul) was founded in 1530 and approved by Pope Clement VII (1523–34). The order's name comes from its ties to St. Barnabas of Milan, whose church was owned by the Barnibites during its early years.

All of these orders were part of the widespread Counter-Revolution intended to reform the clergy with a return to a simple life of poverty and virtue, and to spread Catholicism through education and example. The Church relied less on Inquisitions in regions outside of Italy as the period of the new orders grew and as their influence spread. Many, notably the Jesuits, were successful in preventing the spreading influence of Lutheranism in many parts of Europe.

Censorship of Art in the Counter Reformation

Church leaders had relied on the Inquisition in the past to curtail heresy. In the 16th century, this was no longer possible, so internal reforms were designed within the Counter-Reformation to drastically remake the Church. The growth and approval of new religious orders devoted to piety, poverty and virtue was a major part of this effort, and one that met with considerable success. At the same time, however, the Church continued to believe that it needed to control artistic expression, notably if in their opinion it contradicted Church doctrine. Censorship, not only of books but of other forms of art as well, was part of the Counter-Reformation. While converting by example through the missions of the new religious orders, the Church held onto its older inquisitorial mindset and tried to ensure that unacceptable artistic expression did not corrupt its core doctrines.

This was not an easy task, as artistic expression exploded during the Renaissance. Growing Humanism, science and art were all part of this period, which has no specific start and stop dates but was a part of a general change in Europe. After the period of the Black Plague, the culture in Europe was less dependent on Church leadership for its own definition. People began to express themselves through art, and this presented a problem for the Church, even while the Church itself was one of the major patrons of art. Famed artists including

Leonardo da Vinci, Michelangelo and Raphael contributed to the Christian art of the era. From the 1530s onward, the Church attempted to suppress religious imagery in art. In the final decree of the Council of Trent ending in 1563, the Church took the position that artists were to be instructed in how they portrayed Christ and the saints. The Council ruled that

> no images suggestive of false doctrine, and furnishing occasion of dangerous error to the uneducated, be set up. And if at times, when expedient for the unlettered people; it happen that the facts and narratives of sacred Scripture are portrayed and represented; the people shall be taught, that not thereby is the Divinity represented, as though it could be seen by the eyes of the body, or be portrayed by colors or figures.... Moreover, in the invocation of saints, the veneration of relics, and the sacred use of images, every superstition shall be removed, all filthy lucre be abolished; finally, all lasciviousness be avoided; in such wise that figures shall not be painted or adorned with a beauty exciting to lust; nor the celebration of the saints, and the visitation of relics be by any perverted into revellings and drunkenness; as if festivals are celebrated to the honor of the saints by luxury and wantonness.[2]

The definition of what was acceptable within artistic expression, in the eyes of the Church, can be summarized with four expectations: First, art had to be realistic. Second, it must be clear in what it was showing. Third, art was expected to draw the faithful into devotion. And fourth, art had to conform to the dogma of the Catholic Church in what it portrayed.

The Church position, in part based on its disapproval of Mannerism developing in artistic style, led to an "Anti-Mannerism" movement and eventually to the Baroque style of art. Rome further promoted its control over the arts by serving as patron to artists whose works it approved. The Church objection to Mannerism was based on its subtlety. Church leaders thought the masses would not be able to understand the message in such art. In 1573, a decade after the decree was enacted, artist Paolo Galliari Veronese was brought before the Roman Inquisition and questioned about his painting *Last Supper*. The tribunal questioned him, and part of the transcript of the proceedings reveals the Inquisition's interest in artistic expression:

Q. What is the picture to which you have been referring?
A. It is the picture which represents the Last Supper of Jesus Christ with His disciples in the house of Simon.
Q. Where is this picture?
A. In the refectory of the monks of San Giovanni e Paolo.
Q. Is it painted in fresco or on wood or on canvas?
A. It is on canvas....
Q. Who are the persons at the table of Our Lord?
A. The twelve apostles.
Q. What is Saint Peter doing, who is the first?
A. He is carving the lamb in order to pass it to the other part of the table.
Q. What is he doing who comes next?
A. He holds a plate to see what Saint Peter will give him.

Q. Tell us what the third is doing.

A. He is picking his teeth with a fork.

Q. And who are really the persons whom you admit to have been present at this Supper?

A. I believe that there was only Christ and His Apostles; but when I have some space left over in a picture I adorn it with figures of my own invention.

Q. Did some person order you to paint Germans, buffoons, and other similar figures in this picture?

A. No, but I was commissioned to adorn it as I thought proper; now it is very large and can contain many figures.

Q. Should not the ornaments which you were accustomed to paint in pictures be suitable and in direct relation to the subject, or are they left to your fancy, quite without discretion or reason?

A. I paint my pictures with all the considerations which are natural to my intelligence, and according as my intelligence understands them.

Q. Does it seem suitable to you, in the Last Supper of our Lord, to represent buffoons, drunken Germans, dwarfs, and other such absurdities?

A. Certainly not.

Q. Then why have you done it?

A. I did it on the supposition that those people were outside the room in which the Supper was taking place.

Q. Do you not know that in Germany and other countries infested by heresy, it is habitual, by means of pictures full of absurdities, to vilify and turn to ridicule the things of the Holy Catholic Church, in order to teach false doctrine to ignorant people who have no common sense?

A. I agree that it is wrong, but I repeat what I have said, that it is my duty to follow the examples given me by my masters.[3]

He was ordered to remove the offending images from his painting within three months and at his own expense. This was a typical example of how the Roman Inquisition applied the decrees of the Council of Trent to control artistic expression.

Censorship of Music

The Council of Trent had also ruled that musical expression should be simple and tranquil, and should not excite the faithful or confuse them in any way to distract them from worship. The ruling banished all "lascivious or impure" music from Church services. The result was to delay the development of polyphony in the 16th century. Polyphony is a form of music involving texture of two or more themes or voices performing in harmony with one another. The Council of Trent preferred the older monophonic form of single-voice music without harmony.

The idea of suppressing and controlling music did not originate with the Council of Trent. More than 200 years earlier in 1324, Pope John XXII (1316–34) wrote in his bull *Docta Sanctorum Patrum* (Teachings of the Holy Father) that the new developments in musical expression (polyphony) were not acceptable. He said that

> certain practitioners of the new school, who think only of the laws of measured time, are composing new melodies of their own creation, with a new system of note values, that they prefer to the ancient, traditional music. The melodies of the Church are sung in semibreves and minims and with grace notes of repercussion. Some break up their melodies with hockets or rob them of their virility with discant, three voice music, and motets, with a dangerous element produced by certain parts sung on text in the vernacular; all these abuses have brought into disrepute the basic melodies of the Antiphonal and Gradual [the principal chant books]. These composers, knowing nothing of the true foundation upon which they must build, are ignorant of the church modes, incapable of distinguishing between them, and cause great confusion. The great number of notes in their compositions conceals from us the plainchant melody, with its simple well-regulated rises and falls that indicate the character of the church mode. These musicians run without pausing. They intoxicate the ear without satisfying it; they dramatize the text with gestures; and, instead of promoting devotion, they prevent it by creating a sensuous and indecent atmosphere.... Therefore, after consultation with these same [cardinals], we prohibit absolutely, for the future that anyone should do such things, or others of like nature, during the Divine Office or during the holy sacrifice of the Mass.[4]

So it was that the new art (*ars nova*) of the 14th century was objected to once again in the 16th century and bolstered by the enforcement power of the Inquisition. Polyphony was considered offensive by Church elders, as was the merging between secular and sacred music and musical styles. The use of harmony in vocal music was viewed as lacking solemnity and was called evil; some even called polyphony the music of the Devil or associated it with pagan rites.

Just as artists had devised solutions around Church restrictions by adjusting their style of expression, many composers of the 16th century were able to survive the ban on polyphony. This was accomplished by developing compositions employing polyphony while remaining true to the Church's desire for purity and simplicity of expression, without distractions or sensuality.

The compositions of Giovanni Palestrina were an important step forward in the development of polyphonic music. In 1555, he wrote a six-part mass in polyphonic form called *Missa Papæ Marcelli* (Pope Marcellus Mass), named for the brief-reigning Pope Marcellus II (1555). Even though polyphonic, the mass provided the clarity the Church demanded in sacred music. A Flemish composer named Jacobus de Kerle also wrote polyphonic sacred music late in the 16th century; and Vincenzo Ruffo tried to compromise with the Church dictate against polyphony by employing a chord-based, or homophonic, composition style. Eventually, even the Inquisition stopped trying to censor music and, as polyphonic form was proven to satisfy the concerns expressed by the Council of Trent, the matter was dropped. Polyphony became closely associated with sacred music, notably through famous composers of the Baroque era (1600 to 1750). These included Bach, Vivaldi, Handel and Purcell, among others. All of these prominent Baroque composers were connected with Christianity in their lives and work. Bach started his composition career as a church organist at St. Boniface's Church in Arnstadt, Germany; Vivaldi was a Venetian priest; Handel started out as an organist in a Protestant Church; and Purcell was organist at Westminster Abbey.

In spite of the long standing objection to polyphony on the part of the Church, the beauty and expressive qualities of this style of composition became the standard in both secular and spiritual music. Some of the best-known works of major composers are based on spiritual themes, and eventually the Church abandoned its objections. No longer did composers fear the reach of the Inquisition to prevent polyphonic expression. Just as artists eventually were able to break from the restrictions in expression and style, so did musicians. Both art and music soon were embraced by the Church and today, much of the richest Renaissance art can be found within the Vatican. Art won out over the Inquisition in the end, as the explosion of Renaissance style proved too powerful to stop or censor.

Origins of the Thirty Years' War

The inability of the Church to defeat the Protestant movement through its Counter-Reformation, including new religious orders, overseas missions and continued Inquisitions, led to the ultimate struggle for supremacy in Europe. The Thirty Years' War (1618–48) was in a sense the child of Inquisition, embarked upon as a power struggle in Europe between Catholics and Protestants for control. The war may be viewed in political terms as an armed conflict between European states defined as either Catholic or Protestant, or in geographic and political terms outside of religious belief. However, the Catholic side of the struggle, led by the Holy Roman Emperor and aligned with Catholic states, went to war not purely overly political differences with its Lutheran neighbor states, but specifically as part of the Counter-Reformation. The purpose was not to overrun territory but to eliminate a spiritual competitor.

The Thirty Years' War was a series of expanding conflicts among many countries and coalitions. The sole unifying theme to define each side in this conflict was the distinction between identification as either Catholic or Protestant. What began as a localized conflict over succession in the Bohemian kingdom ultimately encompassed most of Europe's powers. Entire regions were destroyed in the fighting, and in Germany and the Netherlands, famine and disease reduced the civilian populations drastically as a consequence of the lengthy conflict.

The origin of the Thirty Years' War is traced directly to the Edict of Worms nearly 100 years earlier. In 1521, Charles V outlawed Lutheranism and decreed the death penalty for anyone discovered to possess Luther's writings. In spite of this new ruling, Protestants continued to openly declare their faith in areas where Catholics had fallen into the minority. In 1526, Charles asked a general council of the Diet of Speyer to enforce the Edict of Worms, including imposing punishments for heresy. Even so, settlement of the conflict between Catholics and Protestants did not include quelling of one side or the other. The Diet voted to declare a temporary peace during which each state would be allowed to choose whether it would be ruled as Catholic or Protestant. The Diet also called for freedom of religious expression for everyone, including Protestants. This was the first legislative declaration that contradicted the Inquisition and called for an end to persecution based on religious grounds. Luther considered the resulting act of the Diet of Speyer a reversal of his previous conviction for heresy.

The following years several leaders in German states called for the complete extermination of Protestants and a return to Catholicism. This declaration and the responses from Protestant leaders only added to the split among the many Germany sovereign states. The settled decision was that each ruler would declare the official religion of his area in accordance with the majority of those under his rule. Many provinces, including Saxony, Hesse, Prussia, Schleswig-Holstein and Silesia, as well as the cities of Augsburg, Nuremberg, Frankfurt, Ulm, Strasburg, Bremen and Hamburg, all declared themselves Protestant. The larger houses of Austria and the Dukes of Bavaria remained Catholic and challenged the right of other states and cities to abandon Catholicism or to declare themselves Protestant.

In those Protestant states, practicing the Catholic mass was forbidden, and when possible, the ban was enforced by law. Germany was a nation divided along Protestant and Catholic lines. An attempt to reconcile these differences was the Peace of Augsburg in 1555, intended to end the conflict between the two Christian groups. The treaty specified that rulers of all of the 225 German states had the right to choose between Lutheranism and Catholicism, and also to require their citizens to go along with the ruler's decision. Lutherans living in regions ruled by a Catholic bishop would be allowed to continue practicing their faith.

Hostilities ended for the moment, but the underlying conflict between Catholics and Lutherans remained. Calvinism, a major Protestant sect, was spreading through Germany at the time as well, but the Augsburg treaty did not mention any groups other than Lutherans. Conflicts between Germany and other European powers (Spain, France, Sweden and Denmark) added to the complexity of the political situation and made the treaty more fragile as time passed.

The treaty fell apart when some Catholic rulers tried to force Catholicism on Protestant regions. In one of the many conflicts that ensued, the Cologne War (1583–8), the Spanish army expelled the ruling Protestant prince-archbishop and replaced him with Ernst of Bavaria, a Catholic. In Cologne and other states, Lutherans were given a choice: convert to Catholicism or leave the region. The forced conversion policy spread to other regions of Germany. By the beginning of the 17th century, states around the Rhine and south to the Danube were mostly Catholic, and northern German states were Lutheran. Some portions of western Germany were dominated by Calvinists. In many of these states, minority religious groups were persecuted or forced to relocate. The states of Sweden and Denmark were Lutheran, and they supported German Lutheran states out of fear that Catholic forces would eventually overrun them. So the division became geographic, with Protestant states dominant in the North and Catholic states dominant in the South of Germany.

Archduke Ferdinand II of Austria was educated by Jesuits and was a loyal Catholic, even though his lands (Bohemia) were dominated by Protestants. When the nobility of the area rejected Ferdinand's appointment as crown prince in 1617, an open revolt followed. The Bohemian Revolt of 1618–20 became the first of five phases of the Thirty Years' War.

Phases of the Conflict

The Thirty Years' War was not a struggle between two countries or armies for control. It involved most of Europe's states at one point or another, in the following five phases.

Phase 1— The Bohemian Revolt, 1618–25. Protestants, the majority in Bohemia, feared that appointment of a Catholic ruler would lead to the loss of religious freedom. They preferred the appointment of Protestant Frederick V over the Catholic Ferdinand II. Even so, Ferdinand was declared the king of Bohemia when Emperor Matthias died in 1619. The conflict became violent as it spread throughout greater Bohemia, to Silesia, Lusatia and Moravia. Catholics and Protestants took up arms against one another in the expanding power struggle. Fighting escalated as states outside of Bavaria pledged troops in support of one side or the other, drawing in Spain, Austria and the Ottoman Empire. The war continued beyond the initial phase, and the Protestant armies were defeated by 1625.

Phase 2 — The Huguenot Rebellion, 1620–8. As the Bohemian war between Catholics and Protestants played out in Germany, another phase began. The Huguenots, who were located primarily in the southern region of France, rebelled against the central Catholic French government. They tried to establish independent military and political offices and diplomatic offices with foreign governments. This did not occur suddenly; rivalry between Catholic and Protestant centers in France first became violent during the French Wars of Religion (1562–98). After 22 years, the conflict was reignited. The Huguenots were defeated in several battles, and in 1627–8 the conflict drew in the English and led to the Anglo-French War (1627–9). Defeated, England withdrew its support of Protestant causes in Europe.

Phase 3 — The Danish intervention, 1625–9. King Christian IV of Denmark was a Lutheran who had aided Lutheran rulers in the states of Lower Saxony by pulling together an army in support of their cause. Catholic successes in the war caused King Christian to fear that his rule as a Lutheran would be threatened by Catholic interests. He had financed a mercenary army of 20,000 men and built up an additional national army of 15,000 to help defeat Catholic states and to defend neighboring Lutheran rulers. To offset Denmark's army, Ferdinand negotiated with a Bohemian noble, Albrecht von Wallenstein, who pledged his army of as many as 100,000 in exchange for plundering rights in territories he conquered. In 1626, Wallenstein's force defeated the Danes in a series of battles. However, he was not able to take the Danish capital. Negotiations allowed Christian to maintain his rule over Denmark in exchange for giving up his support of Protestant German states. As a consequence, Catholic control spread to a growing number of previously Lutheran areas in Germany.

Phase 4 — Swedish intervention, 1630–5. The Swedish army invaded the Roman Empire in 1630, turning the course of the war against the Catholic side. King Gustav II (Gustavus Aldolphus) was determined to stop Catholic victories over German Lutheran states close to the Baltic Sea. From 1630 to 1634, the Swedish army drove Catholics from most of the Lutheran states. The Swedish army had 42,000 men, but with subsidies from France, it was able to increase its size to 149,000.

The Swedish king and Roman Empire ended hostilities with the Peace of Prague in 1635. The agreement allowed Protestant rulers in Northern Germany to retain power (Protestant-controlled states in southern and western Germany were not included). German princes were not allowed to form future alliances between themselves or with foreign powers. Most parties were satisfied with these terms, with the exception of France.

Phase 5 — The French intervention, 1636–48. France was predominantly Catholic, and although the conflict was mostly focused within Germany, King Louis XIII was a rival to both the Roman Empire and the Spanish monarchy. France signed a treaty with Sweden (the Treaty of Bärwalde) agreeing to pay one million livres per year to support Sweden's army in Germany. The treaty also required that Sweden not make peace with the Roman Empire without approval from France.

When the Swedish army was defeated in 1634, French leaders realized Sweden was not going to be able to keep its promise. France declared war on Spain in 1635 and on the Roman Empire in 1636. The war had expanded beyond the conflict between Protestants and Catholics as this, the longest phase of the Thirty Years' War, began. The Spanish and Empire forces prevailed over several years and nearly overran Paris. In 1643, Louis died and his five-year-old son, Louis XIV, became king, with Cardinal Jules Mazarin as chief minister. The French conflict fell into stalemate and on March 14, 1647, the Truce of Ulm was signed by Bavaria, Cologne, France and Sweden.

The End of the War

After four years of negotiations to end the long conflict, a series of regional treaties went into effect. Casualties were catastrophic in Germany. Over the course of this long war, the population of Germany fell between 15 and 30 percent. In Wüttemberg, 75 percent of the population was lost, and in Brandenburg, about half died. Bohemian and other Czech regions also had substantial losses estimated at one-third of the total population. This included war deaths, losses from disease and famine, and expulsion of Protestants. Property destruction included over 2,000 castles, 18,000 villages and 1,500 towns (one-third of total towns in Germany).[5]

Troop concentrations and movements, displacement of populations, and crowded refugee centers accelerated the spread of diseases in the three decades of conflict. References to "head disease" and "spotted disease" probably signify outbreaks of typhus. Bubonic plague broke out in northern Italy between 1629 and 1631, and in sections of Germany in 1634. In the last decade of the war, many more casualties were caused by an outbreak of dysentery in Germany.

Politically, neither Catholic nor Protestant forces prevailed. Germany remained segmented into many small territories; the decentralized power structure weakened Germany as a part of the Holy Roman Empire. Spain's military and political power diminished as it fought wars both with France and Portugal. France replaced Spain as the strongest military nation in Europe. Sweden also emerged as a new force in Europe as the result of its part in the war.

A series of edicts collectively called the Peace of Westphalia finally ended the Thirty Years' War in 1648 while creating for the first time sovereign states in Europe and setting boundaries. So many of the issues at conflict involved religious freedom. Accordingly, the peace treaty addressed numerous issues involving differences between Protestant and Catholic citizens. The treaty gave Lutherans and Calvinists the right to worship according to their beliefs and to hold office in Catholic-controlled regions. It also ensured that when people emigrated for religious reasons, they would no longer forfeit their property.[6]

The agreed-upon peace concluded the war but did not bring peace between the pope and those who had agreed to it. Pope Innocent X (1644–55) issued a bull, *Zelus domus Dei*, on November 16, 1648,* in which he called the religious provisions of the Peace of Westphalia "null and void, invalid, iniquitous, unjust, condemned, rejected, absurd, without force or effect."[7]

Before the war, political and religious power was shared and overlapped. The war transformed Europe and for the first time, secular rule had the final word over the population and created its own laws. The Church had lost its influence in the legal and political scene. The Thirty Years' War also marked the end of centuries of large-scale religious wars in Europe. In that respect, the

---

*The bull was held up for nearly two years and not published until August 20, 1650.

Thirty Years' War could be considered the Church's last crusade, a failed attempt to eradicate Protestant sects and regain control in the Christian world. Accompanying this end to an era was the loss of European power on the part of the Inquisition. Even in Spain, the once powerful Inquisition was over for the most part. Only in the Papal States did the Church continue to hold the power to place heretics on trial.

End of the European Inquisitions

While the Roman Inquisition continued its efforts at controlling dissent, mostly through censorship, the Spanish Inquisition's era also ended. During Napoleon's domination of Spain (1808–12) the Inquisition was abolished. In 1813, the government declared the Inquisition to be officially over. However, when Ferdinand VII recaptured the Spanish throne in 1814, the Inquisition was brought back, but only briefly. The last heretic executed under the Spanish Inquisition was a school teacher named Cayetano Ripoll, accused of teaching Deism (the belief that a supreme being created the universe but does not intervene in its course and that religious truth is found in observing nature). He was either hanged or garroted on July 26, 1826.[8]

The final step was formal abolishment of the Spanish Inquisition on July 15, 1834, by royal decree. Regent Maria Cristina de Borbon signed the decree in behalf of Isabel II, who was a minor. This step was taken with approval of the head of the Spanish cabinet, Francisco Martínez de la Rosa.

The 18th century also saw the end to the centuries-long witch trials in Europe. A trend developed in which persons assumed to be pretending to be witches were tried under secular laws and were treated more as con artists than as witches. Punishment of witches under the Inquisition had been severe in the past, especially in Germany. The last executions for witchcraft took place in 1738. In Austria, witchcraft trials ended after 1750. Suspicion of witchcraft continued in trials of other crimes. A woman was placed on trial in 1782 in Switzerland and accused of killing her infant child, although she was unofficially suspected of also being a witch. As late as 1863, people were lynched when citizens suspected them of witchcraft. In that year, one of the last accused witches was lynched in Essex, England. A deaf mute known only as Dummy the Witch told fortunes for a living, and was accused by a young girl of bewitching her house. A drunken mob seized him, beat him, and threw him into a river. He died of pneumonia after the attack. Two people, Emma Smith and Samuel Stammers, were charged in the case and in 1864 were sentenced to six months in prison.[9]

The Great Witch Hunt had ended, although its repercussions have extended well into the modern age. During the Nazi era, the witch hunts were cited as "proof" of a Jewish plot against Aryan women. In a 1934 book by Mathilde

Ludendorff, *Christian Cruelty Against German Women* (*Christliche Grausamkeit an Deutschen Frauen*), the exaggerated figure of nine million victims of the "Jewish" plot was claimed. The same charge appeared in 1935 in *The Christian Witch Craze* (*Der christliche Hexenwahn*), in which Jews were charged with executing Aryan women under the guise of accusing them of witchcraft.[10]

The Roman Inquisition was vastly reduced in its power as Church influence shrank. By the end of the 18th century, the office of the Inquisition focused almost exclusively on censoring books and on accusations made against members of the clergy. The Inquisition was never abolished by the Church, although the office's name was changed. In 1908, Pope Pius X (1903–14) shortened the formal title, the Supreme Sacred Congregation of the Holy Roman and Universal Inquisition, to the less incendiary Congregation of the Holy Office. The name was changed once more into the title by which the office of the Inquisition is known today. In 1965, Pope Pius VI (1963–78) renamed the office the Sacred Congregation for the Doctrine of the Faith.

CHAPTER 16

The Modern Office
of the Inquisition

> The Church has the right to inflict corporal punishment, even death.
> — Fr. Marinus de Luca, S.J., *The Institutes of*
> *Public Ecclesiastical Law (Institutionos Juris*
> *Ecclesiasticus Publici)*, Vatican Press, 1901

The long history of the struggle between the Church and its heretical enemies (those who have disagreed with doctrine, as well as witches, disobedient
priests, Jews and others) has not ended. It has only taken on a different face.
This face is less violent than in the past and today lacks the power to tie people to a stake and set them on fire. Even so, the speculation is worthwhile: Has
the Inquisition been modified because of enlightened thinking, or simply
because the Church no longer holds the power to convict and punish?

The Church is an evolving institution. It has changed many times and in
many ways over 2,000 years, and one of the changes has been a slow acceptance
of attitudes and views more tolerant than those of the past. From the beginning a debate took place within the Church concerning the appropriate punishment for heretics (and equally, the appropriate *threat* of punishment to keep
the faithful in line). The early dominant opinion held that excommunication
should be the ultimate punishment for the unrepentant heretic. In the Middle
Ages, this was replaced with the excesses of the Inquisition. Dominican inquisitors, given far too much power and exercising a perverse zeal, took the Church
in a less pacifistic direction, and it seems that the Church could not stop this
trend. Various popes published bulls either in favor of extreme punishments or
in attempts to tone them down. In Spain, the monarchy was in complete control of the process. If the Church had taken a strong position against the Spanish monarchy, history might have been different. However, popes of the day
were acting out of both spiritual and political interests and even if they had been
able to stop or modify the Spanish Inquisition, they would not have been able
to eliminate the anti–Semitism that defined that era.

In many ways, the Church was powerless to stop the course of events; this is true regarding the underlying motives of those in power who selected their victims based on race, superstition or simply the holding of different beliefs. This does not excuse the Church or its leaders, and without any doubt the papacy was behind the persecutions of victims throughout hundreds of years, beginning with the Cathars and ending with Conversos, witches, scientists and artists. The tragic loss of life, property and freedom suffered by thousands has been a great historical and defining flaw of the Church, both as an institution and as a collection of flawed, often far less than infallible individuals.

Views of the Church

In spite of the history of corrupt popes and cardinals, political motives in the guise of religious purpose, and outright prejudice creating victims while hiding behind official sanctity, the Church as an institution has survived. The Church failed to use its power to silence the prejudiced clerics who *individually* drove the excesses of the Spanish Inquisition, or to ensure fair tribunals in France when Dominicans were at the height of their inquisitional power. Instead, various popes and bishops allowed these excesses to occur and failed to protect the individual rights of innocent people. Even so, the Church has survived the worst of its own history. Without excusing the events that took place, the fact that the Church has survived is evidence of deeply held faith among Christians.

The extreme sides in the debate have not been reduced. To this day, these sides continue to present their arguments. The unquestioning faithful insist that anti–Church extremists exaggerate the death numbers and accuse Protestants and secular leaders of worse abuses. They believe that every pope has been divinely appointed and that the Inquisition was an act of God to punish the nonbeliever. They also believe that the Crusades were inspired and commanded by God, speaking through the popes; history, observing the consequences of both Crusades and Inquisitions through history, draws a different conclusion. To the true believer, the revelations of history, even though provable, are themselves a form of modern heresy.

On the other side are those who hate Catholicism and consider the institution (including the pope) to be evil. For many, the Church itself is evil and the Inquisition is evidence that the entire Church as an institution is corrupt and has been at least since the date of its merger with the Roman Empire.

Today, the controversy continues and many cite biblical verses and interpret them to refer to the Roman Catholic Church as the Antichrist. A favorite reference is to the "Whore of Babylon" mentioned in Chapter 17 of the book of Revelation, which many have concluded is a reference to Rome, to the Church, or to the papacy. The references most often cited include the colors worn by priests and cardinals and the wealth of the Church and the popes, the period of worldly and sexual excesses among the popes, anti–Semitism, the number seven (hills of Rome), and other symbols. Among these citations are:

> The woman was clothed in purple and scarlet and decked out with gold and precious stones and perils. In her hand she held a gold cup full of obscenities and the foulness of her fornication [17:4].
>
> Written on her forehead was a name with a secret meaning: "Babylon the great, the mother of whores and of every obscenity on earth" [17:5].
>
> I say that the woman was drunk with the blood of God's people, and with the blood of those who had borne their testimony to Jesus [17:6].
>
> The seven heads and seven hills on which the woman is enthroned [17:9].
>
> For God has put it in their minds to carry out his purpose, by making common cause and conferring their sovereignty on the beast until God's words are fulfilled [17:17].
>
> The woman you saw is the great city that holds sway over the kings of the earth [17:18].[1]

References to Babylon are to the city of Rome in the view of most biblical scholars. These include Catholic commentary on the Jerusalem Bible, Protestant writings about the New International Study Bible, and many other sources. Even in the Bible itself, the meaning of Babylon is clear. Peter concluded his first book, written to the "scattered people of God" in distant lands, with the words, "Greetings from your sister church in Babylon."[2]

The "Whore of Babylon" has been called a reference to the Church or in general to the evils of modern times. During the Reformation, Church leaders cited the same passages and claimed they referred to the Protestant movement. At the same time, Martin Luther (*On the Babylonian Captivity of the Church*, 1520) cited Church corruption as evidence that the reference was aimed squarely at the papacy and the Roman Church. The *Westminster Confession of Faith* (1646) is a major Calvinist publication that also names Roman Catholicism the Whore of Babylon. Even earlier, Frederick I (Frederick Barbarossa) also called the papacy the Whore of Babylon and said the pope was the Antichrist. This occurred during Frederick's conflict with Pope Alexander III (1159–81).

This historical summary of references to the Church is significant in terms of the Inquisition. The power of the Church invited corruption, and as the Church grew as a political and temporal power through its partnership with the Roman Empire, the associations were easy to make. Enemies of the Church — including Protestant leaders — cite Scripture to bolster their beliefs, not only to vilify the Catholic Church but also to make their own case as the legitimate Church preaching the message of Christ. In times when making such statements could lead to trial and execution through the Inquisition, it was dangerous to talk about such ideas. Today, however, with the direct threat of the tribunals removed, critics of Catholicism are free to draw the parallels.

The freedom to voice dissent and enter into debate may be viewed as a cancerous trend by the faithful; or it may be seen as healthy dialogue leading to clarification of faith on either side of the issue. However, one cause for hatred of the Church and for characterizing it as the Whore of Babylon is the Inquisition itself and abuses connected to the institution. The office was feared and hated not only by its victims but also by those who remained silent out of fear that they would come to the attention of an inquisitor. In the worst period of the Inquisition, even a witness arguing in behalf of an accused person (including the accused person's lawyer) could be charged with heresy simply for making a vigorous argument contrary to the tribunal's views. The absolute power held by the inquisitor in those times came with complete arrogance and zeal, making it impossible for the pious inquisitor to see beyond the defiance of the accused, the witness, or the advocate.

The abuse of power not only by inquisitors and tribunals, but also by the interrogators they employed and by bishops, cardinals and popes, explains why throughout Christian history, the Church has been called the Whore of Babylon referenced in the book of Revelation. As the Church gradually lost its temporal power as a result of its excesses and of the corruption in the papacy before the Reformation, the power of the Inquisition ebbed. At the same time, the voices of anti–Church sentiment grew and were expressed through the Protestant movement, Humanism, the Enlightenment and the emergence of the modern secular world.

The evils assigned to the Church extend beyond the Inquisition directly. A large part of the distrust and hatred toward the Church has grown from the many crusades and wars fought in the name of the Church, culminating in the Thirty Years' War, which not only caused great loss of life and property but also cemented the decline of the Roman Church and its Inquisition. Many more victims were generated from many holy wars—starting with early crusades through the war against the Cathars and the Thirty Years' War—than were ever punished by the Inquisition. Anti-Church feelings are derived from many sources beyond the Inquisition itself.

Criticisms of the Church are not limited to the history of injustices of the Inquisition, but include the methods inquisitors employed in interrogation of victims, conduct of trials, and punishments.

The Church's Early Views on Punishment

The question of how "spiritual crime" should be punished has been debated since the earliest times of Christianity. Paul recommended shunning heretics, and early Church theologians favored excommunication as the only appropriate punishment a religious body could appropriately impose on even the worst heretic. The Inquisition, which arose to address the rapid growth of heretical movements during the Church's struggle with Catharism, was the first step in an increasingly severe and punitive approach. The papacy believed that a declaration or threat of excommunication did not work. After all, if a heretic no longer accepted the authority of the Church, excommunication meant nothing of consequence.

A troubling aspect of inquisitorial procedure was the use of torture during interrogations. It is widely acknowledged that given enough physical pain, people will confess to anything to bring the pain to an end. The Church *required* that confessions be given freely and not as the result of torture; but Dominican inquisitors reacted to this restriction by simply placing into the record the statement that the confession complied with this rule, even when it was not the case. When inquisitors were troubled by their involvement in interrogations, either directly or with knowledge about procedures being used by interrogators they hired, they devised the simple solution of absolving one another from any sin associated with mistreatment of prisoners.

The debate concerning appropriate interrogation techniques goes back many centuries and was never settled even by the end of the Roman Inquisition. Knowing his theories to be correct, Galileo nevertheless recanted just to avoid the possibility of more intense interrogation leading to a torture-induced confession resulting in execution. This was a very real possibility, since other scientists had been burned at the stake in recent years at the time of Galileo's trial.

As early as the third century, Tertullian, one of the earliest Christian writers, argued against the use of torture even against a Christian's enemies:

Shall the son of peace take part in the battle when it does not become him even to sue at law? And shall *he* apply the chain, and the prison, and the torture, and the punishment, who is not the avenger even of his own wrongs?[3]

He also believed it was not possible for a good Christian to adhere to Roman law, based on the punishments that could be imposed under that system. Tertullian wrote that a Christian was prevented from "sitting in judgment on anyone's life or character ... condemning ... imprisoning or torturing."[4]

Augustine, the 5th century Christian writer and philosopher, also struggled with the use of coercion. He wrote that the accused

is tortured to discover whether he is guilty, so that, though innocent, he suffers most undoubted punishment for crime that is still doubtful; not because it is proved that he committed it, but because it is not ascertained that he did not commit it. Thus the ignorance of the judge frequently involves an innocent person in suffering.... [T]he wise judge does these things, not with any intention of doing harm, but because his ignorance compels him, and because human society claims him as a judge. And if he is compelled to torture and punish the innocent because his office and his ignorance constrain him, is he a happy as well as a guiltless man?[5]

The Church relied on torture in conformity with Roman law and the Theodosian Code, which extended the use of extreme measure to witnesses if necessary. The law called for torture especially in cases of crimes against the

Roman emperor (*lèse-majesté*), which specified that "tortures shall tear them to pieces."[6]

Even with the severity of Roman law used by Christian courts in early history, it was more common for heretics to be stripped of their property and consigned to a life of poverty (as well as exile and excommunication) as punishment for their transgression. However, a distinction was always made between methods used to arrive at conviction and punishments given as a result. The use of interrogatory torture (termed *De quaestionibus* under Roman law) was carefully defined and restricted, with different rules for free people and slaves and with distinctions drawn between questioning and final punishment. Sixth century Emperor Justinian wrote:

> It is declared in the Constitutions that torture should be considered neither as always trustworthy, nor as always untrustworthy. And as a matter of fact it is a fickle and dangerous business that ill serves the cause of truth [*etenim res fragilis est et periculosa, et quæ veritatem fallat*]. For there are not a few who are possessed of such powers of endurance, or such toughness, that they scorn the pain of torture, so that there is no way the truth can be wrung from them. Others, however, have so little resistance that they will make up any kind of lie rather than suffer torment; and that can lead them to keep changing their story, even incriminating others as well as themselves.[7]

Church Views since the Middle Ages

By the time the Inquisition had begun, the Church view on the use of torture had not changed significantly. In fact, it was simply accepted that inquisitors had to use coercion to get confessions from accused heretics and witnesses. Pope Innocent IV, in his bull *Ad extirpanda*, described heretics as murderers of souls as well as "robbers of God's sacraments and of the Christian faith" who were to be "coerced — as are thieves and bandits — into confessing their errors and accusing others, although one must stop short of danger to life or limb."[8]

A less extreme opinion was expressed only a few years later by Thomas Aquinas, 13th century theologian and Church doctor. He carefully qualified how and when coercion could be used during interrogations of the accused heretic, while avoiding the direct use of the word "torture" to describe his meaning. He explained that

> there are unbelievers who at some time have accepted the faith, and professed it, such as heretics and all apostates: such should be submitted even to bodily compulsion, that they may fulfill what they have promised, and hold what they, at one time, received.[9]

The approval for the use of torture by the papacy (documented in previous chapters) became the sole authority for inquisitors, who went a step further by writing manuals instructing other inquisitors in exactly how torture was to be applied. An accused person, for example, could be tortured to get the initial confession. But that confession had to be given once again after the interrogation had stopped, in the official tribunal itself. A problem arose for the Inquisition when accused heretics argued to inquisitors that they recanted their confessions because they were given under duress. A famous example is that of the Knights Templar in the 14th century. Many of the Knights, arrested and accused of a range of crimes, were brought to interrogators and tortured until they either died or confessed. Many proclaimed their innocence at the time of the tribunal, arguing that their confessions were forced and should not be allowed to stand. Although the sentences were invariably carried out, the careful documentation of tribunal procedures preserves these cases and makes the point that coerced confessions cannot be given equal weight with voluntary admissions or with trials complete with witness testimony, writings and other actual evidence.

By the 18th century, the Church had not evolved much beyond the medieval view of torture as a tool for interrogation for accused heretics. St. Alphonsus Liguori, who has been called the prince of moral theologians, defended judicial torture, writing as an esteemed Catholic moralist. He did not challenge the moral use of torture, but addressed procedures that should be used in late–Inquisition (18th century) interrogations. His analysis of this issue boiled down to three questions:

(1) *When is a judge allowed to order that an accused person is to be tortured?* Answer: This step is allowed when proof cannot be determined by other means, but when some form of partial or semi-complete proof (*semiplenam probationem*) of the person's guilt is in evidence. In addition, some people are exempt from torture, including the elderly, the frail, knights, royal officials, young children or pregnant women.

(2) *How much torture can be applied?* Answer: The greater or more convincing the evidence of guilt, the more severely the person may be tortured; but never so severely that it becomes "morally impossible for him to endure" the resulting pain. If the coercion level goes beyond this threshold, "the confession thus extorted will be involuntary and so must be considered legally null and void." (Alphonsus does not explain how the interrogator is to determine this threshold.)

(3) *Can someone who has already been tortured be tortured again?* Answer: If a confession is not given in the initial session, then he may not be tortured again unless new evidence is discovered. But if the accused confesses and then recants in front of the tribunal, he may be tortured a second or even a third time. If he undergoes three sessions and then recants, he must be set free. The presumption is that all three confessions were forced and involuntary.[10]

The interrogation under the guidelines created by Alphonsus preferred the endurance test over determination of actual guilt or innocence as the deciding factor in setting someone free. These guidelines were used as recently as the 17th century in the Roman Inquisition and in more isolated cases in the 18th century.

In modern times, the topic remains controversial. In 1954, Friar Pietro Palazzini (later a cardinal) appeared to leave the question open. He explained that Catholic

opinion is predominant which takes its stand on the need to safeguard the rights of the human person, by virtue of which the criminal has a right to inviolability in soul and body.... Other reasons are very weighty, especially today when sophisticated investigative methods aided by scientific expertise render much less useful any recourse to methods which, to say the least, are so imperfect. Public opinion, which carries a certain weight among the various means of deciding on specific social goals, is today clearly against the use of torture.... The liceity [legitimacy of human action and its consequences] of torture as afflictive punishment cannot be doubted, given the liceity of the death penalty and that of mutilation and whipping — both equally afflictive.[11]

While Palazzini failed to condemn torture outright, The Vatican Council II did so. It declared in 1965:

All offenses against life itself, such as murder, genocide, abortion, euthanasia and willful suicide; all violations of the integrity of the human person, such as mutilation, physical and mental torture, attempted psychological coercion; all offenses against human dignity, such as subhuman living conditions, arbitrary imprisonment, deportation, slavery, prostitution, the trafficking in women and children, degrading working conditions where people are treated as mere tools for profit rather than free and responsible persons: all these things and others of the same sort are truly appalling, and while they poison human civilization, they debase the perpetrators more than the victims and utterly contradict the honor due to the Creator.[12]

In 1982, Pope John Paul II said in an address to the International Red Cross:

With respect to human rights, I will permit myself to return insistently to the subject of torture and other forms of inhumane treatment. Those governments adhering to the four Geneva Conventions have also committed themselves to the prohibition of such practices, and to allowing delegates of the Red Cross not only to visit detainees but to interview them without the presence of witnesses. It is my wish that, for this purpose too, your missions be accepted in all countries, with a view to eradicating this persistent blight on humanity.[13]

The revised Catechism of the Catholic Church expressed the opinion of the Church concerning the use of torture, while rewriting history to claim that it has always been Church policy to preach clemency and mercy:

#2297. *Torture*, which uses physical or moral violence to extract confessions, punish the guilty, frighten opponents, or satisfy hatred, is contrary to respect for the human person and for human dignity.
#2298. In times past, cruel practices were commonly used by legitimate governments to maintain law and order, often without protest from the Pastors of the Church, who themselves adopted in their own tribunals the prescriptions of Roman law concerning torture. Distressing as these facts are, *the Church always taught the duty of clemency and mercy* [italics added]. She forbade clerics to shed blood. In recent times it has become evident that these cruel practices are neither

necessary for public order, nor in conformity with the legitimate rights of the human person. On the contrary, these practices lead to ones even more degrading. It is necessary to work for their abolition. We must pray for the victims and their tormentors.[14]

In 2005, after centuries of debate, the Church took an even firmer stand when it declared:

In carrying out investigations, the regulation against the use of torture, even in the case of serious crimes, must be strictly observed.... International juridical instruments concerning human rights correctly indicate a prohibition against torture as a principle which cannot be contravened under any circumstances.[15]

After centuries of debate on the issue of torture, the Church took the position in the 21st century that decisions and application of prevailing law over the past 2000 years— notably as part of the Inquisition — were morally and legally wrong. Whether the revised version of history ("the Church always taught the duty of clemency and mercy") is accepted or, in light of the record, rejected, Church policy against torture was stated clearly for the first time. Physical coercion, the best remembered feature of the Inquisition and its tribunals, was no longer an acceptable method for the treatment of criminals.

The Modern-day Inquisition Office

Even with its condemnation of torture, the Church never abolished the Supreme Sacred Congregation of the Roman and Universal Inquisition. On December 7, 1965, Pope Paul VI issued the bull *Integræ servandæ*, officially renaming the Inquisition office the Sacred Congregation for the Doctrine of the Faith (*Congregatio pro Doctrina Fidei*, or CDF). Today, this is the longest-standing office of the Roman Curia.*

The primary duty of the Congregation, according to a declaration in 1988, is

to promote and safeguard the doctrine on the faith and morals throughout the Catholic world: for this reason everything which in any way touches such matter falls within its competence.[16]

The CDF's mission has been greatly changed since the days of the Roman Inquisition. Today, it contains two commissions, the Pontifical Biblical Commission (PBC) and the International Theological Commission (ITC).

The PBC was originally created in August 1901. It was reconstituted as a consultative body on June 27, 1971, via the Apostolic Letter *Sedula cura*. On June 28, 1988, Pope John Paul II placed the PBC under the CDF. Its duties

---

*The other eight are the Congregation for the Oriental Churches, the Congregation for Divine Worship and the Discipline of the Sacraments, the Congregation for the Causes of Saints, the Congregation for the Evangelization of Peoples, the Sacred Congregation for the Clergy, the Congregation for Institutes of Consecrated Life and Societies of Apostolic Life, the Congregation for Catholic Education, and the Congregation for Bishops.

Pope Benedict XVI. Before he became pope in 2005, Benedict (then Cardinal Joseph Ratzinger) was head of the Sacred Congregation for the Doctrine of the Faith, the renamed Supreme Sacred Congregation of the Roman and Universal Inquisition.

include protecting the integrity of Catholicism regarding biblical matters; promoting exposition of sacred books; deciding controversies among Catholic scholars; answering questions from Catholics; improving codices in the Vatican Library; and publishing scriptural studies. Decrees issued by the PBC are not considered to fall within the scope of papal infallibility.

The International Theological Commission (ITC) was created on April 11, 1969. Its most significant action was publication of a document called "Christianity and the Religions." This was the first step in a series of disciplinary actions against members of the clergy. Accused of tolerating or promoting religious pluralism, priests were cautioned to adhere to the doctrines of the Church. In 2004, the ITC published "Communion and Stewardship: Human Persons

Created in the Image of God," which clarified and stated Church positions on creation and evolution. Between 1981 and 2005, Cardinal Joseph Ratzinger headed the ITC. On April 19, 2005, he was elected Pope Benedict XVI, the 265th pope of the Church.

The ITC's steps against religious pluralism included putting an end to local priests' making exceptions to Church doctrine, especially concerning the rules about birth control and divorce for members of congregations, or regarding rules of celibacy for the clergy itself. The Church rule today is that local clergy cannot interpret the rules or allow exceptions based on popular trends or their own opinions.

The CDF also investigates accusations of sexual abuse by members of the clergy. Since 1985, this has taken up much of the CDF's attention as the number of accusations has grown. There were approximately 11,000 accusations filed between 1985 and 2004, the majority between 1992 and 2000.[17]

Priests who defy the requirements of Church doctrine risk being removed from their duties such as administering sacraments; removed from contact with their congregation; or in extreme cases, being removed from their positions. In one case in 2008, a Franciscan friar in Yugoslavia came to the attention of the CDF after fathering a child with a Franciscan sister and later founding a new religious community after claiming he was told to do so by a Marian apparition (which he later admitted to be false). The CDF investigated over several years and in 2008 ordered the friar to have no contact with members of the group he had formed. He was accused of "the diffusion of dubious doctrine, manipulation of consciences, suspected mysticism, disobedience towards legitimately issued orders and charges *contra sextum*."* In this instance, the friar was accused not only of adultery but also of abusing minors and misuse of the sacrament of penance. The friar had also refused to rejoin the Franciscans and reside with them as he had been ordered to do. CDF forbade him from any activities involving the "care of souls," including hearing confessions and preaching, and ordered him to undergo theological training. He was "forewarned that in the case of stubbornness a juridical penal process will begin with the aim of still harsher sanctions, not excluding dismissal, having in mind the suspicion of heresy and schism, as well as scandalous acts *contra sextum*, aggravated by mystical motivations."[18]

Theological Disputes Today

In the intellectual arena, dissenting priests have far more freedom today than ever before to express their opinions, albeit with possible consequences. One prominent priest worth note is Hans Küng, president of the Foundation

---

*The term *contra sextum* refers to violations of the Sixth Commandment ("Thou shalt not commit adultery"), for which Canon 1395 of the Code of Canon Law provides the remedy of dismissal for priests.

for a Global Ethic, who has questioned many of the very basic Catholic doctrines. His most significant dispute with the Church has been his questioning of papal infallibility.

In his book *Infallible? An Inquiry* (1983), Küng noted that popes and ecumenical councils have not always agreed with one another, and explained that the doctrine was not always accepted within the Church itself. In the past, such writings would have doubtlessly brought the offending person before the Inquisition. Today, however, sanctions are far more mild. On December 18, 1979, the Church banned Küng from teaching Catholic theology, but he remains a priest in good standing and was never excommunicated for expressing his dissent. He retired in 1996 but remained an outspoken critic of the Church, especially of the doctrine of papal infallibility.

The Church is contending with a widespread movement within the modern Church called "liberation theology." This is a belief that the primary mission of Christianity is to work to bring justice and equality to the world's poor, and that this mission should be accomplished in the political arena. This highly politically motivated movement is based on the class warfare between rich and poor (nations and well as individuals) and has even been characterized as a conflict on a larger scale between capitalism and Marxism.

The movement is traced to a group founded in 1955. The Latin American Episcopal Conference (*Conselho Episcopal Latino Americano*) began in Rio de Janeiro to promote the political movement within a theological context. The Church position is that this movement is at odds with Catholic social policies for several reasons. Among the most important of these is the association between liberation theology and Marxism, which the Church views as a godless belief system. However, liberation theology remains a strong movement in South America. Pope John Paul II was critical of the movement and disagreed with its characterization of Jesus as a revolutionary as the term is used in modern times. However, he stopped short of condemning the movement outright. When Pope Benedict XVI was head of CDF, he condemned the movement twice (in 1984 and 1986), citing its belief in Marxism and support of armed violence. Some supportive bishops were suspended. Others were excommunicated for expressing belief in liberation theology. The conflict came down to disputes between traditional doctrine and what the Vatican and CDF term the "popular Church." The liberation theology movement continues to present a challenge to the modern Church, although the CDF has little real power to silence such vocal dissent.

The Rehabilitation of Galileo

The Church reactions to the Franciscan friar from Yugoslavia and to Hans Küng demonstrate the broad range of Church reaction to various forms of dissent. Its fairly mild reaction to liberation theology further makes the point that today's CDF is far less powerful or ominous than past Inquisitions. In the case of the Yugoslavian situation, the offenses occurred over more than two decades and the Church did not act swiftly when the facts were first revealed. Church reaction to Küng's disputes was contradictory: He was banned from teaching but left a priest in good standing.

Today, the official Church policy seems to be in a state of confusion. Officials appear uncertain about how to react to situations as they arise. At the same time, the Vatican has taken many steps to resolve its errors of the past. Among these has been a concerted effort to reinstate Galileo, the Inquisition's most famous victim, to the good graces of the Church.

In 1979, Pope John Paul II created a Galileo Review Commission, which took two years to organize and staff. There were four separate groups: exegesis (interpretation of the Bible), culture, and two scientific divisions headed by astronomers (one of whom was a professor at the Vatican Observatory, which houses a $3 million telescope). Over a period of 11 years these four groups debated the issues of Galileo's beliefs and theories. Pope Benedict XIV had already granted forgiveness to the scientist in 1741, and in 1757 scientific works promoting the heliocentric theory were removed from the Index of Prohibited Books. In 1822, Pope Pius VII had also accepted the heliocentric theory and Galileo was again forgiven. Even so, John Paul II apparently believed that his new commission was needed to settle the question of whether Galileo had been right or wrong.

As a postscript to the Roman Inquisition, the commission issued its final report, which stated:

> A twofold question is at the heart of the debate of which Galileo was the center.... The first ... concerns biblical hermeneutics (biblical interpretation).... Galileo rejected the suggestion made to him to present the Copernican system as a hypothesis, inasmuch as it had not been confirmed by irrefutable proof.... Secondly, the geocentric (the sun goes round the earth) representation of the world was commonly admitted in the culture of the time as fully agreeing with the teaching of the Bible.... [C]ertain expressions, taken literally, seemed to affirm geocentrism. "If Scripture cannot err," Galileo wrote to Benedetto Castelli, "certain of its interpreters and commentators can do so in many ways." ... The second aspect of the problem, [is] its pastoral dimension. The pastoral judgment ... was difficult to make ... as geocentrism seemed to be part of scriptural teaching itself.... A tragic mutual incomprehension has been interpreted as the reflection of a fundamental opposition between science and faith.[19]

In other words, the Inquisition would have been less harsh on Galileo if he had simply agreed to present the Copernican theory as a hypothesis and not as fact. Defending the Inquisition, the report asserted that the geocentric belief was widely held in that day and conformed to biblical revelation. The report implies that Galileo went against popular scientific thought of the day, meaning he was more at fault than his inquisitors for ending up under suspicion of heresy.

The 1992 report did not settle the matter. It kept the debate open and questioned the degree of fault that Galileo held for remaining inflexible before the tribunal. The entire Inquisition remained an unsettled and controversial issue as well and in spite of many published apologies, it remains so today.

An attempt to end the era of the Inquisition once and for all occurred in 2004 when Pope John Paul II delivered an address:

> Before public opinion the image of the Inquisition represents ... counter-witness and scandal. In what measure is this image faithful to the reality? Before asking for forgiveness it is necessary to know the facts exactly and to acknowledge the deficiencies in regard to evangelical exigencies in cases in which it is so. This is the reason why the Committee asked for the consultation of historians, whose scientific competence is universally recognized....
>
> The historians' irreplaceable contribution constitutes for theologians an invitation to reflect on the conditions of life of the People of God in their historical journey. A distinction should guide the theologians' critical reflection: the distinction between the authentic "*sensus fidei*" [faithful sense] and the prevailing mentality in a determined period, which might have influenced their opinion.
>
> One must appeal to the "*sensus fidei*" to find the criteria for a just judgment on the past of the life of the Church.
>
> The institution of the Inquisition has been abolished.... [T]he children of the Church must revise with a spirit of repentance "the acquiescence manifested, especially in some centuries, with methods of intolerance and even violence in the service of truth." ...
>
> This spirit of repentance clearly implies the firm determination to seek in the future paths of evangelical testimony of the truth.
>
> On March 12, 2000, on the occasion of the liturgical celebration that characterized the Day of Forgiveness, forgiveness was asked for the errors committed in the service of truth, taking recourse to non-evangelical methods. The Church must carry out this service imitating her Lord, meek and humble of heart.
>
> The prayer I then addressed to God contains the reasons for the petition for forgiveness, which is valid both for the dramas linked to the Inquisition as well as for the wounds they have caused in the memory: "Lord, God of all men, in some periods of history Christians have yielded to methods of intolerance and have not followed the great commandment of love, thus disfiguring the countenance of the Church, your Bride. Have mercy on your sinful children and accept our determination to seek and promote truth in the gentleness of charity, conscious that the truth only imposes itself with the force of truth itself. Through Christ our Lord."[20]

The pope's contrition was offset and brought into question by a report filed by the symposium at the same time, based on an exhaustive study of documents from the Vatican Secret Archives. According to this report, most of the reported instances of torture and execution never occurred; the number of heretics put to death during the Spanish Inquisition was only 0.1 percent of the 40,000 who were accused. Only 99 witches were killed during the witch hunts out of 125,000 trials. The report concluded that the Inquisition saved many lives by preventing secular authorities from executing the accused. In an article about this report, one expert concluded that the Inquisition has been highly exaggerated as part of an attack on the Church:

"Historians can no longer use the topic of the Inquisition as an instrument to defend or attack the Church," said [Agostino] Borromeo, a professor at Rome's La Sapienza University. "The debate has moved to the historical level, with serious statistics."

Borromeo said that the "black legend" begun in Protestant countries against the Inquisition was opposed by a propagandist Catholic apologetics that failed to obtain an objective view.[21]

The conclusion from this symposium was that the Inquisition had been a relatively small incident in historical context.

Although the actual number of those tortured, executed, imprisoned, or robbed of their property can never be known, the extent of abuses has been well documented and supported by the careful and detailed records kept of tribunals themselves and of the many public spectacles accompanying executions. Furthermore, the estimate of casualties issued by the symposium did not count the thousands killed, wounded or displaced during the Albigensian Crusade, the Thirty Years' War or countless other crusades and holy wars accompanying or preceding the Inquisition's tribunals and executions.

Leaving the Inquisition in the Past

In spite of the revisionist claims by some Catholics, John Paul II seemed to want to put the matter of the Inquisition to rest without qualifying or minimizing the Church's abuses. Four years before the pope's public statement in the symposium report, John Paul II was criticized for having apologized too many times. One source reported in the year 2000:

On no fewer than 94 occasions, according to the Italian journalist Luigi Accattoli, Pope John Paul II has publicly admitted that the Catholic Church was guilty of errors in the past. Now, in what Religion News Service calls "a move unprecedented in two millenniums of Roman Catholic history," John Paul has issued a summation of all these apologies. He read the document, "Memory and Reconciliation: The Church and the Mistakes of the Past," at a "solemn ceremony" on March 12, the first Sunday of Lent. A preparatory document, outlining the conditions and limits of the forthcoming apology, was also issued by the Vatican.... Among the Church's errors for which John Paul apologized are divisions within Christianity, forced conversions, ecclesiastical use (and approval) of violence, and anti–Jewish prejudice. The document also says that past errors by Catholics lie at the root of such "evils of today" as the spread of atheism and ethical relativism.[22]

The article calls the pope's apologies a theological and historical quandary. This is based on the infallibility doctrine of the Church. How could the Church have been in error in the past and yet remain infallible both in the past and the present? The article also notes that the pope's apology condemns the Inquisition, even though many past popes (including many who have been declared saints) approved of the institution. Critics were concerned about John Paul's creation of the paradox, potentially giving liberal critics ammunition to support calls for retraction of some doctrines, such as bans on artificial birth control or ordination of female priests. The article noted that

> some members of the Catholic hierarchy have been openly critical of John Paul's binge of apologizing. "As regards the sins of history," Cardinal Giacomo Biffi of Bologna wrote in a 1995 book, "would it not be better for all of us to wait for the Last Judgment?" Biffi also drew attention to the theological distinction between sins committed by individual members of the Church, and the sinless Church itself. John Paul usually makes this distinction clear, and a recent preparatory document for the apology refers to the Church as "holy and immaculate," despite the sins of its members.[23]

The suggestion by Cardinal Biffi that it would be better to wait for the Last Judgment may have been applied equally to persecutions under the Inquisition, whose tribunals tortured and killed accused heretics often on only flimsy testimony and suspicion, on the beliefs of inquisitors who themselves were not willing to let the matter wait until the Last Judgment.

No rational conclusion can be drawn, either from apologies of popes, or for the criticisms leveled by more conservative Church elders. The fact is that Inquisitions occurred, and whether 10,000 were killed or only 10, abuses have been proven through the historical record, and cannot be denied or rationalized. The wrongs committed against the people of Europe and elsewhere, done in the name of God even when other motives were the true guiding force, have tainted the history of the Church. The most recent attempts by popes and symposia to leave the Inquisition in the past have confused the issue. No consensus of opinion has been reached. Indeed, consensus may be impossible.

As an institution, the Roman Catholic Church remains powerful and influential today, but much less so than in the Middle Ages. Perhaps the lesson to be learned from the Inquisition is that any institution, even the Church, will be corrupted if given too much power. The corruption is likely to be the most extreme when power is applied in the name of God.

Epilogue

For the foxes destroy the vineyard of the God of hosts, and the impious rend the seamless robe of Christ. Let God therefore arise, let all his enemies be scattered. And you, most blessed father, since all these things are so manifest, public and notorious that they cannot be hidden by any evasion or defended by excuses, arise in the power of the most High, together with this sacred council, and judge the cause of your spouse and be mindful of your sons. Gird your sword upon your thigh, O mighty one. Set out, proceed prosperously and reign, and say with the psalmist: I will pursue my enemies and crush them, and I shall not return until I consume them. I shall consume and crush them and they will not rise; they will fall at my feet. For it is wrong that so wicked a deed and so detestable a precedent should be allowed to pass by disguised, lest perhaps unpunished daring and malice find an imitator, but rather let the example of punished transgressions deter others from offending.

— Ecumenical Council of Florence
(1438–1445), March 23, 1440

History is, and should be, controversial. Even so, open dialogue concerning dispute of fact is instructive and enables all sides to consider and reconsider their point of view about events of the past. One great flaw in Church policy toward heretical movements has been the consistent refusal to even consider any point of view other than the official, approved doctrine of the day (even though doctrine itself has evolved and changed over time). Many people have been condemned and executed or sent away to prison simply for raising questions about basic beliefs. The belief in the infallibility of the Church and its doctrine created more problems than solutions.

When it comes to writing a history of the Inquisition, the position of the Church is well understood. Heresy is not merely to question doctrine or to express an opposite belief; it is equally heretical to write about events of the past in any way critical of the Church. The current Church leadership continues to question whether the wrongs of the Inquisition were as severe as history has demonstrated, and has even raised questions as to whether the events

263

(including events well documented by the Church) occurred as the record shows. The Church position is that telling the story of the Inquisition (or any other matter that questions Church authority) is simply wrong.

The Church position has always been that books critical of the Catholic doctrine are to be ignored and that good Christians should refuse to read them. An encyclical from the year 1766 written by Pope Clement XIII (1758–69) strongly condemns not only those who write books critical of the Church, but also those who read such books. Clement wrote on the dangers of anti–Christian writings:

> The well-being of the Christian community which has been entrusted to Us by the Prince of shepherds and the Guardian of souls requires Us to see to it that the unaccustomed and offensive licentiousness of books which has emerged from hiding to cause ruin and desolation does not become more destructive as it triumphantly spreads abroad. The distortion of this hateful error and the boldness of the enemy has so increased ... accursed men who have given themselves over to myths ... [and who] vomit the poison of serpents from their hearts for the ruin of the Christian people by the contagious plague of books which almost overwhelms us. They pollute the pure waters of belief and destroy the foundations of religion.... They are abominable in their activity. Secretly sitting in ambush, they draw arrows out of the quiver which they shoot at the righteous in the dark. They have not restrained their impious minds from anything divine, holy, and consecrated by the oldest religion of all time; rather in their attack they have sharpened their tongues like a sword. They have run first of all against God in their pride. Armed with a thick neck, they have strengthened themselves against the Almighty....
>
> It is necessary to fight bitterly, as the situation requires, and to eradicate with all our strength the deadly destruction caused by such books. The substance of the error will never be removed unless the criminal elements of wickedness burn in the fire and perish.... For if it is necessary to avoid the company of evildoers because their words encourage impiety and their speech acts like a cancer, what desolation the plague of their books can cause! Well and cunningly written these books are always with us and forever within our reach. They travel with us, stay at home with us, and enter bedrooms which would be shut to their evil and deception....
>
> [The faithful] should be warned not to allow themselves to be ensnared by the splendid writing of certain authors in order to halt the diffusion of error by cunning and wicked men. In a word, they should detest books which contain elements shocking to the reader; which are contrary to faith, religion, and good morals; and which lack an atmosphere of Christian virtue....[1]

Clement's position was not exceptional; it was a typical expression of Church policy that has been in effect since the 13th century. Today, "heretics," including anyone who writes a history critical of the Church's past, may be ignored or reminded of their loss of salvation. Fortunately the Church's loss of political power has at least done away with the one-sided tribunals of the Dominican Inquisition and the prejudged guilt of anyone under suspicion. Many of the tragic outcomes of tribunals in the 13th century can be easily blamed on ignorance or on a misguided sense of justice. However, in reading the opinions of modern Catholic leadership, one thing is clear: The opinion from 800 years ago continues to prevail today, although the Church is powerless to punish its perceived enemies as it has done in the past.

A few important overall realities have to be kept in mind. These include the fact that today's Church doctrine has not changed much since the time when Pope Gregory IX authorized the first full-blown Inquisition; yet the Church has been ineffective at eliminating heresy, even with the Inquisition. The Cathars and Waldensians have disappeared, but their philosophies endure under different names. Intellectuals like Wyclif and Hus sparked the Protestant Reformation. The Great Witch Hunt that began as an extension of the Inquisition in Germany was only one of many oddities based on superstition, distrust, and zeal. The racial components that lay behind the excesses of the Spanish Inquisition demonstrate that in each instance of persecution based on religion — whether of Cathars, witches, Conversos, or scientists — the stated agenda is not always the true reason for the process. With this in mind, it is understandable that even with the best of intentions a sincere effort to hold the faithful together in a unified belief can easily be twisted. It can even more easily evolve into a form of terrorism in which confessions are coerced under torture, innocent people are sent to prison or burned at the stake, and entire families are robbed of their inheritance and rendered homeless — often on nothing stronger than suspicion or a jealous neighbor's accusation.

By the time the Reformation began and was expressed in its various forms by Luther, Calvin, and the monarchs of England, the Church had already begun to lose the political power it needed to exert complete control through tribunals. Even so, with attention turned to innocuous "offenders" such as Galileo or musicians writing polyphonic music, the Church tried to find new ways to identify its anti-heretical stance and to continue to exert control.

Even with less temporal power than in past centuries, the Church remains an influential and powerful institution. Today, Catholics make up over half of all Christians. The Church now has more than one billion members.[2]

An organization of this size and in so many countries faces a daunting task in attempting to enforce a single doctrine everywhere. Different cultures and development of social beliefs affect how Catholics practice their faith, in spite of the Vatican's desire for a single, unified, and obedient flock. The truth is that the Christian "community" has never existed as a single entity. Heretics have always been found in abundance, as real dissenters from the official doctrine or at the very least as perceived enemies of the Church.

It is tragic that the Church was never able to simply accept dissent as one aspect of free will, and to lead by example so that many of those dissenters might one day return to the Church's claimed doctrine. It is equally tragic that so many lives were destroyed in an effort to force uniformity of belief along all Christians. The Church might have benefitted by taking advice from

Augustine of Hippo, one of the greatest Church philosophers, who wrote 1,600 years ago that

> among [the Church's] enemies lie hidden those who are destined to be fellow-citizens [of the city of God].... Of these, some are not now recognized; others declare themselves, and do not hesitate to make common cause with our enemies in murmuring against God, whose sacramental badge they wear. These men you may today see thronging the churches with us, tomorrow crowding the theatres with the godless. But we have the less reason to despair of the reclamation even of such persons, if among our most declared enemies there are now some, unknown to themselves, who are destined to become our friends. In truth, these two cities are entangled together in this world, and intermixed until the last judgment effects their separation. I now proceed to speak, as God shall help me, of the rise, progress, and end of these two cities; and what I write, I write for the glory of the city of God, that, being placed in comparison with the other, it may shine with a brighter luster.[3]

Chapter Notes

1. Pope Gregory IX, 1227 to 1241: Stage One Begins

1. Frank E. Smitha, "Europe, the Church and Economic Growth to 1300," 2000, *www.fsmitha.com/h3/h10eu.htm*.

2. Pope Lucius III, papal bull *Ad abolendum*, November 4, 1184.

3. J. N. D. Kelly, *Oxford Dictionary of Popes* (New York: Oxford University Press, 2005).

4. *Ibid.*

5. Global Anabaptist Mennonite Encyclopedia Online (GAMEO), *www.gameo.org/encyclopedia*.

6. *The Catholic Encyclopedia*, *www.catholic.org/encyclopedia*.

7. S. Z. Ehler and J. B. Morall, *Church and State through the Centuries* (London: Burns & Oates, 1954).

8. Revelation 6:4 (*Revised English Bible*).

9. Matthew 26:26–28 (*Revised English Bible*).

10. Matthew 16:18–19 (*Revised English Bible*).

11. Pope Gregory IX, *Nova compilatio decretalium* (New Compilation of Decretals), 1234 (first printed in 1473).

12. Pope Innocent III, *Si adversus vos*, 1205.

13. *The Catholic Encyclopedia*.

14. Pope Innocent IV, *Ad extirpanda*, 1252.

15. Thomas Aquinas, Article III ("Whether heretics should be tolerated"), *Summa Theologica* (1265–74).

2. Cathar Beginnings: Challenges in Heresy

1. Cited in Heinrich Denzinger, *Sources of Catholic Dogma*, trans. Roy J. Deferrari (Fitzwilliam NH: Loreto Publications, 1957).

2. Alain de l'Isle, cited in Jacques-Paul Migne, *Patrologiæ cursus completus*, Vol. 210, (1844–64).

3. Matthew 19:13–21 (*Revised English Bible*).

4. Walter L. Wakefield and A. P. Evans, trans., *Heresies of the High Middle Ages* (New York: Columbia University Press, 1990).

5. *Ibid.*

6. Matthew 5:28 (*Revised English Bible*).

7. Anonymous, *De heresy catharoum in Lombardia*, cited in Malcolm Barber, *The Cathars: Dualist Heretics in Languedoc in the High Middle Ages* (Harlow, Essex, UK: Pearson Education, 2000).

8. Gershom Scholem, cited in Steven Bayme, *Understanding Jewish History: Texts and Commentaries* (New York: Ktav, 1997).

9. Peter of Les Vaux-de-Cernay, *The History of the Albigensian Crusade: Peter of les Vaux-de-Cernay's 'Historia Albigensis,'* vol. 1 (1926), trans. W.A. Sibly and M.D. Sibly (Rochester NY: Boydell & Brewer, 1998).

10. Charles Carleton Coffin, *The Story of Liberty* (Plymouth MA: Maranatha, 1987).

11. Bernard Gui, *Inquisitor's Manual of Bernard Gui*, trans. J. H. Robinson, in J. H. Robinson, ed., *Readings in European History* (Boston: Ginn, 1905).

12. J. C. Wolf, *Historia Bogomilorum* (1712).

13. *Le Liber du duobis principiis* (*The Book of Two Principles*), cited in Wakefield and Evans, *Heresies*.

14. Matthew 13:24–28 (*Revised English Bible*)

15. Rainerius Sacconi, *Summa de Catharis et Pauperibus*, cited in Wakefield and Evans, *Heresies*.

16. Peter of Les Vaux-de-Cernay, *History of the Albigensian Crusade*.

17. Mark Gregory Pegg, *The Corruption of*

Angels: The Great Inquisition of 1245–1246 (Princeton NJ: Princeton University Press, 2001); and Peter of Les Vaux-de-Cernay, *History of the Albigensian Crusade.*

18. Barber, *The Cathars*; and Peter of Les Vaux-de-Cernay, *History of the Albigensian Crusade.*

19. Peter of Les Vaux-de-Cernay, *History of the Albigensian Crusade.*

20. Walter L. Wakefield, *Heresy, Crusade and Inquisition in Southern France, 1100–1250* (Berkeley: University of California Press, 1974). Amaury's words paraphrased the Bible, "The Lord knows his own" (II Timothy 2:19, *Revised English Bible*).

21. Christopher Tyerman, *God's War: A New History of the Crusades* (Cambridge MA: Harvard University Press, 2006).

22. Letter from Pope Innocent III, cited in Peter of Les Vaux-de-Cernay, *History of the Albigensian Crusade.*

3. The Dominican Order

1. William Thomas Walsh, *Characters of the Inquisition* (Rockford IL: TAN Books, 1940).

2. Dominican Friars, "A Short Biography of St. Dominic," *http://dominicanvocations.com.*

3. Fourth Lateran Council, 1215, cited in Jonathan Kirsch, *The Grand Inquisitor's Manual* (New York: HarperCollins, 2008).

4. Philip Schaff, *History of the Christian Church* (New York: Scribner's, 1910).

5. Henry Charles Lea, *History of the Inquisition in the Middle Ages* (1964).

6. Pope Gregory IX, *Ille humani generis,* 1231.

7. *Ibid.*

8. Fourth Lateran Council, Canon III.

9. Edward Burman, *The Inquisition: The Hammer of Heresy* (New York: Dorset, 1992).

10. Edward Peters, *Inquisition* (Berkeley: University of California Press, 1989).

11. G. G. Coulton, *Inquisition and Liberty* (1938; reprint, Boston: Beacon Hill, 1959).

12. Cited in Paul Carus, *The History of the Devil and the Idea of Evil from the Earliest Times to the Present Day* (1900).

13. Norman F. Cantor, *Inventing the Middle Ages: The Lives, Works and Ideas of the Great Medievalists of the Twentieth Century* (New York: William Morrow, 1991).

14. Kirsch, *The Grand Inquisitor's Manual.*

15. "Inquisition," Southern Methodist University, *http://faculty.smu.edu/bwheeler/Joan_of_Arc/OLR/crinquisition.pdf.*

16. Cecil Roth, *The Spanish Inquisition* (New York: Norton, 1937, 1964).

17. The Fundamental Constitution, "Purpose" (Clause I), written by Pope Honorius III to Dominic, *Monumenta Ordinis Praedicatorum Historica* (MOPH), January 18, 1221, *www.domcentral.org.*

18. *Ibid.,* Clause IV.

19. Matthew 28:19 (*Revised English Bible*).

4. The Cathars' End and Expanded Inquisitions

1. Philipp von Limborch, *Historia Inquisitionis* (1692).

2. Fourth Lateran Council, 1215, Canon 68.

3. *The Catholic Dictionary* (1887).

4. Council of Toulouse, 1229, Canon 14.

5. *Ibid.,* Canon 1.

6. *Ibid.,* Canon 6.

7. Peters, *Inquisition.*

8. Alan Friedlander, ed., *The Trial of Fr. Bernard Délicieux, 3 September–8 December 1319* (1996).

9. Barber, *The Cathars.*

10. Wakefield and Evans, *Heresies.*

11. Barber, *The Cathars.*

12. Gui, *Inquisitor's Manual.*

13. *Ibid.*

14. *Ibid.*

15. *Ibid.*

16. *Canon Episcopi.*

17. Walter Map, quoted in Wakefield and Evans, *Heresies.*

5. The Age of Wyclif and Hus

1. Kelly, *Oxford Dictionary of Popes.*

2. *The Catholic Encyclopedia.*

3. Norman F. Cantor, *In the Wake of the Plague: The Black Death and the World It Made* (New York: HarperPerennial, 2001).

4. J. H. Robinson, *Petrarch* (1898).

5. Cited in Schaff, *History of the Christian Church.*

6. *Ibid.,* p. 318.

7. Thomas Walsingham, *The St. Albans Chronicle, Vol. I: 1376–1394,* ed. John Taylor and Wendy R. Childs, trans. Leslie Watkiss (New York: Oxford University Press, 2003).

8. *De haeretico comburendo,* 1401.

9. Council of Constance, May 4, 1415.

10. Henry Knighton, *Knighton's Chronicle, 1337–1396,* ed. and trans. by G. H. Martin (Oxford: Clarendon, 1995).

11. Henry Gee and William John Hardy, eds., *Documents Illustrative of English Church History* (1910).

12. John Hus, *The Letters of John Hus*, trans. Matthew Spinka (Manchester: Manchester University Press, 1972).

13. G. R. Evans, *A Brief History of Heresy* (Oxford: Blackwell, 2003).

14. Petr z Mladenovic, *John Hus at the Council of Constance*, trans. with notes by Matthew Spinka (New York: Columbia University Press, 1965).

15. Schaff, *History of the Christian Church*

16. "Vatican Considers Clearing Hus," *The Christian Century*, January 5, 2000.

6. The Great Witch Hunt

1. Schaff, *History of the Christian Church*.

2. Ann-Marie Gallagher, *The Wicca Bible: The Definitive Guide to Magic and the Craft* (New York: Sterling, 2005).

3. Lea, *History of the Inquisition*.

4. Joseph Pérez, *The Spanish Inquisition* (New Haven CT: Yale University Press, 2005).

5. *Ibid.*

6. Pope Innocent VIII, papal bull *Summis desiderantes affectibus*, December 5, 1484.

7. Schaff, *History of the Christian Church*.

8. *Malleus Maleficarum*, Part II, Question I, Chapter 1.

9. *Ibid.*, Part III, Question I.

10. *Ibid.*, Part III, Question XV.

11. Anne Llewellyn Barstow, *Witchcraze: A New History of the European Witch Hunts* (New York: HarperCollins, 1995).

12. Reginald Scot, *The Discoverie of Witchcraft* (1584; reprint, 1930, 1972).

13. Tertullian, *De Cultu Feminarum*.

14. Steven Katz, *The Holocaust in Historical Context* (New York: Oxford University Press, 1994).

15. Isaiah 34:14 (*New Revised Standard Bible*).

16. Dead Sea Scrolls, *Song for a Sage*, ref. 4Q510–511.

17. Ardern Holt, "The Witch," in *Fancy dresses described; or, what to wear at fancy balls*, 1896.

7. The Jews and Conversos of Spain

1. Pope Pius V, *Hebraeorum gens*, February 26, 1569.

2. "Hidden Ireland," *http://hiddenireland.wordpress.com*.

3. Adolf Harnack, *The Expansion of Christianity in the First Three Centuries* (London: Williams & Norgate, 1904).

4. Benzian Netanyahu, *The Origins of the Inquisition*, 2nd ed. (New York: New York Review of Books, 2001).

5. *Ibid.*

6. Fourth Council of Toledo, 633, canon 57.

7. *Ibid.*, canon 63.

8. *Ibid.*, canon 60.

9. *Ibid.*, canon 65.

10. Netanyahu, *Origins of the Inquisition*.

11. E. Ashtor, *The Jews of Moslem Spain* (Philadelphia: Jewish Publication Society, 1973–84).

12. Order of King Enrique II, August 25, 1378.

8. Conversos in the 15th Century

1. Paul of Burgos, *Scrutinium Scripturarum* (1591).

2. Y. F. Baer, *A History of the Jews in Christian Spain* (Philadelphia: Jewish Publication Society, 1961).

3. Council of Basel, Session Twenty, January 22, 1435.

4. José de los Ríos, *The History of the Jews of Spain and Portugal* (1848).

5. Netanyahu, *Origins of the Inquisition*.

6. J. Román de la Higuera, *The Church History of the Imperial City and Region of Toledo* (1290).

7. Pope Nicholas V, papal bull *Humani generis inimicus*, 1449.

8. A. Martín Gamero, *History of the City of Toledo* (1862).

9. *Ibid.*

10. Cardinal Juan de Torquemada, *Tractatus*.

11. *Ibid.*

12. Marcos García de Mora, *Memorial*, cited in Torquemada, *Tractatus*.

13. Lea, *History of the Inquisition*.

9. The Age of Torquemada, the Grand Inquisitor

1. Netanyahu, *Origins of the Inquisition*.

2. Henry Kamen, *The Spanish Inquisition: A Historical Revision* (New Haven CT: Yale University Press, 1997).

3. *Ibid.*

4. Sebastián de Olmedo, *Chronicon magistrorum generalium Ordinis Prædicatorum*.

5. Ferdinand II of Aragon and Isabella I, *The Alhambra Decree*, 1492.

6. António José Saraiva, *The Marrano Factory: The Portuguese Inquisition and Its New Christians 1536–1765*, trans., rev. and augmented Herman Prins Salomon and I. S. D. Sassoon (Leiden: Brill, 2001).

7. Netanyahu, *Origins of the Inquisition*.

8. Lea, *History of the Inquisition*.

9. Netanyahu, *Origins of the Inquisition*.

10. *Ibid.*

10. The Spanish Inquisition after Torquemada

1. Lea, *History of the Inquisition*.

2. Netanyahu, *Origins of the Inquisition*.

3. Kenneth Scott Latourette, *A History of Christianity* (New York: Harper, 1953).

4. Pérez, *Spanish Inquisition*.

5. *Ibid.*

6. *Ibid.*

11. Martin Luther

1. Council of Constance, *Hæc sancta*, April 6, 1415.

2. Pope Clement VI, *Unigenitus*, January 27, 1343.

3. Martin Luther, *Wider Hans Worst* (1541).

4. *Ibid.*

5. Martin Luther, in *Luther's Writings*, ed. J.G. Walch and G. Stoeckhardt (1885).

6. Schaff, *History of the Christian Church*.

7. *Ibid.*

8. V. E. Löscher, *The Complete Reformation* (1720–29).

9. Pope Leo X, *Exsurge Domine*, June 15, 1520.

10. *Ibid.*

11. *Edict of Worms*, May 25, 1521.

12. James Anthony Froude, *Short Studies on Great Subjects* (New York: Scribner's, 1905).

13. Council of Trent, *Canon to be used for the Mass*.

12. Anglicanism and Calvinism

1. "Documents on the changing status of the English Vernacular, 1500–1540," *http://www.ric.edu/faculty/rpotter/statutes.html.*

2. Supremacy Act of 1534.

3. *Abjuration of Papal Supremacy by the Clergy*, 1534.

4. *Book of Common Prayer* (1662).

5. Pope Paul III, *Eius qui immobilis*, August 30, 1535.

6. King Henry VIII, *The Royal Injunctions*, 1536.

7. Pope Pius V, *Regnans in excelsis*, April 27, 1570.

8. Schaff, *History of the Christian Church*.

9. Peters, *Inquisition*.

10. Edward Gibbon, *The History of the Decline and Fall of the Roman Empire*, Ch. LIV (1788–9).

13. The Roman Inquisition

1. Cardinal Caraffa, 1542, cited in Will Durant, *The Reformation* (New York: Simon & Schuster, 1957).

2. John Farrow, *Pageant of the Popes* (1942; reprint, Charleston SC: Forgotten Books, 2008).

3. Alfredo Cardinal Ottaviani, June 14, 1966.

4. Cardinal Joseph Ratzinger, letter to the Archbishop of Genoa, January 1985.

5. John O'Malley, *The First Jesuits* (Cambridge MA: Harvard University Press, 1993).

6. Council of Trent, Session 25, Chapter IV.

14. Galileo and the Center of the Universe

1. In Karl Heim, *Christian Faith and Natural Science* (London: SCM, 1953).

2. Joshua 10:12 (*Revised English Bible*).

3. John Calvin, in Gordon L. Glover, *Beyond the Firmament: Understanding Science and the Theology of Creation* (Chesapeake VA: Watertree, 2007).

4. John Calvin, *Commentary on Genesis*, 1st English ed. (1578).

5. All verses from the *Revised English Bible*.

6. Nicholas Copernicus, Preface, *De Revolutionibus Orbium Coelestium* (1544).

7. *Ibid.*, Chapter 2.

8. *Ibid.*, Chapter 10.

9. Richard S. Westfall, *The Construction of Modern Science* (New York: John Wiley, 1971).

10. Galileo Galilei, *The Assayer* (*Il Saggiatore*) (1623).

11. Acts 1:11 (*Revised English Bible*).

12. Michael Sharratt, *Galileo: Decisive Innovator* (Cambridge: Cambridge University Press, 1994).

13. Galileo's recantation, in Paul Halsall,

Internet Modern History Sourcebook, http://www.fordham.edu/halsall/mod/1630galileo.html.

14. Galileo Galilei, *Two New Sciences* (1638).

15. George V. Coyne, "The Church's Most Recent Attempt to Dispel the Galileo Myth," in Ernan McMullin, ed., *The Church and Galileo* (Notre Dame IN: University of Notre Dame Press, 2005).

16. Pope Pius XII, speech at the Pontifical Academy of Sciences, December 3, 1939.

17. Joseph Cardinal Ratzinger, speech at Sapienza University, Rome, February 15, 1990; and Joseph Cardinal Ratzinger, *Turning Point for Europe? The Church in the Modern World — Assessment and Forecast* (Fort Collins CO: Ignatius Press, 1994).

15. The End of Inquisitions

1. *The Jesuit Portal, www.sjweb/info*, with statistics reported as of January 1, 2007.

2. Council of Trent, 25th Session, December 3–4, 1563.

3. "Report of the Tribunal of the Inquisition, July 18, 1573," trans. Charles Yriate, in Francis Marion Crawford, ed., *Salve Venetia* (London: Macmillan, 1905).

4. Pope John XXII, *Docta sanctorum patrum*, 1324.

5. C.V. Wedgwood, *The Thirty Years War* (1938); and Geoffrey Parker, *The Thirty Years' War* (London: Routledge & Kegan Paul, 1984).

6. The Peace of Westphalia, 1648, cited in W. F. Reddaway, *Select Documents of European History, 1492–1715* (1904), and in Henry Bettenson and Chris Maunder, eds., *Documents of the Christian Church*, 3rd ed. (New York: Oxford University Press, 1999).

7. Pope Innocent X, *Zelus domus Dei*, November 16, 1648.

8. James Maxwell Anderson, *Daily Life During the Spanish Inquisition* (Westport CT: Greenwood, 2002).

9. Montague Summers, *Geography of Witchcraft* (London: Taylor and Francis, 2003).

10. Michael David Bailey, *Magic and Superstition in Europe* (Lanham MD: Rowman & Littlefield, 2006).

16. The Modern Office of the Inquisition

1. All verses from the *Revised English Bible*.

2. I Peter 5:13 (*Revised English Bible*).

3. Tertullian, *De Corona Militis*.

4. Tertullian, *De Idololatria*.

5. Augustine of Hippo, *The City of God (De civitate dei)*.

6. Clyde Pharr, ed. and trans., *The Theodosian Code and Novels and the Sirmondian Constitutions* (1952; reprint, Clark NJ: Lawbook Exchange, 2001).

7. Ramón Vicente, *The Digest of Emperor Justinian* (1874).

8. Pope Innocent IV, *Ad exstirpanda*, May 15, 1252.

9. Aquinas, *Summa Theologica*.

10. Alphonsus Liguori, *Theologia Moralis* (1753–5).

11. Cited in P. Fiorelli, *Enciclopedia Cattolica* (Vatican City, 1954).

12. Vatican Council II, "Respect for the Human Person," December 7, 1965.

13. Pope John Paul II, address, June 15, 1982.

14. "Respect for bodily integrity," *Catechism of the Catholic Church*, 1992.

15. *Compendium of the Social Doctrine of the Church* (Vatican City: Pontifical Commission for Justice and Peace, 2005), article 404.

16. Pope John Paul II, *Pastor bonus*, amending Article 48 of the Apostolic Constitution of the Roman Curia.

17. Thomas J. Reese, "Facts, Myths and Questions," *America, the National Catholic Weekly*, March 22, 2004.

18. "The Father of the Medjugorje Affair Is Removed from Ministry," *Catholic Light*, September 2, 2008.

19. In *L'Osservatore Romano*, November 4, 1992.

20. Pope John Paul II, "Letter on Inquisition Symposium," June 15, 2004.

21. "Balanced History of the Inquisition is Possible, Says Expert," *Zenit*, June 16, 2004, http://zenit.org/151.

22. Tom Bethell, "Is the Pope Overdoing the Apologies?," *Beliefnet*, 2000.

23. *Ibid.*

Epilogue

1. Pope Clement XIII, encyclical *Christianæ Reipublicæ*, November 25, 1766.

2. Sources: *2007 Pontifical Yearbook* (claiming 1.115 billion Catholics worldwide); and *CIA World Factbook* (based on worldwide census reports).

3. Augustine of Hippo, *City of God*, Book I, Chapter 35.

Bibliography

Alcalá, Ángel. *The Spanish Inquisition and the Inquisitorial Mind*. New York: Columbia University Press, 1987.

Ames, Christine Caldwell. *Righteous Persecution: Inquisition, Dominicans, and Christianity in the Middle Ages*. Philadelphia: University of Pennsylvania Press, 2008.

Arnold, John H. *Inquisition and Power: Catharism and the Confessing Subject in Medieval Languedoc*. Philadelphia: University of Pennsylvania Press, 2001.

Baer, Yitzhak Fritz. *A History of the Jews in Christian Spain*. Philadelphia: Jewish Publication Society of America, 1961.

Barber, Malcolm. *The Cathars: Dualist Heretics in Languedoc in the High Middle Ages*. Harlow, Essex, UK: Pearson Education, 2000.

Barstow, Anne Llewellyn. *Witchcraze: A New History of the European Witch Hunts*. New York: HarperCollins, 1995.

Beinart, Haim. *The Expulsion of the Jews from Spain*. Oxford: Littman Library of Jewish Civilization, 2002.

Ben-Yehuda, Nachman. *Deviance and Moral Boundaries: Witchcraft, the Occult, Science Fiction, Deviant Sciences and Scientists*. Chicago: University of Chicago Press, 1985.

Berger, Peter L. *The Heretical Imperative*. London: Collins, 1980.

Berkhof, Louis. *The History of Christian Doctrine*. Carlisle PA: Banner of Truth Trust, 1937.

Bettenson, Henry, and Maunder, Chris, eds. *Documents of the Christian Church*. 3rd ed. New York: Oxford University Press, 1999.

Boorstin, Daniel. *The Discoverers: A History of Man's Search to Know His World and Himself*. New York: Vintage Books, 1983.

Bouwsma, William James. *John Calvin: A Sixteenth-Century Portrait*. New York: Oxford University Press, 1988.

Bowman, Robert. M. "A Biblical Guide to Orthodoxy and Heresy." *Christian Research Journal*, Summer 1990.

Brooke, John L. *The Refiner's Fire: The Making of Mormon Cosmology, 1644–1844*. Cambridge: Cambridge University Press, 1996.

Brown, Colin. *Philosophy and the Christian Faith*. Downers Grove, Illinois: Intervarsity Press, 1968.

Brown, Peter R. L. *The Cult of the Saints: Its Rise and Function in Latin Christianity*. Chicago: University of Chicago Press, 1981.

Burman, Edward. *The Inquisition: The Hammer of Heresy*. New York: Dorset, 1992.

Cameron, Euan. *Interpreting Christian History: The Challenge of the Churches' Past*. Oxford: Blackwell, 2005.

Cantor, Norman F. *Inventing the Middle Ages: The Lives, Works and Ideas of the Great Medievalists of the Twentieth Century*. New York: William Morrow, 1991.

_____. *The Medieval Reader*. New York: HarperPerennial, 1994.

Carroll, Warren H. *The Founding of Christendom*. Vol. 2. Chicago: Christendom, 1987.

Chamberlain, Russell. *The Bad Popes*. Gloucestershire: Sutton, 2004.

Chesterton, G. K. *Orthodoxy*. New York: Dodd, Mead, 1908.

Cipolla, Carlo M. *Before the Industrial Revolution: European Society and Economy, 1000–1700*. New York: W. W. Norton, 1976.

Clifton, Chas S. *Encyclopedia of Heresies and Heretics*. New York: Barnes & Noble, 1992.

Coffin, Charles C. *The Story of Liberty*. (1879.) Plymouth MA: Maranatha Publications, 1987.

Cohn, Norman. *Europe's Inner Demons: An Enquiry Inspired by the Great Witch-Hunt*. New York: Basic Books, 1975.

Collins, Michael. *The Fisherman's Net: The Influence of the Popes on History*. Mahwah NJ: Hidden Spring, 2005.

Coulton, G. G. *The Inquisition*. London: Ernest Benn, 1929; New York: Jonathan Carp & Harrison Smith, 1929.

_____. *Inquisition and Liberty*. (1938.) Boston: Beacon Hill, 1959.

Creighton, Mandell. *A History of the Papacy from the Great Schism to the Sack of Rome*. New York: AMS, 1969.

Daniel, Robin. *This Holy Seed: Faith, Hope and Love in the Early Churches of North Africa*. Harpenden: Tamarisk, 1993.

Denzinger, Heinrich. *Sources of Catholic Dogma*. Trans. Roy J. Deferrari. Fitzwilliam NH: Loreto, 1957.

De Santillana, Giorgio. *The Crime of Galileo*. Chicago: University of Chicago Press, 1955.

Dodds, E. R. *Pagan and Christian in an Age of Anxiety: Some Aspects of Religious Experience from Marcus Aurelius to Constantine*. Cambridge: Cambridge University Press, 1990.

Duffy, Eamon. *Saints and Sinners*. 3rd ed. New Haven CT: Yale University Press, 2006.

Dunn, Richard F. *The Age of Religious Wars: 1559–1715*. 2nd ed. New York: W. W. Norton, 1979.

Durant, Will. *The Reformation*. New York: Simon & Schuster, 1957.

Evans, G. R. *A Brief History of Heresy*. Oxford: Blackwell, 2003.

Fernández-Armesto, Felipe. *Ferdinand and Isabella*. London: Weidenfeld & Nicolson, 1975.

Friedlander, Alan. *The Hammer of the Inquisitors: Brother Bernard Délicieux and the Struggle Against the Inquisition in Fourteenth-Century France*. Leiden: Brill, 2000.

Froude, James Anthony. *Short Studies on Great Subjects*. New York: Scribner's, 1905.

George, Leonard. *Crimes of Perception: An Encyclopedia of Heresies and Heretics*. New York: Paragon House, 1995.

Gerber, Jane. *The Jews of Spain*. New York: Free Press, 1992.

Gitlitz, David M. *Secrecy and Deceit: The Religion of the Crypto-Jews*. Philadelphia: Jewish Publication Society, 1996.

Given, James B. *Inquisition and Medieval Society*. New York: Cornell University Press, 2001.

Gottfried, Robert. *The Black Death and Human Disaster in Medieval Europe*. New York: Free Press, 1983.

Grant, Robert M. *Heresy and Criticism: The Search for Authenticity in Early Christian Literature*. Louisville KY: Westminster, 1993.

Gui, Bernard. *Inquisitor's Manual of Bernard Gui*. Trans. J. H. Robinson. In J. H. Robinson, ed., *Readings in European History*. Boston: Ginn, 1905.

Guitton, Jean. *Great Heresies and Church Councils*. New York: Harper & Row, 1965.

Hamilton, J., and B. Hamilton. *Christian Dualist Heresies in the Byzantine World 650–1450.* Manchester: Manchester University Press, 1998.

Hayward, Fernand. *A History of the Popes.* London: J.M. Dent & Sons, 1931.

Hedrick, Charles W. *Ancient History: Monuments and Documents.* Oxford: Blackwell, 2006.

Hogan, Richard M. *Dissent from the Creed.* Huntington IN: Our Sunday Visitor, 2001.

Hughes, Philip. *A History of the Church.* Vol. 1. Lanham MD: Sheed and Ward, 1948.

Hunt, Dave, and McMahon, T. A. *America: The Sorcerer's New Apprentice.* Eugene OR: Harvest House, 1988.

Johnson, Paul. *A History of Christianity.* New York: Simon & Schuster, 1976.

Kamen, Henry. *The Spanish Inquisition: A Historical Revision.* New Haven CT: Yale University Press, 1997.

Kelly, J. N. D. *Early Christian Creeds.* London: Longman, 1950.

_____. *Oxford Dictionary of Popes.* New York: Oxford University Press, 2005.

Kieckhefer, Richard. *The Repression of Heresy in Medieval Germany.* Philadelphia: University of Pennsylvania Press, 1979.

Kirsch, Jonathan. *The Grand Inquisitor's Manual.* New York: HarperCollins, 2008.

Klaits, Joseph. *Servants of Satan: The Age of the Witch Hunts.* Bloomington: University of Indiana Press, 1985.

Küng, Hans *Infallible? An Inquiry.* New York: Doubleday, 1983.

_____. *Justification: The Doctrine of Karl Barth and a Catholic Reflection.* Trans. Hermann Haring. (1964.) Louisville KY: Westminster John Knox, 2004.

Lambert, Malcolm. *Medieval Heresy.* 2nd ed. Oxford: Blackwell, 1992.

Langbein, John. *Prosecuting Crime in the Renaissance.* Cambridge: Cambridge University Press, 1974.

Latourette, Kenneth Scott. *A History of Christianity.* New York: Harper, 1953.

Laux, John. *Church History.* Rockford IL: TAN Books, 1930.

Lea, Henry Charles. *History of the Inquisition in the Middle Ages.* (1888.) New York: Citadel, 1964.

Longhurst, John B. *The Age of Torquemada.* Lawrence KA: Coronado, 1964.

Mair, Lucy. *Witchcraft.* New York: McGraw-Hill, 1969.

Mansfield, Mary C. *The Humiliation of Sinners: Public Penance in Thirteenth-Century France.* Ithaca: Cornell University Press, 1995.

Martin, Malachi. *The Decline and Fall of the Roman Church.* New York NY: Putnam's, 1981.

Martin, Sean. *The Cathars: The Most Successful Heresy of the Middle Ages.* Edison NJ: Chartwell Books, 2006.

Matthew, Donald. *Atlas of Medieval Europe.* New York: Facts on File, 1983.

Maxwell-Stuart, P.G. *Chronicle of the Popes.* New York: Thames & Hudson, 2001.

McDowell, Josh. *The New Evidence That Demands a Verdict.* Nashville TN: Thomas Nelson, 1999.

McNeill, William H. *Plagues and Peoples.* New York: Doubleday, 1976.

Monter, William. *Frontiers of Heresy: The Spanish Inquisition from the Basque Lands to Sicily.* Cambridge: Cambridge University Press, 1990.

Moore, R. I. *The Birth of Popular Heresy.* London: Edward Arnold, 1975.

Netanyahu, Benzion. *The Origins of the Inquisition in Fifteenth Century Spain.* 2nd ed. New York: New York Review Books, 1995, 2001.

O'Malley, John. *The First Jesuits.* Cambridge MA: Harvard University Press, 1993.

Parkinson, C. Northcote. *East and West.* Cambridge MA: Houghton Mifflin, 1963.

Pegg, Mark Gregory. *The Corruption of Angels: The Great Inquisition of 1245–1246.* Princeton NJ: Princeton University Press, 2001.

Pérez, Joseph. *The Spanish Inquisition.* New Haven CT: Yale University Press, 2005.

Peters, Edward M. *Inquisition*. Berkeley: University of California Press, 1989.

Plaidy, Jean. *The Spanish Inquisition: Its Rise, Growth and End*. New York: Citadel, 1967.

Poliakov, Leon. *A History of Antisemitism*. New York: Schocken, 1974.

Rahner, Karl. *On Heresy*. London: Burns & Oates, 1964.

Ricciotti, Giuseppe. *The Age of Martyrs—Christianity from Diocletian to Constantine*. Rockford IL: TAN Books, 1959.

Roth, Cecil. *The Spanish Inquisition*. New York: Norton, 1937, 1964.

Ryrie, Charles C. *A Survey of Bible Doctrine*. Chicago: Moody, 1972.

Schaff, Philip. *History of the Christian Church*. New York: Scribner's, 1910.

Shannon, Albert C. *The Medieval Inquisition*. 2nd ed. Collegeville MN: Liturgical Press, 1949.

_____. *The Popes and Heresy in the Thirteenth Century*. Villanova PA: Augustinian Press, 1949.

Sharratt, Michael. *Galileo: Decisive Innovator*. Cambridge: Cambridge University Press, 1994.

Shelley, Bruce. *Church History in Plain Language*. 2nd ed. Nashville TN: Thomas Nelson, 1995.

Smith, Preserved. *Luther's Table Talk: A Critical Study*. New York: Columbia University Press, 1907.

Sproul, R. C. *Essential Truths of the Christian Faith*. Wheaton IL: Tyndale, 1992.

Tentler, Thomas M. *Sin and Confession on the Eve of the Reformation*. Princeton NJ: Princeton University Press, 1977.

Thomas, Keith. *Religion and the Decline of Magic*. New York: Scribner's, 1971.

Tomkins, Stephen. *A Short History of Christianity*. Grand Rapids MI: William Eerdmans, 2005.

Tuchman, Barbara W. *A Distant Mirror: The Calamitous 14th Century*. New York: Ballantine, 1978.

Tyerman, Christopher. *God's War: A New History of the Crusades*. Cambridge MA: Harvard University Press, 2006.

Wakefield, Walter L. *Heresy, Crusade and Inquisition in Southern France, 1100–1250*. Berkeley: University of California Press, 1974.

_____, and A. P. Evans, trans. *Heresies of the High Middle Ages*. New York: Columbia University Press, 1990.

Walsh, William Thomas. *Characters of the Inquisition*. Rockford IL: TAN Books, 1997.

Weis, René. *The Yellow Cross: The Story of the Last Cathars' Rebellion Against the Inquisition, 1290–1329*. New York: Vintage Books, 2000.

Weisser, Michael R. *Crime and Punishment in Early Modern Europe*. London: Hassocks, 1979.

Westfall, Richard S. *The Construction of Modern Science*. New York: John Wiley, 1971.

Whitechapel, Simon. *Flesh Inferno: Atrocities of Torquemada and the Spanish Inquisition*. Washington DC: Creation Books, 2003.

Ziegler, Philip. *The Black Death*. London: Collins, 1969.

Index

absolution (in excommunication) 24
Acacius, Patriarch 19
Acta synodi Tridentinae cum Antidoto 203
Acts of the Apostles (bull of 1869) 25
Ad abolendum 13
ad contumacia 72
Ad extirpanda 33, 34, 101, 252
ad hæreticorum exterminium 59
Ad maiorem Dei gloriam 212
Ad nostrum noveritis audientiam 118
Ad perpetua rei memoriam 100
Ad providam 82
Admonitio paterna Pauli III 203
Affair of the Placards 201
Agimet 88
Alberic 30
Albertus Magnus 68
Albigensian Crusade 13, 37, 49–52, 70–72
Albrecht 181
Alexander III, Pope 14–15, 37, 65, 71–72, 249
Alexander IV, Pope 31, 32, 33, 34, 57, 58–60, 67
Alexander V, Antipope 93
Alexander VI, Pope 150
Alfonso VIII, King 55
Alfonso XI, King 127
Alfred the Great 101
Alhambra Decree 150, 159
Alias emanarunt 119
Alumbrados 168–169
Amaury, Arnaud 50–51
Ambrose, Saint writings on heresy 3, 123
Ames, Christine Caldwell 233
Amigos en el Señor 213
Anabaptists 15–16
Anastasius, Emperor 19

Anglican Church 194, 200, 204, 206
Anglo-French War 242
animadversion debita 73
Anti-Heresy Book 16
Apostle's Creed 194–195
Apostolicæ Sedis 24
Appareilamentum 39
Aquinas, Thomas 35, 57, 59, 68, 69, 217, 252
Arbués, Pedro 150
Archimedes 219
Arianism 17–18, 123
Aristarchus of Samos 219
Aristotle 217, 219–220, 221, 223–224
Arnold, William 75
ars nova 239
art censorship 236–238
Arundel, Thomas 193
Ashkanazi Jews 119–120
Assayer 226–227
Augsberg, Peace of 241
Augustine of Hippo: anti-Jewish statements 123; opinions 8, 251; Order 16; rule 16; writings on heresy 3–4, 29, 50, 266
auto-de-fé 6, 34, 61–62, 208, 212
Avignon exile 88
Ayala, Pero López de 137

Babylon captivity 88
Bach, Johann Sebastian 239–240
Bacon, Roger 57
Baptists 15
Barbarossa, Frederick 14, 71–72, 249
Barefoot Carmelites 236
Barnabas of Milan 236
Barnibites 235–236
Bärwalde, Treaty of 243
Bascio, Matteo de 235

Basel, Council of 131, 134–136
Battle of Baziège 50
Beatus Andreas 119
Bebnedictine Order 53–54
Beguins 78, 80–81
Bellarmine, Robert Cardinal 224
bellum sanctum and *bellum justum* 4
Benedict XI, Pope 88
Benedict XIII, Antipope 131–133
Benedict XIII, Pope 119
Benedict XIV, Pope 119, 229, 249
Benedict XVI, Pope 208, 229, 256–258
Benedictus Deus 213
Bernard, Saint 25
Bernard of Charivaux 14
Bezxa, Theodore 202–203
Bishops, Synod of 193
Black Friars 204
Black Legend 204
Black Plague 87–88, 89, 100–101, 105, 127, 152, 179, 236
blood guilt 161
Bloody Mary 191
Boabdil 150
Bogomils 39, 48
Bohemian Revolt 242
Boleyn, Anne 194
Bonaparte, Joseph 172, 245
Bonaparte, Napoleon 172, 245
Bonaventura 57
boni hominess or *bonnes homes* 36
boni veri 32
Boniface VIII, Pope 32, 34, 84–85, 88
Book of St. John 48
Book of Two Principles 48–49
Borromeo, Agostino 261
Bruno, Giordano 221–223
Bubonic plague 244
buon Christiano 180

Burning of Heretics 91, 192
burning times 105

Caccini, Tommaso 224
Cæca et obdurate 119
Cajetan, Cardinal 184
Calvin, John: belief in witches 104; books on the *Index* 207; *Cathecism* written by 167; dispute of heliocentrism 218–219; Inquisition views of 203–205; life 200–203; threat Inquisition 206
cambion 107
Canon Episcopi 81–82
Capuchins 235
Carafe, Giovanni Pietro 236
Caraffa, Giovanni 207
carcere perpetuo 210
Carranza, Bartolomé 169
Castañega, Martin de 103
Catalina, Laws of 132–134
Catechism 167
Catechism of the Catholic Church 254–255
Cathars: *Appareilamentum* 39; book burnings 58; Church reaction 49–52, 78, 85; *Consolamentum* 38; crusade against 49–52, 69; defiance of Church 35, 62; Dominic and 55; *Fraction du Pain* 39; historical context 43–44; in history 7; Inquisition targets 12–13, 60, 66, 71–77; literature 47–49; perfect heretics 37; popularity 36; prominent as heretics 5; society 45–47; theology 37–41; threat to Roman Church 12, 29, 53; yellow cross 69–70
Catherine of Aragon 151, 194
Catholic Monarchs 150
Catholic Revival 234
Celtic Christianity 195
Cena de le Ceneri 221
Cerularius, Michael, Patriarch 41
Charles I, King 152, 155
Charles IV, King 158
Charles V, Emperor 186–187, 213, 240–241
Charles VI, King 131
Charles the Bald, King 101
Charter of the Inquisition 13
Chintila 124
Christãos novos 159
Christian IV, King 243
Christian Cruelty Against German Women 246
Christian Witch Crazy 246
Christianos nuevos 135
Chrysostom, Saint John 4, 122

Church of England 194–195, 199
Cibdad, Juan de la 139
Ciruelo, Pedro 101, 171
Clement IV, Pope 30–31, 34, 118
Clement V, Pope 31, 82, 88
Clement VI, Pope 178
Clement VII, Pope 153, 194, 236
Clement VIII, Pope 119, 121
Clement XIII, Pope 264
Clerics Regular of St. Paul 236
Coeli et terræ 171
Colle, Bonifacio da 236
College of Cardinals 14, 27
Cologne War 241
Company of Jesus 213
Concord of Discordant Canons 29
confessionem esse veram, non factam vi tormentorum 156
Congregation for the Doctrine of the Faith (CDF) 6–7, 207–208, 246, 255
Congregation of Clerks Regular of the Divine Providence (C.R.) 236
Congregation of the Holy Office 246
Congregation of the Index 217
Congregation of the Inquisition 207
Conrad of Marburg 58, 63–65
Conrad of Urach 27
Consejo de la Suprema y General Inquisición 153–154, 171
Consiglieri, Paolo 236
consolamentum 38
Constance, Council of 92–94, 95, 177–178
Constantine I, Emperor conversion 4, 16–17
Constitution of Oxford 91–92
Constitutions of Oxford 193
Conti di Tiene, Gaetano dei (St. Cajetan) 236
Conti, Ugolino de 26–27
Conversos: accused of great heresy 148; accused of plotting assassination 149; away from Spain 164; Christian hatred of 134–135; conversion 144; criminalization 143, 145–146; early Spanish 123; expanded numbers of 126; forced from Spain 160; Inquisition called to investigate 147; laws concerning 135–136; legislation against 141–142; *limpieza* rules imposed on 161; secret recital of Jewish prayers 134; sentiments against 151; suspicions 117; threat of in Toledo 139
Convocations 194

Cop, Nicholas 201
Copernicus, Nicolaus 218–221, 222
corpus juris canonici 29
Cortes 172–173
Cota, Alonso 138
Council of the Suprema 153–154
Council of Thirteen 152
Counter-Inquisition 194–197
Counter-Reformation 189, 234–238, 240
Courtney, William 90
Cranmer, Thomas 194
Credentes 37, 39, 43
crime of defiance 72
Cromwell, Thomas 196–197
Crypto-Jews 140
Cum Hæbræorum militia 119
Cum nimis absurdum 118–119
Cum nos nuper 118–119
Cum sæpe accidere 118
Cum sit absurdum 118
Cuthbert, Bishop 192–193
Cyril of Alexander 123

Danish intervention 243
De absolution a pena et culpa 92–93
De civil dominio 90
De ecclesia 92
De hæetico comburendo 91, 192
De l'Infinito, Universo e Mondi 221
De opera monachorum 16
De quuestionibus 252
De Revolutionibus 220, 229
De Schismate Donntistarum 1
Dead Sea Scrolls 111
Decanus Sacri Collegii 14
decrees of mercy 34
Deism 245
Délicieux, Bernard 75
demiuerge 44
Deza, Diego de 163
Dialogue Concerning the Two Chief World Systems 224–225, 229
Didachus 94
Dominic, Saint 14–15, 28, 53–56
Dominican: conformity between science and theology 217; contradiction 60–61; contrast with Franciscan Order 56–58; Inquisition, 12n, 59–60, 204, 264; inquisitors 28, 30, 58, 65–68, 104, 109, 117–118, 165, 208, 247–248; knowledge and education 85; mission 58–59; Order empowered by Gregory IX 5, 52; Preaching

Friars 16; Protestant movement against 204; rationale for harsh measures 61–63
Donatism 29
dualism 41–43, 44–45, 77–80
Dudum ad nostrum audientiam 118
Dum fidei catholicæ 147–148
Dummy the Witch 245
Durand of Huesca 16
Dynamism 29

Eastern Orthodox Church 19, 41–42, 55
ecclesia non sitit sanguine 59
Ecclesiastical Ordinances 201
Ecomenical Council (Basel) 135–136
Edict of Expulsion 150
Edict of Milan (*Edictum Mediolanensium*) 17
Edict of Worms 186–188, 240–241
Edward VI, King 197–198
Eius qui immobilis 196
Elao, Francisco de 167
Elapso proxime anno 119
Elizabeth I, Queen 191, 196, 198–199, 205
Elvira, Council of 122
Emanavit numer 119
Enchiridion 168
Encinas, Francisco de 167
Enrique II, King 127–128
Enrique III, King 127, 132
Enrique IV, King 141–142, 145–148
Ephesus, Council of 17
Episcopal Inquisition 13, 14–15, 28, 51, 58
epistola decretalis 28–29
Erasmus Roterodamus, Desiderius 167–168, 171
Ernst of Bavaria 241
Erwig 125–126
Espina, Alfonzo de: author of *Fortalicium fidei* 145; kept out of Inquisition process 147; pressure on Enrique 148; quoted by Siliceo 162
Esschen, Johannes van 188
Eugene IV, Pope 100, 118, 143, 147–148
Euphemius, Emperor 19
European Inquisition 245–246
Eusebius 123
Everwin of Steinfeld 36
Ex parte vestra 118
Excommunicamus 60
excommunication 15n, 22–26, 61, 184, 206, 251
Exigit sinceras devotionis affectus 117, 118, 149

exorcism 26
Exsurge Domini 185
Eymeric, Nikcolas 33

Faith Commissions 173
Fawkes, Guy 199
Felix III, Pope 19
femmine indiavolate 102
Ferdinand, King 6, 118, 148–151, 163–165
Ferdinand II, Archduke of Austria 242
Ferdinand II, Grand Duke of Tuscany 229
Ferdinand VII, King 173, 245
ferendæ sententiæ 23
Ferrier (Dominican) 75
Feyerabend, Paul 229
fideles Christi 144
Filioque 42
Florence, Ecumenical Council of 263
Formosus, Pope 25
Formula of the Institute 213
Fortalicium fidei 145
forum externum and *forum sacramentale* 23
Foscarini, Paolo Antonio 221
Foundation for a Global Ethic 257–258
Fraction du Pain 39
Francis, Saint 14–15, 28, 56–58, 235
Franciscan Order 16, 30, 56–58, 81, 85, 208, 235
fraters de poententia 57
Frederick I, Emperor 14, 249
Frederick II, Emperor 16–22, 27, 71
Frederick III, Elector (Frederick the Wise) 183–184, 187–188
Frederick V, King 242
Freemasons 154, 173
French intervention 243
French Prophets 170
Friars Minor 16
Friends of the Lord 213

Galasius, Pope 19
Galileo: *Dialogue* on *Index of Forbidden Books* 225; famous victim of the Inquisition 215; in history 7; later years 228–229; recantation 216, 227, 251; rehabilitation of 258–261; Review Commission 259; scientific revolution 223–225; under threat from the Inquisition 225–228
Galvez, Pero Lope 139–140
García de Mora, Marcos 138–139, 142, 144–145
garrucha 156

geocentric model 218
Gerritszoom, Gerrit 167–168
Ghislieri, Michele 208
Gnosticism 29, 44–45
Gnosticism sect in Spain 153
Gómez Barroso, Pedro 128–129
González de Mondoza, Pedro 149
Grand Armée 172
Grand Inquisitor's Manual 131, 163
Grande y Felicísima Armada 198
Gratian 29
Great Schism 41–42, 86
Great Witch Hunt: aimed at Protestants 206; during Reformation period 200; end 245–246; extension of the Inquisition 265; misogyny 107–112; Spanish 101–104; Waldensians as victims 15, 99–100
Gregorian Mission 195
Gregory I, Pope 19–20, 195
Gregory VIII, Pope 27
Gregory IX: approval of torture 63; canonization of Dominic 56; conflict with Frederick II 16–20, 71; efforts to eliminate heresy 5, 68; established the Inquisition 12–13, 50, 52, 70, 265; *Excommunicamus* bull 60–61; inquisitorial posts granted by 58; letter to bishops 53; life of 26–28; restrictions enacted against Jews 118; *Vox in Rama* bull 64
Gregory X, Pope 30–31, 118
Gregory XI, Pope 91
Gregory of Nyssa 123
Grenada, Treaty of 150
Guil, Bernard 61, 77–80
Gunpowder Conspiracy of 1605 199–200
Gustav II, King 243
Gutenberg, Johannes 46–47
Guzmán, Dominis de (Saint Dominic) 53–54

Hæc sancta 178
Hæresiarcha 94
hæreticatio 40
Hales, Alexander 57
hammer of heretics 54, 158
Hammer of Witches 105–107
Handel, George 239–240
Hartung, Jack 222n
Hebræorum gens 117, 119
heliocentrism 6, 217–219, 221–222, 259
Henry II, Count 64–65
Henry IV, King 92, 192
Holy Office 6, 67, 207, 211–212
Homilies 4

Honorius III, Pope 27, 29, 52, 56, 66, 118
Hospitallers, Knights 82
Huguenot Rebellion 242
Huguenots 200
Humani generis inimicus 141–142
Humanism 112–113, 160, 168–169, 178, 236, 250
Humbert 41n
Humiliati 57
Hus, John 83, 85, 86, 92–93, 177–180
Hussite Church 93, 95

Ignatius of Loyola 168–169, 206, 212–213
Illuminism and Illuminati 167–170
Impia judoerum perfidia 118
imprimatur 207
Index Librorum Prohibitorum 171, 207, 217, 225, 229
infallibility 87
Infallible? An Inquiry 258
Innocent III, Pope: Albigensian Crusade called 50–52; anti–Jewish statements 70; death 27; denial of legal help for accused 31; Fourth Lateran Council called by 15, 55; promotion of execution of heretics 59
Innocent IV, Pope 30, 31, 32, 34, 56, 58, 101, 118, 252
Innocent VIII, Pope 97–98, 104–105, 150, 165
Innocent X, Pope 244
Inquisition 147
Inquisition of Castile 6
Inquisitor's Manual 78
Institutes of Public Ecclesiastical Law 247
Institutes of the Christian Religion 200
Institution of the Christian Religion 167
Integræ servandæ 255
International Red Cross 254
International Theological Commission (ITC) 255–257
Ionan Christianity 195
Isabel II, Queen 245
Isabella 6, 148–151, 163–165
l'Isle, Alain 37, 82

James I, King 199
Jerome, Saint 122
Jerome of Prague 95–96
Jesuit Order 168–169, 212–213, 214, 250
Jews: accomplices to lepers 83; accused of witch hunting conspiracy 245–246; Ash-

kanazi 119–120; blamed for Black Plague 88; compared to witches 109; conspiracy charges against 162; conversion in Spain 123–125; Crypto- 140; expelled from Church states 117; forced conversion 158; papal decrees against 118–120; in Spain 120–123; Spanish society and 125–127; usury charges against 127
Joan of Arc 99–100
João II, King 159
João III, King 159–160
John II of Aragon 148
John XXII, Pope 118, 238–239
John XXIII, Antipope 94
John of Antioch, Saint 4
John of Gaunt 90
John of St. Giles 57
John of the Cross 236
John Paul II, Pope 95, 225, 229, 254–255, 258–260
John the Baptist 40
Juan I, King 128
Juan II, King 136, 137, 140, 145
judicio sumarísino 170–171
judíos escondidos 140
Julius II, Pope 163, 166
Julius III, Pope 162
Juntas da fé 173
Justinian, Emperor 252

Kabbalah 45
Kabbalistic black magic 119
katharos 36
Kerle, Jacobus de 239
King's Duty 90
Kirsch, Jonathan 131, 163
kith and kin 120
Kraemer, Heinrich 105–106
Küng, Hans 257–258, 259

Lancaster, First Duke of 90
Larra, Mariano José de 173
Lateran Council Fourth 15, 55, 60
Lateran Council Second 29
Lateran Council Third 14, 36–37
Latin American Episcopal Conference 258
Laws of Catalina 132–134
la layenda negra 204
Lea, Henry 164
Leo I, Pope 3, 17, 18
Leo IX, Pope 41
Leo X, Pope 168, 182–188
Leonardo da Vinci 236–237
lepers as heretics 83
lèse-majesté 252
Lettera ... sopra l'opinione ... del Copernico 221

Letters on Sunspots 224
Levi, Solomon ha- 131
Liber Antihæresis 16
liberation theology 258
Licet ab initio 207
Liguori, Alphonsus 253
Lilith 109, 111
limpieza de sangre 161
Lollards 89–92, 93, 191, 192–194, 198
Lorini, Niccolo 224
Louis VII, King 52
Louis XIII, King 243
Louis XIV, King 243
Luca, Marinus de 247
Lucero, Diego Rodríguez 163–164
Lucius III, Pope 13–14, 15, 28
Ludendorff, Mathilde 245–246
Luna, Pedro de 131–132
Luther, Martin: beginning of the Reformation 177; belief in witches 104; books on the Index 207; citing Church corruption 249; conflict with Erasmus 168; defiance of Church 166, 183–184; life 180–183, 186; quoted in Table Talk 177; ridicule of heliocentrism 218; Treatise on Christian Liberty 167
Lutherans 155–167, 170

magic 98, 119, 214
Malleus Maleficarum 106–107
Manichaean heretics 78
Manrique, Alfonso 168
Marcellus II, Pope 239
Marcionism 42–43
María-Cristina, Regent 173
Marian Persecutions 191
Marranos 140
Marsh, Adam 57
Martin V, Pope 118
Martínez, Ferrán 127–130, 131
Martínez Bellalo, Francisco 172
Martínez de la Rosa, Francisco 245
Mary I, Queen 151, 191, 193, 198
Mary, Queen of Scots 198
Master of the Sacred Palace 143
Matilda of Tuscany 14
Matthias, Emperor 242
Maurice, Emperor 19
Mayence, Archbishop of 64
Mazarin, Jules 243
Mazzolini, Silvester 183
Medicean planets 223
Medieval Inquisition 12, 20–22, 28, 35, 52, 56
Memorial 144–145
Mennonites 15–16
Merici, Angela de 235

Mexican Inquisition 160
Michelangelo 237
Miltitz, Karl von 184
Milvian Bridge, battle of 16
Mirror of Saxon Laws 29
Missa Papæ Marcelli 239
mitigated dualism 43
Modern-day Inquisition Office 255–257
Monastic Inquisition 28
moral dualism 42
More, Thomas 192–193
Morillo, Miguel de 149
Moriscos 152, 164–165
Morning Star of the Reformation 90, 177–178
Mother of Sciences 28
Muhammad XII, Abu-abdallah 150
murus largus and *murus strictus* 67
music censorship 238–240

Navarre, Council of 103, 170
Nazi era 245–246
Nicaea, First Council of 17
Nicholas IV, Pope 34, 118
Nicholas V, Pope 141, 143–144
nihil obstat 207
Ninety-Five Theses 181–182, 184–185, 187
Numquam dubitavimus 118

Ockham 57
Old Mother Hubbard 111
On the Babylonian Captivity of the Church 249
On the Revolutions of the Celestial Orbs 220, 229
On the Truth of Holy Scripture 90
Optatus of Mileve 1, 3
Opus Evangelicum 90
Order of Frairs Minor Capuchin (OFM) 235
Order of Preachers 53, 56
Order of St. Augustine 16
Ory, Matthias 202
Otto of Brunswick 27
Oxford, Constitution of 91–92

palabras deshonestas 172
Palazzini, Pietro 254
Palestrina, Giovanni 239
palmitem putridum et aridum 95
Papal Inquisition 28, 58
Parens scientiarum 28
Paris, Council of 101
Paris, Treaty of 50, 70, 72
Pastoralis Præerminentiæ 82
Patrini 36
Paul III, Pope 6, 159, 196, 203, 207, 212–213, 220, 235

Paul IV, Pope 118–119, 171, 208–209, 217, 236
Paul V, Pope 224
Paul VI, Pope 207–208, 255
Paul of Burgos 131–133
Paul of St. Père de Chartres 50
Paulicians 39
Pauline Index 207, 217
pauper Christi 57
Pauperes Catholici 16
Pedernales, Juan Martínez 161
Perfecti 37, 39, 43, 52
A Perfit Description of the Coelestiall Orbes 221
perinde ac cadaver 212
perpetua servitus indæorum 30
perpetuo commorari 34
Peter, Cistercian monk 45
Peter, Saint 27, 180, 182
Peter of Castelnau 50
Peter of Les Vaux-de-Cerney 50
Peter of Mladovice 94
Peter of Verona (Peter Martyr) 60, 76
Peters, Edward 147
Petrarch 89
Philip II, King 149, 169, 198
Philip IV, King 82
Philip of Swabia 27
Pius II, Pope 143, 147–148
Pius IV, Pope 70, 169, 207, 209, 213, 234
Pius V, Pope 117, 118–119, 169, 198, 208
Pius VI, Pope 246
Pius IX, Pope 25
Pius X, Pope 246
Pius XII, Pope 229
Plaza, Fernando de la 148
Pontifical Biblical Commission (PBC) 255–256
Pontifical Council for Culture 225
Poor Brethren of Penitence 80–81
Poor Catholics 16
Poor Fellow-Solders of Christ 82
Poor Men of Lombardy 57
Poor Men of Lyons 14–15, 57
Poor Priests 89
Pope's Power 90
Portuguese Inquisition 159–160
Postilla super totam bibliam 90
potro 156
Pracura officii inquisitionis heretice pravitatis 61
Prague, Peace of 243
Preaching Friars 16
Priscillian, Bishop 3
Probe te meminisse 119
Probst, Jacob 188
procedure at Inquisition tribunals 31–32

Processis inquisitionis 61
purgatory 15, 40

Raceswinth 124–125
Rainerius 38
Raphael 237
Ratzinger, Joseph, Cardinal 208, 229, 256–257
Raymond of Peñaforte 29, 35, 76
Rebelión de las Germanías 152
Reconquista 150
Reformation: beginnings 87, 177, 178; Lollards contribution 193; outgrowth of Wyclif and Hus 92, 96, 177–180; root causes 179; sects accused of witchcraft 105; spread 166
Regans in excelsis 198
Regensburg, diet of 214
Regimini militantis ecclesiæ 213
Regino of Prüm 81–82
Religiosan vitam 56
Revolt of the Brotherhoods 152
los Reyos Católicos 150
Righteous Persecution 233
Rinn, Andreas von 119
Ripoll, Cayetano 245
Roman Curia 14, 255
Roman Inquisition: Counter-Reformation during 234; established 6, 207–209, 214, 255; expansion of 214–215; focus on Reformation foes 217; Jesuit involvement in 212–213; procedures under 210–212; reaction to the Reformation 206–207; reduced in power 246; view of Galileo 226, 259–260
Roman Republic 215
Romanists 39
Ruffo, Vincenzo 239
Ruiz de Medina, Juan 149
Rule of Saint Augustine 16
Rule of Saint Francis 81

Sachsenspeigel 29
Sacred College of Cardinals 14, 27
sæculari judicio relinquere 34
salvo conductus 93
San Martín, Juan de 149
sanbenito and *coroza* 210
sanctum Officium 67, 207
Sand Reckoner 219
Sarmiento Pero 136, 139–144
Schmidt, Charles 36
Scotus Duns 57
Scultetus, Hieronymus 181
Secret Supper 48
sede vacante 14
Sedes apostolic 118

Sedula cura 255
Sentencia-Estatuto 140–144
sequere naturam 112
sermo 34
Servetus, Michael 201–203
servitus cameræ imperialis 30
Seyn, Count of (Henry II) 64
Si adversus vos 31
Siena, Bernard de 102
Sigismund, Emperor 93–94
Siliceo 161–162
Simon of Trent, Saint 119–120
Singulari noblis consoldtioni 119
Sippenhaft 120
Sisebut 123–124
Sisenaud 124
Sixth Crusade 22
Sixtus IV, Pope 6, 112, 117, 118, 149, 165
Sixtus V, Pope 171, 198
Smith, Emma 245
Smith, Preserved 177
Society of Jesus (SJ) 168–169, 212–213, 235
sola scriptura 235
sophronisterion 34
sorcerers as heretics 81–82, 101, 104, 153, 170, 208, 214
Spanish Armada 198
Spanish Inquisition stage in history 5–7
Spanish witch hunts 170–172
Speyer, diet of 241
Spiritual Exercises 206
Sprenger, Johann 105–106
Stammers, Samuel 245
Stephen VI, Pope 25
strappado 156
Studia Humanitatis 113
Stupor Mundi 21–22
Der Stürmer 120
Sufficere debuerat perfidioe judoerum perfidia 118
Summa de Ecclesia 143
Summa de penitentia 76
Summa Theologica 69, 217
Summis desiderantes affectibus 97, 104
Supremacy Act of 1534 194
Supreme Council of the Inquisition 103, 171, 209, 210
suum vigorem morale 207
Swedish intervention 243
Swinthila 124
Synod of Bishops 193

Table Talk 177
Talavera, Hernando de 164
Talmud 111, 119, 121
Tarragona, Council of 70
Templar, Knights 82, 253
Teresa of Ávila 236
Tertullian 195, 251

Tetzel, Johann 180–181, 184–185
Theatines 235–236
theodicy 42–43
Theodoric, Emperor 17, 19
Theodosian Code 251–252
Theodosius, Emperor 4, 17
Thirty-Nine Articles of Religion 196
Thirty Years' War 234, 240–245, 250
Thonon, Municipal Register of 25
toca 156
Toledo, Councils of 124, 126, 142
Toledo riots of 1449 137–138, 143
Torquemada, Alvar Fernández de 143
Torquemada, Cardinal Juan de 141, 143–146
Torquemada, Tomás de: abuses 58; appointment as Grand Inquisitor 6, 149, 165; death 163; hammer of heretics 158; hatred of Jews 163; life 158–159; nephew of Cardinal Torquemada 141, 149, 158; procedures of Inquisition 155; report to Queen Isabella 149
tortura del agua 156
torture: applied to repeat offenders 211; Augustine's views 251; authorized by Innocent IV 101; authorized by Pius V 208; authorized by Pope Gregory IX 63; Catechism explanation of 254–255; confessions gained under 106–107, 153, 251; expanded under Spanish Inquisition 117–118; expanded use for Cathars 73; *garrucha* device 156; guidelines in 18th century 253; Knights Templar confessions 82; methods 63–65; ordered by Recceswinth 124; *potro* device 156; Tertullian's views 251; *tortura del agua* device 156; use supported by Torquemada 158; used sparingly 98; victims' patron saint 119; witchcraft confessions 105
Toulouse, Council of 29, 70–71
Tournon, Cardinal 201
Tours, Council of 37
Tractatus 143–144
Tre Savii sopra eresia 209
Treatise on Christian Liberty 167
Trent, Council of 189, 190, 203, 207, 213–214, 217, 234–235, 238–239

Trialogus 90
Tridentine Index 217
Turbato corde 118
Twelve Conclusions of the Lollards 192
Two New Sciences 228–229

Ulm, Truce of 243
Unam Sanctam 84–85
Unigenitus 178
Urban II, Pope 27
Urban IV, Pope 30–31, 32, 33, 67
Urban VIII, Pope 224, 227, 229
Ursulines 235
Ut commissi vobis officii 32

Valdenses ydolatræ 100
Valdéz, Fernando de 171
Vatican Council II 254
Vatican Secret Archives 260–261
Vaudès, Pierre 14
Vaux Pierre de 14
Venice, Treaty of 71–72
Vera christiannæ pacificationis et Ecclesiae reformandæ ratio 203
Vergentis 51
Verona, Council of 15
Veronese, Paolo Galliari 237–238
vicari foranei 208
Visigoth Arianism 123
Vision of Isaiah 91
Vivaldi, Antonio 239–240
Voss, Hendrick 188
Vox in Rama 64

Waldensian Idolatry 99–100
Waldensians 14–16, 45, 62, 78, 85
Waldo, Peter 14–15
Wallenstein, Albrecht von 243
Wenceslaus, King 93
Western Schism 88
Westminister Confessions of Faith 249
Westphalia, Peace of 244
Whore of Babylon 248–250
Wicca 100
William of Puylaurens 45
witchcraft 3, 5, 7, 81–82, 87, 96, 98–101, 104–105, 107–108, 111
Worms, diet of 186
Wyclif, John 83, 85, 86, 89–90, 177–180

yellow cross 69

Zelus demus Dei 244
Zeno, Emperor 19
Zoroastrianism 43